Gamification for Product Excellence

Make your product stand out with higher user engagement, retention, and innovation

Mike Hyzy

Bret Wardle

BIRMINGHAM—MUMBAI

Gamification for Product Excellence

Group Product Manager: Alok Dhuri

Publishing Product Manager: Uzma Sheerin

Senior Editor: Nithya Sadanandan

Technical Editor: Maran Fernandes

Copy Editor: Safis Editing

Project Coordinator: Manisha Singh

Proofreader: Safis Editing

Indexer: Manju Arasan

Production Designer: Alishon Mendonca

DevRel Marketing Coordinators: Deepak Kumar and Mayank Singh

Business Development Executive: Puneet Kaur

First published: September 2023

Production reference: 2290923

Published by Packt Publishing Ltd.

Grosvenor House

11 St Paul's Square

Birmingham

B3 1R.

ISBN 978-1-83763-838-3

www.packtpub.com

Endorsements for *Gamification for Product Excellence*

An eye-opening exploration of how gamification can supercharge product development. This book is an excellent read for anyone passionate about creating exceptional user experiences.

Nir Eyal, author of Hooked: How to Build Habit-Forming Products

'Gamification for Product Excellence' is one of the most holistic and comprehensive books on modern Gamification. I highly recommend it for product leaders!

Yu-kai Chou, Creator of The Octalysis Framework, and Author of Actionable Gamification - Beyond Points, Badges, and Leaderboards

'Gamification for Product Excellence' thoughtfully navigates the intricate landscape of gamification, emphasizing ethical considerations to ensure a well-rounded approach for product development.

Marc Lane, Attorney and Author of The Mission-Driven Venture: Business Solutions to the World's Most Vexing Social Problems

Mike Hyzy and Bret Wardle's book 'Gamification for Product Excellence' takes readers from Asteroids to Easter eggs as they explore both the history and psychology of gameplay while sharing with readers important principles like the power of rewards, voting, storytelling, and even the power of losing—or averting loss! This book isn't just for product managers, but anyone looking to create a more engaging business experience through gamification.

Geoff Thatcher, Founder and Chief Creative Officer at Creative Principals and Author of The CEO's Time Machine

Description

Are you trying to build a product that your audience loves to use? Game mechanics and psychology have been used for decades to increase engagement, convert users to buyers, and increase audience retention. Learning when and where to implement these tools can take your product from the middle of the pack to a must-have!

This book begins by helping you get a clear understanding of gamification, its key concepts, and how product managers can leverage it to drive user engagement in non-game scenarios. As you progress through the chapters, you'll learn different gamification frameworks, mechanics, and elements with structured ways to implement them while designing a successful gamification strategy tailored to a business case. You'll get a chance to implement and test the designed strategy prototype with the users for feedback. You'll also discover how to sell your strategy to stakeholders to get full buy-in from the top down, along with how to gamify your product development process to drive innovation, engagement, and motivation.

By the end of this book, you'll be primed to harness the power of gamification, and will have benefited from proven case studies, best practices, and tips, ensuring you are well-equipped to apply gamification principles to your work as a product development professional.

What you will learn

- Explore gamification and learn how to engage your user with it
- Gain insights into the functionality and implementation of different gamification frameworks
- Master specific game elements and mechanics that can be used to improve user experiences
- Design a successful gamification strategy to test your hypothesis and develop a business case
- Implement and test the prototype you've created with users for feedback
- Say the right words to sell your gamification strategy to stakeholders
- Use design thinking exercises and game elements to improve the product management process

To my parents, my wife, my mentors, and my daughter, Vivian: your unwavering support, love, and belief in me have been the driving force behind my journey. Thank you for inspiring me to pursue my passions and for being the pillars of strength in my life. This book is dedicated to each of you, as you have played an integral role in shaping who I am today. Your presence brings joy and meaning to my life, and I am grateful for the laughter, love, and endless encouragement you provide.

– Mike Hyzy

This book is dedicated to the two pillars of my life: my incredible wife and my fantastic children. To my wife, who has provided unwavering support, inspiration, and love throughout this journey; thank you for standing by my side, for understanding my passions, and for being my lifelong friend. To my children, thank you for sharing my love for gaming, for indulging me on nostalgic adventures, and for embracing the classics that came well before your time.

– Bret Wardle

Foreword

There isn't a single aspect of our digital lives untouched by product management. As unsung (and often underappreciated) heroes of our new, tech world, product people toil in relative obscurity to create experiences that are fun, engaging, functional, and ultimately successful.

Accomplishing this can be a challenge – both because of the cynicism and distraction of users, and also the exhausting rhythm of life in the PM function. In a sense, the opportunities to use fun and engagement to motivate and succeed exist on both sides of the equation.

Gamification provides a perfect platform to accomplish this, regardless of which aspect of product management demands improvement. As a system of behavioral design, gamification delivers a wide range of frameworks, tactics, and techniques that can radically transform any system and its users into something with positive growth and satisfaction.

In this book, Wardle and Hyzy have neatly organized extensive information about gamification and how to use it, filtered through the lens of utility in product management. This is no simple task, as decades of research and practice have generated an exceptionally broad field of tools, techniques, and approaches to creating engagement using the best ideas from games.

Without a doubt, your organization, processes, and products can benefit from gamification approaches. And this book will be a worthy and comprehensive guide to your journey along the way.

Gabe Zichermann

CEO, Gamification Co

Contributors

About the authors

Mike Hyzy is a highly experienced product strategist and principal consultant with a proven track record of delivering results. Throughout his career, he has demonstrated exceptional leadership skills, guiding cross-functional teams to successful product launches and driving growth for his clients. With a deep understanding of the product development landscape, Mike is known for his ability to develop and execute effective product strategies, bringing innovative products to market. Mike holds key certifications, including an NPDP certification from the Product Development and Management Association, a CSPO certification from the Scrum Alliance, and a Foresight Practitioner certification from the Institute for the Future.

Bret Wardle is an advocate for the convergence of design psychology in games and software. This includes concepts such as understanding similarities between professional e-sport players and software power users and studying the societal changes invoked by using "hi-scores" in e-commerce platforms. He finds joy in implementing these findings to make products and experiences people love to use! He started his career as a game designer and has since moved over to primarily software and product design. Bret has worked within organizations as large as Electronic Arts, and as small as two-person start-ups. Bret is Nielsen Norman Group Masters certified, as well as holding a PMC-V certification from the Pragmatic Institute.

About the reviewers

Amad Amin is a senior product executive whose career has spanned financial services, IoT, e-commerce and marketplace, SaaS, and HealthTech. He has a proven track record of success in creating innovative digital solutions for enterprise and global accounts. He has expertise in managing highly complex systems of interdependencies, leading product development and design, and directing cross-functional teams, including clients, domain experts, applications professionals, and technical engineers. He holds multiple patents. When he is not working on products, he hosts the If I Could podcast.

Brad Sytsma has worked in the employee recognition and engagement space for the last decade. As a product manager in the employee engagement industry, Brad coordinates with Terryberry's development, marketing, sales, and customer success teams to design and improve product features on Terryberry's web and mobile employee engagement platforms. Outside of the world of products, Brad is an actor and playwright who enjoys telling stories rooted in the human experience.

Danny Spillman is a chief innovation officer and chief people officer. Throughout his career, he has always matched the excitement of attempting the impossible with a profound commitment to team unity.

On the technical side, he has led innovation strategies that yielded novel programs and products. Most often, these have been within a corporate incubator environment, where he had the freedom to fulfill a corporate vision with very few cultural restraints. With this type of autonomy, he nurtured a number of SaaS products with Spillman Technologies, which catapulted the company to eight figures of annual revenue and Inc. 5000 ranks for fastest-growing private companies for seven years running, with the company growing by 49% from 2009 to 2012 alone. In short, the company leaned on him to shift its mindset, break down corporate norms that nearly prevented a foray into the SaaS space, and promote a company ripe for acquisition by Motorola in 2016.

Whitney Shirk is a highly skilled and accomplished product manager with a passion for innovation and customer-centric product development. With over 15 years of experience in the tech industry, Whitney has successfully led and delivered numerous product initiatives from conception to launch.

Whitney is based out of Chicago, USA. You can reach out to her at whitney.shirk@gmail.com.

Table of Contents

6

Designing a Gamification Strategy   121

10

Gamifying Your Product Development Processes   223

11

Case Studies and Best Practices   261

12

The Future of Gamification   291

Index   311

Other Books You May Enjoy   324

Preface

This book will be incredibly utilitarian to specialists across the product development life cycle, such as designers, UX strategists, engineers, and data scientists, and covers areas specific to those roles.

The PM, as defined by us, wears many hats and is responsible for a wide range of activities, including, but not limited to, market research, product development, product positioning pricing, and go-to-market releases. They are the "glue" in the cross-functional team, managing designers, engineers, marketers, and sales teams with different degrees of authority, sometimes none at all. The role motivates and drives the vision, so the teams involved in the processes are aligned and contribute to a successful product, determined by the KPIs created in the strategy process. The PM also monitors product performance through qualitative and quantitative feedback, through platforms and processes such as analytics, and by gathering customer feedback to guide future product development efforts. And who is in charge of tracking that?

The role of the PM has evolved significantly over time. As technology has continued to expand and evolve, the role of the PM has expanded and evolved as well.

In the past, overseeing the development and launch of a single product or product line was the role of a PM. PMs may be responsible for a wide range of products and services today. The position may work across multiple teams and departments to ensure the successful development and launch of products.

As technology has become more advanced and users have become more sophisticated, the role of the PM has become increasingly focused on user-centered design. PMs must understand the needs and motivations of users and use this information to guide the development of products that meet those needs and use gamification as a tool to do so.

With the rise of big data and analytics, the role of the PM has become more data-driven. PMs use data and metrics to inform product development decisions and may conduct experiments and A/B tests to evaluate the effectiveness of different product features and strategies.

PMs may have worked in isolation in some cases, with limited collaboration across teams and departments. Today, the PM role is much more collaborative. PMs must work closely with designers, engineers, marketers, and other stakeholders to ensure that products have triumphant development and release of products and platform development.

PMs are considered leaders and educators in development methodologies, whether Agile, Scrum, Lean Six Sigma, Lean Startup, or others. With the increasing pace of technological change, the role of the PM has become more focused on becoming an expert in methodologies and rapid iteration.

PMs must be able to work quickly and efficiently to develop and launch products and must be able to adapt to changing market conditions and user needs.

Product management roles have grown 32% in the two-year period from August 2017 to June 2019.

The average salary of a PM is $127,979 but is more than $250,000 at companies such as Meta and Amazon.

Being a PM is listed as one of the top 10 best jobs, according to Glassdoor.

So why does this matter?

As the popularity of being a PM continues to rise, so do the expectations and responsibilities. The ongoing joke among PMs is that if the product does well, we get none of the credit, and if it goes wrong, we get all of the blame. The key word in the role is *responsibility*.

To be an elite PM, you need to master the core functions, have a high level of emotional intelligence, and understand basic concepts in design, engineering, law, economics, policy, data, and marketing as they relate to your product. Gamification is a special set of knowledge and skills that give you a competitive advantage over your peers.

Who this book is for

If you are a product manager, product leader, or product designer weaving gamified experiences and crafting exceptional digital products from conception to reality, then this book is the absolute right pick for you. The topics covered will enable you to level up your products and unleash their full potential through gamification. All the gamification strategies and frameworks discussed in this book can be practically applied across different domains with ease.

What this book covers

Chapter 1, Gamification Basics, provides an overview of the fundamentals of gamification and its applications in various domains.

Chapter 2, Gamification for Product Teams, explores how gamification can be utilized to enhance product team performance and collaboration.

Chapter 3, Gamification Frameworks and Experts, explores different gamification frameworks and models for designing effective gamified experiences.

Chapter 4, Understanding Your User, covers strategies for understanding user behavior and preferences to tailor gamification elements accordingly.

Chapter 5, Game Mechanics and Psychology, provides an in-depth analysis of various gamification elements and mechanics to create engaging experiences.

Chapter 6, Designing a Gamification Strategy, provides a step-by-step guide to crafting a comprehensive gamification strategy for a specific context.

Chapter 7, Implementing Your Gamification, covers best practices for implementing and evaluating the effectiveness of a gamification strategy.

Chapter 8, Challenges and Limitations in Gamification, examines the challenges and limitations of gamification and how to address them.

Chapter 9, Selling Your Gamification Strategy, covers techniques for effectively presenting and convincing stakeholders to adopt a gamification strategy.

Chapter 10, Gamify Your Product Development Process, shows how to integrate gamification into the product development life cycle for better outcomes.

Chapter 11, Case Studies and Best Practices, provides real-world case studies and examples of successful gamification implementations.

Chapter 12, The Future of Gamification, provides a glimpse into the future trends and potential advancements in the field of gamification.

To get the most out of this book

In this book, you'll learn how to integrate game mechanics into your product development process to drive better user engagement and retention. Whether you're an experienced PM or new to gamification, we'll provide the knowledge and real-life examples to help you create a compelling business case for gamification. By the end of the book, you'll be equipped to design practical game mechanics into your user experience and achieve higher levels of user satisfaction and success.

Conventions used

> **Tips or important notes**
> Appear like this.

Get in touch

Feedback from our readers is always welcome.

General feedback: If you have questions about any aspect of this book, email us at customercare@ packtpub.com and mention the book title in the subject of your message.

Errata: Although we have taken every care to ensure the accuracy of our content, mistakes do happen. If you have found a mistake in this book, we would be grateful if you would report this to us. Please visit www.packtpub.com/support/errata and fill in the form.

Piracy: If you come across any illegal copies of our works in any form on the internet, we would be grateful if you would provide us with the location address or website name. Please contact us at copyright@packt.com with a link to the material.

If you are interested in becoming an author: If there is a topic that you have expertise in and you are interested in either writing or contributing to a book, please visit authors.packtpub.com.

Share Your Thoughts

Once you've read *Gamification for Product Excellence*, we'd love to hear your thoughts! Scan the QR code below to go straight to the Amazon review page for this book and share your feedback.

https://packt.link/r/1837638381

Your review is important to us and the tech community and will help us make sure we're delivering excellent quality content.

Download a free PDF copy of this book

Thanks for purchasing this book!

Do you like to read on the go but are unable to carry your print books everywhere?

Is your eBook purchase not compatible with the device of your choice?

Don't worry, now with every Packt book you get a DRM-free PDF version of that book at no cost.

Read anywhere, any place, on any device. Search, copy, and paste code from your favorite technical books directly into your application.

The perks don't stop there, you can get exclusive access to discounts, newsletters, and great free content in your inbox daily

Follow these simple steps to get the benefits:

1. Scan the QR code or visit the link below

https://packt.link/free-ebook/9781837638383

2. Submit your proof of purchase
3. That's it! We'll send your free PDF and other benefits to your email directly

1
Gamification Basics

Although the term gamification is relatively new, the concept has been around since well before the computer age. And beyond that, humans have enjoyed games since the beginning of recorded history. As with any knowledge, it is important to understand the past to lead toward the future. And rather than start in the early 2000s when the word gamification was first uttered, you should understand why humans enjoy games, and how they can make even mundane tasks feel like important accomplishments. By doing that, you can start to harness the power of gamification to build products that people love to use, talk about, and engage with regularly.

In this chapter, we will cover the following topics:

- Introduction to gamification
- History of gamification
- Key concepts of gamification
- Where gamification stands today

Introduction to gamification

Take a second and think about one of the best memories you have with friends or family. It doesn't need to take long. It could be something recent, or something from your past. Now that you can picture that memory in your head, think about what you and/or the people around you are doing. It may be tied to a significant event in your life (graduation, marriage, the birth of a child, etc.). If it is not one of those significant events, there is a decent chance that this memory involves some form of game, or at least the idea of play. On the other side of that, there is an incredibly small chance that your favorite memory involved you using some form of business software!

Why is it that we fondly remember playing a game of flag football with our family, our first vlsit to a great vacation spot, or sitting around a table with friends playing D&D, poker, dominoes, or any other number of games? Why do we not as easily recall the last time we absolutely crushed it on a work spreadsheet? Games are fun. As humans, we love the concept of playing. It allows us to relax and hyper-focus on a few key elements, as opposed to the many tasks we may juggle on a normal day. But what if we could make the applications we use act more like games, and less like work? That is what gamification is, and what we will explore in this book.

Games as a business

Games are no longer just childish toys either (to be honest, they never were). Gaming has grown to be a giant industry. In 2021, games generated $198 billion (source: `https://www.liquidweb.com/insights/video-game-statistics/`). That is more than books ($126 billion), music ($22.5 billion), and movies ($45 billion) combined! Of the four segments within the entertainment industry, games is the only one with steady year-over-year growth in the last decade. With numbers like that, it's hard to deny that people enjoy playing games and are willing to pay for experiences that bring that joy.

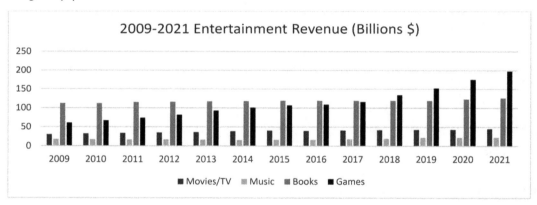

Figure 1.1 – Entertainment industry revenue from 2009-2021

Humans enjoy playing games and the challenge, reward, and satisfaction that come with it. But what does that mean for product design? Well, to be honest, a lot. After all, games are products too, with development teams, designers, quality assurance, and tight deadlines, just like their software counterparts. In the early days of software and video game history, those two products were relatively far from each other, but those worlds are colliding. It seems like every major corporation now has a game division or is doing some work in that space. On the flip side, many game publishers are also starting to build their own software platforms (Steam, EA, Epic, and others). And with these crossovers comes employee experience between platforms. It is a natural progression for some software to feel more game-like and for games to start incorporating more software practices. But when those game elements start to bleed into product design and development, we have what is now known as **gamification**.

Gamification basics

Gamification is a process that involves adding game-like elements and psychology to traditionally non-game activities or products in order to increase engagement, motivation, enjoyment, and fun. Examples of gamification in various industries and fields include loyalty reward programs, apps that offer positive feedback for completing goals, educational software that makes learning fun and interactive, and productivity tools that use game mechanics to motivate employees to complete work. Chances are you are using multiple products each day that includes these types of elements. Did you purchase your morning coffee today? If so, how close are you to earning your next "free drink"? To further that, did you buy your coffee from a specific place knowing you would earn more or better rewards? That is the effect that gamification can have on our brains. Let's say you made your own coffee this morning... was that decision based on any sort of financial tracker telling you to save money by avoiding the high prices of coffee shops? Or maybe making it yourself just gives you a sense of pride that helps you get your day started right, making you more productive. Gamification is happening all around us, all the time.

Gamification has become a widely recognized and effective approach to engaging and motivating users in a variety of contexts, not just coffee! This starts with initial marketing tactics and continues through the customer journey down the entire path. Game techniques can be applied to any industry in some capacity. Many people think of more "fun" products first, such as fitness, shopping, and leisure, but it can be just as effective in a serious context as well. Did you know that many emergency call centers (911) are timed on how quickly they can assess and triage their calls? By doing this, they know who the top performers are and can better understand how they could improve their efficiency in getting high-priority cases taken care of and moving lower-priority cases to a non-emergency department. Gamification also continues to evolve and expand as new technologies, advancements, and psychological research are developed.

As we discuss the topics throughout this book, examples and lessons will lean toward the role of a product manager (or one of many similar titles). And although this book leans toward that role, it is important to understand that the lessons are just as easily applicable to almost every role on a product or development team. Designers and artists can use gamification to capture users' attention and help introduce features, functions, or important tasks. Programmers can use games to help collaborate on estimates or take part in hack-a-thons to sharpen their skills. Marketing can benefit from using game psychology to drive a great call to action for potential users. Even quality assurance can use these concepts to motivate and incentivize its teams. These are just a few examples, but anyone can apply these lessons to their product, their work, or their life.

It is also worth noting that we will not only highlight a ton of real-world examples of gamification in practice but we will also refer to a couple of theoretical products as well, one of which will be a social media application like Facebook, LinkedIn, or the platform previously known as Twitter. That application will be referred to as **Product Management Media** (**PMM**). The other is a fitness and wellness app like you might see from companies such as Nike or Weight Watchers. We will call it **Hi-Z Fitness**. We will see these products throughout their life cycles, from ideation and design to feature inclusion and refinement, and potentially take a quick look at marketing gamification for when the product is ready to ship. As topics are discussed, think about how you might implement the ideas in these products, and see whether you can figure out the approach that might be taken before you read about it!

History of gamification

The term gamification seems to have first emerged in 2002, when Nick Pelling, a British programmer and game designer used the term in a blog post to describe the process of using game design mechanics and techniques to make non-game activities more engaging. He was specifically trying to design a game-like interface for ATM machines at the time. However, the term did not initially gain widespread popularity. But, as a concept, gamification was taking place far before the term was established. And more so, as a culture, we have enjoyed games for much of our existence. Before we can discuss how game design theory might be applied to other practices, it is worth looking back at how games themselves got to be an over $200 billion industry… and that goes *way* back!

The birth of games

Humans have played games for thousands of years. In fact, archaeologists in the Middle East have discovered dice and other gaming artifacts that are thought to be over 3,000 years old! Chinese texts reference other tile-based games that date back to roughly the same time frame. The beginnings of card-based games can also be traced back to China, nearly 1,000 years ago, during the Tang Dynasty (618-907 AD). One of the earliest card games was the "leaf game," which used paper cards decorated with intricate designs, and players would compete to form winning card combinations. The game spread through trading routes to other parts of Asia, and eventually to Europe. As the social aspect took hold, more and more people wanted to get in on the fun, and, over time, the various games evolved and became popular pastimes. Why humans love games can be hard to pinpoint, but many studies, including a 2021 study titled *Stress-Reducing Effects of Playing a Casual Video Game among Undergraduate Students* (source: `https://www.ncbi.nlm.nih.gov/pmc/articles/PMC7952082`), have found that playing casual games can be nearly as stress reducing as meditation.

In Europe during the Middle Ages, playing cards were often handcrafted and featured religious symbols or figures. The four suits we know today (hearts, diamonds, clubs, and spades) evolved from the different social classes in medieval Europe, with hearts representing the clergy, diamonds representing the wealthy merchants, spades representing the nobility, and clubs representing the peasants. During the Renaissance, playing cards began to feature the royal figures we know today, with kings, queens, and jacks representing various historical and legendary rulers. The earliest known European card game was called **Karnöffel**, which was played in Germany, and the game is still played today as Schafkopf. As the popularity of card games increased, new games and variations emerged, such as poker, bridge, and gin rummy. Even Nintendo, who many consider the grandfather of the modern video game industry, got its start making Japanese playing cards all the way back in 1889.

Games as motivators

Games continued to be played and shared, but 1896 saw one of the first instances of game mechanics being applied to a non-game context. S&H Green Stamps were small stamps that you could collect by purchasing goods at local grocery stores, gas stations, and department stores. Users could take their collected stamps and add them to a "saver book," which could be redeemed for prizes once filled up. The S&H company would sell these stamps to those retailers, and in turn, the retailers would use them to try and drive business by advertising themselves as a green stamp rewards shop. The program continued for nearly a century and became the basis for nearly all rewards programs that followed. Despite their eventual decline around the 1970s, S&H Green Stamps remain a popular cultural icon and are often referenced in movies and television shows set in the mid-20th century. The stamps are also collected by vintage memorabilia enthusiasts and can often be found for sale at antique shops and flea markets. This program is widely credited for laying the groundwork for all the loyalty programs that came after.

Figure 1.2 – Boy Scout merit badges

In 1908, the Boy Scouts of America organization introduced the merit badge system that it still uses today. This system allows its members to earn one of more than 130 badges by testing their proficiency in a number of skills, including first aid, camping, and swimming. There are more badges added every year and they now include specialized topics such as robotics, cybersecurity, and even game design. The importance of this sort of system is twofold. Not only do you as a user have a clear path to testing your own proficiency in a topic but you also get a physical good that allows you to show your expertise to others easily. This sort of system continues throughout our entire life with job titles, college degrees, and trade certifications. At a psychological level, seeing someone with a bunch of letters after their name is not much different from seeing your childhood friend showing off their sash with all their merit badges.

Gaming goes electronic

The beginnings of arcade and coin-operated games can also be traced back to the early 1900s when simple mechanical devices such as slot machines and pinball machines were introduced into bars and amusement parks throughout the United States. One of the earliest arcade games was Skee-Ball, which was introduced in 1909 and became a popular attraction at amusement parks around the country. Other games such as shooting galleries, mechanical horse races, and fortune tellers followed. More and more games were introduced as the decades passed and consumers showed more of an appetite for this type of entertainment. By the 1940s, the coin-operated arcade game industry was a lucrative business, and popular leisure activity for many adults and children alike. These early arcade and coin-op games paved the way for the modern arcade industry, which exploded in popularity in the 1980s with the introduction of video games such as Pac-Man and Donkey Kong. Although games have been played for thousands of years, it is important to understand video games in particular in relation to gamification, as the explosion of personal computers and the video game industry are closely tied to one another, and especially to what we think of today as gamification.

> ### Asteroids (1983)
>
> This was the first game to feature a high score list, where you could enter your initials. Adding this type of feature gave this game a high replay value, as when someone bested your score, you were compelled to try to get back on top. In the world of coin-operated gaming, this replay value added directly to the amount of money the game could make.
>
> Asteroids can still be found in many arcades/barcades around the world. If you cannot access it in the wild, you can find many ports of the game online with a quick search. Try playing this or a similar game with your friends and/or family and see what kind of competition arises from it. The sense of pride in being #1 will surely come out in several people and can be a strong motivator to play the game over and over!

As the history of gaming and gamification design shifts from the physical to the digital world, the growth and popularity increase exponentially. With the dawn of the computer age, gaming followed right behind. Created in 1945, ENIAC is considered to be one of the first computers, and used over 17,000 vacuum tubes. Competitors to this system were quick to follow, including EDSAC and EDVAC. It didn't take long for people to use this new technology for fun, as what is often considered the first video game was created in 1952 at the University of Cambridge on the EDSAC system. It was called **OXO** and was a digital version of tic-tac-toe. Following that were two of the other earliest games: Tennis for Two was a game for a pair of players created in 1958 that used an oscilloscope. The gameplay was meant to simulate a game of tennis, which might sound familiar to anyone who knows a thing or two about Atari. *Spacewar!* (1961) was also a two-player game, and considered by some to be the first true video game as it used a joystick for control and could be run on a PDP-1 computer, which was the first to use a cathode-ray tube display.

Games in the home and everyday life

Over the next 30 years, both personal computers and video games became more popular and more advanced. Two of the most successful early personal computers were the Apple II, released in 1977, featuring color graphics and a keyboard, and the IBM PC, released in 1981, which featured an open architecture and could be customized by users, paving the way for the widespread adoption of computers in the workplace. Video game consoles were trying to make the same impact in homes as personal computers, but the price was hard to justify for many families. Companies such as Mattel, Coleco, and Magnavox all released their own gaming consoles, but the market was dominated by Atari's 2600 console. This is attributed to several things, including successful marketing strategies and partnerships with retailers such as Sears and Toys "R" Us. Atari also had a few popular game franchises, including Pong, Space Invaders, and Pac-Man, which consumers knew from their local arcades. This success led to a waterfall of companies trying to get a piece of the home gaming market pie, and a flood of poorly made games entered the market. Personal computers were the smarter choice for those families facing the difficult economic times of the early 80s. Because of these factors, the video game industry crashed, and many felt it may never recover.

Why is an over-40-year-old crash of a similar industry important? Gamification itself went through a similar downturn in the early 2010s. Points, badges, and leaderboards were being thrown on everything and the strategy was half-baked across many gamified products. Consumers were getting bored with it, and several tech strategists had tossed gamification out as a fad. The same could be said for the bursting of the dot-com bubble in the early 2000s. Just because a company had a flashy new website, didn't make it a wise investment. It is important to remember this as we learn gamification techniques. These are not band-aids for poor product design. And if implemented without understanding, they can be as detrimental as they are valuable.

The mid- to late 80s was when personal computers, gaming, and gamification hit their stride and really started to gain consumer traction. Technology was moving incredibly fast, and product design as an industry was growing right along with it. Many of the designers we look up to today shaped the industry during this timeframe: Dieter Rams, Don Norman, Alan Cooper, Jakob Nielsen, and more. Businesses were constantly searching for a way to give their experience a leg-up over the competition. Because of this, we saw the beginnings of many programs still running today. American Airlines was the first to offer a "frequent flyer" program, earning customers rewards for loyalty to their service. The hotel industry quickly followed suit and Holiday Inn became the first in that industry to do the same. Many restaurants already implemented some form of loyalty reward, but McDonald's had another idea.

In 1987, it partnered with Hasbro and began a promotion using Monopoly intellectual property. Over the years, this promotion continued (last offered in 2019) and has been attributed to increasing McDonald's sales during the promotion timeframe by as much as 5%. If you have never heard of this promotion, customers could receive game pieces by purchasing certain menu items, such as Big Macs, fries, and drinks, as well as certain promotional items, such as large sandwiches or value meals. The game offered customers the chance to win prizes by collecting game pieces that corresponded to properties on a Monopoly board.

In 1985, Nintendo revitalized an otherwise dying video game industry with the release of its Nintendo Entertainment System in the US. Requiring game publishers to meet the Nintendo Seal of Approval made sure that the games were of high quality, and that helped to earn consumer trust after it was lost during the earlier industry crash. By 1990, 30% of Americans had an NES in their homes. This created a generation of children that grew up on games. The acceptance and enjoyment of that industry go hand in hand with gamification techniques gaining any sort of traction.

Connectivity in game design

The growth of the technology industry during the 1990s and early 2000s was defined by connectivity. The birth of the internet and the drastic expanse of mobile phone ownership meant that users were only minutes away from communication with anyone in the world, and by the early 2000s, those minutes had become seconds. Although connected games had been around since 1978 (Multi-User Dungeon One, or MUD1), with the launch of online gaming platforms such as Xbox Live, friends could join each other across the globe to share these fun experiences and/or compete for bragging rights. The rise of social media during this time mirrored those same sentiments. Friends and family were breaking down geographic walls and interacting with one another in real time no matter where they were. The fact that we are social beings is no longer an afterthought and, with the new age of product design, that connectivity needs to be considered and planned from the start.

Products were being made for these new connected platforms. But for many people these activities were limited to work, school, or a home office where access to a connected PC was possible. But in a move that changed the world, Apple released the iPhone in 2007. What was previously tied to a desktop PC could now be done anywhere. As we saw with the video game industry in the late 70s, everyone was rushing to build apps for the new platform, and quality suffered because of it (and arguably still does). But the smartphone platform is alive and well, and consumers are ultra-conscious of the products they use on the platform. Engagement is key, and many of the most installed apps drive that engagement with some form of gamification. This may come in the form of the social aspect of apps such as TikTok, Instagram, or Snapchat or the personal customization of products such as Spotify, YouTube, and Netflix. Many people prefer the sense of accomplishment and reward of applications such as Duolingo, Habitica, or Nike Training Club. All of these utilize some form of gamified design, and although it is rarely called by that name, consumers look for these types of experiences. And for us as product owners, the bottom line is that many studies have shown that it drives engagement, loyalty, and in turn revenue!

Key concepts in gamification

Gamification can be, and is often, used to describe many things. Sometimes, it is a distinct feature added to a product such as a progress tracker. But it can also be the use of subtle psychological cues to help nudge a user down a desired path such as offering a coupon for creating an account on an e-commerce platform. It could also be something bolder, such as a fast-food restaurant offering a scratch-off ticket that could reward you with anything from a free drink to a cash prize. Game design is all around us, and that becomes evident the second you start paying attention to it and looking for it. As more and more products adopt gamified techniques, the lines between what could be considered gamification and what is simply experience design become more and more blurred. But for the lessons in this book, most of what we now consider gamification techniques fall into one of five broad categories:

- Reward systems
- Progress tracking
- Narrative and storytelling
- Social engagement
- Game psychology

Reward systems

Reward systems are likely the most common use of gamification today. Point redemption and punch cards are two very common ways to build reward systems. The most common version of this likely comes in the form of loyalty reward points. Almost every food and entertainment brand has its own loyalty program now, offering items as simple as free food to entries to win elaborate prizes. If you spend much time in the US Intermountain West, you might be familiar with the Maverick brand. These gas station/food stops offer a point system that allows you to spend smaller points on free food, or you can go big and enter to win some one-of-a-kind items, including branded trucks, RVs, and motorcycles. Systems such as this give the user a choice and make it feel more empowering as opposed to a simple "buy X get X free" system. One of the keys to implementing a well-received reward system is the use of surprise and delight. This approach involves surprising users with potentially unexpected rewards or experiences. When everything is a scheduled and predictable outcome, users can quickly become bored of the grind. By creating moments of surprise and delight, you can create a positive emotional connection with your users, which can lead to increased engagement and loyalty.

Progress tracking

Often paired with reward systems is the idea of progress tracking. This is the concept of showing users how far they have come and how much progress they have made. Games need to provide instant feedback to players on their actions as it is critical for keeping users informed, engaged, and motivated. The easiest software implementation might be to simply show a progress bar in a web form letting the users know how much of the form they have filled out, and what is left to go. By providing visual feedback on their progress, users are more likely to stay motivated and continue progressing toward the goal within your app or product. These systems can become significantly more complex than a percentage-complete visual. Prodigy is a math learning program for children that plays more like a role-playing video game than your standard math worksheet. By completing problems, you progress your character's level. Within the system, you can always see how close you are to leveling up, and with each problem you solve, that meter grows. Children see that progress and are compelled to try just one more battle, then another, then maybe just one more. They want to see the reward at the end of the progression. Our sense of progress and accomplishment is incredibly powerful. Think about the last time you completed a large project at home or work. How did you feel? Did you reward yourself afterward?

Narrative and storytelling

One of the key components of most video games is strong narrative and storytelling that engages players and immerses them in a fictional world. Products can leverage similar elements to make more engaging and memorable experiences. Narrative can help to solidify the user's sense of purpose and meaning and help them connect emotionally with the product. It has also been shown that humans retain information more effectively when it is delivered in a narrative format. Storytelling can also be used to explain complex features or concepts in a fun and engaging way. Epic Win is an app that uses fun and exciting stories and character development to help you with your daily routine. By completing the tasks you set up for yourself each day, you earn **experience points** (**XP**) that allow you to unlock things and progress on your own epic story. This continuation of the story motivates users to keep their streak alive. Can you remember the last show you binge-watched on your favorite streaming platform? Did you click **Next Episode** when you knew you had other stuff you could be doing? Our human interest in stories drives engagement and draws us in. What if we could binge our yardwork in the same way? What if the passion we had for the latest season of our favorite show translated into clearing out our overloaded inbox?

Social engagement

Games often have a strong social component. Sometimes, it is cooperative; other times, it is competitive. It can even be a simple sharing mechanic where the interaction is passive. Gameplay can take place online or in the same room. Product gamification can use social engagement mechanics in many of the same ways. User-generated content, sharing, and collaboration can be an easy way to foster a sense of community and social connection among users. You can tap into the power of social influence by creating social challenges or group activities. We have a natural desire for competition and cooperation. You can motivate users to stay engaged with your app or product by using features such as daily or weekly leaderboards. TikTok has grown to gigantic proportions using several social gamification techniques. To begin with, TikTok is simply a platform for hosting content and everything within is user generated. All of the videos you see have someone on the other end who decided they wanted to put that content into the world. Many of the videos that go viral on the platform tie heavily into social emotions such as humor, admiration, curiosity, and attraction. And with each social interaction you perform within the app (likes and shares), the algorithm gets more refined at knowing what you want to see. Do you have a favorite restaurant? Do you prefer to go to that restaurant alone, or share the experience with friends? Is it exciting to talk about the food and atmosphere with someone who has never been there? Our desire to share information and ideas to help others can be an incredibly powerful motivator.

Waze (2006)

Waze started with a single goal and statement: "Outsmarting Traffic, Together." At that point in history, driver assistance products were for singular users. Waze looked to disrupt that concept with the idea that if people worked together, they could make a better product that was always being updated by its own users. The idea inspired users to join together to make a better driving experience.

Give the Waze app a try. Use it for a trip to and from work, or on a road trip. Pay attention to the social cues the app gives you. Give other "Wazers" a honk as you pass by, report cars stopped on the shoulder of the road, or warn other drivers of a speed trap. That feeling you get when either helping other drivers or thanking a driver that helped you can be a rewarding experience!

Game psychology

After reading the aforementioned examples, you might be thinking that all of it could be considered psychology, and you'd be correct. In reality, nearly all design is psychology. Interface aesthetics rely heavily on psychological concepts such as the Gestalt principles. Marketing uses concepts such as scarcity and authority to drive the call to action. And product design is heavily tied to psychology of all kinds. Even though all gamification is centered around psychology, it is worth keeping a separate game psychology grouping as there are principles that may not be tied directly to one of the four above. For instance, the concept of flow, as written about by Mihaly Csikszentmihalyi, refers to a state of complete absorption and engagement in an activity, where people become fully immersed and lose track of time. In gaming, this occurs quite often, as users become so immersed in gameplay they even forget to eat and sleep. Csikszentmihalyi identified several key factors that can help foster the experience, including clear goals and feedback, a sense of control and autonomy, a feeling of challenge and skill, and a sense of immersion and focus. You can see a similar set of factors in the study of **Self-Determination Theory (SDT)**.

In summary, the core concept of SDT is that humans are motivated by three basic psychological needs:

- **Autonomy**: Autonomy refers to the desire to be in control of one's own life and make choices that are consistent with our values and interests

- **Competence**: Competence is the desire to feel effective and capable in one's actions

- **Relatedness**: Relatedness refers to our need to feel connected to others and to experience a sense of belonging

According to this psychological theory, satisfying these three basic psychological needs can lead to greater intrinsic motivation, improved performance, and greater well-being. Free Rice is a quiz platform that allows you to earn rice for answering questions correctly. This rice is then donated to the World Food Program (technically, the monetary equivalent of the rice is donated since the charity itself can do more with money than sacks of rice). The educational platform had over 8 million users from 135 countries in 2022. There have been over 214 billion grains of rice donated to date! Users get nothing by participating other than a sense of competence and relatedness.

As you continue through the examples discussed and learn more about gamification, try and think about which of these areas each concept might fit. Usually, there is a little bit of crossover between a few of them.

Where gamification stands today

Over the years, gamification has been described in many ways. Some may view it as the future of product and software design, while others toss it to the side as just another gimmick. As you read this book, you may find that some of the examples speak to you, and others do not. That is one of the key lessons: every application and product is different. What might work for one doesn't work for others. There is no real prescriptive application for gamification to any given product you might be working on.

Gamification ethics and planning

It is also important to remember that gamification can be used for both good and bad. Encouraging a user to eat more healthily by rewarding them with real-world items would likely be considered positive by most consumer standards. However, designing a system that encourages someone to pay more and more money for a slight chance of earning something valuable (such as a "loot box") is bordering on gambling and can be incredibly psychologically addictive. Although, in the short term, consumers may like that serotonin hit when they get something big, over the long term, they will grow increasingly weary of these types of systems. It is up to us as product designers, user experience designers, programmers, and marketers to be responsible in the way we use these tools.

Gamification also has its own set of limitations. Adding a leaderboard and/or a point system to a problem does not fix the problem; it is not a miracle cure. Implementing gamified design needs to be done intelligently and with an understanding of your users, team, and product. The types of game elements used affect the outcome differently. In a 2017 research article titled *"How gamification motivates: An experimental study of the effects of specific game design elements on psychological need satisfaction,"* the researchers found that varying the specific types of elements could yield statistically significant changes to behaviors and the perception of user's tasks (source: `https://www.sciencedirect.com/science/article/pii/S074756321630855X`). This means that simply adding gamification for the sake of it may create more problems than good if not applied properly. Gamification aside, when design is rushed, any application is destined to fail and no amount of high scores can change that. These types of features are also rarely added after the fact and made to be successful. Implementing some of these systems and working the psychology into your designs takes foresight. This must be planned from the onset, not just a feature you get to down the road when your numbers are not hitting the target you expected.

Industry acceptance

Despite these limitations, some of the world's largest software companies now have some form of game division and cross-train their staff in game design techniques and psychology. Microsoft has dived fully into embracing games as a technology and revenue driver with Xbox and the Games Pass service. Google is always looking to expand its brand, and although Stadia failed to reach customers as planned, there is always work being done in that space. Meta, like Microsoft, has made incredibly large investments in the convergence of games and software with its acquisition of Oculus and the development of the Horizon Worlds platform. The goal is a single piece of hardware that you can do work, play games, socialize, and shop on… a new "personal computer," but in the realm of virtual reality. Amazon has even launched its own gaming service in Luna and is trying to compete with all of these offerings. Previously, you saw a hard division of industry between game development and tech development. That world and skill set are colliding. Product, engineering, design, and marketing jobs all now require experience with platforms that check these boxes.

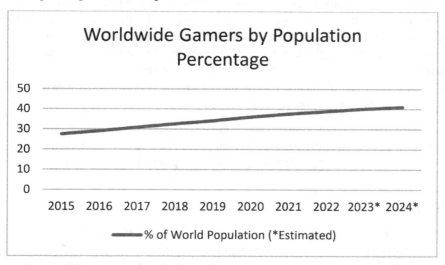

Figure 1.3 – Yearly percentage of population that plays video games

Consumers are facing these same types of convergence. Someone labeling themselves as a gamer used to come with a negative connotation, but as Generation X and Millennials get older, the percentage of people who grew up with and still regularly play games is inching closer and closer to a global majority. What this means to us is that users of our products now have baked-in knowledge of how some of these things work. There no longer needs to be high-level explanations of the concepts. If a user sees a score or progression tracker, there is an immediate understanding of how that works.

Since the early days of our civilization, we have searched for enjoyment and fun. Was this for a change of pace from the more stressful parts of our day-to-day lives? Or, did we simply crave the social aspect that games naturally bring? As we play games, and share that experience with others, we are constantly adapting and adjusting to make it feel unique to the players in the game. As we build more and more of these types of systems, we continue to learn more about what can be improved. As consumers continue to use these systems, their own wants and needs will shift as well. Gamification within product design has moved well beyond the points, badges, and leaderboards it was in the early 2000s. This is because consumers grew bored of it, and desired something new, just like they would with games in general. Technology is moving faster than even creators can keep up with, and the design of products needs to understand this pace to try and build longevity into the systems we use.

Static features themselves age incredibly quickly in this space, but if thought is put into designing the overarching systems, we can have more longevity. Take, for instance, a simple deck of playing cards. As discussed earlier, they have been around longer than any of us, yet are still owned and used by a large part of the population around the globe. The games we play with them (features) may come and go, but the cards themselves (the system) remain. Do you have any games in your life that friends or family have established a set of "house rules" for? Changing a few rules here and there to be more inclusive or easier to play is incredibly common for games. Quite often, games even take on a whole new role that was not the designed intention. Game designers call this emergent behavior, and understanding the eccentricities of it could be a whole new book (and likely is). It is through these adaptations that games evolve and grow. In some instances, business software has done the same. There is an entire community of people across the globe that uses Microsoft Excel to create art. There are a few people that use gameplay footage from games such as The Sims to create movies. Gamification is more than just rewarding users for tasks. If you provide a good toolset, and keep the limitations to a minimum, in the words of Dr. Ian Malcom, "Life, uh… Finds a way."

You may have started this book looking to understand more about points, badges, and leaderboards. But there is more to gamified design than that – a lot more. Looking beyond those things is how we can embrace the future of this style of product design and make products that the audience loves to use.

Summary

Gamification involves adding game-like elements to non-game activities to increase engagement, motivation, and enjoyment. Games have a strong appeal as they offer challenge, reward, and satisfaction, leading to their widespread popularity. The gaming industry has grown significantly, generating more revenue than books, music, and movies combined. The convergence of gaming and software development has given rise to gamification as a powerful tool in the product design process. Gamification can be applied in various industries and roles, enhancing customer experiences and employee motivation.

From ancient dice and card games to modern video games, gaming has evolved. The introduction of reward systems such as S&H Green Stamps laid the foundation for loyalty programs, which led to adopting more game elements in non-game situations. Personal computers and arcade games surged in the 1980s, followed by home video game consoles. The 1990s and early 2000s marked the era of connectivity, with the rise of the internet and mobile devices. Human's current level of connectivity and access to digital devices has changed the landscape, making both games and gamified apps more accessible. By harnessing the design psychology games have utilized for centuries, you can boost engagement, loyalty, and revenue.

Gamification ranges from distinct features such as progress trackers to subtle psychological nudges. Five main categories of gamification emerge: reward systems (punch cards and memberships), progress tracking (badges and achievements), narrative and storytelling (avatars and user profiles), social engagement (leaderboards and share buttons), and game psychology (Easter eggs and boss fights). Each category taps into human motivations and emotions, fostering engagement and connection with users. We will go into significantly more detail about these in *Chapter 5.*

Viewed by some as the future of product design and others as a mere gimmick, the implementation of gamification by product designers, user experience professionals, programmers, and marketers is crucial to both its acceptance and its usefulness. Gamification's limitations demand intelligent integration and foresight, as it is not a quick fix for dragging performance. As major software companies invest in game divisions and cross-train staff, a convergence between gaming and technology has emerged. By embracing the dynamic nature of gamified systems, product designers can build longevity and surpass static solutions.

In the next chapter, we'll discuss how not only your product can utilize gamified design but also how you can work the same concepts into the activities and artifacts you use with your cross-functional teams. By doing so, you can super-charge not only your product but also the speed and efficiency at which you build it as well.

Further reading

Boskamp, Elsie, *25 Gamification Statistics [2023]: Facts + Trends You Need to Know*, Zippia, 2022, https://www.zippia.com/advice/gamification-statistics/.

2

Gamification for Product Managers

In this chapter, we will cover the persona of the product manager we are writing for and other roles that apply to this content. We'll take a deep dive into the competencies and skills of product managers. In those areas, we will discuss their relationship with gamification and briefly overview where the skills relate to gamification, so it's clear what the role entails and who is responsible for managing the areas of product development we will be covering.

Product managers can use gamification to increase user engagement, motivation, and adoption of their products. We'll cover why user engagement is one of the most, if not *the* most, vital metrics to judge a product's value.

We will show how design elements such as points, levels, rewards, and challenges enhance the UX and drive desired behaviors, termed **nudges** in non-game contexts, such as the products you are responsible for developing.

By using gamification in their product development efforts, product managers can create more engaging, motivating, and effective products to differentiate themselves from competitors and stand out in a crowded marketplace.

We'll also create a fictional app to show how the core principles of gamification for product managers increase the value of the technology you are building.

In this chapter, we're going to cover the following main topics:

- Product Manager Core Competencies
- Elite Eight Skills for Product Managers
- The 3 core principles

By the end of the chapter, you will know how to be a better product manager by incorporating gamification into your product work. You will understand how to drive user engagement by tapping into human motivations and psychology and will know about the concept of nudges and how you can design them to influence user behavior. Additionally, you will learn about the potential of gamification to break the status quo and revolutionize the way we interact with technology, creating more engaging and personalized experiences for users. These skills and insights will enable you to develop more effective and impactful gamification strategies for your products and will help you stay ahead of the curve in a rapidly evolving industry.

Product manager core competencies

Product management is a complex and multi-disciplinary field that requires a wide range of skills and competencies. To successfully implement gamification strategies, product managers must have a deep understanding of the core competencies and elite skills that are required to develop, launch, and manage successful products. These skills and competencies are essential to creating gamified experiences that are engaging, effective, and aligned with business goals and objectives. By developing these skills and competencies, product managers will be able to design and implement gamification strategies that drive meaningful user behaviors and outcomes, and that help to differentiate their products in a competitive market.

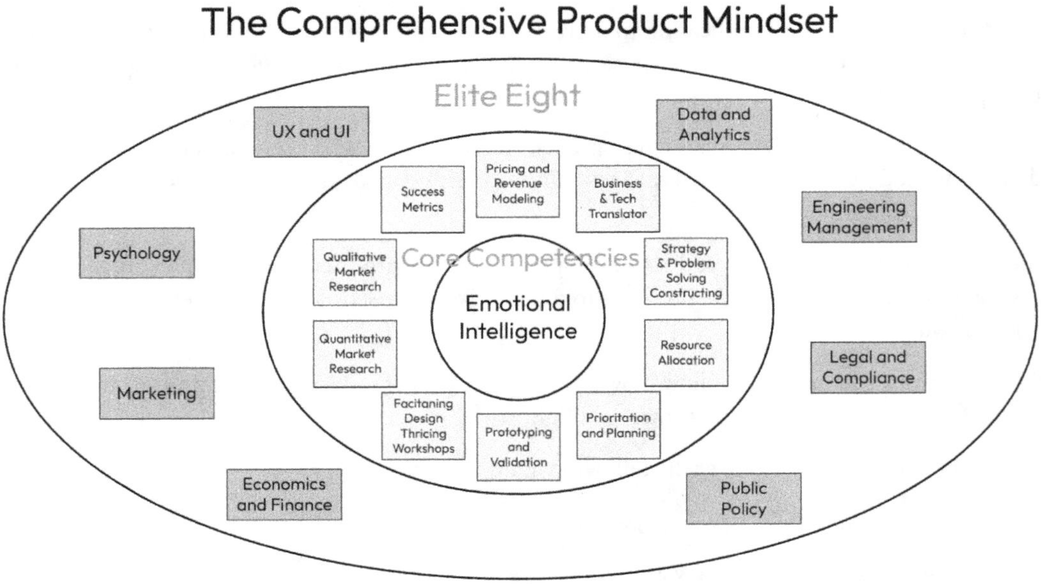

The Comprehensive Product Mindset

Figure 2.1 – Comprehensive product mindset

The top 10 core competencies of product managers are as follows:

- **Qualitative market research**:

  - Focus groups: A research method for gathering feedback from a group of potential or existing users about a product or service.

  - In-depth interviews: A research method for obtaining detailed insights and feedback from individual users about their experiences and needs.

  - Ethnography: A research method for observing and understanding user behavior and culture in their natural environment.

  - Customer site visits: A method for product managers to gain firsthand insights about how customers are using a product or service.

  - Social media: A platform for product managers to monitor and engage with users, as well as to gather feedback and insights about user needs and preferences.

- **Quantitative market research**:

  - Market sizing: Estimating the potential size of a target market for a product or service.

  - Surveys: Collecting data through a set of standardized questions to gain insights into customers' attitudes and behaviors.

  - Concept tests: Testing the appeal and potential success of a new product or service idea with potential customers.

  - Consumer panels: A group of customers who are regularly surveyed or studied to provide ongoing feedback on products or services.

  - Data and analytics: The collection and analysis of data from various platforms to gain insights and inform decision-making in product management.

- **Facilitating design-thinking workshops**:

  - Problem validation: Process of testing and validating the problem statement by gathering feedback from potential users or stakeholders to ensure that the problem being addressed is a real, important, and relevant one that requires a solution.

  - Hypothesis testing: Creating a set of assumptions about the problem and solution, then testing them through experimentation and data analysis. Validating your ideas, identifying potential risks and challenges, and refining the solutions based on feedback from users.

  - Ideation: Participants generate a large number of ideas and potential solutions to the problem statement through brainstorming and other creative techniques.

  - Innovation: Developing a novel, valuable, and feasible solution that addresses the problem statement and meets user needs. This involves synthesizing insights and ideas from the previous stages, prototyping, and testing the solution with users.

- **Prototyping and validation**:

  - Requirements gathering: Collecting and documenting information about what the product should do, based on user needs and business goals.

  - Running design sprints: Structured process for generating and testing ideas in a short amount of time, to rapidly iterate and improve the product or feature idea.

  - Clickable prototype: Simulated version of the product that users can interact with, allowing for feedback and testing before building the full product.

  - Proof of concept: A working prototype that demonstrates the feasibility of a product or idea, typically used to secure funding or support for further development.

- **Feature prioritization and roadmap planning**:

  - Prioritizing your product in the portfolio: Determining how your product aligns with the company's overall strategy, prioritizing it within the product portfolio, and allocating the appropriate resources to ensure its success.

  - Prioritizing product features: Using data, customer feedback, and market trends to prioritize which features are most important to build and when to build them.

  - Roadmaps: Documents that communicate the vision and direction of the product, align teams on priorities, and provide transparency to stakeholders on what will be delivered and when.

  - Dependencies and risk management: Identifying dependencies between teams and managing potential risks that could impact the product's development and launch. You must also have contingency plans in place to mitigate any potential roadblocks.

- **Resource allocation**:

  - Negotiation: Communicating and compromising with stakeholders to achieve desired project outcomes. Product managers must negotiate for project resources and new business goals in order to successfully implement and launch a product.

  - Project resource demand: Accurately estimating and communicating the resources required to execute a project, including staffing, budget, and time, to ensure that the team has what it needs to succeed and that stakeholders are well informed.

  - New business goals: Having a strong understanding of the company's business goals and objectives, and being able to align the product roadmap with those goals to ensure that the product is contributing to the company's overall success. This includes being able to identify opportunities for growth and new markets to enter and allocate the necessary resources to make it happen.

- **Strategic thinking and problem solving**:

  - Understanding the market and competition: Possessing a deep understanding of the market and competition to make informed decisions and position their product in a way that differentiates it from competitors. Keeping up with market trends, customer needs, and industry advancements.

  - Setting a vision: Setting a clear vision for their product, outlining the goals, target audience, and objectives that the product must achieve. A well-defined vision can provide direction and align stakeholders toward a common goal.

  - Solving complex problems as they arise: Identifying and solving complex problems related to your product. You must have strong problem-solving skills to identify root causes, analyze data, and develop and implement effective solutions that align with the overall product vision and objectives.

- **Translator between the business and technology teams**:

  - Brevity communication: The ability to communicate ideas and information concisely and clearly, making sure that all parties involved understand the key points and objectives.

  - Constructing arguments: The ability to build and articulate compelling arguments in support of a particular position or decision, using logic, evidence, and persuasive techniques.

  - Presentation design: The ability to create engaging and effective presentations that communicate key messages and information to diverse audiences, utilizing visual aids, storytelling, and other techniques to enhance understanding and retention.

- **Pricing strategy and revenue modeling**:

  - Price elasticity and psychology: The concept of price elasticity refers to the sensitivity of demand for a product or service in response to changes in its price, while psychology refers to the study of human behavior and how it influences decision-making. Together, product managers need to understand how these two factors interact to inform pricing strategies that maximize revenue while remaining attractive to customers.

  - Revenue model options: There are various revenue model options available to product managers, such as subscription-based, freemium, pay-per-use, or advertising-based models. Product managers need to evaluate the pros and cons of each revenue model option to determine the most effective and profitable approach for their product.

  - **Customer lifetime value (CLV)**: The estimated amount of money a customer will spend on a product or service over the course of their relationship with the company. Product managers need to understand how to calculate CLV and use it to inform pricing decisions and marketing strategies that aim to retain and attract high-value customers.

- **Defining and tracking success metrics**:

  - Metrics by category: The process of categorizing different types of metrics, such as usage metrics, financial metrics, and customer satisfaction metrics, to evaluate the performance of a product and inform decision-making.

  - Selecting metrics: The process of selecting the most relevant and effective metrics to measure the success of a product based on business goals and objectives.

  - Tracking and reporting: The process of continuously monitoring and measuring the selected metrics, analyzing the data, and presenting the findings in a clear and actionable format to inform decision-making and optimize the performance of a product.

Gamification will tie into almost all of the core functions in one aspect or another if you choose to bring it into your product development strategy. In the chapters ahead, we will link gamification to the core functions of a product manager.

Product managers' emotional quotient (PMEQ)

Product managers need to have a high level of emotional intelligence or a high **emotional quotient (EQ)** since the primary functions of their job are representing the voice of the customer, managing a cross-functional team, and managing up to business stakeholders. EQ is the ability to manage your emotions and those of others, which is essential for building effective working relationships, managing conflicts, and driving successful product development.

To understand how to successfully utilize gamification in your product, you must have excellent relationship management skills to find the necessary information and insights on your user's wants and needs. You need to develop empathy for the user and get a deep understanding of their needs and motivations. EQ gives you an empathetic ear and will give you the insight to design your game mechanics in a way that meets your users' needs and innovates on the art of the possible.

Product management is a fast-paced and rapidly changing environment. EQ will help you navigate ambiguity and develop resilience to satisfy your stakeholders' needs and concerns about implementing something they may need to be more familiar with. You'll also need to develop and manage relationships with your stakeholders because they will be the ones who likely sign off on your gamification strategy and are the gatekeepers for product launches, budgeting, and other administrative functions.

Product managers must be able to work effectively with a wide range of people with different skills, personalities, and perspectives. Relationship skills are essential for selling the team on your vision of a gamified product or feature, managing conflicts, negotiating sprint priorities, and keeping the team aligned and motivated to reach your goals. Emotional intelligence can help product managers build strong, collaborative teams by understanding and appreciating the strengths and differences of team members. Also, you work closely with designers and engineers daily.

"Elite eight" product manager skills

Finally, there are the "elite eight" skills of a product manager. Product managers don't have to be experts in these areas, but they need to be well versed in the languages to work with the teams who are the experts in these areas, and they need to know the specifics of how these areas relate to their success. We will look into these skills in the following subsections.

User experience (UX) and user interface (UI) design

As it relates to gamification, this combined area is one of the two most important to understand – so important, we wrote a whole chapter on it. If gamification fits your strategy, UX and UI should be considered in your solution's structure and design to help users meet their goals.

UX

UX refers to a user's overall experience while interacting with a product, service, or system, including their emotions, perceptions, behaviors, and responses. UX design enhances user satisfaction by improving the usability, accessibility, and desirability of the product or system, considering the users' needs, preferences, and expectations.

The UX strategy is the long-term plan that guides the design and development of a product or service to provide an optimal UX. It involves research, analysis, and planning to align the product's features, functions, and design with the users' needs, goals, and use context.

In the context of a product manager's role, the UX strategy plays a crucial part in defining and prioritizing product features and improvements. A product manager is responsible for guiding a product's development, launch, and ongoing management, ensuring it meets user needs and business objectives. The UX strategy helps product managers do the following:

- **Understand users**: Conduct research to gain insights into users' needs, preferences, and pain points, which inform product decisions and priorities

- **Develop user personas**: Create fictional representations of the target users to empathize with their needs, motivations, and behaviors and guide product design

- **Create user journeys and scenarios**: Map out the various steps, interactions, and touchpoints users have with the product, identifying opportunities for improvements and innovation

- **Prioritize features and improvements**: Use insights from UX research to prioritize and make informed decisions about the features and enhancements that will significantly impact user satisfaction and business objectives

As stated, this journey starts with empathically understanding your users' wants, needs, and motivations. Once you understand that, you and your team must design the solution, which is the art and science of where UX, game mechanics, and product management meet. You need to leverage the art of UX and game design with the science of UI best practices, your technological capacity, and the business case.

When thinking about gamification, the first step is to see whether it is a viable solution for your use case. Will gamification theory or game mechanics help your users solve their need and drive your business case? A helpful tip is to be involved with market research and investigate your potential users. Once you understand their needs, compile a few rudimentary designs that showcase your gamification hypotheses for a solution. Bring these back to the user, and test your hypotheses early and often.

UI

UI design creates a digital product or system's visual elements and interactive components, such as websites, mobile applications, or software programs. UI design aims to create an aesthetically pleasing and functional interface that facilitates smooth and efficient user interactions, making it easy for users to achieve their goals and complete tasks.

UI design is closely related to UX design, as both disciplines aim to create a seamless, enjoyable experience for users. While UX design focuses on the product's overall user journey and usability, UI design addresses the specific visual and interactive components that enable users to interact with the product effectively. UI design encompasses several aspects, including layout, color schemes, typography, icons, buttons, and other interactive elements. It focuses on the presentation and interactivity of the product, ensuring that the interface is visually appealing, user-friendly, and consistent with the brand's identity.

In the context of a product manager's role, UI design plays a vital part in the development and success of a digital product. A product manager guides a product's development, launch, and ongoing management, ensuring it meets user needs and business objectives. UI design helps product managers do the following:

- **Define visual and interactive requirements**: Collaborate with UX designers to translate user needs and goals into visual and interactive elements that are easy to use and understand

- **Maintain consistency and branding**: Ensure the UI design adheres to brand guidelines and design systems, providing a consistent experience across all touchpoints and platforms

- **Stay current with UI trends and best practices**: Keep updated with the latest developments in UI design, technologies, and methodologies, ensuring the product's interface remains modern, engaging, and competitive

- **Validate and iterate designs**: Test UI design prototypes with real users, gather feedback, and make data-driven improvements to enhance usability and user satisfaction

- **Oversee design implementation**: Work with development teams to accurately implement the UI design mechanics, addressing any discrepancies or issues that may arise during the development process

You should have an in-depth understanding of prototyping and usability testing to know whether the game mechanics work. You should be able to speak the language with your designer around current trends and best practices in user-centered design, design thinking, customer journey mapping, interaction design, and visual design.

Psychology

Design is the heart of gamification, and psychology is, well, its brain. It's the other most vital skill to understand while developing your gamification strategy. With your market research and UX discovery, you should have a good idea of your persona and their behaviors. The inspirational design blends into both areas since you have to know the wants and needs of the user to be able to design something that is emotionally engaging for them and is aesthetically pleasing, and drives the user's brain to resonate with the design.

When you start getting into the psychology of your user, you should understand the principles of persuasion and influence and be able to use these principles in your product design and experience to drive user engagement and adoption ethically. The subtle art of persuasion is also a tactic you will want to know when working with marketing and advertising teams. One of the best books written about this was the groundbreaking *Influence* by Robert B. Cialdini, Ph.D., which is widely referenced and taught in both product management and consulting. The six fundamental ways in which people are influenced are as follows:

- **Reciprocity**: The principle of reciprocity suggests that people are more likely to comply with requests or demands if they feel they have received something of value first. In other words, if you do something for someone else, they are more likely to do something for you in return.

- **Authority**: The principle of authority suggests that people are more likely to comply with requests or demands from someone perceived as an authority figure. This figure could include someone with expertise, experience, or credentials in a particular area.

- **Commitment and consistency**: The principle of commitment and consistency suggests that people are more likely to comply with requests or demands if they have already made a commitment or taken a position consistent with the request. For example, if someone has already made a small commitment to a cause or idea, they are more likely to make a more significant commitment in the future.

- **Social proof**: The principle of social proof suggests that people are more likely to comply with requests or demands if they see that others like them are doing the same thing. In other words, the actions and opinions of others influence people to take or not take specific actions.

- **Liking**: The principle of liking suggests that people are more likely to comply with requests or demands from people they like or find attractive, hence the popularity of the influencer role on social media. This "influencer" could include people who are similar to them, have given them compliments, or have built a rapport with them.

- **Scarcity**: The principle of scarcity suggests that people are more likely to comply with requests or demands if they believe that the opportunity is rare, unique, or valuable. In other words, people are motivated to take action when they believe they need to catch up on something desirable or limited in availability.

Overall, these six fundamental patterns describe the important ways people are influenced and persuaded to comply with requests or demands. By understanding these patterns, individuals can develop more effective strategies for influencing and persuading others.

And that gets us to the primary goal of developing a gamification strategy...**motivation**. An elite product manager understands what motivates users to use and engage with products. They can use this knowledge to create motivating and rewarding products for users; gamification techniques such as leaderboards and rewards programs are vital tools we will explore in this book.

Engineering management

An elite product manager has a strong understanding of software development methodologies, and since digital technology is the focus here, those methodologies are going to primarily be Agile frameworks, with variations such as Scrum, SAFe, Kanban, *The Lean Startup* method by Eric Ries, *Spotify* by... Spotify, **Rapid Application Development (RAD)**, **Extreme Programming (XP)**, and others that people claim they do they do but really they practice Waterfall. For the purposes of this book, we will be hypothetically developing in Agile and Lean and giving examples that fit one of the frameworks.

For a refresher, Scrum, Agile, and Lean are all software development methodologies that aim to streamline the development process and deliver high-quality software products efficiently. Here are some of the similarities and differences between these methodologies.

Similarities

- **Iterative and incremental**: All three methodologies follow an iterative and incremental approach to software development, focusing on continuous improvement and delivering working software quickly

- **Collaborative**: All three methodologies emphasize collaboration between team members, focusing on teamwork, communication, and shared ownership

- **Customer-focused**: All three methodologies prioritize the needs and expectations of the customer, with a focus on delivering value and meeting user needs

Differences

- **Scrum**: Scrum is a specific framework within the Agile methodology that emphasizes iterative development, cross-functional teams, and frequent feedback. It is based on a set of roles, ceremonies, and artifacts and aims to deliver a potentially shippable product increment at the end of each sprint.

- **Agile**: Agile is a comprehensive and flexible methodology emphasizing collaboration, flexibility, and responsiveness to change. It is based on values and principles and includes several frameworks, such as Scrum, Kanban, and XP.

- **Lean**: Lean is a methodology that emphasizes maximizing value while minimizing waste. It aims to eliminate inefficiencies and streamline processes, focusing on delivering value to the customer and continuous improvement. Delivering value, eliminating waste, and continuous improvement are the core principles of this methodology.

Overall, Scrum, Agile, and Lean all share a common goal of delivering high-quality software efficiently and collaboratively. However, they differ in their specific approaches, with Scrum being a specific framework within Agile that emphasizes cross-functional teams and frequent feedback. Agile is a flexible and adaptable methodology that prioritizes collaboration and responsiveness. Lean is a methodology that emphasizes value delivery and waste elimination. Gamification fits into all these with frequent feedback and doing more with less.

With your understanding of the engineering frameworks, you should understand the basic definitions of user stories, acceptance criteria, technical architecture, **application programming interfaces (APIs)**, tech debt, code reviews, unit testing, **quality assurance (QA)**, **user acceptance testing (UAT)**, release management, and DevOps.

It will be a bonus if you come from engineering and understand how to code or have a deep understanding of architectural and cloud platforms; this will set you up to master the technical product manager position.

Data and analytics

A product manager understands big data and analytics and can use data to inform product development decisions. But the modern product manager has multiple platforms to understand, depending on where or who they work for. Also, data and analytics tools are constantly evolving, and you must be up to speed with the changes.

There is also a vast selection of options out there now. For example, Adobe Analytics uses multiple tools and functions to track, measure, and analyze customer interactions. It allows businesses to track customer behaviors and preferences, measure marketing campaigns' effectiveness, and identify improvement areas in their digital experiences. Mixpanel is a web and mobile analytics platform that provides real-time data processing, user behavior tracking, and A/B testing capabilities. Businesses use it to focus on product and UX optimization. Hotjar is a web analytics and user feedback tool that provides heatmaps, session recordings, and user surveys. It allows businesses to identify areas of a website that need improvement and to collect user feedback to guide their optimization efforts. I picked these examples because I have used them and had successful experiences. There are many more platforms to explore to see which fits your organization, needs, goals, and price points.

Product managers may also have to make their dashboards, building and populating databases that connect to Microsoft Power BI or Tableau. Please create your dashboard when displaying a product with game mechanics (which we will get into in more depth in a later chapter). The data and analytics you will need to be successful in your gamification journey are as follows:

- **Measuring engagement**: This is your most crucial tracking mechanism. It would help if you were tracking metrics such as user participation, time spent on the platform, and game completion rates. How are your users engaging with your product?

- **Continual improvement**: Analyze user feedback, performance data, and exits to identify areas where product teams can optimize their gamification by adjusting the difficulty level of challenges, adding new features, or optimizing the UX.

- **Objectives and key results** (OKRs): When you decided to gamify your product or feature, you had a business goal you were trying to achieve, such as revenue growth, retention, or a number of sessions. By tracking the costs and benefits of your gamification, you can determine the **return on investment** (ROI), and whether it provided the key results you planned on and sold to your stakeholders.

- **Team health**: Develop internal metrics to track releases, the health of your process, the pulse of your team, and the quality of code and architecture. You can only build a product successfully with an engaged team producing quality work and working together effectively.

When building a gamification strategy, you may use artificial intelligence and work with data scientists to build machine learning models that power your game mechanics. It's important to understand that data scientists work differently than engineers, have unique skill sets and challenges, and require their management techniques. Data scientists may only sometimes prefer Agile methods due to data science projects' unique challenges and workflows. Unlike Agile methods emphasizing rapid iteration and continuous delivery, data science projects often require significant data preparation and exploration, which can be time-consuming and unpredictable. The focus of Agile methods on quickly delivering working software may not leave sufficient time for rigorous testing and QA, which could compromise the integrity of data scientists' models and analysis.

Additionally, data science projects often require experimentation and research to explore different approaches and hypotheses, which may be limited in an Agile environment due to the pressure to deliver results quickly. However, many data science teams have successfully adopted Agile methods by adapting them to fit their unique workflows and needs, demonstrating that the success of any project management approach will depend on the specific context and the preferences of the team involved. Before you begin your gamification development, talk with your data scientists and set expectations for project execution.

You might be working with a data team or teams to ensure that products are designed and launched in a way that maximizes user engagement and drives business growth. Data analytics, data mining, data visualization, data-driven decision-making, **key performance indicators** (KPIs), metrics, A/B testing, cohort analysis, funnel analysis, segmentation, data governance, and data privacy are all terms that should be on your radar.

Marketing

Undertaking a gamification strategy requires a strong understanding of marketing principles, including brand management, customer acquisition, and user engagement. As a product manager, you should work closely with marketing teams to ensure that products are launched and promoted to maximize user adoption and market share.

As the product manager who drives the vision and understands the users' pains, gains, and motivations, you should be the marketing team's key to unlocking their messaging potential. You can relate the message to stop the pain points or motivations of the user; you can explain how the game mechanics work and why people would love to use them.

Marketing plays a critical role in the success of a gamification strategy by promoting the product and engaging users. Gamification relies heavily on marketing to drive user acquisition and engagement and promote the product's unique features and benefits.

One of the key ways that marketing can support a gamification strategy is through user acquisition. By promoting the gamified elements of the product through targeted campaigns, social media, and other channels, marketing can drive awareness and interest in the product. Your marketing strategy is fundamental in the early stages of the product launch when building an initial user base is critical.

In addition to user acquisition, marketing can also help to keep users engaged with the product by promoting ongoing gamification events and features. For example, by promoting challenges, leaderboards, and rewards, marketing can incentivize users to continue using the product and engage with its gamified elements. Focusing your marketing campaign on the fun aspects of your game mechanics can increase user retention and drive ongoing engagement with the product.

Another essential role of marketing in a gamification strategy is brand building. By promoting the product's gamified elements and unique features, marketing can help build the product's brand and create a robust and engaging identity that resonates with users. The tactical marketing focus can help to differentiate the product from competitors and build a loyal user base that is more likely to continue using the product over time. And remember, as the product manager, you are the brand as well. So things you do on social media affect the brand of the product you represent.

Marketing can also gather user feedback on the gamification strategy and product features. Product managers can improve their gamification strategy by working with the marketing team to monitor user feedback and sentiment. The findings from this collaboration clearly identify areas where product managers could enhance the existing gamified experience or additional features could be added. Marketing can share this information with the product development team to inform future iterations and improvements.

Finally, marketing can help track key metrics such as user engagement, acquisition, and retention. By monitoring these metrics, marketing can evaluate the success of the gamification strategy and make data-driven decisions about how to refine and optimize the strategy over time.

By working closely with marketing teams, product managers can leverage their expertise in user acquisition, engagement, and brand building to help promote and enhance the gamification strategy, ultimately leading to increased user adoption, engagement, and retention. Through ongoing collaboration between product and marketing teams, gamification can be a powerful tool for driving business growth and user satisfaction.

Brand management, market research, customer acquisition, customer retention, customer engagement, marketing automation, inbound marketing, outbound marketing, **search engine optimization** (SEO), **pay-per-click** (PPC) advertising, content marketing, and social media marketing are all terms that should be on your radar with the marketing teams.

Legal and compliance

An elite product manager understands the legal and regulatory landscape in which their products operate and understands issues such as data privacy, security, and intellectual property. They work closely with legal teams to ensure products comply with relevant laws and regulations.

Legal and compliance matter to a product manager who is using gamification because gamification often involves collecting and using user data, which can raise legal and regulatory issues around data privacy, security, and intellectual property. Failure to comply with relevant laws and regulations can result in significant legal and financial consequences for the company, as well as damage to the company's reputation and user trust.

Specifically, legal and compliance matter in the following ways:

- **Data privacy**: Gamification often involves the collection and use of user data, such as personal information, behavioral data, and other sensitive information. Product managers must be aware of relevant data privacy laws, such as GDPR or CCPA, and ensure their gamification strategy complies with these laws. Areas to focus on may include the following:

  - Obtaining user consent

  - Implementing appropriate data security measures

  - Ensuring that you or the company does not utilize user data for purposes beyond what is disclosed in the company's privacy policy

- **Intellectual property**: Gamification often involves the creation of original content, such as game mechanics, graphics, and other visual elements. Product managers need to be aware of relevant intellectual property laws, such as copyright and trademark laws, and ensure that their gamification strategy is not infringing on the intellectual property rights of others. Your responsibility may involve conducting thorough research to ensure that the gamification elements are original or obtaining permission to use copyrighted materials. On the other hand, if you create something so original that it justifies registering a copyright or trademark, work with your legal team to protect your intellectual property.

- **Consumer protection**: Gamification strategies can potentially exploit users through misleading or deceptive practices. Product managers must be aware of relevant consumer protection laws, such as the FTC Act, and ensure their gamification strategy is transparent and not misleading. Your due diligence may involve the following:

  - Clearly communicating the game's rules

  - Disclosing any fees or costs associated with the game

  - Ensuring that false claims or promises do not mislead users

- **Industry standards**: Gamification often involves using industry standards, such as Open Badges or Game On, with their own guidelines and best practices. Product managers must be aware of these industry standards and ensure that their gamification strategy complies with them. We will cover many of these in this book, and you are well on your way to conducting research by reading this book. You should also be open to consulting with industry experts to ensure that your gamification strategy aligns with industry best practices.

Example – Hi-Z Fitness App

Background: Hi-Z Fitness App is a mobile application designed to help users track their workouts, set fitness goals, and stay motivated through gamification features such as leaderboards, badges, and rewards. The app collects personal information, such as users' names, email addresses, workout data, and location information.

Challenge: As the product manager for Hi-Z Fitness App, you need to ensure that the app complies with data privacy and security regulations, such as the **General Data Protection Regulation (GDPR)** in the European Union and the **California Consumer Privacy Act (CCPA)** in the United States. Additionally, the app should respect intellectual property rights when implementing gamification elements such as badges and rewards.

Solution: To address these challenges, the product manager took the following steps:

- Collaborated with the legal team to review the app's data collection, storage, and processing practices to ensure compliance with GDPR, CCPA, and other relevant regulations. The outcome included implementing features that allow users to access, delete, and modify their personal information and opt out of data sharing with third parties.

- Partnered with the appropriate partners to conduct a thorough risk assessment to identify potential security vulnerabilities and implemented security measures to protect user data, such as data encryption, access controls, and regular security audits.

- Worked with the design team to create original gamification elements such as badges and rewards, avoiding potential intellectual property infringement issues arising from using copyrighted or trademarked material.

- Received a clear and comprehensive privacy policy and terms of service from the legal team, explaining how the app collects, uses, and shares user data and the measures taken to protect users' privacy and security to which they have access.

- Implemented an ongoing compliance monitoring program, ensuring that changes to legal and regulatory requirements are promptly addressed and the app remains compliant.

Outcome: By working closely with the legal team and taking a proactive approach to legal and regulatory compliance, the product manager was able to successfully launch the Hi-Z Fitness App with gamification features that complied with data privacy, security, and intellectual property laws. As a result, the app avoided potential legal and financial consequences and built trust with users, contributing to its success and growth in the competitive fitness app market.

As a product manager, data privacy, intellectual property, patents, trademarks, copyrights, data security, GDPR, CCPA, the **Children's Online Privacy Protection Act (COPPA)**, FTC regulations, compliance, terms of service, and privacy policy should be terms on your radar when talking to legal.

Economics and finance

An elite product manager understands basic economic concepts such as supply and demand, price elasticity, and market competition. They work closely with business teams to develop effective pricing strategies and ensure products are priced to maximize profitability. Their understanding of supply and demand and market competition can help product managers design gamification strategies that stand out in a crowded market. Understanding the behavior of consumers and competitors can help a product manager to identify areas where their gamification strategy can differentiate them from the competition.

Pricing strategies are a core competency in product management, but knowing price elasticity is a significant upgrade when figuring out how responsive demand is to changes in price. One of the game mechanics is having a rewards system for users that complete specific objectives or tasks. The price elasticity of the product can impact the effectiveness of the incentive. There is a balance between how much you pay for the service and the value of the reward you may receive. And the price is only sometimes financial. Some products may ask you to collect data or personal information in exchange for rewards.

Financial incentives tie into rewards, which tie into psychology. It's helpful to understand the basic principles of behavioral economics, such as decision-making biases and heuristics. Product managers can use this knowledge to develop products designed to overcome these biases and drive user behavior in specific ways.

For example, many gamification strategies offer users rewards or financial incentives in exchange for completing certain tasks or achieving specific goals. By understanding decision-making biases and heuristics, product managers can design these incentives in a way that is likely to motivate users and drive engagement.

Some examples of decision-making biases and heuristics that product managers may consider when developing gamification strategies include the following:

- **Loss aversion**: People tend to be more motivated by the fear of losing something than the possibility of gaining something. Product managers may design gamification strategies emphasizing the potential loss of rewards or status to motivate users to act.

- **Social proof**: The behaviors of others influence the thoughts and actions of people all of the time. Product managers may design gamification strategies that highlight the actions of other users, such as displaying leaderboards or sharing social media posts, to encourage users to participate.

- **Status quo bias**: People prefer the status quo, even if it is not the best option. To overcome this bias, product managers may design gamification strategies that encourage users to try new behaviors or break old habits.

> **Duolingo (2012)**
>
> Touting itself as the #1 way for someone to learn a new language, Duolingo hit the public app stores in 2012. The application has over 60 million monthly average users and is full of gamification examples.
>
> Download the Duolingo app and give it a try. Within the first couple of minutes, you are encouraged to learn a new language using a number of gamification cues. One of the most powerful strategies Duolingo uses however is the "Number of Consecutive Days" streak counter. By logging in and completing one lesson a day, you can keep this streak alive. See how far you can take your streak. At what point does the loss aversion take effect for you? Did you make it to 5 days? 20? Even higher? The longer that streak becomes, the harder you will try and keep it, which can be a powerful method for staying fresh in the mind of your users.

Using their behavioral economics knowledge, product managers can design gamification strategies that are more likely to drive user engagement and achieve business goals. They can create incentives and rewards tailored to specific decision-making biases and heuristics to maximize the gamification strategy's effectiveness.

Finally, the last section of utilizing your economic skills is internal. To get your product or feature funded, you will have developed (or should be developing) a business case. In the business case, you will have to show your stakeholders the value of your product. Developing financial metrics on CLV, CAC, profit margins, and ROI is an essential aspect of product management, mainly when designing gamification strategies:

- **Customer Lifetime Value (CLV)**: CLV is a metric that measures the total value a customer will bring to a company over the course of their relationship. To calculate CLV, product managers must take into account the average revenue per customer, the length of the customer relationship, and the costs associated with serving that customer. By understanding the CLV of their customers, product managers can allocate resources better and develop gamification strategies that maximize the long-term value of each customer.

- **Customer Acquisition Cost (CAC)** : CAC is a metric that measures the cost of acquiring a new customer. To calculate CAC, product managers must consider the total cost of sales and marketing activities related to acquiring new customers over a given period, divided by the number of new customers acquired in that period. By understanding the CAC, product managers can better allocate resources and develop gamification strategies tailored to drive user acquisition cost-effectively.

- **Profit margins:** Profit margins are a metric that measures the difference between revenue and costs associated with a product. Product managers must understand the costs associated with developing and marketing a product and the revenue generated from sales to calculate the profit margin. By understanding the profit margins associated with different products or services, product managers can make informed decisions about resource allocation and develop gamification strategies designed to maximize profitability.

- **Return on Investment (ROI):** ROI is a metric that measures the financial return on a particular investment, such as a gamification strategy. To calculate ROI, product managers must consider the costs associated with developing and implementing the gamification strategy and the financial benefits resulting from increased user engagement, retention, and profitability. By understanding the ROI of a gamification strategy, product managers can make informed decisions about resource allocation and can optimize the strategy to maximize ROI.

Product managers must have a deep understanding of financial metrics to develop effective gamification strategies. Product managers can make informed decisions about resource allocation and develop gamification strategies tailored to meet specific business goals by calculating and analyzing metrics such as CLV, CAC, profit margins, and ROI. By leveraging financial metrics, product managers can create gamification strategies that are engaging for users and profitable for the company.

Product managers should understand the core concepts of supply and demand, pricing strategies, cost-benefit analysis, market competition, market segmentation, loss aversion, CLV, CAC, revenue, profit margin, break-even point, and ROI.

Public policy

Product managers must understand the political and regulatory environment when designing gamification strategies. An elite product manager must be well versed in consumer protection, environmental regulations, and industry standards and work closely with policy teams to ensure that products are compliant with relevant policies and regulations.

Political and regulatory issues may impact the design of gamification strategies. For example, gamification strategies that involve financial incentives or rewards may need to comply with industry standards or government regulations that dictate how rewards are distributed or used. Additionally, gamification strategies may involve public policy issues, such as health and safety regulations, impacting how the product is designed and marketed.

Stakeholder management is also crucial to product management, particularly when designing gamification strategies. Product managers must work closely with their leadership team to align with external stakeholders, such as policymakers, industry groups, and consumer advocates, to ensure the gamification strategy is well received and supported. Policy advocacy is more of a support role that may involve lobbying efforts to shape policy or engage with stakeholders to address concerns or gain support.

Overall, an elite product manager must understand the political and regulatory landscape in which their products operate to design effective gamification strategies. Product managers can ensure that gamification strategies comply with relevant regulations and laws and address potential stakeholder concerns by working closely with policy teams and legal experts. Your role ultimately helps to build trust and credibility with users and stakeholders and can drive greater user engagement and business success.

Product managers should understand the core concepts of consumer protection, environmental regulations, industry standards, government regulations, compliance, lobbying, public policy, political landscape, and stakeholder management.

To reiterate, we reviewed the top 10 core competencies, the emotional intelligence quotient, and the "elite eight" skills of product managers. You may have just started in product management and are still learning the core competencies, or you may be a seasoned pro and have mastered all skills and then some. This overview shows how gamification ties to all aspects of a product manager's role and responsibility. It is a skill that requires tremendous work and insight but also provides tremendous opportunity. We wrote this book to help you navigate the journey and become a better product manager using best practices and gamification techniques.

How this book fits into your product career

Layering in the gamification best practices on top of 0ur core competencies, a high level of emotional intelligence, and elite product manager skills will make you a better product manager. Harnessing the transformative power of gamification is not an isolated endeavor but a holistic strategy that requires the synergy of various competencies, perspectives, and skills. This approach is encapsulated in the following arguments:

- Argument 1: You can incorporate your gamification strategy into your core competencies. When doing market research, you will now have more insight and can ask users how they feel about specific game mechanics such as levels or leaderboards. As you build your solution, you have a toolbox of gamification features you can insert into your prototype or proof of concept. When you are workshopping, you can use success stories around gamification to stimulate new ideas and innovation.

- Argument 2: As a product manager with emotional intelligence, you understand the importance of researching with empathy to truly understand the user and their needs, whether they like to play games or not. Human-centered design is being able to use the game mechanics and solutions to solve a problem for your user. Relationship management with your teams allows you to bring your gamification vision to life by motivating and leading your team. And it also allows you to sell the vision to your stakeholders to get the clearance and funding to build a successful product or feature with game mechanics.

- Argument 3: Understating the "elite eight" skills of product managers will give you insight into all the areas you need to be connected to make your product successful. Each of the "elite eight" is a team you should be working with, and if you are in a smaller company, knowing what should be done in these areas will be critical to your success. Each of these areas plays a crucial role in gamification, some more than others, but they are all essential for success. You want to pay attention to all of them because you don't want to create a fantastic product that users love, only to have it shut down due to legal implications or, much worse, get sued.

Gamification increases user engagement

So now that we have the expectations of the product manager out of the way, let's get into why gamification, when utilized correctly in a situation where it is valuable, can be a game changer (pun intended).

If you are in charge of developing and launching a product and feature, and you build the most unique, incredible, fantastic product or feature ever, and no one uses it, you didn't succeed at your job. When we develop products and features, we want people to use them. Gamification can help you with that.

User engagement refers to the level of involvement and interaction with a product or service. It measures how often and how deeply users engage with the product and can include metrics such as time spent using the product, frequency of use, number of actions taken, and social sharing.

For product managers, user engagement is a critical factor in the success of their products. High levels of engagement indicate that users find value in the product and are likely to continue using it, which can lead to increased revenue and user retention. Additionally, engaged users can become brand advocates, sharing their positive experiences with others and driving new user acquisition. Product managers must understand user behavior and preferences to design engaging products that meet their needs. They must also constantly monitor user engagement metrics and use this data to make informed decisions about product development, marketing, and customer support. Overall, user engagement is a crucial metric for measuring the success of a product and is essential for building a loyal user base.

Here are the reasons why people use digital products and how they succeed:

Needs:

- Solves a real problem or meets a genuine need
- Offers a unique value proposition or competitive advantage
- Has a clear target audience and addresses their specific pain points

UX:

- Is user-friendly and easy to understand/use
- Provides an intuitive and seamless UX

- Offers reliable and consistent performance
- Has a high-quality and visually appealing design

Reputation:

- Generates positive word-of-mouth and customer referrals
- Has a strong brand identity and reputation

Evolving:

- Is scalable and adaptable to changing needs
- Continues to innovate and evolve based on user feedback and market trends
- Maintains a competitive edge through ongoing research and development

Benefits of gamification for user engagement

Gamification increases user engagement by leveraging psychological principles of motivation and reward to encourage users to engage with a product or service. By incorporating game-like elements, gamification creates a sense of competition and achievement that motivates users to interact with the product or service more frequently and for extended periods.

Gamification also provides a sense of accomplishment and progression, which can be particularly effective for products that involve repetitive or mundane tasks. By offering rewards and recognition for completing these tasks, gamification can make them more enjoyable and satisfying for users.

Additionally, gamification can increase user engagement by tapping into social dynamics. Multiplayer games and social leaderboards can create a sense of community and encourage users to interact with each other, fostering a sense of belonging and loyalty to the product or service.

Overall, gamification can be a powerful tool for product managers to increase user engagement and retention, ultimately leading to tremendous business success.

Let's take a fictional example, a social media app for product managers called **Product Management Media** (**PMM**), and show how gamification can significantly increase user engagement on a digital product:

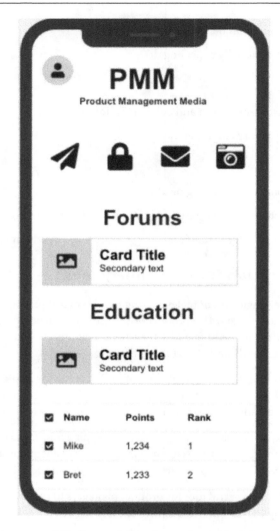

Figure 2.2 – Product Management Media – social media app for product developers and creative teams

Why the app was created

Its unique value proposition is that it's the only social media and education platform for product development professionals. It creates a space where users can learn about product development, share stories with their peers, and learn from the community. Gamification helps its value proposition by giving points for the messages and insights you share with the community and badges for education or articles you post. As people earn more points for posting and connecting, they are more engaged, as are the others that read it. Since the users know that new content on the platform posts constantly, they are more likely to open the app more frequently, therefore driving higher engagement.

UX

In PMM, the structure to progress through the app contains levels, so once you complete the tasks for a level, you progress to the next one. The structure is easy to understand because progressing through a game is familiar to the user. As a user, I read three articles and posted a story about my favorite product launch so that I could progress to the next level. The structure provides an initiative and seamless UX that the user falls right into and doesn't take brainpower to navigate. When a user wins a reward, progresses to a level, or accomplishes a mission in the app, visually striking effects fill the screen, congratulating the user and getting them excited by design.

Reputation

The next gamification tactic is widespread, and I'm willing to bet you've seen this a couple of times before. PMM will send you a coffee mug for inviting 5 project managers to the platform, a T-shirt if you invite 25 friends to the platform, and an all-expense paid trip to spend a weekend on Mars with Elon Musk if you invite 1,000 project managers to the app. The reward is a gamification technique to increase user engagement on the app; more users inviting more users will drive more engagement, driven by the psychology of the rewards. And sometimes, it's a social status play as well; you definitely want to be seen in your PMM T-shirt at the next product management meetup in your area.

Evolving

PMM continues to evolve, and it does that by keeping a close relationship with users and their needs. It just sent out a super fun survey to all of its users; there are quirky questions to keep them engaged, a progress bar so they can stay informed of their accomplishments throughout the journey, and then a reward at the end, a chance to win a $1,000 Amazon gift card. Does this sound familiar to you? Gamification tactics are more common than you might realize, and they are common because they work.

It also gamifies its continual feedback loop. Within the app, when you accomplish a task or move up a level, there is a benefit popup for you to submit feedback, and you'll get points for submission.

Through the survey and the feedback mechanism included in the app, you've learned that product managers think formal education is way too expensive and want some informal training programs embedded in PMM so they can get certified in certain sections of the "elite eight" product skills. You've gamified the feedback process to gain insights that help you grow your product, competitive edge, and user engagement.

The impressive user engagement numbers got around the tech community, and you've just secured your next round of investment funding! Woohoo!

For product leaders, you can also gamify your product research and development. Have your teams participate in a pitch competition, where they collect research, form a business plan, and then pitch to you and other members of the leadership team what their idea for the next big thing will be, based on completion of the feedback loop and market research they have done on their own. The social and competitive factors will drive fresh new ideas, and the rewards can be feasible: dinner with the leadership team or "Pitch Winner 2023" pullovers. Break your team out of their comfort zone, and if timing allows, even run a design sprint, popularized by Jake Knapp of Google Ventures. You can run a half-week or half-day version of the design sprint based on your team's availability and the priority of the new features.

Gamification can be a highly effective strategy for increasing user engagement by incorporating game mechanics and elements into non-game contexts, making them more interactive, immersive, and enjoyable. To successfully implement gamification, product managers must design experiences that appeal to users' intrinsic motivation and emotions, while providing a sense of achievement, progress, and reward. You can achieve gamification parity by offering personalized and engaging experiences that encourage users to pick your product in the first place and stay engaged, fulfilling your engagement and retention goals as a product manager.

The benefits of gamification extend beyond just increasing user engagement. It can also provide valuable feedback and data to product managers, allowing them to refine and improve their products over time. To effectively leverage gamification, product managers should carefully consider the specific goals they want to achieve and design the gamified experiences accordingly. By doing so, they can create a more compelling and enjoyable UX that drives engagement, fosters brand loyalty, and ultimately, contributes to the product or service's success.

Gamification can give "nudges" to desired behaviors

The trifecta of the product development process is always present when starting a project. How do we build something that solves a pain point for the user, makes financial sense for the business, and is technically feasible? Concerning the first two, you may have to design your product in a way that gives subtle "nudges" to get the user to do something that will solve their pain point or make sense for the business.

Nudge theory is a concept that has gained popularity in recent years, especially in the fields of economics, psychology, and public policy. The theory's basis is that nudges can influence people to make better decisions through small, subtle stimuli rather than coercion or outright mandates.

The origins of the nudge theory can trace back to the work of Nobel Prize-winning economist Richard Thaler and legal scholar Cass Sunstein, who wrote a book in 2008 called *Nudge: Improving Decisions About Health, Wealth, and Happiness*. In the book, Thaler and Sunstein argue that people often make poor decisions due to cognitive biases and heuristics. You can design to overcome these biases through small changes in the choice architecture or how people present choices.

One of the critical concepts in nudge theory is the idea of default options. Default options refer to the option presented to people if they do not actively make a choice. By changing the default option, such as making the more beneficial plan the default, a designed nudge pushes people toward making better decisions without thinking about it actively. For example, if I asked a person to choose between two types of insurance plans, they may default to the plan that requires the least effort to sign up for or the plan that is presented to them first.

Another important concept in nudge theory is framing. **Framing** refers to the way in which choices are presented to people and how this can influence their decision-making. For example, if a marketing manager runs a campaign for a product as "healthy" rather than "low in calories," people may be more likely to choose it because it appeals to their desire for health and wellness.

Nudge theory applies in various contexts, from public policy to healthcare to marketing. In public policy, governments have used nudges to encourage people to make healthier choices, such as by placing healthy food options at eye level in vending machines or by adding warning labels to cigarettes. In healthcare, nudges can encourage patients to take their medication as prescribed or to schedule important screenings and checkups.

In marketing, companies have used nudges to influence consumer behavior, such as by offering free trials or using social proof to demonstrate the popularity of a product. For example, a company may show how many people have purchased a product or how many positive reviews it has received to nudge potential customers toward purchasing.

One of the critical advantages of nudge theory is that it is non-invasive and respects people's autonomy. Rather than telling people what to do or forcing them to make confident choices, nudges make it easier for people to make better decisions. However, some critics of the nudge theory argue that it can be manipulative and that people may only sometimes be aware of the nudges driving them to take specific actions.

In conclusion, nudge theory is a powerful concept that can improve decision-making and behavior in various contexts. By understanding the cognitive biases and heuristics that people are prone to and using small, subtle nudges to encourage better choices, product managers can create more engaging, effective, and user-friendly products. However, it is essential to be mindful of the ethical implications of nudging and to ensure that people's autonomy is continually respected.

Pokémon Go (2016)

Pokémon is one of the most well-known franchises of all time, with a **trading card game (TCG)** and multiple video games, TV series, and movies. But when Pokémon Go was released for mobile devices in the summer of 2016, things changed. What was once focused on gamers and anime fans was now being introduced to millions of new users. The game went on to be one of highest grossing mobile games of all time, capturing both long-time Pokémon players and a new audience and generation as well.

Give Pokémon Go a try. If you have an account from that magical summer of 2016, dust it off! If not, make a new account and play through your first couple of level-ups! Pay attention to the nudges given to get you to spend money in the game. Although you can play and enjoy Pokémon Go without spending any money at all, there are definitely subtle pain points that encourage you to drop a few dollars here and there to power up your experience. Pay attention to a few specific mechanics such as Raids, Egg Hatching, and both Item and Pokémon Storage.

A product manager can use gamification to create nudges encouraging users to make confident choices or take specific actions. For example, a product manager might use a progress bar or a completion meter to nudge users to complete a particular task or achieve a specific goal within the product. This nudge can create a sense of accomplishment and progress, increasing user engagement and motivation.

Another way a product manager can use gamification for nudges is through rewards. By rewarding users for taking certain actions or completing certain tasks, a product manager can create a positive reinforcement loop that encourages users to continue engaging with the product. For example, a product manager might offer badges, points, or other virtual rewards for completing specific tasks or achieving certain milestones within the product.

A product manager can also use gamification to create social nudges that leverage the power of social influence to encourage users to engage with the product. For example, a product manager might use leaderboards or social sharing features to encourage users to compete with friends or share their achievements on social media. This type of nudge can tap into users' desire for social validation and create a sense of community and connectedness around the product.

In addition, a product manager can use gamification to create feedback nudges that give users real-time feedback on their actions and choices within the product. For example, a product manager might use a pop-up message or a visual cue to let users know when they have made a good choice or achieved a certain milestone within the product. This type of nudge can create a sense of immediate feedback and reinforcement, which can increase user engagement and motivation.

Overall, gamification can be a powerful tool for product managers to create nudges that encourage users to engage with their products meaningfully. By leveraging game mechanics and elements, product managers can create a more engaging, motivating, and rewarding UX that drives user behavior and delivers business value.

Let's open PMM back up and apply nudge theory to a feature.

As the product manager of PMM, your new investors gave you the goal of 50,000 posts on the app each hour. You want to "nudge" users to post more, so you set up a leaderboard in the app. Users can now see who posts the most by day, week, month, and year. Leaderboards are motivating because they tap into several vital psychological drivers. One of the main drivers is the desire for social comparison and recognition. When people see their name on a leaderboard, they feel a sense of accomplishment and recognition for their achievements, which can be a powerful motivator. In addition, leaderboards provide a sense of competition, which can motivate people who are naturally competitive or enjoy a challenge.

Another psychological driver that makes leaderboards effective is the desire for status and achievement. Seeing their progress tracked and measured against others can create a sense of accomplishment and a desire to continue improving. Leaderboards can be particularly effective when users work toward a specific goal or objective, such as the elite product manager status in PMM.

Finally, leaderboards can tap into people's intrinsic motivation to succeed and improve. When people see how their posts contribute to their progress and success, they are more likely to continue working toward their goals. This social motivator can be particularly effective when combined with other motivational elements, such as rewards and feedback, which are already actively built into the product.

Overall, leaderboards are a powerful tool for nudging users and driving engagement in PMM. By tapping into psychological drivers such as social comparison, competition, and achievement, product managers can create a more engaging and motivating experience for their users.

Gamification differentiates your product and breaks the status quo

Gamification in digital products can break the status quo and revolutionize how we interact with technology. By incorporating game-like elements and mechanics into non-game contexts, gamification creates a more engaging and personalized experience for users while encouraging them to take specific actions and behaviors.

At its core, gamification is about tapping into human motivation and psychology. By providing users with a sense of progress, achievement, and reward, gamification can appeal to their intrinsic motivation and drive, encouraging them to continue engaging with the product or service. You can achieve optimal gamification design through various mechanisms, including point systems, badges, leaderboards, and other forms of recognition and feedback.

At its core, you are developing a more fun product for the user while also solving one of their pain points. In the case of PMM, you are making them better product managers and doing it in a way that doesn't feel like work.

One of the critical benefits of gamification is that it allows product managers to nudge users toward desired behaviors and outcomes. By framing specific actions or choices as more desirable or rewarding, gamification can influence users to make decisions that align with the product's goals and objectives. For example, a health and fitness app might use gamification to encourage users to exercise more frequently by offering rewards and recognition for hitting certain milestones or achieving specific goals.

Another way in which gamification can break the status quo is by fostering a sense of community and social interaction. By incorporating social features such as leaderboards, challenges, and collaborative tasks, gamified products can create a sense of belonging and competition among users, encouraging them to engage with the product regularly and share it with their friends and followers. This engagement can be particularly effective in contexts such as e-learning, where gamification can help students feel more connected to their peers and more motivated to learn and succeed.

Overall, the key to successful gamification is to strike the right balance between engagement and usefulness. While gamification can undoubtedly be entertaining, it must also serve a specific purpose and offer tangible value to users. Product managers need to be strategic in their approach to gamification, carefully considering the specific behaviors and outcomes they want to encourage, and designing gamified experiences that are both engaging and effective.

To do this, product managers must deeply understand their users' motivations, preferences, and behaviors. They must also be able to design gamified experiences that are intuitive, user-friendly, and aesthetically appealing while also incorporating feedback and data-driven insights to improve the UX over time continuously.

Finally, product managers must be willing to experiment and iterate, testing different gamification strategies and approaches to see what works best for their specific product and user base. Product managers can use gamification to break the status quo and create more engaging and effective digital products that drive meaningful user behaviors and outcomes by being open to feedback and being willing to pivot as needed.

Summary

We discussed the core competencies of a product manager and the skills they need to be world-class, and how gamification relates to those skills. Can you imagine if we removed all the gamification features from PMM? A user would log in and see sparsely updated content because there needs to be manufactured motivation for users to post or share with their friends. A product manager wouldn't add new features because the feedback loop brings back barely any insight. After all, a vital driver of the user's motivation is gone.

The strategic implementation of gamification sparked a chain of engagement among users, inspiring them to generate content and share knowledge. This dynamic not only fostered a sense of achievement and joy but also proved so impactful that users enthusiastically spread the word to friends and colleagues. The result was a remarkable enhancement of PMM's reputation. As a product manager, you capitalized on this momentum to introduce premium features, including education and certification programs. These additions were born out of the continuous feedback loop you established by enticing users with rewards, showcasing the strategic value of gamification.

To reiterate, gamification is essential to your job as a PM because it's going to help you accomplish the three critical principles that are crucial to your role:

- Gamification will drive engagement because the experience is fun, the gameplay will entice users log in to your app, and they will have fun doing it so they will do it more often

- Gamification will enable you to nudge users to do mission-critical things for the app; besides driving engagement, this can be mission-critical for driving purchases, medication adherence, or socially impactful actions

- Gamification breaks the status quo – don't create a boring app that feels like a chore

In the next chapter, we will dive into the understanding game mechanics and gamification frameworks. Now that we understand how a gamification strategy benefits product managers, we can discover the keys to the first step, which we briefly touched on here: knowing your user to see where and how gamification will benefit their experience and solve pain points.

3
Gamification Frameworks and Experts

As we discussed in *Chapter 1*, the concepts behind gamification go back a long way. And because of that, many have built frameworks and other thought processes around several of the concepts that game design touches. There is no single framework that is applicable across the board; you must find the bits and pieces that work for your product. Having a basic understanding of the frameworks that exist can help you find the pieces that make sense for you. Throughout this chapter, you will learn about several existing frameworks and key individuals within the field of gamification design.

We will cover the following main topics:

- Gamification frameworks and methodologies
- Additional players in the game

Gamification frameworks and methodologies

A framework or methodology is a holistic way to take on gamification (or any task, for that matter). Some of the frameworks we will discuss are a little older than others, and some are more widely known. But all of them offer some guidance into how you could build gamified design into your product or service. Your tendency might be to gravitate toward one or two frameworks that sound appealing to you, and in some cases, that might be fine, but understanding each of the concepts within might provide you with something that could be easily applied to your project. The explanations provided are overviews, and with each framework, there might be a whole book's worth of explanations. If any of the frameworks herein seem like they might work, it is worth seeking out further detail.

The MDA framework

The MDA framework is a formal approach to understanding games and their design. The MDA framework was introduced in a paper titled *MDA: A Formal Approach to Game Design and Game Research*, presented at the 2001 Game Developers Conference. The authors (Robin Hunicke, Marc LeBlanc, and Robert Zubek) aimed to create a universal language for game design that could be understood by both developers and researchers. It can be used to analyze existing games, design new games, and research the nature of games. The framework has been used by game designers, researchers, and educators to better understand games and to improve the design of new games. It provides a way to think about games in a structured way. It can help designers to identify the key elements of their game and to understand how those elements interact with each other. By doing this within product design, we can start to understand much of the same as users progress through a system, just as a player would a game. **MDA** stands for **Mechanics, Dynamics, and Aesthetics**, representing the three essential elements of games:

- **Mechanics**: This refers to the rules, systems, and components that make up a game. They encompass the actions, behaviors, and interactions available to the players. Mechanics can include game elements such as movement, scoring, resources, and abilities. Analyzing mechanics helps in understanding the tangible aspects of a game and how players interact with them.

- **Dynamics**: These are the emergent behaviors and patterns that arise when players engage with the mechanics of a game. They describe the actions, choices, and consequences that unfold during gameplay. Dynamics are influenced by how players interpret and respond to the mechanics, leading to a range of experiences and outcomes. Analyzing dynamics helps in understanding the player's experience and the flow of the game.

- **Aesthetics**: This is the emotional responses, feelings, and overall experience that players derive from the game. It encompasses the sensory and psychological aspects, including the enjoyment, challenge, immersion, and engagement evoked by the game. Analyzing aesthetics helps in understanding the subjective and experiential aspects of a game.

The MDA framework also highlights several core concepts that are crucial in game design and gamification:

- **Decomposition**: The framework encourages the decomposition of a game into its mechanics, dynamics, and aesthetics to better understand its underlying components and how they contribute to the overall experience

- **Iterative Design**: The framework promotes an iterative design process where designers can analyze and refine the mechanics, dynamics, and aesthetics to achieve the desired player experience

- **A Player-Centric Approach**: The framework places a strong emphasis on understanding the player's experience and designing games that elicit specific emotions and engagement

- **A Holistic Perspective**: By considering the interconnectedness of mechanics, dynamics, and aesthetics, the framework helps designers create cohesive and engaging game experiences

The MDA framework provides a valuable lens for understanding games and designing engaging experiences. By breaking down games into mechanics, dynamics, and aesthetics, the framework offers a structured approach to game analysis and design. It has been widely adopted in the gamification community and serves as a foundation for creating compelling and immersive game experiences.

The Fogg Behavior Model

The Fogg Behavior Model was introduced by B.J. Fogg, a leading researcher, author, and founder of the Behavior Design Lab at Stanford University. B.J. Fogg has dedicated his career to studying and understanding human behavior and how technology can be designed to influence and change behaviors. The framework was first presented in his book *Persuasive Technology: Using Computers to Change What We Think and Do*, published in 2003. Through his research and contributions to the field, B.J. Fogg has become a prominent figure in the study of behavior design.

The Fogg Behavior Model is based on the premise that three elements—motivation, ability, and triggers—must converge at the same moment for a behavior to occur. Each of these elements plays a crucial role in shaping behavior and can be leveraged to design effective gamification experiences:

- **Motivation**: The desire or willingness of a person to engage in a particular behavior. It can be influenced by intrinsic factors such as personal goals, desires, or values, as well as extrinsic factors such as rewards, recognition, or social influence. Designers can enhance motivation by aligning the gamified experience with the user's intrinsic motivations and providing appropriate rewards and incentives.

- **Ability**: Represents the user's capability to perform the desired behavior. It considers factors such as physical ability, knowledge, skills, and available resources. Designers can enhance the ability by simplifying the desired behavior, providing clear instructions, removing obstacles, and offering support and resources to facilitate the desired action.

- **Triggers**: Cues or prompts that initiate the desired behavior. They can be divided into two types: external triggers and internal triggers. External triggers are external stimuli that prompt behavior, such as notifications, reminders, or calls to action. Internal triggers, on the other hand, are internal thoughts, emotions, or habits that prompt the behavior. Designers can use well-timed and carefully designed triggers to prompt and reinforce the desired behavior.

The Fogg Behavior Model highlights the importance of understanding and addressing motivation, ability, and triggers to influence behavior effectively. By designing gamification experiences that align with users' motivations, enhance their abilities, and employ strategic triggers, designers can drive the desired behaviors and create engaging experiences. The model emphasizes the need for simplicity, relevance, and context-awareness in behavior design.

The SCARF Model

The SCARF Model was introduced by David Rock, an esteemed author, speaker, and neuro-leadership expert. He first presented the framework in a 2008 article titled *SCARF: A Brain-Based Model for Collaborating with and Influencing Others*. The article, published in the NeuroLeadership Journal, quickly gained recognition for its insightful perspective on human social behavior and its implications for collaboration and influence. SCARF is an acronym representing five core domains that influence human social behavior:

- **Status**: This refers to our relative position within a social hierarchy. People are highly sensitive to their status and its impact on their interactions. The framework suggests that enhancing individuals' perceived status can positively impact motivation and engagement.

- **Certainty**: Relates to our sense of predictability and control over the environment. Humans have a natural inclination to reduce uncertainty and seek stability. Providing clear rules, expectations, and feedback can enhance motivation and reduce stress.

- **Autonomy**: The degree of control and freedom individuals have over their actions and decisions. When people feel empowered and have a sense of autonomy, they are more likely to be motivated and engaged.

- **Relatedness**: Pertains to social connection and the quality of relationships. Humans are social beings, and positive social interactions can foster motivation and well-being. Building a sense of community, encouraging collaboration, and creating opportunities for social connection can enhance engagement.

- **Fairness**: The perception of equity and justice. People have a strong desire for fairness and are highly attuned to unfair treatment. Promoting fairness in gamified experiences can boost motivation and trust among participants.

By considering the SCARF domains in gamification design, practitioners can create experiences that address users' social needs and promote positive engagement. Understanding how these factors influence motivation and behavior allows for more effective design decisions. The SCARF Model's contribution to the gamification field lies in its ability to deepen our understanding of the social dynamics at play and guide the design of more effective and impactful gamified experiences.

HEXAD User Type Framework

The HEXAD framework was first introduced by Andrzej Marczewski, a renowned gamification expert and consultant. It gained notable traction and recognition around the early 2010s.

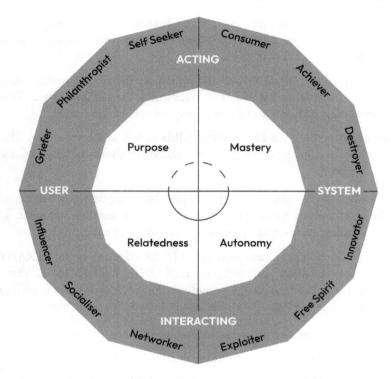

Figure 3.1 – Visual breakdown of the HEXAD framework for user types

Although the HEXAD framework is primarily attributed to Andrzej Marczewski, who conceptualized and devised the model, it is essential to acknowledge the broader gamification community's contributions and feedback, which have shaped and refined the framework over time. Through discussions, practical implementations, and collaborative efforts, various professionals and enthusiasts have contributed to the ongoing evolution and application of the HEXAD framework. The HEXAD framework revolves around six primary user types, each driven by distinct motivational factors. These user types represent different profiles of individuals engaging with gamified systems:

- **Humanist**: Motivated by social interactions, relationships, and helping others. They seek collaborative experiences and value the sense of belonging and community within gamified environments.

- **Explorer**: Driven by curiosity, discovery, and the pursuit of new experiences. They enjoy uncovering hidden elements, exploring different paths, and engaging with challenges that offer novel opportunities.

- **Achiever**: Motivated by setting and reaching goals, earning rewards, and gaining recognition for their accomplishments. They thrive on challenges and strive for mastery, seeking tangible achievements within the gamified system.

- **Architect**: Motivated by the creative aspects of gamification. They enjoy designing, customizing, and shaping their experiences. Architects value the ability to influence and impact the game's mechanics, rules, and overall structure.

- **Director**: Motivated by control, power, and influence. They enjoy leading others, making strategic decisions, and assuming leadership roles within the gamified system. Directors seek opportunities to exert authority and guide the experiences of other users.

- **Socializer**: Motivated by social connections, collaboration, and competition. They thrive in social environments, enjoying interactions with other users, forming alliances, and engaging in friendly competition.

The HEXAD framework offers a user-centric perspective for designing gamified experiences. By understanding the diverse motivations of users, designers can tailor their approaches to cater to different user types, creating more engaging and personalized experiences.

It is also worth noting that there have been some recent (2023) additions to the HEXAD framework to include six more user motivations, aptly called the HEXAD-12. The HEXAD-12 framework aims to provide a more nuanced understanding of user motivations and behaviors in gamified experiences. The additional player types in the HEXAD-12 framework include the following:

- **Philanthropists**: Motivated by altruism and making a positive impact

- **Gamblers**: Driven by taking risks and seeking uncertain outcomes

- **Collectors**: Motivated by the acquisition and collection of in-game items

- **Role-players**: Engaged in creating and immersing themselves in fictional identities and narratives

- **Manipulators**: Motivated by exerting influence and control over the game system or other players

- **Thrill-seekers**: Driven by excitement, intense experiences, and adrenaline rushes

The HEXAD-12 framework offers an expanded understanding of user motivations, allowing designers to tailor gamified experiences to a wider range of player preferences. By recognizing and accommodating these additional player types, gamification practitioners can create even more personalized and engaging experiences.

Spotify (2008)

If you use a music streaming service, there is a roughly one in three chance that service is Spotify. Over 500 million people worldwide use Spotify to stream music. As mentioned in the chapter, it isn't about finding just one of these frameworks and using that one, and only that one. Spotify does a great job of layering a number of the concepts discussed. It makes a point of truly trying to understand how each individual person uses its product.

If you do not use it already, give Spotify a try. Make a playlist, listen to some of the suggested music, and try sharing songs with friends. Spotify has a great mix of productivity, customization, and social features. Every person uses Spotify a little differently, and it does a great job of tailoring the experience for your use case. Whether you listen to music, podcasts, or anything else, it works to fill your needs. If you can continue your use until early December, you will even get a fun report detailing your very own Year in Review. As you try the product out, try and see where you fit in the HEXAD framework. Are you a Humanist/Socializer that is always sharing new music with friends? Or are you more of an Explorer, listening to the daily mixes and trying to discover your next favorite artist?

The Octalysis Framework

The Octalysis Framework was developed by Yu-Kai Chou, a renowned gamification expert and behavioral designer. Chou introduced the framework through his blog posts and webs1te, which gained significant attention in the gamification community. His expertise in behavioral psychology and game design led to the creation of Octalysis around 2013.

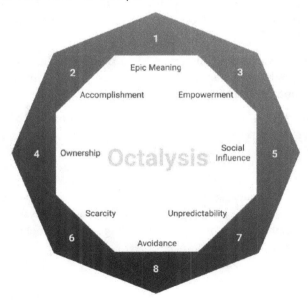

Figure 3.2 – Template for the Octalysis Framework

Octalysis derives its name from the eight essential core drives that motivate human behavior. These core drives are organized into an octagonal framework, providing a systematic approach to analyzing and designing engaging experiences. The framework identifies the underlying motivations that drive people to take certain actions and provides insights into how to leverage those motivations in gamified systems:

- **Epic Meaning and Calling**: This core drive is about finding a sense of purpose and meaning in our actions. It involves aligning activities with a greater cause or mission that resonates with the individual.

- **Development and Accomplishment**: This core drive revolves around the desire for growth, progress, and mastery. It motivates individuals to strive for achievements, challenges, and personal development.

- **Empowerment of Creativity and Feedback**: This core drive focuses on the human desire to express creativity, make choices, and receive feedback. It involves providing users with opportunities for self-expression and offering meaningful feedback on their actions.

- **Ownership and Possession**: This core drive taps into the innate desire to possess and own things. It involves creating a sense of ownership, control, and scarcity within a gamified system.

- **Social Influence and Relatedness**: This core drive revolves around the need for social connections, belonging, and influence. It includes elements such as social interaction, collaboration, competition, and recognition from others.

- **Scarcity and Impatience**: This core drive leverages the psychological principle of scarcity and the fear of missing out. It involves creating a sense of urgency, limited availability, and time-based rewards.

- **Unpredictability and Curiosity**: This core drive focuses on the human fascination with the unknown and the desire for exploration and discovery. It involves incorporating elements of surprise, mystery, and curiosity within a gamified system.

- **Loss and Avoidance**: This core drive is based on the motivation to avoid negative outcomes or loss. It includes elements such as the fear of missing out, the fear of failure, and the desire to avoid penalties or negative consequences.

The Octalysis Framework offers a comprehensive approach to understanding and leveraging human motivations in gamification. By analyzing and incorporating the eight core drives, designers can create engaging experiences that motivate users to take the desired actions. Octalysis has become a widely adopted framework in the gamification community, providing a valuable tool for crafting compelling and motivating gamified systems.

The Hooked Model

The Hooked Model was introduced by Nir Eyal in his book *Hooked: How to Build Habit-Forming Products*, published in 2014. Eyal is an author, lecturer, and expert in behavioral design and product psychology work and draws from his research and experience in the tech industry, where he observed patterns of user behavior and sought to understand the underlying principles that make certain products and experiences habit-forming. The Hooked Model consists of a four-step loop that aims to create habit-forming experiences:

- **Triggers**: These act as the initial cue that prompts a user to act. Triggers can be either external (external stimuli such as notifications or calls to action) or internal (internal thoughts or emotions triggered by a specific situation). Triggers play a crucial role in capturing the user's attention and initiating the habit loop.

- **Action**: After being triggered, users engage in a particular action. This action can be a simple behavior or a series of behaviors that the user performs in response to the trigger. The action should be easy to perform, requiring minimal effort or cognitive load.

- **Variable Reward**: The third step of the Hooked Model involves providing users with a reward or positive reinforcement for their actions. What makes this step powerful is the use of variable rewards—rewards that are unpredictable in their timing or nature. Variable rewards create anticipation and keep users engaged by triggering the brain's pleasure-seeking mechanisms.

- **Investment**: The final step in the Hooked Model focuses on getting users to invest in the experience. This can involve activities such as leaving personal data, customizing preferences, building virtual assets, or establishing social connections. Investments increase the user's commitment to the product or experience, making it more likely for them to repeat the habit loop in the future.

The Hooked Model introduces several core concepts that are essential in creating habit-forming experiences. By leveraging triggers, actions, variable rewards, and investment, designers can create habit-forming products and gamified systems that capture users' attention, foster repeated engagement, and drive long-term behavior change. To learn more, visit `https://www.nirandfar.com/hooked`

The RAMP framework

The RAMP framework was introduced by Andrzej Marczewski (you may recognize the name from the HEXAD user types) in his book titled *Even Ninja Monkeys Like to Play: Gamification, Game Thinking, and Motivational Design*, published in 2015. Marczewski's work draws from his extensive research and practical experience in the field of gamification. His contributions to the gamification community have helped shape the understanding and application of motivational design principles. **RAMP** stands for the following key components: **Rewards**, **Achievements**, **Missions**, and **Progression**:

- **Rewards**: A fundamental aspect of gamification that serves as an incentive to motivate and engage users. The RAMP framework encourages the use of both intrinsic and extrinsic rewards. Intrinsic rewards are related to the inherent enjoyment or satisfaction derived from an activity, while extrinsic rewards are tangible benefits provided as recognition or incentives.

- **Achievements**: Powerful tools for fostering engagement and motivation. They represent specific milestones or goals that users can strive to accomplish. The RAMP framework suggests the use of a well-defined achievement system that includes various levels of difficulty, clear objectives, and meaningful rewards tied to each achievement.

- **Missions**: This refers to tasks or challenges that users undertake within a gamified system. They provide a sense of purpose and direction, guiding users through a series of meaningful activities. The RAMP framework emphasizes the importance of designing missions that are engaging, varied, and aligned with users' interests and aspirations.

- **Progression**: Tracking and showcasing users' progress throughout their journey. The RAMP framework encourages the use of progress indicators, such as experience points, levels, or badges, to provide a visual representation of users' advancement. Progression serves as a motivational driver by giving users a sense of growth, mastery, and accomplishment.

The RAMP framework offers a comprehensive approach to enhancing engagement and motivation through gamification. By leveraging rewards, achievements, missions, and progression, practitioners can design gamified experiences that tap into users' intrinsic motivations, provide a sense of purpose and accomplishment, and ultimately, drive long-term engagement and behavior change.

SAPS Reward Framework

The SAPS Reward Framework stems from the visionary mind of Gabe Zichermann, a prominent thought leader and expert in gamification. Renowned for his contributions to the gamification landscape, Gabe Zichermann introduced the framework to the world in his book "Gamification by Design," which was co-authored with Christopher Cunningham and published in 2011.

The SAPS Reward Framework is rooted in the principle of understanding and leveraging intrinsic motivation to drive desired behaviors. The framework's name is an acronym that represents its core elements:

- Status: This element involves recognizing and enhancing a player's social status within a community or context. Players are motivated by achieving higher status levels and earning respect from peers.

- Access: This component emphasizes granting exclusive access to certain features, content, or privileges as rewards. The allure of gaining access to something unique or special fosters engagement and motivation.

- Power: This aspect empowers players with authority, control, or decision-making capabilities. The ability to influence outcomes and shape the experience can be a compelling motivator.

- Stuff: Material rewards, virtual or tangible, such as badges, points, or virtual goods, fall under this category. These rewards satisfy players' desire for collectibles and tangible proof of their achievements.

The SAPS Reward Framework emphasizes tapping into players' intrinsic motivations. By recognizing the power of intrinsic motivation and strategically designing reward systems that align with human psychology, the framework has provided a structured and effective approach to fostering engagement and driving desired behaviors.

RECIPE Framework

The RECIPE framework was conceptualized by Scott Nicholson, a scholar, educator, and gamification advocate. The framework was first introduced in his article "A RECIPE for Meaningful Gamification" published in 2015. This landmark article unveiled a fresh approach to gamification by emphasizing the importance of meaningful experiences.

The RECIPE framework is a structured guide that prioritizes the creation of meaningful and impactful gamified experiences. It is founded on six core elements, each represented by a letter in the acronym RECIPE:

- **Reflection**: Help users find other items, people, and past experiences that can deepen engagement and learning
- **Engagement**: Encouraging users to discover and learn from each other within the system you've created
- **Choice:** Developing systems that give the users control of what they do and where they go
- **Information**: Using game design psychology to drive how data, context, and concepts are displayed to users.
- **Play**: Giving users the ability to explore, learn, succeed, and fail within the boundaries of your system
- **Exposition**: Create a narrative for users that is integrated with the real-world setting, and allowing them to create their own

By emphasizing the significance of meaningful experiences and holistic design, the RECIPE framework transcends the conventional focus on points and rewards. The framework resonates deeply with educators, designers, and practitioners aiming to create gamified experiences that have a lasting impact on participants' lives.

The Game Thinking Framework

The Game Thinking Framework was introduced by Amy Jo Kim, a respected game designer, entrepreneur, and author. Kim has extensive experience in the field of game design, having worked with notable companies such as Electronic Arts and Netflix. She is also the author of the book *Game Thinking: Innovate Smarter & Drive Deep Engagement with Design Techniques from Hit Games*, published in 2018. In her book, Amy Jo Kim presents a comprehensive framework for applying game design principles to create meaningful and engaging experiences.

The Game Thinking Framework offers a systematic approach to designing products and experiences that leverage the power of games. It draws upon game design principles and user-centered design methodologies to create engaging and compelling experiences for users. The framework consists of several key components:

- **Player Insight**: Involves gaining a deep understanding of the target audience, their motivations, needs, and desires. By empathizing with players and understanding their preferences, designers can create experiences that resonate with them on a meaningful level.

- **Game Design**: Focuses on the core mechanics and dynamics that make a game engaging and enjoyable. This includes defining the goals, rules, challenges, and feedback mechanisms that shape the experience. By applying game design principles, designers can create experiences that are inherently fun, compelling, and rewarding.

- **Smart Feedback**: This refers to the timely and relevant feedback provided to players throughout the experience. It includes clear and actionable information about their progress, achievements, and areas for improvement. Well-designed feedback mechanisms keep players engaged, motivated, and in a state of flow.

- **Rapid Iteration**: Involves an iterative and agile approach to the design process. It emphasizes quick prototyping, testing, and learning from user feedback. By iterating on design concepts and incorporating user insights, designers can refine and improve their gamified experiences over time.

The Game Thinking Framework places a strong emphasis on player-centric design, ensuring that the experience is tailored to the needs and desires of the target audience. It encourages designers to create experiences that are engaging, meaningful, and provide a sense of progression and mastery. The framework also highlights the importance of continuous learning and iteration to refine and enhance the user experience.

The PBL Model

The PBL Model, also known as the **Player-Behavior-Loop Model**, was introduced by a team of researchers and designers including Sebastian Deterding, Rilla Khaled, Lennart Nacke, and Dan Dixon. Sebastian Deterding is a renowned researcher and designer specializing in gamification and game design. Rilla Khaled, Lennart Nacke, and Dan Dixon are experts in player experience and interaction design. The PBL Model was presented in the *Gamification: Toward a Definition* paper in 2011, contributing to the growing field of gamification. The PBL Model consists of three key components: player, behavior, and loop. Let's explore each component in more detail:

- **Player**: The individuals who engage with the gamified experience. Understanding the player's motivations, preferences, and needs is crucial for designing effective gamification. This component highlights the importance of user research and player-centered design, ensuring that the experience caters to the target audience's desires and expectations.

- **Behavior**: Actions, interactions, and activities that players engage in within the gamified system. This component emphasizes the significance of defining clear and meaningful behaviors that align with the desired goals. By identifying the target behaviors, designers can create mechanics, challenges, and incentives that encourage players to exhibit those behaviors.

- **Loop**: The iterative and cyclical nature of the gamified experience. It encompasses the feedback, progression, and rewards mechanisms that keep players engaged and motivated. The loop creates a continuous cycle of challenge, action, feedback, and reinforcement, fostering a sense of achievement, progression, and ongoing engagement.

The PBL Model emphasizes the importance of understanding players' motivations and designing engaging experiences that drive the desired behaviors. By considering the players' needs and preferences, defining meaningful behaviors, and creating an engaging loop of challenges, feedback, and rewards, designers can design gamified experiences that captivate and motivate players.

6D Framework

Kevin Werbach, a prominent figure in the gamification domain, introduced the 6D Framework. The framework debuted in his book "For the Win: How Game Thinking Can Revolutionize Your Business" co-authored with Dan Hunter and was published in 2012. The content is also covered in Werbach's course on gamification offered through Coursera and the University of Pennsylvania.

The 6D Framework encapsulates six critical building blocks that guide the design and analysis of gamified experiences:

- **Define business objectives:** Start by understanding what you want to achieve. If you do not have concrete KPIs you plan to improve, there is no measurement for success.

- **Delineate target behaviors:** Now that you understand why you are implementing a gamified system, what exactly do you anticipate that players will do, and how will you measure them? Your expected actions from players should align with the business goals you defined.

- **Describe your players:** Define who is using your system. This can be a persona as was discussed before, but the type of player you are looking for needs to be defined.

- **Devise activity cycles:** The game begins with a starting point, providing players with an entry into the experience. In the initial stages, ensure simplicity to attract players and provide clear directions. As the game advances towards mastery, the complexity gradually intensifies. It's important to note that each action triggers feedback, which, in turn, kindles the motivation to undertake subsequent actions. The incorporation of loops and branching trees adds layers of engagement.

- **Don't forget the fun:** One of the most important questions to ask yourself on any gamification project: Is the system fun. Would players participate if there weren't any rewards?

- **Deploy the appropriate tools for the job:** After understanding what you are doing and why, you can pick the suitable game mechanics and motivations to achieve your goals. Choosing game elements before this point would be like packing a suitcase for a trip where you do not know the destination.

The 6D Framework has impacted the gamification landscape by offering a structured approach to designing, implementing, and evaluating gamified experiences. Its emphasis on understanding users, aligning game elements with motivations, and utilizing data-driven insights has empowered organizations across industries to enhance user engagement, foster behavioral change, and achieve desired outcomes.

4 Keys 2 Fun

The 4 Keys 2 Fun framework was developed by Nicole Lazzaro, a renowned game designer and researcher known for her work on emotions and player experience. Nicole Lazzaro has dedicated her career to understanding the emotional impact of games and how they can be harnessed to create compelling user experiences. The framework was first introduced in her research paper *Why We Play Games: Four Keys to More Emotion Without Story*, published in 2004, solidifying its position as a seminal resource for understanding the emotional aspects of games.

The 4 Keys 2 Fun framework explores four primary keys or dimensions that contribute to the enjoyment and engagement of game experiences. These keys provide insights into the emotional experiences players seek when engaging with games:

- **Hard Fun**: The satisfaction derived from overcoming challenges and obstacles. It encompasses the thrill of problem-solving, strategic thinking, and skill mastery. Hard Fun engages players by providing them with meaningful and rewarding challenges that test their abilities and offer a sense of accomplishment. This type of fun can lead to emotions like boredom, frustration, or fiero (Italian word for the the feeling of pride in an epic win).

- **Easy Fun**: The pleasure players experience through curiosity, exploration, and discovery. It involves the joy of exploring new environments, uncovering hidden secrets, and engaging in playful experimentation. Easy Fun captivates players by providing them with a sense of wonder, freedom, and the opportunity for creative expression. This type of fun can lead to emotions like curiosity, wonder, and surprise.

- **Serious Fun**: The emotional depth and impact that games can have on players. It includes the range of emotions players experience during gameplay, such as excitement, suspense, surprise, and even sadness or empathy. Serious Fun engages players by immersing them in captivating narratives, compelling characters, and thought-provoking themes. This type of fun can lead to emotions like excitement, focus, and relaxation.

- **People Fun**: Social and interpersonal aspects of gameplay. It encompasses the enjoyment derived from collaboration, competition, and social interaction with other players. People Fun engages players by fostering social connections, enabling cooperative or competitive play, and facilitating meaningful social experiences within the game context. This type of fun can lead to emotions like laughter, naches (Yiddish word for the pride a parent or mentor feels in seeing success), and schadenfreude (a German word for the the feeling of joy derived from the misfortune of others).

The 4 Keys 2 Fun framework emphasizes the importance of understanding and designing for the emotional experiences players seek in games. By incorporating elements that address the dimensions of Hard Fun, Easy Fun, Serious Fun, and People Fun, designers can create engaging and enjoyable gamified experiences that resonate with players on an emotional level. The framework guides designers to consider the emotional impact of their designs, leading to more compelling and meaningful user experiences.

As you can see, there are a lot of frameworks to study and learn. There is a lot of overlap in the ideas, however, so finding the right balance for your product isn't as hard as it may seem. If you have a social app such as our hypothetical Product Manager Media app, it may be important to understand what the primary HEXAD user types are for your users. For something more like our Hi-Z Fitness app, you will rely heavily on motivation and rewards for your users accomplishments (SAPS Reward framework). And if the frameworks and their creators aren't enough, there are a few more experts worth knowing about.

Monopoly (1935)

One of the most recognizable brands in all of gaming, Monopoly has been around for the better part of a century! It has been translated into many different languages and adapted to over 200 licensed and localized versions. A lot of the fun, and frustration, comes from Monopoly's layered mechanics. It is a simple concept of movement (via dice) and money, but its complexity comes from the players' strategy.

Play a round of Monopoly with a few friends (if you can, finish it). Pay distinct attention to the layering of rules and mechanics. The first trip around the board starts off pretty simple, with lots of rolling dice and the gathering up of properties. After a few trips around the board, things start getting more complex, with rent payments and bargaining. Think about many of the concepts discussed as part of a framework. What are your and the other players' HEXAD player motivations? How does the game convey the "leader"? Are there any of the eight Octalysis core drives that seem particularly prominent? Which of the 4 Keys 2 Fun are most prominent or is there a bit of all of them? With any game that has stood the test of time as Monopoly has, it is worth looking deeper at the design of the underlying systems to understand how a game can still be so loved as it approaches 100 years old.

Additional players in the game

Not all of the experts in the field of gamification have an established methodology. In addition to all the creators we just mentioned, there are several other thought leaders it is worth knowing about if you plan on diving into gamification. These are people that have done extensive research in the field of game design, psychology, and/or human behavior.

Jane McGonigal

Jane McGonigal is a prominent figure in the field of gamification, renowned for her groundbreaking work in designing games that have a positive impact on individuals and society. Her work revolves around the concept of "serious games," which are games designed for purposes beyond entertainment. McGonigal believes that games have the potential to address important social, psychological, and environmental issues, and her contributions reflect this belief.

One of McGonigal's notable contributions is her book, *Reality Is Broken: Why Games Make Us Better and How They Can Change the World*, published in 2011. In this influential work, she explores the positive impact of games on individuals and society, highlighting how they can motivate and engage people in ways that traditional approaches often fail to achieve. The book sheds light on the potential of gamification to solve real-world problems, improve well-being, and foster collaboration.

One of the central themes in McGonigal's work is the idea of harnessing the power of games to motivate and empower individuals. She emphasizes the concept of "gameful thinking," which involves adopting a playful and optimistic mindset to tackle challenges in everyday life. McGonigal advocates for the integration of game elements, such as goals, rules, feedback, and social interaction, into various contexts to enhance motivation, resilience, and problem-solving skills.

Jane McGonigal's contributions to the gamification community have had a profound impact on the way games are perceived and utilized for positive change. Her work has inspired researchers, designers, and organizations to explore the potential of gamification beyond mere entertainment and to harness the motivational power of games to solve real-world problems. McGonigal's vision and passion for using games for positive impact continue to inspire and shape the gamification landscape.

Celia Hodent

Celia Hodent is a renowned expert in the field of **user experience** (**UX**) and game design. With her extensive knowledge and expertise, she has made significant contributions to the gamification community. Hodent has a background in psychology and cognitive science, which she applies to her work in creating engaging and user-centered game experiences. She has worked with major game companies, including Ubisoft, where she served as the director of UX for the renowned game franchise *Assassin's Creed*.

One of Hodent's notable contributions is her emphasis on the importance of cognitive psychology in game design. Her insights help game designers understand how players think, learn, and make decisions, enabling them to create more intuitive and enjoyable game experiences. Hodent's book, *The Gamer's Brain: How Neuroscience and UX Can Impact Video Game Design*, published in 2017, is a significant resource in the field of game design and gamification. In this book, she explores the cognitive processes and psychological aspects that influence player engagement and immersion. She provides practical insights and guidelines for designing games that effectively engage players and optimize the user experience.

Celia Hodent's work revolves around the intersection of UX and game design, focusing on understanding user psychology and applying cognitive science principles. Some of the key concepts and approaches she emphasizes include the following:

- **User-Centered Design**: Hodent advocates for placing the player at the center of the design process. By considering the needs, motivations, and preferences of the target audience, game designers can create experiences that resonate with players and keep them engaged.

- **Cognitive Load Management**: Hodent emphasizes the importance of managing cognitive load in game design. By understanding the limitations of human attention and memory, designers can optimize the game experience by presenting information in a clear and digestible manner.

- **Flow and Engagement**: Hodent explores the concept of flow, where players experience deep immersion and a sense of effortless engagement. She provides insights into how to design games that offer the right level of challenge and feedback to maintain players' flow state.

Celia Hodent's work in the field of UX and game design has been instrumental in shaping the gamification community. Through her emphasis on cognitive psychology, user research, and user-centered design, she has helped elevate the standard of game experiences, resulting in more engaging and immersive games.

Mihaly Csikszentmihalyi

Mihaly Csikszentmihalyi is a prominent psychologist known for his groundbreaking work on flow theory and optimal experience. His research and insights have had a significant impact on the field of gamification and the understanding of human motivation and engagement.

Csikszentmihalyi's pioneering work centers around the concept of "flow," a state of deep immersion in and focused concentration on an activity. He conducted extensive research to understand the conditions that lead to optimal experiences, where individuals feel a sense of enjoyment and fulfillment. Csikszentmihalyi's book, *Flow: The Psychology of Optimal Experience*, published in 1990, is a seminal work that explores the concept of flow in depth. In this book, he delves into the psychological and emotional aspects of flow and provides practical guidance on how to create environments and activities that foster flow experiences. His insights have been instrumental in shaping the design of games that capture players' attention and keep them immersed in the gameplay.

Mihaly Csikszentmihalyi's work on flow theory has introduced several key concepts and approaches that are relevant to the gamification community. These include the following:

- **Flow State**: Csikszentmihalyi describes flow as a state of complete immersion in an activity, where individuals lose track of time and feel fully absorbed in the task at hand. Designing game experiences that offer a flow state is crucial for maintaining player engagement and enjoyment.

- **Challenge-Skill Balance**: According to Csikszentmihalyi, flow is achieved when the level of challenge matches an individual's skill level. Designing games that provide an appropriate balance of challenge and skill is essential to keeping players engaged and motivated.

- **Clear Goals and Feedback**: Csikszentmihalyi emphasizes the importance of clear goals and immediate feedback in promoting flow. Games that provide clear objectives and offer continuous feedback on players' progress enhance their sense of control and keep them engaged.

Mihaly Csikszentmihalyi's contributions to the gamification community cannot be overstated. His theory of flow has had a profound influence on the understanding of motivation and engagement in game design. The principles derived from his work have been widely adopted by game designers and gamification practitioners to create captivating and immersive experiences. Csikszentmihalyi's research and insights have garnered international recognition, receiving numerous awards and honors for his contributions.

Summary

There are many existing frameworks and methodologies, and a lot of experts in the field of gamification. By studying these existing concepts, we can start to quickly implement features and concepts into our products knowing that an established method may already be applicable. After reading all the various frameworks, you will see that there is extensive overlap between them all.

It is also worth noting that, as a young field, things are changing incredibly fast, and frameworks can be introduced and changed quickly. This book provides a bit of a snapshot in time, but as a student of gamified design, you should always be seeking out the latest information. As we progress through this book, you may notice parts of these frameworks being used in examples or exercises. See if you can spot them and tie them back to a particular framework.

Within many of these frameworks, you likely noticed a heavy focus on understanding the user, which is crucial to any project, especially so for building gamification into a product. Different user types will respond better or worse to different types of game mechanics. A big part of knowing what tactics and frameworks might work for your project is understanding your users, which we will discuss next.

Further reading

- Hunicke, Robin; LeBlanc, Marc; and Zubek, Robert, *MDA: A Formal Approach to Game Design and Game Research*, 2001, `https://users.cs.northwestern.edu/~hunicke/MDA.pdf`

- Fogg, BJ, *Persuasive Technology: Using Computers to Change What We Think and Do*, Morgan Kaufmann, 2003

- Rock, David, *SCARF: A Brain-Based Model for Collaborating with and Influencing Others, 2008* `https://schoolguide.casel.org/uploads/sites/2/2018/12/SCARF-NeuroleadershipArticle.pdf`

- Chou, Yu-Kai, *Actionable Gamification: Beyond Points, Badges and Leaderboards*, 2015

- Eyal, Nir, *Hooked: How to Build Habit-Forming Products*, Portfolio, 2014

- Marczewski, Andrzej, *The Gamification Design Handbook: Even Ninja Monkeys Like to Play*, 2023

- Zichermann, Gabe; Cunningham, Christopher, *Gamification by Design: Implementing Game Mechanics in Web and Mobile Apps*, O'Reilly Media, 2011

- Werbach, Kevin; Hunter, Dan, *For the Win, Revised and Updated Edition: The Power of Gamification and Game Thinking in Business, Education, Government, and Social Impact*, Wharton School Press, 2020

- Kim, Amy Jo, *Game Thinking: Innovate smarter & drive deep engagement with design techniques from hit games*, 2018

- Deterding, Sebastian; Khaled, Rilla; Nacke, Lennart; and Dixon, Dan. *Gamification: Toward a Definition*, 2011, `http://gamification-research.org/wp-content/uploads/2011/04/02-Deterding-Khaled-Nacke-Dixon.pdf`

- Lazzaro, Nicole, *Why We Play Games: Four Keys to More Emotion Without Story*, 2004, `https://gamemodworkshop.com/readings/xeodesign_whyweplaygames.pdf`

- Nicholson, Scott, *A RECIPE for Meaningful Gamification*, 2015 `https://scottnicholson.com/pubs/recipepreprint.pdf`

- McGonigal, Jane, *Reality Is Broken: Why Games Make Us Better and How They Can Change the World*, Penguin Books, 2011

- Hodent, Celia, *The Gamer's Brain: How Neuroscience and UX Can Impact Video Game Design*, 2017

- Csikszentmihalyi, Mihaly, *Flow: The Psychology of Optimal Experience*, Harper Perennial Modern Classics, 2008

4

Understanding Your User

The ultimate success of your product truly depends on your users—these are the people who will use it, promote it, and spread the word about its benefits. Building a product in a vacuum, without considering user perspectives, is a risky move that can lead to wasted resources and missed opportunities. We've seen this happen time and again when product managers become enamored with the latest technology or a stakeholder has a "game-changing" idea that ultimately doesn't resonate with users.

In this book, we stress the importance of considering your users at every step of the product journey—from the early stages of brainstorming and prototyping to the final stages of the product life cycle. We emphasize that a product leader's role isn't just about being on the cutting edge of technology—it's also about meeting and exceeding user needs.

Consider, for instance, the introduction of a powerful new technology, such as ChatGPT. It has the potential to revolutionize the way we do business, but that doesn't mean it should be blindly adopted without thought. Before integrating this technology into your product, it's crucial to understand how it aligns with the needs and desires of your user base. It's not enough to just know what the technology can do—you need to comprehend how it will enhance the user's experience, meet their needs, and align with your product's vision. In the end, a product's success isn't about the most innovative tech, but about the user value it delivers.

This chapter will explore the essential market research methods enabling you to understand your users truly. Market research, often called the **Voice of the Customer (VOC)**, encompasses various techniques and tactics to gather valuable insights about your end users. We will delve into the most prominent qualitative and quantitative data collection methods, discussing the advantages and disadvantages of each. These techniques will uncover deep insights into user motivations and behaviors.

Building upon this understanding, we will then guide you through creating valuable personas and applying the **Jobs to Be Done (JTBD)** framework. These tools will empower you to design experiences that cater to your users' unique needs and aspirations.

This chapter will equip you with the knowledge and tools to conduct effective market research, gain insights into user motivations and behaviors, create personas, leverage the JTBD framework, and ultimately, translate these insights into meaningful experience design. By putting the user at the center of your product development journey, you will be well positioned to create exceptional products that resonate with your target audience. To summarize, we will go through the following:

- Market research, data, and collection methods

- Understanding user motivation and behavior

- Creating personas and JTBD

Market research, data, and collection methods

Market research is pivotal in informing strategic decisions and driving product success in the ever-evolving product development universe. Among the essential components of market research are primary and secondary research methodologies. Each approach offers unique benefits and contributes to a comprehensive understanding of markets, consumers, and competitors. This section will delve into the intricacies of primary and secondary research, highlighting their differences, methodologies, and critical considerations.

Primary research

Primary research involves the collection of firsthand information directly from the source. It is a tailored and custom approach focusing on specific research objectives and questions. Businesses gain direct insights into consumer preferences, behavior, and opinions by conducting primary research. This data is original, specific to the research purpose, and collected through surveys, interviews, observations, and experiments.

Methods and techniques

Primary research encompasses various methods, including quantitative and qualitative approaches, which we will dive deeper into in a moment. Quantitative methods involve the collection of numerical data that you can analyze statistically. This may include surveys with closed-ended questions, structured observations, or experiments with control groups. On the other hand, qualitative methods provide deeper insights into consumer experiences, motivations, and perceptions. Examples include in-depth interviews, focus groups, and ethnographic research.

Advantages of primary research

Primary research offers several advantages. It enables businesses to gather current and relevant data that aligns precisely with their research objectives. The data collected is unique to the organization and provides a competitive edge by uncovering new insights. Primary research also allows for direct consumer interaction, fostering a deeper understanding of their needs and preferences. Additionally, it provides the opportunity to validate or challenge existing assumptions and hypotheses.

Limitations of primary research

While valuable, primary research can be time-consuming and resource-intensive. It requires careful planning, execution, and analysis. Sample selection, survey design, and participant recruitment can present challenges. Moreover, biases and subjectivity may arise, necessitating rigorous data validation and analysis techniques.

Secondary research

Secondary research involves analyzing and synthesizing existing data and information gathered by others. It examines sources such as published reports, industry studies, government publications, academic research, and online databases. Secondary research provides a comprehensive understanding of the market landscape, industry trends, and consumer behavior.

Sources

Secondary research draws from many sources, including books, journals, websites, market reports, industry databases, and news articles. These sources offer a wealth of information and insights previously collected and analyzed.

Advantages of secondary research

Secondary research offers several advantages, including cost-effectiveness and time efficiency. Existing data can be readily accessed, saving resources you would have required for primary data collection. Secondary research also provides a broader context, allowing organizations to benchmark their performance, identify industry trends, and understand competitor strategies. Moreover, it aids in the identification of research gaps and guides the formulation of research questions for primary research studies.

Limitations of secondary research

Although valuable, secondary research may have limitations. The following are examples of those limitations:

- Alignment with research objectives: Secondary research may need to be carefully evaluated and selected to ensure it aligns precisely with the organization's research objectives, and may not serve all of them

- Timeliness and accuracy: Consider the timeliness and accuracy of the data, as it may not always be up to date or comprehensive

- Potential bias: Be aware of the possibility of bias in the original data sources, requiring critical analysis and verification

In summary, primary and secondary research are distinct methodologies that offer different perspectives and insights. Primary research provides firsthand data customized to the organization's objectives, enabling direct consumer interaction. On the other hand, secondary research offers a broader context by leveraging existing data sources to provide comprehensive market insights. Both approaches are valuable in market research, and the selection of primary or secondary methods should be based on research goals, available resources, and the desired depth of understanding. Organizations can utilize primary and secondary research effectively to unlock a wealth of market intelligence, consumer behavior insights, and competitive advantage.

You should adopt a holistic approach to maximize the benefits of primary and secondary research. Integrating both methodologies allows for data triangulation, validating findings, and gaining a comprehensive understanding of the market landscape.

Qualitative versus quantitative methods

In market research, two fundamental data types and methods are often employed: qualitative and quantitative. These approaches offer distinct perspectives and techniques for understanding consumer behavior, preferences, and market dynamics. Let's delve into each type to understand their characteristics and applications.

Qualitative data and methods

Qualitative research focuses on gathering non-numerical data to explore and understand individuals' underlying motivations, attitudes, and behaviors. It aims to provide rich, descriptive insights into the nuances and complexities of human experiences. Qualitative methods are typically flexible, allowing researchers to adapt their approach based on the context and research objectives. The following subsections cover some standard qualitative methods.

In-depth interviews

This involves conducting one-on-one interviews with individuals to explore their thoughts, opinions, and experiences in detail.

Here are some advantages:

- Rich and detailed data: In-depth interviews allow for open-ended questioning, enabling participants to provide detailed responses and share rich information about their experiences, opinions, and attitudes.

- Flexibility: Interviewers can probe deeper into specific topics, allowing for a more comprehensive understanding of participants' thoughts and behaviors.

- Contextual understanding: Interviews can capture participants' experiences within their contexts, providing a deeper understanding of the factors influencing their perspectives and behaviors.

- Uncovering underlying motivations: In-depth interviews can uncover participants' underlying motivations, beliefs, and emotions, shedding light on the *why* behind their actions.

Here are some disadvantages:

- Limited sample size: In-depth interviews are resource-intensive and time-consuming, making conducting them with many participants impractical. The sample size is typically smaller compared to quantitative research methods.

- Potential interviewer bias: The interviewer's presence and questioning style can influence participants' responses, leading to potential bias. It requires skilled interviewers to maintain neutrality and avoid leading participants.

- Subjectivity: Qualitative data from in-depth interviews can be subjective and influenced by participants' perceptions and interpretations. Generalizing findings to a larger population may be challenging.

Here are some examples of their value:

- Exploration of complex topics: In-depth interviews provide an opportunity to explore complex phenomena, uncover nuances, and gain a deeper understanding of participants' experiences and perspectives.

- Human-centered insights: By engaging directly with participants, in-depth interviews enable researchers to gain a deep understanding of their needs, preferences, and challenges, informing the development of human-centered solutions.

- Informing decision-making: In-depth interviews provide valuable qualitative data that can inform strategic decision-making, product development, marketing strategies, and other areas where understanding the target audience is crucial.

Focus groups

This involves facilitating group discussions with a few participants to uncover shared perspectives and dynamics within a specific target audience.

Here are some advantages:

- Interaction and group dynamics: Focus groups allow participants to engage in group discussions, exploring different perspectives, ideas, and experiences. The interactive nature of focus groups can generate insightful discussions and uncover collective insights.

- Synergistic effects: The group setting can stimulate participants' thinking, encourage them to build upon each other's ideas, and generate new perspectives that may not emerge in individual interviews.

- Efficient data collection: Focus groups provide an opportunity to collect data from multiple participants simultaneously, making it a time-efficient method for gathering various opinions and experiences.

- Nonverbal cues: Besides verbal responses, focus groups capture nonverbal cues such as body language, facial expressions, and tone of voice, providing deeper insights into participants' emotions and reactions.

Here are some disadvantages:

- Influence of group dynamics: Group dynamics can impact participants' responses and influence individual opinions, potentially leading to conformity or dominant voices overshadowing others. Careful moderation is required to ensure a balanced and inclusive discussion.

- Limited depth of individual responses: Due to time constraints and group interactions, participants may need more time to provide in-depth responses or fully articulate their perspectives.

- Potential social desirability bias: Participants may feel inclined to conform to social norms or provide socially desirable responses in a group setting, affecting the authenticity of their feedback.

- Sample representativeness: Focus group participants may only sometimes represent the full diversity of the target population, and the findings may not be generalizable to a larger audience.

Here are some examples of their value:

- Idea generation: Focus groups are effective for generating new ideas, exploring innovative concepts, and brainstorming solutions, leveraging the collective creativity of the group.

- Perceptions and attitudes: Focus groups provide insights into participants' perceptions, attitudes, and opinions on specific topics or products, helping organizations understand how their target audience views specific issues.

- Pre-testing materials: Focus groups can pre-test and refine prototypes, concepts, or marketing materials before more comprehensive implementation, gathering feedback to inform improvements and iterations.

Ethnographic research

This involves immersing researchers in users' natural environments to observe and understand their behaviors, beliefs, and cultural influences.

Here are some advantages:

- Deep understanding of culture and context: Ethnographic research allows researchers to immerse themselves in the natural social and cultural context of the participants, providing a deep understanding of their beliefs, values, behaviors, and practices.

- Rich qualitative data: Ethnographic research generates rich, detailed, and descriptive data through observations, interviews, and field notes. This qualitative data helps uncover nuanced insights you need to capture through other research methods.

- Participant perspective: Ethnographic research emphasizes the participant's viewpoint, giving voice to their experiences, perceptions, and interpretations of their culture and practices.

- Holistic approach: Ethnographic research takes a holistic approach, considering the interconnections between different aspects of participants' lives, such as family, work, social relationships, and community dynamics.

- Long-term immersion: Ethnographic studies often involve extended periods of fieldwork, allowing researchers to develop relationships with participants, gain trust, and capture the dynamics of everyday life over time.

Here are some disadvantages:

- Time-consuming and resource-intensive: Ethnographic research requires significant time and resources due to prolonged fieldwork, participant observation, interviews, and data analysis.

- Researcher subjectivity: Researchers' interpretations and biases may influence the data collection and analysis. Transparency and reflexivity are crucial to minimizing subjectivity.

- Limited generalizability: Ethnographic research focuses on specific contexts and cultural groups, making generalizing findings to broader populations challenging. The emphasis is on in-depth understanding rather than statistical representation.

- Ethical considerations: Ethnographic research raises ethical concerns, such as informed consent, privacy, and cultural sensitivity. Researchers must navigate these considerations and maintain ethical practices throughout the study.

Here are some examples of its value:

- Cultural insights: Ethnographic research provides deep cultural insights, uncovering the values, norms, rituals, and practices of a specific group or community. This understanding is valuable for designing culturally appropriate products, services, and interventions.

- Contextualized decision-making: Ethnographic research helps decision-makers understand the context in which they will use the products or services will be used, ensuring a more informed and contextually relevant approach to design and development.

- Innovation and problem-solving: Ethnographic research uncovers unmet needs, challenges, and opportunities within a specific cultural context, providing insights for innovation and problem-solving in various domains.

Social media and online tools

Social media, app stores, and other online research platforms give you a massive community to engage with and listen to your users.

Here are some advantages:

- Wide reach and accessibility: Social media platforms and online tools provide access to a vast and diverse population of users, allowing researchers to reach a larger audience than traditional research methods.

- Large volume of data: Social media platforms generate an enormous amount of data, offering researchers a wealth of information for analysis and understanding user trends, preferences, and sentiments.

- Cost-effective: Conducting research through social media and online tools can be cost-effective compared to traditional methods, as it eliminates the need for physical resources, such as printing surveys or conducting face-to-face interviews.

- Targeted research: Social media platforms and online tools provide features that allow researchers to target specific demographics, interests, or user segments, enabling more precise and targeted research.

Here are some disadvantages:

- Representativeness and sampling bias: Research conducted through social media and online tools may suffer from sampling bias, as not all platform users may be represented in the data. It is crucial to consider the selected platform's limitations and biases and its user base's characteristics.

- Lack of control over data quality: The data collected from social media and online tools may vary in quality, as it relies on users' voluntary participation and the accuracy of their responses. Researchers must be cautious and validate the data to ensure its reliability and integrity.

- Privacy and ethical concerns: Researchers must be mindful of privacy concerns when collecting data from social media platforms and online tools. Respecting users' privacy and obtaining informed consent is essential to maintain ethical research practices.

- Data volume and analysis complexity: The vast amount of data collected from social media and online tools can be overwhelming, requiring robust data analysis techniques and tools to extract meaningful insights effectively.

Here are some examples of their value:

- Real-time insights: Social media and online tools allow researchers to gather real-time insights into users' opinions, preferences, and behaviors, providing timely information for decision-making and product development.

- User-generated content: Social media platforms and online tools provide access to user-generated content, including reviews, comments, and discussions, which offer rich qualitative data and valuable feedback.

- Consumer sentiment analysis: By analyzing social media data, researchers can gain insights into consumer sentiment, identifying trends, positive and negative feedback, and emerging issues related to products or services.

- Market research and competitor analysis: Social media and online tools enable researchers to monitor competitors, track industry trends, and gain a competitive advantage by understanding consumer perceptions and market dynamics.

- Rapid testing and feedback: Researchers can leverage social media and online tools to quickly test ideas, concepts, and prototypes, gathering feedback and insights from a broad audience within a short timeframe.

Qualitative research allows for in-depth exploration and the discovery of new insights that can drive innovation, uncover unmet needs, and inform the development of user-centered solutions. It provides a rich narrative and context, highlighting the *why* behind consumer decisions and behaviors.

Quantitative data and methods

Quantitative research focuses on numerical data and statistical analysis to uncover patterns, trends, and relationships within a large sample size. It aims to provide objective and measurable insights, often in the form of numerical data. Quantitative methods are typically structured, allowing for standardized data collection and rigorous statistical analysis. The following subsections cover some standard quantitative methods.

Surveys

This involves administering questionnaires to many participants to gather data on opinions, attitudes, preferences, and behaviors.

Here are some advantages:

- Wide reach: Surveys allow researchers to reach many participants, making it possible to collect data from a diverse sample and obtain a broad range of perspectives.

- Structured data collection: Surveys provide a structured format for collecting data, allowing for standardized responses and easy quantification of results. This facilitates data analysis and comparisons across different participants or groups.

- Efficiency: Surveys are a time-efficient research method; participants can complete them at their convenience, and data collection can be automated using online survey tools.

- Anonymity and confidentiality: Surveys provide participants with a sense of anonymity, which can encourage honest and open responses, particularly when addressing sensitive or personal topics.

Here are some disadvantages:

- Limited depth: Surveys may need more depth of qualitative research methods, as they often focus on obtaining concise and specific information. They may not capture the nuances, emotions, or contextual details that qualitative methods such as interviews or observations can provide.

- Potential for response bias: Surveys are susceptible to response bias, where participants may provide socially desirable answers, over-report or under-report certain behaviors, or exhibit acquiescence bias (tendency to agree with statements). Researchers must know potential biases and employ techniques to minimize their impact.

- Limited opportunity for clarification: Surveys provide limited opportunities for participants to ask clarifying questions or seek further information. This can limit the understanding of complex concepts or lead to the misinterpretation of questions.

- Non-response bias: Surveys may suffer from non-response bias, where participants who choose not to participate differ systematically from those who do. This can affect the generalizability of the findings.

Here are some examples of their value:

- Quantitative data collection: Surveys effectively collect quantitative data, allowing researchers to measure and quantify attitudes, opinions, behaviors, and demographics. This enables statistical analysis and supports data-driven decision-making.

- Standardized data: Surveys enable researchers to collect data in a standardized format, facilitating comparisons, trend analysis, and benchmarking across different populations or periods.

- Cost-efficient data collection: Surveys can be a cost-effective method, especially when conducted online using survey platforms that offer features such as skip logic, randomization, and automated data collection and analysis.

- Versatile research tool: You can use surveys at different stages of the research process, from exploratory research to hypothesis testing, market research, customer feedback, and the evaluation of interventions or programs.

Experiments

This involves conducting controlled experiments to test hypotheses, measure cause-and-effect relationships, and assess the impact of variables on user behavior. Here are examples of different types of experiments commonly used in research:

- **Randomized Controlled Trial (RCT)**: In an RCT, you randomly assign participants to two or more groups, with the experimental group(s) receiving a specific intervention or treatment and the control group receiving no intervention or a placebo. For example, a pharmaceutical company testing the efficacy of a new drug may conduct an RCT by randomly assigning participants to either receive the drug or a placebo and then compare the outcomes between the groups.

- A/B testing: A/B testing, or split testing, involves comparing two product versions, web pages, or marketing campaigns to determine which performs better. For example, an e-commerce website may test two versions of its checkout process (A and B) to see which leads to higher conversion rates. You randomly assign users to either version A or B, and their behavior and outcomes are compared to identify the most effective design.

- Quasi-experiment: A quasi-experiment is similar to an experiment but lacks random assignment of participants to groups. You use this when randomization is not feasible or ethical. For example, a researcher studying the impact of a school intervention program may select two similar schools—one implementing the intervention and the other serving as a comparison. The researcher can compare outcomes between the two schools to assess the program's effectiveness.

- Field experiment: Field experiments are conducted in real-world settings, allowing researchers to observe and manipulate variables while participants engage in their natural environment. For instance, a social scientist interested in studying the effect of a particular messaging campaign on voting behavior may conduct a field experiment by implementing the campaign in selected neighborhoods and comparing voter turnout with control areas.

- Quasi-experimental time series design: This design involves measuring the same variables over a continuous period before and after an intervention or treatment. Researchers use this design when randomization is impossible or when examining long-term effects. For example, a researcher investigating the impact of a policy change on crime rates may collect crime data before and after the implementation of the policy to assess its effectiveness.

- Factorial design: A factorial design involves manipulating multiple independent variables simultaneously to understand their combined effects. For instance, a psychologist interested in studying the impact of both rewards and competition on task performance may design a factorial experiment with two independent variables: rewards (present/absent) and competition (present/absent), resulting in four experimental conditions.

- Single-case experimental design: You use single-case experimental designs when studying an individual or small group over time. The design involves repeated measurements during baseline and intervention phases. For example, a therapist may use a single-case design to assess the effectiveness of a specific treatment by measuring behavior before and after the intervention.

These are just a few examples of the many types of experiments used in research. Each type has its purpose, strengths, and limitations, and researchers select the most appropriate design based on their research question, context, and available resources.

Here are some advantages:

- Causality: Experiments allow researchers to establish causal relationships between variables by manipulating an independent variable and observing its effects on the dependent variable. This helps determine cause-and-effect relationships more reliably than other research methods.

- Control over variables: Experiments provide researchers with a high level of control over variables, allowing them to isolate and manipulate specific factors of interest while keeping other variables constant. This control enhances the internal validity of the study.

- Replication and generalizability: Experiments can be replicated to verify findings and test the generalizability of results across different settings, populations, or contexts. This strengthens the reliability and external validity of the research.

- Quantifiable data: Experiments often yield quantifiable data, making it easier to analyze and interpret results using statistical techniques. This allows for the precise measurement and comparison of variables, enhancing the objectivity and rigor of the study.

- Hypothesis testing: Experiments are well suited for hypothesis testing, as researchers can directly test specific hypotheses by manipulating variables and comparing the outcomes. This helps validate or reject hypotheses and advance scientific understanding.

Here are some disadvantages:

- Artificiality: Experiments are often conducted in controlled settings, which may limit the external validity or generalizability of the findings to real-world contexts. The artificiality of the experimental environment may affect participants' behavior and responses.

- Ethical considerations: Some experiments may involve manipulating variables or exposing participants to certain conditions that could raise ethical concerns. Researchers must prioritize participant well-being and ethical guidelines throughout the study.

- Resource-intensive: Conducting experiments can be resource-intensive, requiring careful planning, allocation of resources, and coordination. They may involve participant recruitment, data collection, and analysis costs.

- Demand characteristics: Participants may modify their behavior or respond based on their perception of the experiment's purpose or expectations (demand characteristics), potentially impacting the validity of the findings. Researchers need to address and minimize such biases.

Here are some examples of their value:

- Establishing causality: Experiments provide a solid basis for establishing causal relationships between variables, essential for understanding the impact of interventions, treatments, or manipulations.

- Rigorous testing of hypotheses: Experiments allow researchers to test specific hypotheses and theories by manipulating variables and systematically observing the effects. This helps validate or refine existing theories and contributes to scientific advancement.

- Quantitative analysis: Experiments generate quantitative data, enabling researchers to analyze and interpret results using statistical techniques. This provides precise and objective measurement, allowing for robust statistical inference.

- Replication and validation: Experiments can be replicated to validate findings and test the generalizability of results. Replication increases the reliability and confidence in the observed effects.

- Practical applications: Experimental research provides valuable insights to inform evidence-based decision-making and practical applications in various fields, such as medicine, psychology, marketing, and education.

Behavioral tracking

This refers to the systematic data collection and analysis of users' behaviors, actions, and interactions within a digital environment. It involves capturing and recording various user activities, such as clicks, navigation paths, time spent on specific pages, and interactions with elements or features of a website or application.

Here are some advantages:

- Data-driven insights: Behavioral tracking gives organizations valuable insights into user behavior, preferences, and patterns. By analyzing user actions and interactions, organizations can gain a deeper understanding of their audience and make informed decisions to improve their products or services.

- Personalization: Organizations can personalize the user experience by tracking user behavior. They can tailor recommendations, content, and features based on individual preferences, creating a more engaging and relevant user experience.

- Testing and optimization: Behavioral tracking enables organizations to conduct experiments and A/B testing. They can measure the impact of design, features, or marketing strategy changes by analyzing user behavior and making data-backed optimizations.

- Performance measurement: Behavioral tracking allows organizations to measure and monitor the performance of their products, campaigns, or marketing efforts. By tracking key metrics, they can assess the effectiveness of their strategies and make data-driven improvements.

However, there are also some disadvantages and ethical considerations associated with behavioral tracking:

- Privacy concerns: Behavioral tracking raises privacy concerns as it involves collecting and analyzing user data. Organizations must ensure compliance with privacy regulations and obtain user consent to address privacy concerns.

- Data security: Organizations must implement proper data security measures to protect the collected data from unauthorized access or data breaches.

- Transparency and trust: Organizations should be transparent about their tracking practices and provide clear options for users to opt in or opt out. Building trust with users is crucial to maintain a positive relationship.

- User consent and control: Organizations should respect user preferences and provide mechanisms for users to control their data. Users should have the ability to opt out of tracking if they desire.

- Data accuracy and interpretation: It is essential to ensure the collected data's accuracy and interpretation. Misinterpretation or biased conclusions can lead to incorrect assumptions or decisions.

Here are some examples of its value:

- Enhanced user experience: By analyzing user behavior, organizations can gain a deeper understanding of their users' needs, preferences, and pain points. This insight allows them to design and optimize their products and services to deliver a more tailored and engaging user experience.

- Improved decision-making: Behavioral tracking enables data-driven decision-making. Organizations can use the collected data to identify trends, patterns, and correlations, helping them make informed decisions about product features, marketing strategies, and business goals.

- Increased conversion rates: Organizations can identify areas where users may drop off or abandon their journey by understanding user behavior. They can then implement targeted interventions or optimizations to improve conversion rates and drive user engagement.

- Personalization and customization: Behavioral tracking facilitates personalized experiences. Organizations can leverage user data to provide customized recommendations, content, and offers, enhancing user satisfaction and fostering long-term engagement.

- Competitive advantage: Behavioral tracking allows organizations to stay ahead of the competition by understanding user preferences and market trends. By leveraging data-driven insights, organizations can develop innovative products, deliver exceptional user experiences, and gain a competitive edge on the market.

Facebook (2004)

As we delve into the world of behavioral tracking and statistical analysis, the social media titan Facebook provides a compelling example. Since its inception in the mid-2000s, Facebook's journey from a simple communication platform to an influential multi-market entity, now rebranded as Meta, is a narrative familiar to most of us. Facebook, and most social media in general, is notorious for tracking user behavior.

Everything you do on the platform changes your propensity for seeing different content, being shown specific ads, or encouraging you to connect with certain people. As you use this, or any social platform, pay attention to how your ads change by clicking on items. Notice how your feed of information may change based on what you like. Data is being collected all around us to change the experiences we have, and as time goes on, privacy laws will likely become more and more strict. The ethical dilemma is worth considering now as this landscape changes fast. Do you have a way to collect usage data without encroaching on privacy?

Statistical analysis

This involves applying statistical techniques to analyze numerical data, such as regression analysis, correlation analysis, or hypothesis testing.

Here are some advantages:

- Objective and reliable: Statistical analysis provides an objective and systematic approach to analyzing data, ensuring reliability and minimizing bias in interpreting results

- Data-driven decision-making: By applying statistical techniques, researchers can uncover patterns, relationships, and trends within the data, enabling informed decision-making based on empirical evidence

- Generalizability: Statistical analysis allows researchers to generalize findings from a sample to a larger population, providing insights that you can apply to a broader context

- Precise and quantifiable: Statistical analysis provides precise measurements and quantifiable results, allowing researchers to draw meaningful conclusions and make accurate predictions

Here are some disadvantages:

- Assumptions and limitations: Statistical analysis relies on certain assumptions and may have limitations based on collected data, sample size, or underlying statistical models. Researchers should be cautious of these limitations when interpreting results.

- Complexity: Statistical analysis techniques require expertise and knowledge of statistical methods and software tools. Improper application or misinterpretation of statistical techniques can lead to erroneous conclusions.

- Time and resources: Statistical analysis can be time-consuming and resource-intensive, mainly when dealing with large datasets or complex statistical models.

Here are some examples of its value:

- Insights into customer behavior: Statistical analysis allows researchers to uncover patterns and trends in customer behavior, preferences, and attitudes. This information helps organizations understand their target market, identify customer segments, and make data-driven product development, marketing strategies, and customer satisfaction decisions.

- Performance evaluation: Statistical analysis enables organizations to assess the performance and effectiveness of their marketing campaigns, pricing strategies, and sales initiatives. By analyzing key performance indicators and conducting statistical tests, organizations can identify areas of improvement and optimize their strategies for better business outcomes.

- Forecasting and predictive analytics: You use statistical analysis to develop predictive models that forecast future trends and outcomes. This allows organizations to anticipate market changes, customer demand, and business opportunities, enabling proactive decision-making and strategic planning.

- Evidence-based decision-making: Statistical analysis provides objective evidence and quantifiable insights, helping organizations make informed decisions based on empirical data rather than assumptions or intuition.

Quantitative research provides a systematic and objective approach to understanding market trends, quantifying consumer preferences, and measuring the impact of interventions. It allows for generalizations and predictions based on a larger sample size and enables data-driven decision-making.

The choice between qualitative and quantitative research depends on the research objectives, the nature of the investigated problem, and the available resources. In many cases, combining both approaches, known as mixed methods, can provide a comprehensive and robust understanding of the market, consumer behavior, and product opportunities.

Sample size and sampling methods

Determining an appropriate sample size in market research is crucial as it represents the subset of the target population from which you will collect the data. Since gathering feedback or testing every individual within a group is often impractical, researchers use sampling methods to select a representative sample that can provide reliable insights. Next, we'll look at an expanded explanation of sample size and sampling methods.

Sample size

Sample size refers to the number of participants or data points included in a research study. It is determined based on various factors, such as the research objectives, desired precision level, expected population variability, and available resources. A larger sample size generally leads to greater statistical power and increased confidence in the findings. Conversely, a smaller sample size may introduce higher levels of uncertainty and decreased generalizability.

Researchers often employ statistical formulas or online tools to determine an appropriate sample size. These formulas consider factors such as the desired confidence level, the margin of error, and the expected variability in the population. By inputting these parameters, researchers can calculate the minimum sample size required to achieve their desired level of precision. However, it is essential to note that sample size calculations are based on assumptions about the underlying population, and you should consider the actual sample size within the constraints of the research context.

Sample size example

Assuming you want to estimate the proportion of satisfied customers with a 95% confidence level and a margin of error of ±3%, you can use the following formula to calculate the required sample size:

Sample size = $(Z^2 * p * (1 - p)) / (E^2)$

In this example, Z represents the Z-value corresponding to the desired confidence level. For a 95% confidence level, the Z-value is approximately 1.96.

Confidence Level Z-Value

80% 1.282

85% 1.440

90% 1.645

95% 1.960

99% 2.576

p is the estimated proportion of satisfied customers (using a conservative estimate or a pilot study result).

E represents the desired margin of error as a decimal (3% would be 0.03).

For example, assume you estimate the proportion of satisfied customers is 0.7 (70%) based on prior knowledge or assumptions. Plugging these values into the formula, we have the following:

- Sample size = $(1.96^2 * 0.7 * (1 - 0.7)) / (0.03^2)$
- Sample size ≈ 381

In this case, you would need a sample size of approximately 381 respondents to estimate the proportion of satisfied customers with a 95% confidence level and a margin of error of ±3%. This sample size calculation ensures that you have sufficient data to draw statistically reliable conclusions from the survey.

Remember that this is a simplified example, and there may be additional factors to consider depending on the specific research context, such as the survey design, population characteristics, and anticipated response rates. We recommend consulting statistical resources or a statistician to ensure accurate sample size calculations for your research study.

Sampling methods

Sampling methods are techniques used to select individuals or elements from the population to be included in the research study. The goal is to ensure that the sample is representative of the broader population, allowing for generalizations and inferences. Here are a few standard sampling methods:

- **Probability sampling**: Probability sampling methods involve random selection, where each individual in the population has a known and non-zero chance of being included in the sample. Examples include simple random sampling, stratified sampling, and cluster sampling.

- **Non-probability sampling**: Non-probability sampling methods do not rely on random selection and may introduce some bias into the sample. Use these methods when it is difficult to obtain a random sample or when specific subgroups need to be targeted. Examples include convenience sampling, purposive sampling, and snowball sampling.

- **Sampling techniques in online research**: Additional sampling methods have emerged with the rise of online research. These include quota sampling, where participants are selected to match specific characteristics in predetermined proportions, and panel sampling, which involves recruiting and using a pre-existing group of participants for multiple research studies.

The choice of sampling method depends on factors such as the research objectives, the target population, the available resources, and the desired level of representativeness. You need to carefully consider the strengths and limitations of each method to ensure the validity and reliability of their findings.

Let's move on to understanding your users' motivations and behaviors.

Understanding user motivation and behavior

Market research is pivotal in uncovering the motivations and behaviors that drive user engagement and decision-making. Product teams can gain valuable insights into user preferences, needs, and desires by employing various research methods. This section explores how market research methods can be effectively utilized to understand user motivations and behaviors, ultimately informing the design and development of successful products and experiences.

Triangulating insights and bridging the qualitative-quantitative divide

It is often advantageous to combine qualitative and quantitative research methods to gain a comprehensive understanding of user motivations and behaviors. Triangulating insights from different sources allows researchers to validate findings, identify converging patterns, and explore the interplay between user attitudes and actions.

Complementary nature of qualitative and quantitative insights

Qualitative and quantitative research play distinct yet complementary roles in understanding user behavior. Qualitative research delves into the *why* behind user behavior by exploring their experiences, motivations, and perceptions through interviews, focus groups, and observations. It allows researchers to capture rich, nuanced insights and uncover underlying reasons for user preferences and actions.

On the other hand, quantitative research provides statistical rigor and scalability by collecting numerical data from a larger sample size. Surveys, user analytics, and experiments are standard quantitative research methods that generate measurable data on user behavior, preferences, and outcomes. You can analyze the data statistically to identify patterns, correlations, and trends.

Combining qualitative and quantitative approaches bridges the gap between subjective experiences and objective data, resulting in a more comprehensive understanding of users. Product teams gain a holistic view of user behavior and motivations by integrating qualitative narratives with quantitative metrics.

Integrating qualitative and quantitative research allows for triangulation, combining insights from both approaches to validate findings and ensure a more comprehensive understanding of users. Product teams can derive actionable insights that inform strategic decision-making by synthesizing qualitative narratives and metrics. This combination enables a deeper understanding of user behavior, motivations, and needs, leading to more effective product development and customer-centric solutions.

Validating and generalizing findings

Triangulating qualitative and quantitative insights is a powerful approach that allows researchers to strengthen the validity and reliability of their findings by integrating different research methods. This convergence of insights from multiple sources enhances the overall quality and robustness of the research, reducing the risk of biased interpretations and providing a more comprehensive understanding of the research topic.

The convergence of insights from qualitative and quantitative sources enables researchers to validate their findings across different research methods. Researchers can identify consistencies, inconsistencies, or complementarity between the two data types by comparing and contrasting the results. This process of triangulation enhances the reliability and trustworthiness of the research outcomes, as it reduces the potential for biased interpretations that may arise from relying on a single method.

Moreover, integrating qualitative and quantitative data allows for a more comprehensive analysis of the research topic. It enables researchers to uncover hidden insights, gain a deeper understanding of complex phenomena, and explore different dimensions of the user experience. By triangulating insights, researchers can generate a more holistic and nuanced picture, capturing the research topic's breadth and depth.

Applying market research insights to drive product excellence

The ultimate goal of understanding user motivations and behaviors through market research is to inform the design and development of products and experiences that resonate with users. Applying the insights gained from market research allows product teams to create user-centric solutions that drive engagement, satisfaction, and business success.

Designing compelling user experiences

Market research insights guide the design of user experiences by aligning them with user motivations, needs, and desires. Product teams can identify key pain points, feature preferences, and interaction patterns by integrating qualitative and quantitative findings. This knowledge enables the creation of intuitive interfaces, personalized features, and engaging gamification elements that captivate users and enhance their experience, which we will cover in-depth in *Chapter 6*.

Tailoring marketing and communication strategies

Understanding user motivations and behaviors empowers product teams to develop targeted marketing and communication strategies. Organizations can deliver compelling campaigns that effectively drive user acquisition, engagement, and retention by identifying the messaging, channels, and incentives that resonate with users. Market research insights also facilitate the identification of user segments, allowing for tailored marketing approaches that address specific needs and preferences, which we will cover in more depth in *Chapter 9*.

Iterative improvement and continuous innovation

Market research serves as a foundation for iterative improvement and continuous innovation. By regularly gathering feedback, measuring user satisfaction, and tracking user behaviors, product teams can identify areas for enhancement and refine their offerings accordingly. Market research insights help organizations adapt to evolving user needs, anticipate trends, and stay ahead of the competition by delivering innovative products and experiences, which we will cover in *Chapter 7*.

Understanding user motivations and behaviors through market research is critical to successful product development. By leveraging qualitative and quantitative research methods, product teams can comprehensively understand user preferences, needs, and desires. These insights inform strategic decision-making, drive user-centric design, and enable organizations to create products and experiences that resonate with their target audience. By continuously refining and improving based on market research insights, organizations can achieve product excellence and establish long-lasting relationships with their users.

Creating user personas and Jobs to Be Done

Designing gamification for your product requires a deep understanding of your target users. User personas and **JTBD** are valuable tools in this process. User personas bring the characteristics and behaviors of your target audience to life, providing insights for creating experiences that resonate with their needs. The JTBD framework helps identify the specific goals users aim to achieve when using a product. By understanding these goals, we can align gamification elements to address user needs effectively and create engaging experiences. By focusing on user personas and JTBD, we ensure that our gamification strategies are tailored to user motivations, driving meaningful engagement and achieving business goals.

Personas

Personas are a standard framework of user experience design. Alan Cooper first popularized them in his book *The Inmates Are Running the Asylum: Why High-Tech Products Drive Us Crazy and How to Restore the Sanity*, which has been influential in user-centered design and persona development. Cooper emphasizes the importance of creating personas based on a deep empathy and understanding of the target users. He advocates for personas that represent real individuals, complete with names, photos, and detailed descriptions of their goals, motivations, and behaviors. Cooper believes personas should serve as a shared understanding among stakeholders and guide design decisions throughout product development.

Personas can be a valuable component of the design process. However, it is essential to approach their creation with care and precision to ensure their effectiveness. Outdated or irrelevant information can render personas useless or even detrimental. Therefore, it is crucial to have accurate and up-to-date data when developing personas. Additionally, avoid overgeneralization and stereotyping, as personas should represent a group of users without bias or assumptions.

> **Mass Effect 2 (2010)**
>
> **Role-Playing Games (RPGs)** are known for using multiple character archetypes, and *Mass Effect 2* is no exception. Within this game, you can build a squad using over 10 different characters. Each has stats, a storyline, physical traits, and more. The game is set in outer space, so there is no shortage of characteristics available to use. The storytelling in the franchise is wonderful, and many feel part two is the best of the series.
>
> If you can get your hands on this game, it is worth playing through, as the storytelling alone is a masterclass in narrative design. But, specifically, pay attention to all of the characters and races within the various planets. Each character profile acts much like a persona, with details about the character, key information, demographics, and more. Reading over each character's bio could set you up nicely for knowing exactly how you could best use them in any situation, much like a persona for your product should.

When creating personas, keep the users' goals in your mind. Ensure that your personas align with the specific objectives and tasks users aim to accomplish. This way, your design decisions will more likely address their needs and priorities.

To make personas truly valuable, it is vital to validate them through testing. By testing your personas with real users, you can verify their accuracy and relevance. This validation process ensures that your product is designed for the right end users, increasing its chances of success.

This comprehensive guide will explore the process of building user personas for product development. We will delve into the importance of personas, discuss the steps involved in creating them, and highlight best practices along the way. Additionally, we will provide a case study and practical examples to illustrate how you can apply personas in a real-world context.

Let's begin our journey into the world of user personas.

Step 1 – research and data collection

The first step in building user personas is conducting thorough research and data collection. This involves gathering information about your target audience through various methods, as we covered at the beginning of the chapter.

Case study example: Let's consider "Hi-Z Fitness." We want to create user personas to better understand their target audience, which includes fitness enthusiasts of all ages and fitness levels. We conduct surveys, interviews, and competitor analysis to collect data on user preferences, fitness goals, exercise routines, and motivations.

Step 2 – data analysis and pattern identification

Once you have collected the necessary data, the next step is to analyze it and identify patterns, trends, and insights. Look for commonalities, recurring themes, and significant variations in the data that can help you understand your target audience's diverse needs and behaviors.

Qualitative data can be analyzed by categorizing responses, identifying recurring keywords or phrases, and clustering similar insights. Quantitative data, on the other hand, can be analyzed using statistical techniques such as frequency analysis, correlation analysis, and data visualization.

By analyzing the data, you can start identifying the key characteristics and traits defining your target audience's user segments. Look for demographic information, psychographic attributes, goals, pain points, and behavioral patterns from the data.

Case study example: We analyze survey responses and interview transcripts in the Hi-Z Fitness case study. We discover that their target audience can be divided into three primary segments: young professionals seeking weight loss, older adults focused on maintaining overall fitness, and athletes aiming for performance improvement. We also identify common motivations, such as wanting to improve health, tracking progress, and achieving personal goals.

Step 3 – persona creation

With the data analysis complete, it's time to create your user persona. User personas are fictional representations of your target users that encapsulate their key characteristics, motivations, goals, and behaviors. They provide a tangible and relatable way to understand your audience and make user-centered design decisions. You can also include what type of gamer they are, as discussed in *Chapter 3*.

To create user personas, give each persona a name and a photo. This helps humanize the personas and makes them more relatable to the product team. Then, write a detailed description of each persona, including their demographics, background, goals, challenges, preferences, and behaviors. The more detailed and realistic the personas, the more effectively they will guide product development and gamification decisions.

Case study example: In the Hi-Z Fitness case study, the team creates three user personas:

- Sarah, a 28-year-old environmental scientist looking to lose weight and improve her overall fitness

- James, a 55-year-old music executive aiming to maintain his fitness and manage stress

- Emily, a 42-year-old competitive athlete striving for performance improvement

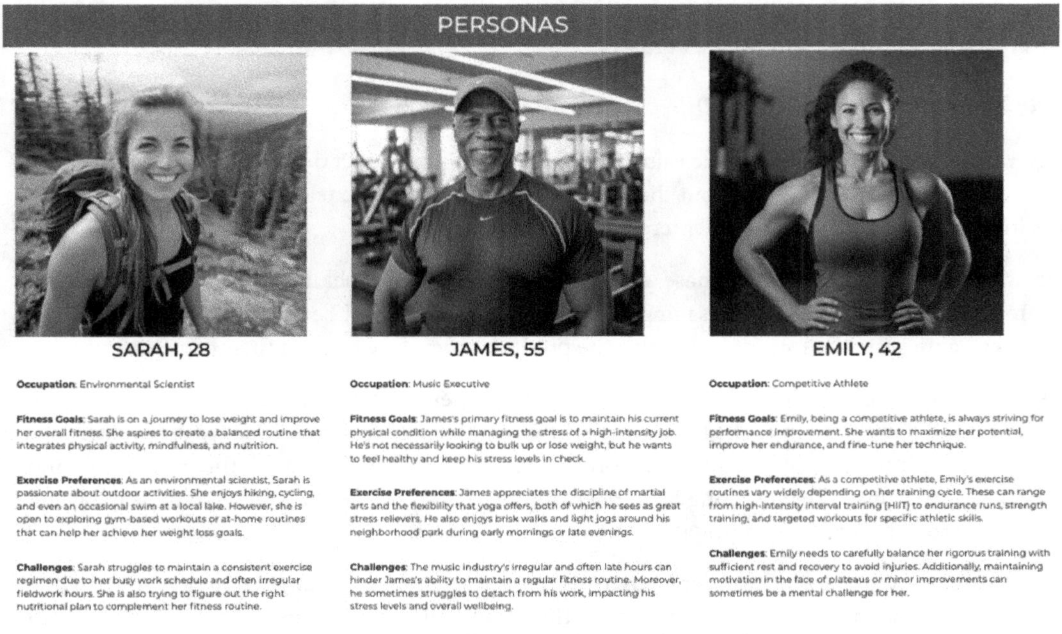

Figure 4.1 – Overview of personas (images from Midjourney)

Each persona is accompanied by a photo and a detailed description that includes their age, occupation, fitness goals, exercise preferences, and challenges they face. The personas clearly represent Hi-Z Fitness's target users, allowing the team to empathize with their needs, design a product that meets their expectations, and understand their behaviors and motivations for the gamification strategy.

Step 4 – persona validation

After creating the user personas, it is essential to validate them to ensure their accuracy and reliability. Validation involves sharing the personas with stakeholders, such as team members, users, and subject matter experts, and gathering feedback to refine and enhance the personas. This feedback helps validate that the personas accurately represent the target audience and align with their needs and behaviors.

Validation can be done through workshops, focus groups, or individual interviews where stakeholders provide input and insights about the personas. Gathering diverse perspectives and ensuring that the personas resonate with various stakeholders is essential.

Case study example: In the Hi-Z Fitness case study, the team conducts a validation workshop inviting internal stakeholders, including designers, developers, and marketers, to review and provide feedback on the personas. They also interview potential Hi-Z Fitness users to validate whether the personas accurately represent their goals, motivations, and challenges. The feedback gathered during validation helps refine the personas and ensure accuracy.

Step 5 – persona application

Once validated, the personas become valuable tools for guiding product development decisions. They serve as a reference point throughout the design process, helping the team understand user needs, prioritize features, and make user-centered design choices.

During the product development phase, refer to the personas when making decisions about product features, user interface design, messaging, and marketing strategies. Use the personas to empathize with users, anticipate their needs, and tailor the product experience to meet their expectations.

Case study example: In the Hi-Z Fitness case study, the personas are regularly referenced during the design and development of the fitness app. The design team uses the personas to guide decisions about the app's interface, layout, and functionality, ensuring that it aligns with the preferences and goals of each persona. The marketing team refers to the personas to develop targeted messaging and communication strategies that resonate with the user segments.

Building user personas is a critical step in user-centered design and product development. By creating personas, product teams can deeply understand their target audience, uncover user motivations and behaviors, and make informed design decisions. User personas humanize the design process, enabling teams to empathize with users and create products that address their needs and preferences.

Remember, personas are not static entities. They should be continuously updated and refined as new insights emerge. Regularly revisit and validate your personas to ensure they remain accurate and representative of your evolving user base.

Now, there is an alternative to personas, and depending on who you speak to in the product development community, a necessary companion to personas.

JTBD

While personas have long been a popular tool in user-centered design, some product leaders prefer using the JTBD framework as an alternative approach. The JTBD framework focuses on understanding users' underlying motivations and desired outcomes when they "hire" a product or service to get a job done. Here are a few reasons why product leaders may prefer JTBD over personas:

- Outcome-focused: JTBD emphasizes the desired outcomes or goals users try to achieve rather than focusing solely on their demographic characteristics or behaviors. Product teams can align their solutions more effectively with user needs by understanding the desired outcomes.

- Flexibility: Personas are typically static representations of user archetypes, whereas JTBD allows for a more dynamic and adaptable approach. With JTBD, the focus is on understanding the context and situation in which users have a specific job to be done. This flexibility enables product teams to uncover new opportunities and adapt their solutions accordingly.

- Market segmentation: While personas are often used to segment the user base, JTBD can provide a more granular understanding of market segments based on the specific jobs users are trying to accomplish. This segmentation helps product leaders identify under-served needs and target their solutions more precisely.

- User-driven innovation: The JTBD framework encourages product teams to focus on the user's desired outcomes and find innovative solutions to help them achieve them. This user-centric approach can lead to breakthrough innovations and a deeper understanding of user motivations.

- Alignment with product strategy: JTBD aligns well with the strategic goals of a product organization. By understanding the jobs users are trying to get done and the outcomes they desire, product leaders can make informed decisions about feature prioritization, product positioning, and go-to-market strategies.

It's important to note that personas and JTBD are not mutually exclusive approaches. They can complement each other, and product leaders can choose to use one or both, depending on their organization's specific needs and product. We would choose both. Ultimately, the goal is to gain a deep understanding of users' motivations, behaviors, and desired outcomes to create products that genuinely meet their needs.

This comprehensive guide will walk you through implementing JTBD, providing practical steps and insights to help you apply this framework successfully.

Step 1 – understanding the concept of JTBD

The fundamental principles of the JTBD framework are as follows:

- Focus on the job: JTBD emphasizes understanding the actual job or task customers are trying to accomplish rather than solely focusing on the product or solution itself. It shifts the perspective from features and functionalities to the underlying problem customers seek to solve.

- Context matters: JTBD recognizes that customer needs and preferences can vary depending on the context in which they are trying to accomplish a job. Understanding a job's specific circumstances, constraints, and motivations allows for more accurate problem-solving and solution design.

- Outcome-oriented: JTBD focuses on the desired outcome or results that customers are looking to achieve. It encourages product teams to design solutions that deliver the desired outcome effectively, regardless of the specific features or attributes of the solution.

- Customer progression: JTBD recognizes that customers go through a progression of jobs, starting from an initial struggle or need and progressing toward a desired outcome. Understanding the stages and steps involved in this progression helps product teams identify opportunities for intervention and improvement.

- Jobs are stable, solutions evolve: JTBD suggests that jobs remain relatively stable over time, while the solutions or products used to accomplish those jobs can evolve. By understanding the core job, product teams can innovate and improve solutions without being limited by the current offerings on the market.

- Emotional and social factors: JTBD acknowledges that emotions and social factors significantly affect customers' job completion. Customers often seek solutions that provide emotional satisfaction or meet social expectations. Considering these factors in solution design can enhance customer engagement and satisfaction.

By embracing these fundamental principles, product teams can better understand customer needs, design solutions that align with those needs, and drive meaningful innovation in their products and services.

Step 2 – conducting user research to identify jobs

User research plays a crucial role in understanding customer needs. Explore various research methods to gather insights, such as customer interviews, behavior observation, and feedback analysis. By analyzing this information, you can identify the core jobs customers are trying to accomplish and uncover their pain points and motivations.

Step 3 – crafting effective job statements

Once you have identified the essential jobs customers are trying to accomplish, it is crucial to articulate them clearly and concisely. A well-defined job statement effectively captures the essence of customer needs and provides a foundation for solution design. Here are the components of a well-defined job statement and some guidelines for crafting effective statements:

- Verb: Start the job statement with an action verb that describes the core activity the customer wants to accomplish. For example, verbs such as "organize," "manage," "learn," or "connect" can be used to articulate specific actions.

- Object: Specify the object or subject of the job, which represents the focus or target of the customer's action. This could be a problem, task, goal, or need that the customer wants to address. For example, "finances," "project timelines," or "customer relationships" could be the objects of the job.

- Context: Consider the context in which the job is performed and include any relevant details that impact how the job is executed. Contextual information can provide a deeper understanding of the job and help refine the solution. For example, consider factors such as time constraints, environmental conditions, or specific user characteristics.

- Outcome: Clearly articulate the desired outcome or result the customer wants to achieve by completing the job. This outcome represents the ultimate goal or benefit the customer is seeking. It could be increased efficiency, improved satisfaction, cost savings, or any other positive outcome.

When crafting effective job statements, keep the following guidelines in mind:

- Be specific: Use precise language and avoid vague or general terms. The job statement should convey the specific action, object, and outcome.

- Keep it concise: Aim for brevity and clarity. Avoid unnecessary details or extraneous information that may dilute the essence of the job.

- Customer-focused: Frame the job statement from the customer's perspective, focusing on their needs, goals, and aspirations. This helps maintain a user-centric approach throughout the solution design process.

- Test and refine: Iterate and refine the job statements based on user feedback and insights. Validate that the statements accurately capture the customer's perspective and effectively communicate their needs.

Here's an example of a well-defined job statement:

Job: Manage personal finances effectively

Components:

- Verb: Manage
- Object: Personal finances
- Context: Within a limited monthly budget
- Outcome: Achieve financial stability and savings goals

In this example, the job statement clearly expresses the action (`manage`), the object (`personal finances`), the context (`within a limited monthly budget`), and the desired outcome (`financial stability and savings goals`). This statement provides a concise and focused understanding of the specific job customers are trying to accomplish concerning their finances.

By using such well-defined job statements, product teams can gain insights into their customers' core needs and motivations. This understanding allows them to design products and experiences that effectively address the customers' financial management challenges, support their goals, and deliver meaningful value.

Step 4 – mapping customer journeys

Visualizing the customer journey is crucial in identifying the key touchpoints and pain points where customers encounter challenges. It helps product teams gain a holistic view of the customer's experience from start to finish and enables them to identify opportunities for improvement.

To visualize the customer journey, follow these steps:

1. Define the stages: Break down the customer journey into distinct stages that align with the typical progression of a customer's interaction with your product or service. Typical stages include awareness, consideration, purchase, onboarding, product usage, and support.

2. Map touchpoints: Identify customers' various touchpoints or interactions with your product or brand at each stage of the journey. This can include visiting your website, signing up for a trial, using specific features, contacting customer support, and more. Ensure you capture both digital and offline touchpoints.

3. Understand customer goals: Determine the customer's goals and motivations at each journey stage. What are they trying to achieve or accomplish? What challenges do they face? By understanding their goals, you can align the JTBD with the corresponding stages 4nd touchpoints.

4. Link jobs to touchpoints: Identity which JTBD are relevant to each touchpoint along the customer journey. For example, if a customer is in the onboarding stage, their job might be to "get up and running quickly." Link this job to the specific touchpoints where they interact with your onboarding process.

5. Identify pain points: Within each stage and touchpoint, pinpoint the pain points or areas where customers encounter challenges or frustrations. These pain points can prevent customers from accomplishing their jobs effectively or efficiently. Understanding these pain points is critical for designing solutions that address customer needs.

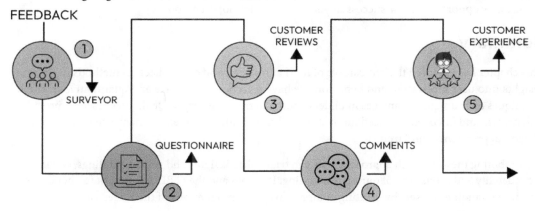

Figure 4.2 – Customer journey map example

By visualizing the customer journey and linking the identified jobs to specific stages and touchpoints, you gain insights into the opportunities to improve the customer experience. This exercise helps you understand how your product can effectively address customer needs and pain points at each stage, ensuring that your solutions align with their goals and provide a seamless and valuable experience. You can find many other books and online resources that will give you more insight on how to journey map effectively. Here are two of our favorites:

- *Mapping Experiences: A Guide to Creating Value through Journeys, Blueprints, and Diagrams* by James Kalbach: https://www.amazon.com/Mapping-Experiences-Complete-Creating-Blueprints/dp/1491923539

- Nielsen Norman Group: https://www.nngroup.com/

Step 5 – validating and refining JTBD

Testing and validation are crucial steps in the JTBD process. Use the methods we covered in the chapter to test job statements with customers, gather feedback, and iterate on your initial findings. Leverage data and analytics to validate and refine the identified jobs based on real customer insights.

Step 6 – applying JTBD in product development

Start applying the JTBD framework in the product development life cycle. From ideation and solution generation to prioritizing features and designing user experiences, understanding the JTBD framework can guide decision-making and drive innovation. We will cover this in detail in *Chapter 6*.

Implementing JTBD is a powerful approach to understanding customer needs and driving product innovation. Product teams can design solutions that truly resonate and deliver value by identifying the core jobs customers are trying to accomplish. This comprehensive guide has provided the necessary steps and insights to effectively implement JTBD. Embrace this customer-centric framework and unlock new opportunities for success in your product development journey.

Summary

This chapter has explored the critical role of market research and data collection methods in gaining insights into user motivation and behavior. We have seen how qualitative and quantitative research techniques offer unique advantages in understanding users more deeply. Qualitative research provides rich context and uncovers nuanced motivations, while quantitative research enables the identification of general preferences and trends.

By combining these research approaches, we can triangulate insights and validate findings, enhancing the reliability and robustness of our understanding. Personas and the JTBD framework further deepen our understanding of users by creating comprehensive representations of their needs and goals.

Personas allow us to empathize with users and design experiences catering to their requirements. The JTBD framework helps us focus on the outcomes users seek and design solutions that address those needs effectively. By visualizing the customer journey and identifying touchpoints and pain points, we can align our product offerings with user needs throughout their experience.

The next chapter will delve into the exciting world of game mechanics. *Chapter 6* will combine the insights from market research, personas, JTBD, and game mechanics to design a gamified product that engages and motivates users. By leveraging these powerful tools, we will create an experience that meets user needs and surpasses their expectations.

5
Game Mechanics and Psychology

We have discussed gamification history, methodologies, and understanding your users, but what about the actual gamification mechanics? What things can you, as a product development professional, implement to make your product more engaging? The short answer is a lot!

We will discuss several popular ways game mechanics are used outside of games in this chapter, but this is not meant to be an exhaustive list. The best way to understand how to create fun is simply to get out and try some things. This chapter will give a *lot* of examples of where that exploration may start.

In this chapter, we will cover the following topics:

- Reward systems
- Progress tracking
- Narrative and storytelling
- Social engagement
- Game psychology

Reward systems

Reward systems can be a powerful motivator. By rewarding your users, you can drive several valuable KPIs, including daily/weekly/monthly average users, retention rate, transaction values, and referrals, to name just a few. There are several ways to reward users, but the most successful rely on having meaningful and attainable rewards. You can accomplish that by using one or more of the tactics discussed in this subsection.

A product such as our hypothetical Product Manager Media product would rely on many of these features. The goal of any social platform is to motivate others to spread it to their friends and family. Providing the users with rewards for continued use can encourage them to log in daily and see what's new.

Point redemption

These systems rely on users earning points or credits for activities. This can be a transaction, filling out a profile, answering questions to better tailor ads, or any number of things. Point systems work particularly well if you want to reward several different activities (as opposed to *just* purchases). One of the trickiest parts of these systems, however, is working out the earning and redemption economy.

Figuring out which activities are worth which points can take some adjusting over time. And calculating the value of the items that can be redeemed may take iteration as well. By paying attention to what your users are doing, you can likely find where possible balance issues might be. If users are completing a certain task at a significantly higher percentage than others, it might be that the reward-to-work ratio for that task is a little high. You can always make changes and move forward as needed or add a special bonus for certain tasks at different points in the year or sales cycle.

One of the more common industries to see this style of system is airline purchases. With each flight, you earn points for additional flights, on-flight items, and more. Because the price of each flight can vary significantly, this type of system is used more often in this industry than something such as a punch card, which we will discuss next.

Punch cards

Like point redemption, punch cards rely on users earning items to perform activities. The main difference is that punch cards are generally used when the item earning the punch is the same item that is redeemed. If there is a large variance in the items earning punches, you can have users game the system by making several small item punches and then redeeming them for a large item reward. For this reason, many companies have moved to a point system, which comes at the cost of complexity. If you have a simple product line, punch cards can be an easy-to-understand system for users of all demographics, as shown in *Figure 5.1*:

Figure 5.1 – Example punch card for a coffee shop

Punch cards are used a lot in the beverage industry since the cost of various drinks doesn't usually vary too much. If a user purchases 10 coffees, the 11th is free! It is simple to understand, and users know immediately how to earn a reward and what that reward will be, which can often be the downside to more complicated point-based systems.

Referral systems

One of the metrics that reward systems aim to improve is user referrals. If users earn great things by using your product, they are likely to tell others they know. If you want to drive that behavior even further, or you are a new business looking to quickly scale, rewarding current users for bringing in new clients can be a great way to do that. One of the hang-ups of these types of systems is making sure users get credit when credit is due. If someone makes a referral and the system doesn't properly capture and reward that referral, it can have an even worse effect than not having the system in the first place. This can happen for several reasons. Maybe the user didn't sign up by clicking the specified link, or they used a different email address when signing up. If that credit doesn't make it to the referral, you may end up losing the original customer.

Many **Software-as-a-Service (SaaS)** vendors use this system as part of their subscription model. If you refer a new user that signs up for the service, you can earn yourself a free month of service or similar. Music streaming services, communication tools, and project management platforms are all known to drive retention and new business using this model.

Content unlocks

As users become more and more advanced within your system, it can be advantageous to reward them for that progression. Unlocking new features or cosmetics as they progress can feel like a fun little reward. This could come in the form of items for their avatar (discussed later), or even potential new features in the software that beginning users do not have access to. It is important to make the reward match the work; otherwise, the feeling of accomplishment can be underwhelming. It is also worth considering several smaller rewards at shorter tiers, rather than having a single large payoff after a lot of work, especially in the beginning stages of onboarding. This will keep user anticipation high and encourage early use of the system.

One example would be rewarding any user that reaches a milestone with content to use inside or outside the platform. Maybe by using the system for five consecutive days, they earn a badge they can share on social media or a wallpaper image for their phone or computer. Many e-commerce sites will open a few additional features if you create a free account on the site, such as wish lists or free returns.

Memberships

On the surface, memberships may feel a bit like content unlocks, but the key difference is the concept of paid not earned. Within this type of system, rewards are given as an add-on for being a premium/paid member. It is worth noting that in the world of multiplayer gaming, there is a heated debate about the value of "pay to win" type features. If a player can simply pay a fee to unlock more powerful items in the game (thus allowing them a higher chance to win), much of the skill gets turned on its head. Product designers must be careful not to offset the balance between different user types when implementing a similar system. For paid memberships to succeed, the return on investment must be very clear to users. Without a clear value added compared to non-member shopping, it will be an uphill battle.

Several social media platforms are starting to take this approach by unlocking new functionality for paying or premium users. Allowing paid users additional tools or features can lead to increased premium accounts, but can also cause resentment in non-paying users, just like the multiplayer game example mentioned previously. It is important to weigh up the value before trying something like this. Many online retailers are attempting to follow the Amazon Prime example as well and offering a paid upgrade to your shopping account by offering things such as discounts on purchases, free returns, and/or free shipping.

Community recognition

As users level up their skills, a major opportunity emerges: to acknowledge their achievements and contributions within the community in a meaningful and special manner. If you put in the time to be an expert at something, it feels good to earn that recognition. This will build loyalty, and potentially earn new users if that recognition is shared with others.

One of the best and longest-running versions of this comes from eBay. Since its inception, eBay has needed a way for shoppers to recognize good and trusted sellers from potentially dangerous ones. Thus, the "star" system was born. With each product you sold, buyers could give you positive or negative feedback. The more positive ratings you got, the higher your star rating was. Your star could even change color and style the higher you got. Those that were professional eBay sellers were quickly recognized on the platform and were noticed on all their listings because of the fun star icon. Not only were trusted community members rewarded for their use but the shoppers got value from the system as well.

Purchase matching

A lot of products might require you to load funds into your account. When this is the case, giving you a matching bonus on your first deposit can be a fantastic way to push you past any hesitation and get you excited about signing up. Most of the time, this "free money" comes with the stipulation that it must be used in the system and cannot be withdrawn, thus increasing the likelihood the user never leaves with an actual reward. As a motivator, however, it doesn't get much more powerful than free money.

Online gambling and sports book systems are notorious for using these types of systems. Many of these products will match your first deposit up to as much as a few hundred dollars. To the user, this feels like free money, and to an extent it is. Ultimately, these products know that the longer you play with them, the higher the chance that money comes back to them. And, since the barrier of entry is a bit higher to get an account set up, they know switching products is rough. By offering these matches, they hope to get you as a user for the long term, where they can more than make up the matched amount.

Random loot

Sometimes, you may not want to wait for a user to perform some large action to reward them – you may be aiming for a quick conversion. Random rewards (or loot drops) are a way to accomplish that. This concept centers around the idea of giving users a quick varying reward early in the journey. This can be on the first entry to your product, or possibly even before that in the form of an offer attached to an ad, driving users to the product. It could be a spin of a prize wheel, a scratch-off coupon, or any number of activities. This type of reward can be incredibly fun for users. However, the perceived value of rewards given with no work is generally low (regardless of *actual* value). Although traditionally used at the beginning of the user journey due to the lack of information and action by the users, these systems can also be used later in the funnel. Adding random rewards to each promotional email, giving users a free daily spin of the coupon wheel, or just choosing subsets of traffic to reward a percentage off coupon can yield an increase in conversion. Maybe give something like this a try in an A/B Test, as we will discuss further in *Chapter 7*.

This type of system can be found all over e-commerce retailers. Many sites offer some form of entry coupon or email sign-up reward. The most successful versions of this activity make the reward fun to attain, even if simple. Spinning a prize wheel or scratching a coupon can go a long way in making the user feel as if this is personalized to them. If this is indeed something they may encounter multiple times, however, there needs to be actual randomness to the rewards; otherwise, users will quickly see through the game and feel that the uniqueness to them is gone.

Progress tracking

Users like to know where they stand within a system or product. This takes place on both a macro and micro level and can be a comparative rank against others, or simply knowing where they stand in a process or cue. By informing users of their progress or giving them updates for key events along the way, you can encourage continuation and avoid frustration. Rewarding long-term usage in this way can also help users feel appreciated and continue to push that progression to become an even more loyal user. Progress can be tracked in several ways. This can be visual, such as badges, numerical, such as completion percentages, or in even more creative ways.

Points

Unlike the point redemption mechanic discussed earlier, sometimes users simply earn points to show their status within a system. In this iteration, points are not earned to be spent but used to show your acumen within the system. Using a point system like this can add small rewards to all the little tasks along the way to set up a level-increase badge or achievement, which we will discuss shortly. This helps a user keep those bigger progress trackers in sight, while still encouraging the use of the product. When points turn into a high-score list or a leaderboard, you cross the realm into social mechanics, which we will also discuss later.

Although points are often used to redeem, there are a few examples of simply earning a score without that side of the mechanic. eBay has been using its star rating to keep track of seller feedback since its inception. With each positive review you earn as a seller, you get a +1 added to that star count. This lets buyers know that you are experienced on the platform and provides a sense of trust.

Leveling

Often used in conjunction with the concept of points, users can also unlock skill levels or character levels. By accruing a certain number of points, completing a set of tasks, or simply sticking with a product for a distinct amount of time, users could be viewed as more of a power user than a beginner. That sense of accomplishment can go a long way in helping a user continue with a product that they otherwise might not. The sense of loss becomes even greater when they reach a level that took them months or even years to reach.

Duolingo is well known for incorporating a leveling system within the platform. As users become more skilled at a language, they earn additional levels in said language. Many users cite this and their streak accomplishments as the top motivation factor for continuing use of the platform. Some users might try and reach level 25 in the language they want to focus on, but other users will try and reach level 10 in three or more languages. The challenge is for the users to create themselves, so long as you've built the system.

Badges

When a user completes an important task, many systems will honor that accomplishment with a badge. These may be displayed on your profile page or within your avatar in some way. Allowing users to share their accomplishments with others can even further drive new users to the platform. Earning these rewards along the path to becoming a power user helps the customer know that they are progressing in the system and that they are on the right path. It also furthers their loyalty to the product since it is a tangible mark of progression that is hard to give up if they were to move platforms.

Learning platforms utilize these badges particularly well. Maybe you earn one with each course or unit you complete. Alternatively, they could be tied to streaks of daily usage. Small visual representations of progress can make us feel good about what we have done and unleash that inner child within us searching for our gold star!

Achievements

Achievements are very similar to badges but, generally, they are rewarded for going outside of the normal progression. These are incredibly useful for power users, or those that have completed the normal set of actions. Their goal is to push the user beyond normal progression and cement their status as a true professional! As a designer, these can be incredibly fun to come up with as they require you to think beyond the golden path and consider what accomplishments someone might come across if they were using the system in ways beyond how a normal user would.

Figure 5.2 – Microsoft Xbox gamer scorecard

As shown in *Figure 5.2*, this concept was perfected within Microsoft's Xbox gaming system, where players had a subset of tasks that were beyond normal gameplay for each game they played. Earning these stretch goals was often quite a challenge, and each one earned you a gamer score. This became a right of passage to prove how skilled you are as a gamer.

Completion scores

At a micro level, users want to know where they are in a process such as a job application, user survey, profile completion, or account sign-up. Knowing where they stand in the grand scheme of things helps lessen the blow of what might be an arduous task. It also lets them know when they may need to take a break in the case of a longer process. Games have used these concepts for a long time, but mostly as a point of bragging rights (for example: "I beat Super Metroid with a 100% completion rate").

Professional social profiles use completion scores to let users know when they have entered a good amount of their credential information. Users are compelled to ent3r more and more data about themselves to reach that 100%. And if that data is being used per governing laws, it can be valuable for things such as ads, tailoring content, and helping users find other profiles they like.

Step counters

Like a completion score, step counters provide users with a quantifiable metric for how far they have come, and what is left. Users can very quickly relate to seeing something such as "Step 5 of 7" – we have been learning fractions since the third grade after all. This helps users know what is left and can make the process feel more in their control and avoid surprises along the way. How many times have you filled out a web form, clicked next, and been met with another unexpected page of details? It can be frustrating.

These are particularly useful when several larger steps are needed in areas such as job applications, medical questionnaires, user surveys, and more. Letting the user know what they are embarking on can help ease any frustration or a sense of being caught off guard.

Completion rewards

Although we discussed rewards earlier, it is worth noting that offering rewards as part of task completion can be a highly effective way to decrease the drop rate of your users. Nobody likes filling out forms or detailed information, but if we know something is waiting for us at the end, the burden feels worth it as opposed to frustrating.

E-commerce sites are notorious for offering coupons when signing up for email lists. Although users need to put in a bit of personal information for a 10%, 15%, or 20% off coupon, many are willing to do so, especially if they are nearing a purchase. These types of rewards are generally even *more* effective when the reward is something the customer is in a spot to utilize immediately, such as sitting on the cart page about to check out.

Tests of knowledge

Along the user journey, it is often worth checking in to make sure that what has been taught was learned. Games do this often, many times putting a difficult challenge at the end of each level or area. This gives the users a way to prove their skills. This can feel rewarding but also helps designers know that key information was retained and can be used. It is worth noting that this concept should be viewed slightly differently than "boss fights," which we will discuss a bit later. Tests of knowledge are to check that key information was retained after being taught. A boss fight is specifically meant to be a difficult challenge, using a wider array of skills. Tests of knowledge are also usually a mental challenge, such as a quiz or test, rather than a battle that might include action, timing, and other skills.

Opening tutorials are a key example of this mechanic in action. Both games and software use them often to make sure the basics are fully understood. If a user can learn the most used path through the software (usually referred to as the "golden path"), then the retention rate takes a significant jump. By guiding them closely through this once, then asking them to prove what they have learned engagingly, you can raise that retention rate as well.

Accomplishment splashes

One way to add whimsy and fun to an otherwise stale system is giving users fun animations or splashes when a task is completed or a checklist is cleared. This small but effective reward boosts dopamine in our body and provides a quick boost of happiness to help users continue with their tasks. These can range from subtle to fairly over the top; just try and keep in mind what type of users your product has and the type of activity that earns this reward. It may not be professional or effective to have an animation of confetti play when a user completes a task that may be sad or otherwise strongly emotional.

Email clients are starting to use quick and clever messages/images when you clear an inbox. We all have an unruly list of emails all or most of the time, and that refreshing message when we finally get around to clearing that out can be incredibly rewarding.

Asana (2012)

Asana is a collaborative work management software company that provides a platform for teams to manage their projects, tasks, and workflows. Over the years, Asana has continued to evolve its product offerings, introducing new features and integrations to meet the changing needs of modern workplaces. It has established itself as a prominent player in the work management software market, competing with other tools in the project management and collaboration space.

Give Asana a try for a small personal project or as a test run for a larger project. Many product professionals have their tool of choice for this type of work but specifically pay attention to when you close out tasks in the system. Every so often, you may catch a unicorn or other animal cross the screen as a bit of a "hooray!" to complete that task. This is a simple interaction, but after a long sprint retrospective meeting, it can brighten the mood!

Save points

For an incredibly long time, games relied on several devices for saving your game so that you could come back later. After all, some games may take hundreds of hours to complete. This was done in the form of codes, adding batteries to cartridges for saves to be stored, and including in-game locations to save and exit the game.

Many gamers in the 80s and 90s remember panicking to find a save point as our parent(s) called us for dinner. Now, these saves happen automatically in games for the most part, although there is some fantastic retro nostalgia in playing a game that has a code to return you to where you were. Products do not necessarily function the same way, but we should consider where games came from in this regard. If your user is performing a task that requires a lot of work, cautiously and consciously pay attention to when and how that work is being saved. One of the most frustrating things that can happen in software is the loss of work. This should not be yet another thing our users must pay attention to since we have the technology to make things such as auto-saving the norm. However, that nostalgia from an old-school code such as the one shown in *Figure 5.3* can sometimes be entertaining:

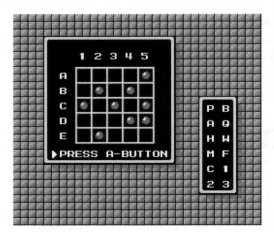

Figure 5.3 – Code entry screen from Megaman 2

Be it Microsoft Office, or Google's Office suite of products, auto-saving is the gold standard for anything that might constitute hours of work. If you ask anyone in your office older than about 35-40 whether they have ever lost hours of work because of not saving, the answer is likely yes and will be followed by a long and story about how frustrating it was. We are past many of the storage and usability issues that caused these problems, and products should not put that burden on their users.

Anniversary call-out

Sometimes, progress within a product doesn't necessarily come with accomplishments, just time. Letting users know how long they have been with you can be a fun little reward. Many of the products we use every day we forget when we started. It can be refreshing to get a small reminder of just how long it has been. You can also gain a sense of pride for being one of the earliest adopters out of your friends and colleagues.

Not only can this be a fun reminder for users, but in some cases, it can help your users gain trust in one another. Twitter (or "X" if you are riding that crazy train) notoriously shows other users when any given account joined the platform. This can be used to help determine the credibility of an account, or just for bragging rights.

Narrative and storytelling

Humans love great stories. Games are successful because of these stories, and, more specifically, because of the role the player has in how these stories unfold. The interaction between the player and the game world makes a story told via a game much more powerful than other mediums such as movies or books. Your product has the advantage of having that same opportunity. Many of the mechanics here would be perfect for an application such as Hi-Z Fitness. This app would rely on motivating the user by telling their story of progress. Giving the user updates on how their day, week, month, or year is progressing can act as motivation and potential continued use.

Let your users make the product their own and tell their own story using your platform. This can create a strong sense of loyalty, increase engagement, and make your product one that users do not want to leave. Storytelling may not seem like something most software does, but you would be surprised what common design elements are used frequently that, if done well, can tell the story of your product, your company, or your users.

Customer reviews

Many sites and products use customer reviews, but how are those displayed and sorted? All of that data can be used as a storytelling device. Users want to hear what others have to say, especially if it is compelling and tells a relatable story. Rather than hiding customer reviews and comments at the bottom of a page, take a few of the most relatable ones and use them to tell the story of what your product does for other users. How does it help solve their problems? How has it improved their life or business? How could they not live without it?

Any product leader should have a bank of customer comments about the product they own, whether they are published or not. Just like you see on the front of books or movie posters, take the most compelling and highlight them for others to see.

Environmental, Social, and Governance

Many potential customers will make it to your website to evaluate your product, but what about investors looking to value your company beyond that? **Environmental, Social, and Governance (ESG)** is a way to tell the story of the company behind the product. Do you use sustainable goods? Do you have a philanthropy policy? What about a **Diversity, Equity, and Inclusion (DEI)** policy? All of these and more tell the story of your brand. Customers are becoming more and more aware of the company behind the products, and if you have a great story to tell, let that shine through!

There are many examples of companies that have leaned heavily into the ESG storytelling side of their business. Ultimately, ESG was a set of data and resources for investors, but as users become savvier about the products they buy, it will continue to grow beyond that. Many companies now have public-facing pages dedicated to ESG resources, including Meta, Apple, Microsoft, and countless others. Your brand has a story to tell, and that story can influence purchase decisions of consumers. Do not be afraid to tell it!

Year in review

For products that get used every day, it can sometimes be hard to remember how much we accomplish in a year. But as a user, seeing those accomplishments laid out in front of you at the end of the year can be very rewarding. Games will often give similar breakdowns upon completion, tracking favorite weapons or characters, total play time, and completion percentages. Most people use non-game products more than games, but we rarely see the big picture of what we have done. In some cases, it might depress us (nobody wants to know how many hours they've spent editing spreadsheets), but in other cases, knowing what we accomplished with our efforts could be inspiring. How many files did I work on? What was my favorite hotkey? How many days did I open the software? Countless points of data could be tracked for this type of storytelling and, in addition, could be analyzed for usage data.

Spotify was the first mainstream app to pull this off with great success. Many of Spotify's over 500 million users look forward to their year in review each December. Many users take pride in sharing how big of a fan they are of certain artists or genres. Others like to brag about the crazy amount of music or podcasts they've listened to. Spotify has made a point of weaving stories into their product, and even better for the users is that it is *their* story being told and shared.

Inventory systems

One staple of games, especially in the role-playing genre, is an inventory system. What items are you taking with you to battle, since space is limited? This system forces players to think about what is and isn't important to them. Although it may have been in the past, this is no longer a system limitation and is implemented as a gameplay mechanic. Software may not have the same restraints, but in some cases, should it? When the user has countless sets of tools at their disposal, would it be worth them choosing a select few to tackle the job at hand?

Adobe Creative Suite handles this particularly well. This product has countless tools within it. Even the programs themselves are sectioned off for specific use cases. You wouldn't edit videos with Photoshop or touch up photos with InDesign. To even further the segmentation of tools, users can customize the tool panels they have open at any given time. Maybe you have a specific layout in Illustrator for print design that includes things such as Align, Layers, and Fonts, or a tool layout for graphic design that focuses on Colors, Shapes, and Pen tools. The user is free to organize their inventory of toolsets to fit the job.

User profiles

Allowing users to set up an area with their information creates a sense of story for themselves. They can write a bio, add links to other content, list some of their favorite things, or even make a collection of items they love to purchase on the site. Telling your own story is an engaging way to interact with a platform and then foster connections between users.

All social media platforms function this way; without profiles, there is no way to connect and interact with others. But many e-commerce platforms are starting to do this as well – allowing users to share their wish lists, create curated content for others to look at and buy from, or simply give recommendations and/or reviews for various items on the site. Sites such as eBay and Etsy are centered around seller and creator profiles, allowing anyone to get in and tell a story while selling the goods they create.

Avatars

The concept of avatars within products can have a fairly large range of customizability. At one end, users can simply upload a profile image. The other end of that scale is a full character design you might see more traditionally in games. These and everything in between have their place in products. Detailed avatar creators work well for more whimsical platforms, specifically where you might share that avatar across the platform or see it often. Users will not spend time creating something that is never seen. Thus, if you do not plan to have it prominently used or displayed, a profile image will suffice. In either case, allowing the user to choose the way they want to be depicted in a system can go a long way in them telling their own story:

Figure 5.4 – Example Bitmoji

Bitmoji (as shown in *Figure 5.4*) made an entire product around the concept of avatars, allowing users to truly customize them to their heart's content. From there, users are encouraged to add their newly designed Bitmoji to several platforms. These little avatars can be sent in messages or emails, shared on social media, or even made part of video content on various platforms. Bitmoji even has an SDK for adding a user's avatar to games. When something can be reused on several platforms, the time needed to add details pays off for users. The more time someone spends on something like this, the more they will want to share that work in fun and meaningful ways.

Sims 4 (2014)

The Sims franchise has been around for over 20 years and has been played by more than 70 million people worldwide. Many Sims players enjoy playing through a life they can create from scratch. The Sims, more than most games, puts you in nearly full control of the story. Create a Sim, choose a town, build a house, and live a lifestyle of your choosing… there is something for nearly all players.

The Sims 4 has been made available as a free-to-try game through the EA store, allowing many new players to try it out. Although it has features *way* beyond the character creator, it still boasts one of the most powerful avatar and character creators around. You can fully customize the look and characteristics of your Sim, choose their various outfits, and even pick traits that affect how they interact with the world around them. Although this level of granularity might be a bit much for most product users, it is worth checking out what is possible if you turn avatar creation up to 11.

Mentor

You may be familiar with the classic literary template of the "Hero's Journey" (also called the Monomyth). If not, you should spend some time to familiarize yourself with it as it is an incredibly common template used in game storytelling especially. But the concept of a mentor helping the user along comes from this template. When a user is faced with a large task, providing them with a guide or mentor to help break things down can provide structure, motivation, and guidance to what may seem like a challenge. Doing so allows you to pace the experience in a way that guides success, as well as provide crucial information or storytelling when you want. Often, the mentor is viewed as an expert user, and with enough practice or repetition, the user can surpass or become a mentor.

Mentorship is being used quite a bit in the workplace. Many companies offer a mentorship program, where a senior or director-level role might work with a junior-level employee for some amount of time. This may include shadowing tasks or simply having weekly discussions about how situations were or could be handled. This allows employees to learn and build relationships with one another. The mentor gains valuable skills as well, which help them become better leaders and experts in their field.

Abandonment capture

Within your product, it can be hard to determine why a user did what they did. Quite often, a user will abandon a task, and as a product leader, you will likely have very little idea as to why. Users may return on their own, other times not. Acknowledging that something was left in a sort of half-done state can be very valuable for a product. This could be saving the partial data that had been entered on a longer form, or keeping track of where the user was in a purchase journey. Helping to get a customer back to where they left off when they return can be a breath of fresh air to the user, especially if they had to leave abruptly. In some cases, they may have forgotten, and do not return. In this case, some circumstances warrant reaching out to them as a reminder of where they left off if you have account details sufficient to do that (email is the most common). Because you do not know the reason for leaving, you can have a little fun with the narrative to fit your product. Let users know they are welcome back to complete the task in a way that is fun and fits your brand.

Within e-commerce, this has become a very common practice for cart abandonment. Users that add items to their cart have shown at least some desire to purchase, which places them deep in the funnel. If you have their email in some way, it has proven valuable to give them a nudge about returning to complete the purchase. In some cases, the cart was being used as a bit of a holding pen and there was no intention to buy. In some cases, within our busy lives, we simply get sidetracked and forget to finish our browsing. These are the times when a small nudge can help bring us back to wrap it up.

User research artifacts

Within product management, several artifacts are created that tell a story about the user and their journey within the product. All of these are storytelling and narrative devices to a certain degree. If proper research is done and made into a compelling format to guide the design and ideation process, you have built a powerful story about your potential user. Although the upfront time to create these artifacts properly can be large, they truly are powerful in helping you understand the story of your users.

Empathy maps, personas, journey maps, user stories, and more are all narratives about the user and their journey with the product. These should be utilized by the entire team as the narrative that's depicted is a powerful tool to aid decision-making in the process. Just like you might read a book or watch a movie and be able to guess what each character might do next, your user research artifacts should do the same. Use these to anticipate the next move of the users in your product's story.

Social engagement

Allowing your product to be shared between friends, family, colleagues, and even rivals can be an incredibly powerful thing. When users hear about a great product from someone they trust, they want to try it for themselves. Allowing for interaction between two or more people within your product can directly add value to the product. Metcalfe's law states that the financial value or influence of a system of users is proportional to the number of users connected to that system. Building these types of social interactions can positively impact things such as daily/monthly average users, new sign-ups, retention rate, and time using the product.

Both of our hypothetical products could focus on a number of these systems. Product Manager Media is all about social engagement and relies on users interacting with each other to have any product at all. These systems can be used to drive those interactions and motivate users to become more prominent on the platform. For Hi-Z Fitness, the motivation that comes with competition is a known driver for the target demographic. Providing a way for users to track and compare how they are doing could help push them to log in daily and track their progress so that they can reach the top of a leaderboard, or just compete against their own best days, weeks, or months. Many of the mechanics discussed here would be a great fit for either of these products.

High scores

Trying to beat your own personal best may not seem like a "social" tool at first glance, but even trying to improve ourselves likely leads to further interactions with others. This might be searching out tutorials, asking others for help, or just discussing these scores with other potential users. Simply allowing someone to benchmark their progress in a product is a great motivation to improve as a user, and once a user has months or potentially years of this data stored on your platform, it becomes a very hard proposition to switch products as well, creating a very sticky product.

The traditional high score may be a relic of the arcade gaming era, but you can still find it on a few platforms. Fitness trainers are a great example of tracking your own personal best without specifically comparing to others automatically. This benchmarking helps push users to reach further than they have and creates an emotional tie to your product when they succeed. Many products that use some form of score display these against other users for friendly competition, which leads us to the next concept.

Leaderboards

Most people enjoy friendly competition with others, and when you take the concept of high scores and publicly display them against other users, you can create just that. Leaderboards take individual high scores and weigh them against others. This could be comparing against a select group of friends, comparing to all users, or any combination in between using filters or settings. Much like high scores, once a user reaches a certain status on a public board, they are apt to continue using the product. Nobody enjoys restarting their progress once they have established a presence on a certain platform.

One user demographic that responds particularly well to friendly competition is sales orgs. Many sales tracking and CRM products have implemented performance leaderboards. Sales reps are already motivated by high performance since bonuses and commissions make up a good amount of their salary. Providing an additional motivator within team competition has been shown to improve this performance. We will discuss this in even further detail in the next chapter!

Live collaboration

Allowing multiple users to collaboratively work within a file is a great way to increase user or license sales. In this connected world, awkwardly passing files back and forth for review doesn't make a lot of sense. By allowing this live collaboration, you add direct value to your users, as well as encourage all members of the team to use the product.

When games moved from a single console to online play, there was a drastic change in the industry. Software has had the potential for this same change for a while, but several industries still haven't made that switch. Design and creativity suites are notorious for having collab features. Creativity has a hard time waiting for passing a file back and forth. There is incredible value to these live edits, especially in the new remote workforce. Many companies look for these types of features when purchasing systems as a large percentage of their workforce may not work in the same office anymore.

Share button

One of the easiest forms of social interaction is a simple share button. Although the concept is easy, users have a lot of versatility in where they share whatever content they want. Sending to a chat with friends, saving to a cloud drive, posting to social media, and more can all be done with a simple and generally understood interaction. When users share content from your product with others, they are sharing an open door for others to join in. Ultimately, it is free marketing.

Any media platform now offers the share icon and feature. Images, text, videos, and more can now be sent to friends and family all over the world. Peek at nearly any application you use, and most will allow this interaction. In the connected world we live in, the share feature is now as common as the save feature.

Voting

Allowing users to add a +1 to ideas, content, or even other users can create a sense of ownership. By placing a vote, users feel empowered by the products they use. This empowerment can add loyalty, but only if the things that are leading vote-getters get action. An important piece of voting is that it must serve its purpose. Without a plan to act on the so-called winner, voting is fruitless and will quickly lose credibility and fail. If acted upon, however, it can create a great sense of community among users.

Voting has been implemented in several product management boards. Some of these tools allow for a public-facing roadmap of features potentially in the backlog, being worked on, and those that are released. By making these things public, you allow actual users to place votes on what they would like to see. If cultivated properly and acted upon, there are several benefits to not only the users but also you as a product leader. Votes are a quick and quantifiable way to justify the prioritization of the features or ideas that your users want!

Reactions

When content can come from anyone and anywhere within a product, there needs to be a way to regulate it. Reactions provide users a way to quickly and easily voice their opinion, as well as allow a community to self-regulate content on a platform. Early iterations of this in software were limited to simply "liking" something, but now, many companies have implemented a multitude of reaction options. Like, dislike, celebrate, support, and more are all common options.

Although social media platforms are the most common place for these reactions, we are starting to see them make their way to more and more platforms. As mentioned previously, this is anywhere you may want to quantify a sentiment to content. One place where quantification could be valuable is in customer comment data. Any product that offers a wiki or feedback forum can easily cultivate the most popular sentiments by allowing all users to react to other comments. This data can be used to directly impact roadmap prioritization or simply cherry-pick high-ranking ideas or features for further research.

Chat

One thing that games acknowledged long ago was that users do not read manuals. If anything, gamers may pick up the occasional strategy guide, but even those are near extinct within the age of information we live in. Users will reliably take a more social approach to asking questions and getting answers. Googling a topic or searching for a YouTube video about a product feature is the new standard... both of which exit users from your product. For the same effect, and without bouncing someone from your product, many platforms are implementing chat features within the software. And with the advancements in text-based AI models, these chats no longer even need to be staffed by a human 24/7.

Outside of actual products, many sales websites for purchasing products have implemented chat for potential buyers. Rather than asking Google about a product, prospects can stay on site and have controlled and cultivated answers. This data can also be used to further refine the site, working many of the frequently asked questions into site content to create a clearer message. Even in the form of text, this personalized social interaction can be incredibly valuable. Users will opt to use chat where they feel heard over reading a static FAQ nearly every time.

Friends and follow

Many products allow you to build a list of friends. The purpose of this could be to curate content based on the people you friend or follow. It could be to allow for quick connection to preferred collaborators. Users want to surround themselves with similar people and allowing them to do so within your product can start to create communities within.

This is not for every product. Friends and followers are only as valuable as the data or content they can share. Social media relies on this type of system as much as any online game does. But moving beyond the obvious, think about other **business-to-business (B2B)** software. There are several software tools where similar businesses or buildings that are in proximity geographically might want shared data. Casino security systems are a great example as the users and personnel within these systems are a tight-knit group. If someone is removed from a gaming facility for cheating, the casino across the street likely does not want that player either. By sharing data between their systems, things like this could be shared between the two.

Game psychology

Many of the previous examples are specific features you could implement in your product, but games, like products, are more than just features. There is a complex set of psychological principles and concepts that help users learn, understand, recall, and master a product. Games only have about 5-10 minutes to capture the user's attention, so they rely a bit more on these principles. There are several design psychology principles that both games and product UX already employ regularly that are not worth reiterating here since most product leaders are experienced with them. But if you have not learned any of the following, they are also worth understanding:

- Gestalt Design Psychology
- Dieter Rams' Ten Principles for Good Design
- Jakob Nielsen's Heuristics for Interaction Design
- Don Norman's Principles of Interaction Design

Between these design philosophies and the game psychology mechanics mentioned here, you can have quite a versatile set of design psychology in your toolkit. Using these can help your product with first impressions, user onboarding, daily use motivation, encouraging flow in user actions, and more.

Clues

Nobody likes being told exactly what to do. This is the reason Clippy from Microsoft Office 97 didn't last long. Users do not mind subtle hints, but in the end, they want to figure things out for themselves, or at least feel like they did. Finding that line can be tricky, but if you make a point of observing users, you can start to see what actions predicate others. When users start to perform some of these indicators, you can start to nudge them or, even better, simply give them a way to speed up the process. Once you understand these triggers, they can also be used to cut off behavior you want to prevent (moving to a competitor product, for instance).

When shopping online, many users will utilize the cart as a compare/contrast wish list. In some cases, when sites realize users are adding several very similar items to the cart, they may ask whether the user wants to use a compare a product feature or create a wish list for the items. But as we said previously, in some instances, this might be too forceful. Maybe you simply queue an introduction to the value of the wish list feature, or you offer a coupon for any item from your wish list. This lets the user connect the dots themselves, feeling like they have mastered the system.

Layering

Games famously use power-ups to take early mechanics and modify them for countless possibilities. Once a user has learned and committed an action to memory, it is significantly easier to add slight modifications to what already exists to make it feel more powerful.

This concept is how products such as Adobe Creative Suite help their users understand and remember the hundreds of tools available to use in any one of their products. In Photoshop, for instance, there are several tools just for selecting – Drag Selection, Color Wand, Lasso, and more. In addition, users can modify the selection tool so that it's additive or subtractive.

Experimentation

Mundane and tedious tasks can be a killer for usability. They do not foster any creativity and can stifle user flow. The best products (and games) allow users to solve even basic tasks. Letting users experiment with new tools or methods can create new paths to productivity. If you allow this sort of experimentation, you must allow for a quick recovery if things go bad. In most computer products, that may be as easy as pressing *Ctrl + Z*, but for physical goods, that is not always the case. Even in tech, relying on undo might not be enough. Maybe users want to try a few things side by side and compare. Maybe one experiment they want to try is 20-30 steps deep; how far back does undo go in your system? Sure, maybe they just create a new file, but should they have to? Thinking about and planning for this type of exploration in products can create a product that users love to solve problems with.

Music, film, and graphic software rely on tracks or layers to compose complicated pieces of art. By adding new tracks to a composition, an artist can try out a new instrument, sound, or effect. If it works great, you keep the track. If not, you can delete the track and try again. This fosters a great sense of experimentation as you are never destroying previously fine-tuned details. You're simply keeping what is good and dropping what doesn't work.

Ambiance

The main characteristic that games rely on that is often overlooked in software or other products is a sense of ambiance. Primarily, this is a combination of aesthetics and acoustics. Products take great pride in their design aesthetics to the point of making them beautiful. But do the looks tell a story? Do you know what software does by simply looking at its color palette? Games also rely on music to tell a story. As of 2023, there is now a Grammy Award for Best Score Soundtrack for Video Games, and many would argue that is well overdue. When was the last time the audio of a software or product caught your attention? Many gamers will listen to their favorite game soundtrack as often as their favorite artist's latest album. Non-game products are hard-pressed to say that.

One area that is starting to at least lean into the virality of audio is video-short products such as TikTok. Songs have gone on to top the charts and earn increased sales simply because they caught the ears of creators and viewers on the platform. Others can then call on the same track for their video, and the viral beat spreads. Soon, these songs are played outside of the platform and start to gain traction beyond the videos themselves.

Repetition

If you want users to learn and remember an action, having them repeat the action a few times can help. If you can vary the methods by which they use it, they can start to understand the versatility in addition to committing it to memory. Products can have a wide range of actions. Some have only a few, while others can be complex. The key to users learning with this repetition is that you focus on only a couple of interactions at a time. Start with the most basic of actions, and then add more as the user's skill improves.

If you have ever played Super Mario Bros, think back to that first level. A whole lot of run and jump and run and jump. By the end of the level, however, as a user, you know 75% of the game. Now, think about your first time using social media; what did you do? Scroll and "like" and scroll and "like," repeating the core actions over and over. Within minutes, you know how the product works, and can easily recall that the next time you log in.

Super Metroid (1994)

Released on the Super Nintendo Entertainment System nearly 30 years ago, Super Metroid is still considered one of the best games within one of the most iconic franchises in gaming. Super Metroid's unique gameplay has cemented it in gaming history and has started an entire genre of games based on this style of play (Metroidvania, named after both the Metroid and Castlevania franchises).

Super Metroid is a master class in user onboarding. Users do not have any kind of manual or documentation, yet within the first 10-15 minutes, you know almost everything you need. Sure, the puzzles get harder, and the powers get upgraded, but the core of run, jump, and shoot remains throughout. If you cannot find a way to play it yourself, you can always check out Bret Wardle's 2022 talk from TEDxSaltLakeCity to hear why Super Metroid is a perfect example of **Clues, Layering, Experimentation, Ambience, and Repetition** (or **CLEAR** for short).

Landmarking

As games became less linear, it became difficult for players to keep track of where they were and needed to go. In a complex system or product, the same problem exists. Both games and non-game products have similar ways to address this. Landmarking involves using visual, easy-to-recognize items so that the user knows where they are and where they have been.

Games often use maps to help orient a player. Many websites include a site map as well to help find where they need to go. But the most powerful form of landmarking in products is consistency in design. Several standards make any design carry a certain level of familiarity. When placing a logo in the top left, it is expected to take you home. Key standard iconography can also help you navigate a site. Icons for things such as save, share, cart, and settings are nearly identical across all platforms. As a product leader, it is important to understand these landmarks.

Easter eggs

The entertainment industry is notorious for adding hidden content for users. This hidden content is referred to as an Easter egg. Sometimes, this is a fun message, maybe some additional content, or maybe a peek behind the scenes or into the future of a franchise. Widely considered to be the first instance of this was the designer of the video game *Adventure* hiding his name on the Atari 2600 game. At the time, Atari did not publicly credit their creators, and Warren Robinett was feeling a bit rebellious. He created a secret room in the game that could only be reached by following several unconventional moves in the game. Upon reaching that room, you could see his name (as shown in *Figure 5.5*). Little things like this can capture new users, and let existing users feel like they are part of an in-crowd. It can be a fun little freshen-up from the usual day-to-day usage that resonates with any user that likes things shaken up:

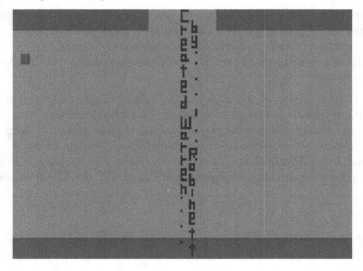

Figure 5.5 – The original Easter egg from the game Adventure on the Atari 2600

Google is notorious for hiding mini-games and information within their doodle on the Google home page. Once found, you can often see them circulating social media so that users can try and get to them before the experience changes. This drives traffic to the site and builds a sense of whimsy for the brand among its users. Any user who finds it feels a sense of pride for having cracked the code.

Emergent behavior

As we briefly discussed in *Chapter 1*, emergent behavior is the idea that a game, product, or anything is used in a way different from its intended use. As a game designer, you may purposely leave some of the systems within a game open-ended, allowing players to stretch the rules and use their imagination to solve puzzles or challenges. This can lead to several emotions within the user. There is a sense of pride and accomplishment, as well as the drive to take on whatever the next challenge is. One of the tricky things about emergent behavior, however, is that it cannot be directly built into the product as that would imply the behavior being designed. However, when you are building systems and features, you can design them in a way that leaves room for creativity. Allow features to overlap. Do not actively prevent systems from being used in places you did not consider the primary use case. By doing so, experienced users can and will find a way to do some creative stuff and they will feel like superstars for doing so.

Excel is used to make spreadsheets, right? What if I told you that there was a whole community out there using Excel, and its ability to fill in cells with color, to make entire animations? Rather than using pages of a workbook to segment numbers and data, they are used in the frames of an animation. This exists, and some of the stuff being done with it is incredible. Some may argue it's not a professional tool or even the best tool for the job, but it is accessible to nearly everyone.

> **Minecraft (2011)**
>
> Open world sandbox game originally developed by Mojang Studios, which was acquired by Microsoft in 2014. Considered the best selling video game of all time, with a staggering 238 million copies sold, and more than 100 million monthly active players.
>
> Minecraft features a robust set of intertwined game systems, but little to no designated tasks or objectives. Your job in Minecraft is to have fun. The terrain is procedurally generated, meaning no two realms are the same. If you like action you can explore and fight hordes of creatures. If you want to be a farmer or fisher you can do those tasks in relative peace. If you just want to build incredible houses and other items you are free to do that as well. Minecraft is the ultimate example of emergent gameplay. Give it a try and see which activities you find are most enjoyable for you.

Boss fights

In gaming, after the long grind of building your character and completing all the tasks asked of you, there is the final challenge. It is the culmination of all the prior knowledge you have learned. It is where you put your skills to the ultimate test. It is the final boss. These moments, and the potential lesser bosses before this, are often some of the most epic moments in a game. The stakes are high, and things happen fast. You must learn to recall potentially all that you have learned to this point. But when things go right and you beat the challenge, there truly is no greater payoff. Does this mean that users should be forced to slay a dragon before they save their files? Well, maybe, but probably not. But what are these "Aha!" moments in your product? At what point does the student become the master? And if there is that moment in your product, how do you celebrate the accomplishment? When a user can piece together all that they know and complete a momentous task, it deserves to be celebrated. And as product leaders, we should strive to have these types of moments available to our users.

Although it may not feel like it when you are in the moment, big rush shopping days are very similar to this. Users come to shop for the best deals of the year at a limited-time event. They put their knowledge of prices, coupon strategy, search filters, site and store layouts, and more to the ultimate test in the hopes that they can be one of the select few who gets to walk away with a limited-time deal before the time or stock runs out. This can be as big of an adrenaline rush as anything. Think about the last time you snagged a great limited-time deal. Shopping for the holidays or just during Amazon Prime Days has this sort of effect. eBay and other auction sites try and capture this moment for every product, or at least they did. However, if every enemy you come across is a boss fight, the risk and reward aren't the same. That is why even eBay started using things such as "Buy It Now." The scarcity of the boss fight is what makes it the boss fight.

Combos

Within gaming, combos are the manifestation of "things are more powerful together." By chaining or grouping a set of actions, the result is greater than the sum of their parts. This can be utilized to increase average order size, target sales in specific departments, or more. Many triggers might use this chain action concept as well. When a user performs action A, then B, then C, offer them a coupon or open a new path.

Many retailers are starting to pair purchases for discounts or provide rewards after a set of other actions. Some examples might include things such as 5 purchases in a month for a $5 gift card, saving $2 when you purchase any variety of chips and dip, or spending $50 on cleaning products to receive a free dishtowel set.

Summary

Although more than 40 mechanics and features were described here, this is not meant to be an exhaustive list. There are countless ways that games engage and create fun for their players. Hopefully, at least a few of the mechanics here apply to your products. But it is important to continue learning. The best way to learn about what makes games fun is to simply play more games. There are limitless experiences out there, and countless ways to divide them up. Find your favorite genre and preferred art style, try online versus offline gameplay, competitive or cooperative, and more. In the same way that you as a product leader likely evaluate any product as you use it, do the same with any game you play. What makes it fun? What kept you playing? Would you recommend it to friends, and why? Discovering the things that make games great for yourself is the best way to learn, and if you are curious about where to start, try any of the examples we cite throughout this book. Once you can start to understand what things engage the types of users you have, you can begin the process of designing your product's gamification strategy, which is exactly what we will be discussing next.

Further reading

- Koster, Raph, *Theory of Fun for Game Design*, O'Reilly Media, 2013
- Tekinbas, Katie Salen; Zimmerman, Eric, *Rules of Play: Game Design Fundamentals*, The MIT Press, 2003
- Rogers, Scott, Level Up! The Guide to Great Video Game Design, Wiley, 2014

6

Designing a Gamification Strategy

Welcome to *Chapter 6*, where will we start to put everything together. We covered the history of gamification, principles of product development, gamification frameworks, understanding the importance of designing for your end user, and game mechanics and elements. Now, we will use the two examples we've been using throughout this book, Hi-Z Fitness and Product Management Media, and design the gamification features step by step and explain the process along the way using examples from the previous chapters. There won't be additional theory – we'll just be putting the previously discussed ideas into action so that you can build products and features that appeal to your users. By doing so, you will see increased engagement and retention.

We will cover the following topics in this chapter:

- Setting goals and objectives
- Defining success metrics
- Choosing the right game mechanics
- Creating a game loop
- Building a reward system
- Incorporating gamification into the user experience

Setting goals and objectives

Whether you are a product manager, consultant, or entrepreneur, you report to someone. A boss, client, or investor may want an explanation of what you are developing and why. So, remember to always start with the goal in mind. Setting clear goals and objectives for your product is essential for its success. Goals provide a sense of direction and purpose, guiding your team's efforts and ensuring alignment toward a shared vision. On the other hand, objectives break down those goals into actionable and measurable targets, allowing you to track progress and evaluate the effectiveness of your strategies.

Defining OKRs

Objectives and Key Results (OKRs) offer a robust framework that aligns teams, fosters accountability, and drives results.

Objectives are aspirational and begin to capture the overarching vision and direction of the product. These objectives must be ambitious, inspiring, and aligned with the organization's strategic priorities. Ensure objectives are cascaded to individual teams and employees, creating a sense of purpose and shared commitment.

Key results are measurable outcomes that track progress toward the defined objectives. They are specific, measurable, and time-bound, providing clarity and focus for individuals and teams. Key results should be challenging yet attainable, encouraging a stretch mindset and driving innovation. By regularly tracking and updating key results, you can monitor progress and make data-driven adjustments to stay on track.

OKRs foster a culture of transparency, focus, and alignment within product teams. By establishing clear objectives and key results, teams are empowered to prioritize their work, make informed decisions, and collaborate effectively. The iterative nature of OKRs allows for continuous learning, adaptation, and improvement, ensuring that efforts remain aligned with more significant organizational priorities.

Gamification itself is not the goal. Instead, the focus should be on driving specific business, social, or environmental outcomes and gaining the support of your team and stakeholders. It's important to note that you can have multiple goals for your gamification efforts. Let's take the example of Hi-Z Fitness to illustrate this point.

Example

Hi-Z Fitness has two main goals:

- The first goal is to drive more users to sign up for premium fitness features, which include gamified elements. To achieve this, Hi-Z Fitness adopts a subscription-based business model.

- The second goal is more social. The aim is to encourage users to spend a certain amount of time exercising in the app. Your research shows that if users spend a specific amount of time exercising, their risks for certain health issues decrease by a certain percentage.

The dual goals reflect a social enterprise business model with a double bottom line, prioritizing profit and people. The objective of the gamification design for Hi-Z Fitness is to boost premium usage of the application and "nudge" users to exercise more.

On the other hand, **Product Management Media** (**PMM**) follows a revenue-maximizing business model. The primary goal is to maximize site transactions, which operate on a pay-per-use model. There is no monthly subscription fee, but users can purchase level-ups, premium badges, boosts, training courses, and other items. Additionally, PMM generates revenue through advertisements and selling its APIs to other businesses. In this case, there are both business and engagement goals. The objective is to have as many users as possible on the site and to use gamification to keep them engaged and benefitting from the knowledge shared within the community. Therefore, the gamification objective for PMM is to ensure that users can fulfill their purpose of connecting with other product managers, sharing their stories, participating in discussions, and accessing available training programs.

You should align gamification with specific goals and business models. It can drive revenue, boost engagement, and achieve desired outcomes. Organizations can effectively utilize gamification to enhance their products and services by defining clear objectives and designing gamification strategies.

Defining success metrics

Key Performance Indicators (**KPIs**) and OKRs are strategic measurement tools that help organizations track progress and achieve their goals. KPIs serve as the compass guiding organizations, teams, and individuals toward their goals. Derived from strategic objectives, KPIs are quantifiable metrics to measure progress, evaluate performance, and steer businesses in the right direction.

KPIs provide a robust framework for assessing performance and propelling businesses toward success. These metrics go beyond surface-level measurements, cutting through vanity metrics to reveal meaningful insights. By aligning KPIs with specific business objectives, you can gain invaluable data to drive action, make data-driven decisions, and uncover areas for improvement.

Creating an effective KPI framework for a product-driven organization requires careful planning and consideration. Here are the key steps to follow:

1. **Align to your OKRs**: Start by clearly articulating your overarching business goals and strategic objectives, which we covered in the previous section.

2. **Identify critical success factors**: Determine the key areas or factors that contribute significantly to the success of your product-driven organization. These may include revenue growth, customer satisfaction, user engagement, product quality, market share, or operational efficiency. Identify the critical success factors that align with your business goals and will drive your organization's success.

3. **Select relevant KPIs**: Based on the critical success factors, choose the most relevant ones to measure and track progress towards your objectives. Ensure your selected KPIs are meaningful, actionable, and aligned with your business goals. Consider lagging indicators (measuring historical performance) and leading indicators (predicting future performance) to gain a comprehensive view.

4. **Establish a baseline and targets**: Set a baseline for each KPI, representing the current performance level. Then, establish realistic and ambitious targets or benchmarks you aim to achieve within a specific time frame. These targets should be challenging yet attainable, providing motivation and a sense of purpose for your teams.

5. **Monitor, analyze, and act**: Regularly monitor and analyze the performance against your KPIs. Identify trends, patterns, and areas of improvement. Celebrate successes and address any performance gaps or deviations from targets. Use the insights from KPI analysis to inform decision-making, prioritize initiatives, and drive continuous improvement.

6. **Review and refine**: Review and refine your KPI framework to ensure its relevance and effectiveness. Adjust or refine the KPIs as your organization evolves to reflect changing priorities or strategic shifts. Seek stakeholder feedback and incorporate lessons learned to improve your KPI framework continuously.

The difference between KPIs and OKRs lies in their nature and usage. KPIs are typically more focused on measuring ongoing performance and progress against specific targets, while OKRs are more future-oriented and aim to set ambitious goals and drive significant outcomes. You primarily use KPIs to monitor and manage day-to-day operations, while OKRs provide a framework for setting and achieving strategic objectives in the longer term.

Now that we understand what KPIs and OKRs are, let's create KPIs and OKRs for Hi-Z Fitness and PMM.

OKRs for Hi-Z Fitness

Organization: Hi-Z Fitness

Type: OKRs

Objective: Enhance user engagement

Key results:

1. Increase the average number of workouts completed per user by 20%.

2. Achieve a 30% increase in user-generated content, such as shared workout routines and achievements.

3. Improve user satisfaction with gamified features, targeting a rating of 4 out of 5 in user feedback.

KPIs:

1. **Conversion rate**: Increase the percentage of free users who upgrade to premium subscriptions by 15%.

2. **Monthly active users**: Maintain a consistent growth rate of 10% in the number of active users each month.

3. **Churn rate**: Reduce the monthly user churn rate by 20% to improve user retention.

4. **Average session duration**: Increase the average time spent by users in the app by 15% to indicate higher engagement.

5. **Customer satisfaction score**: Maintain a satisfaction score of 8.5 or above on a scale of 1 to 10 based on user surveys.

OKRs for PMM

Organization: PMM

Type: OKRs

Objective: Expand user community and interaction

Key results:

1. Increase the number of registered users by 30% through targeted marketing campaigns.

2. Achieve a 20% growth in active user participation in community discussions and forums.

3. Launch three new training programs or courses to provide additional value and engagement for users.

KPIs:

1. **Revenue growth**: Achieve a 15% increase in overall revenue compared to the previous year.

2. **Conversion funnel efficiency**: Increase the conversion rate at each customer journey stage by 10%.

3. **User retention**: Maintain a monthly user retention rate of 85% or higher.

4. **Ad click-through rate**: Improve the click-through rate on ads by 20% to drive more user engagement.

5. **API usage**: Increase the number of businesses utilizing the API by 25% through targeted marketing efforts.

By setting and regularly reviewing these KPIs and OKRs, Hi-Z Fitness and PMM can track their progress, measure success, and align their efforts with their strategic objectives.

Habitica (2013)

This is an online task management application that incorporates heavy elements of a traditional **role-playing game (RPG)**. The player collects items, such as gold and armor, and gains levels to increase their skills. Rewards are achieved through completing real-life goals in the form of keeping/dropping habits, completing tasks, and finishing to-do items.

Once you understand the concept of OKRs and KPIs, you can start to make an informed guess at what those are for the applications you use each day. Try out Habitica for a week or so and try and guess what the application's KPIs are. Can you pinpoint what a long-term strategy might be for that team (OKR)? Are any of the hooks you come across compelling enough to make you a long-term user? Habitica has a heavy game influence. Think about how this might feel if that design was more subtle. Or would you enjoy it more if it leaned even heavier into that traditional game design?

Selecting your personas and JTBD to design around

In the previous chapter, we emphasized the significance of understanding user motivations and behaviors through market research. Now, we will move forward and identify our champion users, the individuals who have a strong need for our product or feature. These users are so passionate about solving the problems that they overlook initial design flaws and technical difficulties upon launch. They become the advocates who utilize our product and spread the word about its value.

To effectively engage and retain these champion users, treating them well and establishing ongoing communication is crucial. Regularly engage with them to gather feedback, address their concerns, and showcase that you are actively working on improving the product. You build trust and loyalty among these valuable users by demonstrating your commitment to continuous enhancement.

Creating a persona for your users further enhances your understanding of their needs, preferences, and pain points. This persona helps you empathize with their unique circumstances and tailor your product offering to serve their requirements better. Additionally, employing the **Jobs to Be Done (JTBD)** framework allows you to focus on the specific problem your users are looking to solve, enabling you to design a solution that effectively addresses their needs. It is important to note that any product might have several different types of key users, and each might have a persona. However, we are focusing on just one for these examples.

We will delve into the process of creating personas and applying the JTBD framework, combining these techniques with the power of gamification to design a compelling and user-centric product experience.

Persona for the eco-fit enthusiast

Persona: Vivian - the eco-fit enthusiast

Name: Vivian Rae

Age: 38

Occupation: Environmental scientist

Background:

Vivian is a dedicated environmental scientist passionate about sustainability and healthy living. She spends her days conducting research and advocating for eco-friendly practices. However, she often finds balancing her work commitments with her well-being challenging as she spends long hours in her research lab.

Fitness goals:

Vivian's primary fitness goal is maintaining a healthy lifestyle and improving her overall well-being. She aims to achieve a balanced and active routine that aligns with her eco-conscious values. She strives to be physically fit, mentally sharp, and energized to impact the environment positively.

Exercise preferences:

Vivian prefers outdoor activities that allow her to connect with nature while staying fit. She enjoys running or cycling in parks, practicing yoga in serene environments, and hiking on weekends. She seeks workout routines that benefit her body and improve her mental clarity and environmental awareness.

Challenges:

One of Vivian's main challenges is finding the time and motivation to exercise consistently amid her busy schedule. She often feels overwhelmed with work-related responsibilities and needs help prioritizing her personal fitness goals. Additionally, she occasionally faces difficulties accessing sustainable fitness resources that align with her environmental values.

Behaviors:

Vivian is disciplined and organized, trying to incorporate physical activity into her daily routine. She tracks her workouts and progress using fitness apps and wearable devices to stay motivated and accountable. She actively seeks information and resources related to sustainable living and integrates them into her fitness practices.

Motivations:

Vivian is motivated to lead a healthy and environmentally conscious lifestyle. She believes that caring for herself is connected with caring for the planet. Vivian seeks fitness solutions that support her physical well-being and resonate with her values of sustainability and eco-friendliness.

Life goals:

Vivian's life goals revolve around positively impacting the environment and promoting sustainable practices. She aspires to educate others about the importance of environmental conservation and inspire them to adopt eco-friendly habits. Vivian's ultimate aim is to create a healthier and more sustainable future for future generations.

By understanding the persona of Vivian, Hi-Z Fitness can tailor the gamification features and experiences we have previously discussed to align with her goals, preferences, and motivations. This persona serves as a guiding representation of the target user, ensuring that the gamified product effectively engages and supports individuals such as Vivian on their fitness journey while promoting sustainability.

JTBD for Vivian – the eco-fit enthusiast

1. **Job**: Achieve a balanced and sustainable fitness routine.

   - **Motivation**: Vivian wants to maintain a healthy lifestyle that aligns with her eco-conscious values

   - **Desired outcome**: Find fitness solutions that support her physical well-being while minimizing her environmental impact

2. **Job**: Overcome time and motivation constraints to exercise consistently.

   - **Motivation**: Vivian wishes to prioritize her fitness goals amid her busy work schedule.

   - **Desired outcome**: Discover effective strategies and tools that help her stay motivated, manage her time efficiently, and maintain a consistent exercise routine

3. **Job**: Access sustainable fitness resources and eco-friendly workout options.

   - **Motivation**: Vivian seeks fitness solutions that align with her environmental values

   - **Desired outcome**: Find fitness programs, apps, or equipment that promote sustainability, use eco-friendly materials, and support ethical practices

4. **Job**: Connect with a community of like-minded individuals focused on fitness and sustainability.

   - **Motivation**: Vivian wants to engage with others who share her passion for fitness and the environment

   - **Desired outcome**: Discover platforms or communities where she can connect with fellow eco-conscious fitness enthusiasts, share experiences, exchange tips, and support each other's journey

---

By understanding Vivian's JTBD, Hi-Z Fitness can design its gamification features and user experience to fulfill these needs. The design includes the following:

- Personalized workout recommendations

- Eco-friendly challenges

- Progress tracking with sustainability metrics

- Access to eco-conscious fitness resources

- Opportunities for community engagement with like-minded individuals

Now, let's take a look at the same for PMM and see how its users are motivated.

Persona for PMM – the data-driven innovator

Name: Chet Ripley

Age: 26

Job Title: Associate data product manager

Background:

Chet Ripley is a passionate and ambitious associate data product manager professional. With a bachelor's degree in computer science and a strong interest in data analytics, Chet embarked on a career path that combines his love for technology and product development. He joined PMM to further develop his skills in data-driven decision-making and make a meaningful impact in product management.

Goals:

Chet is driven by several key goals that shape his professional journey. Firstly, he aims to master the art of data-driven product development by leveraging data insights to inform and drive strategic decision-making. Additionally, Chet strives to advance his career in product management, taking on more significant roles and contributing to strategic product initiatives. Lastly, he is motivated to deliver innovative solutions that meet customer needs while pushing the boundaries of innovation and driving business growth.

Product development skills:

Chet has honed skills that enable him to excel as an associate data product manager. He possesses a strong analytical mindset and is proficient in data analysis and interpretation. Chet is well-versed in Agile methodologies and understands the importance of iterative development and continuous improvement. He translates customer insights into actionable product requirements and employs data-driven decision-making processes to inform strategic product decisions and validate hypotheses.

Challenges:

Chet faces several challenges in his role as an associate data product manager. Firstly, he must balance incorporating advanced technical capabilities and ensuring the product remains user-friendly and accessible. Navigating stakeholder expectations and competing priorities is another challenge since Chet works closely with various stakeholders and must effectively manage their expectations while prioritizing the product roadmap. Additionally, keeping up with evolving industry trends and emerging technologies is crucial for Chet to remain competitive in the fast-paced industry.

Behaviors:

Chet's behaviors shape his approach to work and collaboration. He is highly analytical and detail-oriented, meticulously analyzing data and paying attention to even the smallest details to drive accurate insights and decision-making. Chet's curiosity and eagerness to learn are evident as he actively seeks opportunities to expand his knowledge and skills. He is a collaborative team player who thrives in cross-functional environments and enjoys collaboration with colleagues from different departments. Chet takes a proactive and resourceful approach, staying informed about emerging trends and technologies relevant to his role and seeking ways to apply them in his work.

Motivations:

Chet is motivated by several key factors. Firstly, he is driven by the desire to make a positive impact by contributing to the development of innovative product solutions that positively impact users' lives and drive business success. He is also motivated by driving customer satisfaction and loyalty through data-driven insights that enhance the user experience. Lastly, Chet is motivated by the opportunity to advance his career and become a respected leader in product management, continuously improving his skills and taking on more significant responsibilities.

Life goals:

Beyond his professional aspirations, Chet has personal goals that shape his overall life journey. He strives for personal and professional growth, seeking opportunities to expand his knowledge, develop new skills, and become well-rounded. Chet aims to maintain a healthy work-life balance and prioritize personal well-being and career growth.

Overall, Chet Ripley is a dedicated and ambitious associate data product manager who brings a data-driven mindset and a passion for innovation to his role at PMM. With his analytical skills, collaborative approach, and determination to make a positive impact, Chet can contribute to the organization's success and drive strategic product initiatives.

JTBD For Chet – the data-driven APM

1. **Job:** Leverage data insights to inform and drive strategic product decisions.

   - **Motivation:** Chet aims to collect and analyze relevant data, extract actionable insights, and translate them into effective product strategies

   - **Desired outcome:** Make informed decisions that drive product success and business growth

2. **Job:** Develop user-centric products that meet customer needs and deliver an exceptional user experience.

   - **Motivation:** Chet aims to understand user preferences, pain points, and behaviors, translating them into actionable product requirements and driving product enhancements

   - **Desired outcome:** Create products that address user needs, generate positive user experiences, and drive customer loyalty

3. **Job:** Monitor the competitive landscape and stay updated on emerging trends, technologies, and industry best practices.

   - **Motivation:** Chet aims to conduct a competitive analysis to identify product differentiation and innovation opportunities

   - **Desired outcome:** Stay ahead of the competition and contribute to the organization's competitive advantage

4. **Job:** Pursue career growth and development within the field of product management.

   - **Motivation:** Chet aims to continuously develop his skills, expand his knowledge, and seek opportunities for career advancement

   - **Desired outcome:** Grow as a product manager, take on new challenges, and make a meaningful impact in the industry

Chet's JTBD provides a clear framework for navigating his role as an associate data product manager at PMM. By understanding these jobs and their underlying motivations, Chet can prioritize his efforts, make informed decisions, and contribute to the organization's success while advancing his professional growth.

As previously mentioned, for this book, we are only giving one example for each product. We recommend creating three to six personas with their JTBD, depending on the time, resources, and scope of the project you are undertaking. Now that we have established our examples, let's choose our game mechanics, which we learned about in *Chapter 5*.

Choosing the right game mechanics

In the world of gamification, a fascinating concept exists known as **the game within the game**. It revolves around strategically selecting and testing game mechanics, creating captivating prototypes, and the art of weaving compelling narratives that captivate and influence your audience. To truly understand the power of this approach, let's take a closer look at some of the greatest games of the last decade: God of War, Spider-Man, Call of Duty, and Fortnite.

God of War and Spider-Man stand out not only for their stunning graphics and immersive gameplay but also for the incredible stories embedded within them. These games masterfully combine engaging narratives with stellar game design, creating an experience that keeps players engrossed and motivated to progress through missions and uncover more captivating storylines.

On the other hand, Call of Duty and Fortnite take advantage of the social mechanics of gaming. They leverage features such as multiplayer modes, leaderboards, and badges to foster a sense of pride and competition among players. These social elements add a layer of engagement and excitement, driving users to connect with others, strive for higher ranks, and achieve recognition.

Chrono Trigger (1995)

Chrono Trigger is an RPG that was released by SquareSoft, originally for the **Super Nintendo Entertainment System (SNES)**. Chrono Trigger was a critical and commercial success upon release and is frequently cited as one of the greatest video games of all time.

If you want your examples to be a little older than the last decade, check out Chrono Trigger. It is often considered to be one of the most flawless combinations of storytelling and gameplay. Before games had fancy graphics to draw in an audience, those two things were what hooked a player. Give it a try and see if you prefer gameplay or storytelling. Maybe it's the seamless combination of them both. Pay close attention to how the many different characters interact, and how audio design is used to set a mood.

When considering your gamified product, it is essential to understand your target users and define your primary game mechanics. Are you aiming for a more social experience that encourages user collaboration and competition? Or are you focused on individual progress and achievement? Understanding the preferences and motivations of your users is crucial in determining the game mechanics that will resonate with them.

To make informed decisions about your game mechanics, you must do the following:

- Rely on thorough research and user feedback
- Study your target audience to uncover what motivates and engages them the most
- Analyze successful products and games in your industry or with similar demographics to identify patterns and mechanics that have proven effective

By gathering this knowledge, you can design game mechanics that align with your users' preferences and enhance their overall experience.

Remember, the *game within the game* is about more than just entertainment. It has the potential to drive desired behaviors, increase user engagement, and create meaningful connections with your audience. By carefully crafting your game mechanics and understanding the elements that resonate with your users, you can create an experience that keeps them returning for more.

Next, we will explore how game mechanics and elements intertwine to shape the design of a gamified product that aligns with user motivations and behaviors. Get ready to embark on a journey where psychology, design, and technology converge to create engaging experiences.

Hi-Z Fitness

We made sure not to include the fitness enthusiast persona for Hi-Z Fitness. Our research shows this persona is going to the gym regardless of what we design and will crush those leaderboards, bro. The persona we highlighted has a million things going on in their personal life, so just exercising for 30 minutes, 4 times a week is a significant accomplishment. By comprehending and profoundly understanding our users and implementing appropriate metrics, we can effectively gauge the impact of our gamification techniques and determine if we are truly making a difference. Our design strategy with Hi-Z Fitness is to design game mechanics into most of the technology's core features. First, we will identify our main game mechanics and the technology's core features and then give some examples of complementary secondary mechanics.

Gamification toolbox – primary

We have chosen to focus on portraying the story of achieving an optimal, healthy life through exercise alongside our users. In this book, we will not exclusively align with a single persona; instead, we will design for multiple personas. As a result, we will weave together the stories of a diverse group of users embarking on their fitness journey, presenting them with compelling statistics and visual elements throughout the user experience. Even with multiple personas, we use data to focus on telling a personalized story; we aim to keep users engaged and help them envision the success they can achieve.

Notifications and in-app popups are triggers to keep users focused on their fitness journey. Understanding that our users often struggle with busy schedules and prioritizing exercise, we leverage these triggers to prompt them to take action. The desired action may involve one of the following:

- Opening the app
- Selecting an exercise to complete
- Manually inputting their workout
- Syncing their activity tracker

To ensure consistent user engagement, notifications can update users on their progress, levels, or any other important information to keep them engaged. Just don't overdo it; too many notifications and the user will turn them off, and you've lost one of your most powerful tools.

Leveling

In a fitness-focused app, you can implement various levels, many of which you may have already encountered if you've used fitness apps. However, our approach to leveling will differ from the conventional approach. Rather than tying levels to performance, we want to embrace the uniqueness and diversity of our users. We will base our leveling system on the activity tracked per week. The design allows us to reward users based on their commitment and effort, regardless of their fitness levels or preferences.

For example, we would structure our leveling system as follows:

- **Level 1**: Less than 10 minutes of tracked activity per week
- **Level 2**: 10-30 minutes of tracked activity per week
- **Level 3**: 30-45 minutes of tracked activity per week
- **Level 4**: 45-60 minutes of tracked activity per week
- **Level 5**: 60-75 minutes of tracked activity per week
- **Level 6**: 75 - 90 minutes of tracked activity per week
- **Level 7**: 90-120 minutes of tracked activity per week

- **Level 8**: 2-3 hours of tracked activity per week
- **Level 9**: 4-5 hours of tracked activity per week
- **Level 10**: 6+ hours of tracked activity per week

This leveling system ensures that we reward users for consistent engagement in activities that align with their fitness goals, regardless of the intensity or duration. Whether lifting weights or going for a brisk walk, the focus is on recognizing and celebrating their commitment to improving their fitness. Not all users might be able to reach the highest level, but even competing against what they did last week, month, or year motivates engagement. In this way, the mechanic can be effective for multiple personas.

Badges

While we want to ensure a collective sense of achievement, we also recognize the importance of personal accomplishments. To address this, we will utilize badges to recognize individual achievements. Each badge will represent a significant milestone or accomplishment, such as completing a 5k run, finishing a marathon, or even conquering an Ironman event (maybe one day it will replace the leg tattoo!). By earning these badges, users will feel a sense of recognition for their feats. The badge system will also facilitate connections among users with similar interests and achievements. When encountering someone with badges for expertise in activities such as fencing, kayaking, and extreme yoga, users may find a sense of kinship and shared passions they can bond over.

User profiles

To further enhance the user experience, we can create user profiles that showcase each individual's level, score, and earned badges. These profiles will highlight their unique strengths, areas of expertise, and the communities they are connected to. This approach draws inspiration from popular online games such as World of Warcraft, where players' profiles showcase their skills and abilities. However, in our case, the user's skills and abilities will be aligned with different aspects of a healthy lifestyle routine.

Points

Lastly, we will incorporate a points system into our toolkit. Users can earn points by engaging in eco-friendly workouts, such as exercising outdoors instead of using a treadmill during summer. They can also earn points by logging into the app several times monthly, submitting success stories, and uploading their workout routines. We use points as a powerful incentive tool that you can tie to physical and financial rewards. Accumulating points will provide a sense of progress and achievement and create opportunities for users to unlock desirable benefits.

By combining badges, user profiles, and a points system, we can create a dynamic and engaging gamification experience for our users. This approach encourages collective and individual accomplishments, fosters connections among like-minded individuals, and offers incentives for sustained engagement. As users progress in their fitness journey, they will unlock badges, showcase their expertise, and earn valuable points, further motivating them to pursue a healthy and active lifestyle.

Gamification toolbox – secondary

Accountability can be a powerful psychological motivator when embarking on significant life changes. Our fitness app will leverage social tools to help users hold themselves accountable for their fitness goals.

Share button

By allowing users to share their profiles with family and friends, they can track each other's progress within the app. This transparency fosters a sense of accountability and encourages individuals to stay committed to their workouts. Moreover, users can choose to track the progress of their family and friends, creating a supportive and motivating environment.

Friends and follow

To further enhance accountability, we will provide the option to form groups within the app. Users can create groups with their friends or family members, allowing them to set collective fitness goals. This group dynamic fosters a sense of camaraderie and healthy competition, driving each member to push themselves toward achieving the shared objectives. Additionally, users can connect with a designated trainer who acts as an authoritative presence within the group, providing guidance and support.

Mentor

In his influential book *Influence: The Psychology of Persuasion,* Robert Cialdini explores the powerful impact of authority on human behavior. He reveals that people are more likely to agree to specific actions when they perceive an authoritative figure endorsing or guiding those actions. This psychological principle has significant implications for our fitness app.

By incorporating an authoritative figure, such as a professional trainer, within the group dynamic, we tap into this natural inclination for obedience and conformity. The presence of a knowledgeable and experienced authority figure lends credibility and expertise to the group. Users are more inclined to trust and follow the guidance provided by this authoritative figure, fostering a sense of confidence and motivation.

The role of the trainer goes beyond mere guidance and instruction. They are influential, inspiring individuals to push beyond their limits and stay committed to their fitness goals. With their expertise, they can provide valuable insights, personalized advice, and ongoing support to each group member. Their authority carries weight, reinforcing the importance of staying on track and adhering to the shared fitness objectives.

Leaderboards

In addition to individual and group accountability, we will introduce a group leaderboard feature. This leaderboard will be specific to each user's group, showcasing their collective progress and achievements. The more intimate nature of this leaderboard, focused on the goals and members of the group, further enhances motivation and engagement within the group dynamic.

Tip: Generic, general leaderboards are not effective. Using them strategically to make the most of a leaderboard would be best. For instance, public leaderboards at gyms tend to favor fitness enthusiasts who can work out frequently, leaving little opportunity for others to compete. Here are some tips to optimize the effectiveness of leaderboards:

- **Meaningful metrics**: Define metrics that align with your KPIs. Consider factors such as workout frequency, duration, calories burned, or achievements unlocked. These metrics should directly contribute to the leaderboard rankings.

- **Regular rotation and periodic challenges**: Keep leaderboards fresh and engaging by regularly rotating them. For example, if you have a leaderboard for workout minutes logged, consider rotating it weekly to allow new participants to reach the top. Additionally, incorporate periodic challenges and events, such as a mindful medley highlighting yoga, meditation, and tai-chi.

- **Milestones instead of leaderboards**: Shift the focus from leaderboards to milestones. Create goals anyone can achieve over time, such as reaching 10,000 miles on a bike or running on a specific treadmill. This approach instills a sense of accomplishment and uses scarcity to tap into your fitness enthusiasts since not everyone will reach these milestones. You can have a 100k miles club that will appeal to certain users but not impede the overall leaderboard functionality and usability.

- **Personalized leaderboards**: Enable users to create their groups or teams and have a collective leaderboard for comparison. This design tactic fosters a sense of camaraderie, motivation, and accountability within the group. Users will strive to contribute their effort to ensure their team's success and maintain their position on the leaderboard.

By implementing these strategies, you can make leaderboards more engaging and effective. Avoid the pitfalls of generic leaderboards and focus on meaningful metrics, regular rotation, milestone achievements, and personalized experiences. These techniques tap into users' motivation, encourage friendly competition, and foster a sense of community and achievement.

Random loot

A secondary reward you can insert into the gamified experience includes a lottery system. When users complete a specific action or milestone, they are entered into a prize draw. This approach keeps costs down while providing extrinsic rewards. To enhance the experience, ensure transparency by showcasing the profiles of users who have won prizes and what they have won. This experience creates excitement and motivates users to participate.

Test of knowledge

Quizzes are another effective gamification tactic. For example, during the workout experience, you can drop clues related to the exercises. After users complete a set of weights, present them with a question related to an object of similar weight, offering multiple-choice answers. This surprise adds an element of fun and rewards users for their engagement and attention to detail. These are small mini accomplishments that lead up to the many larger tasks such as badges and levels.

Live collaboration

With the prevalence of workout videos on social media platforms such as Facebook, Instagram, and TikTok, it's essential to leverage this trend. Research indicates that your target persona is active on these platforms, so consider integrating a feature that aligns their level, score, and badges with a video. Users can either live stream their workouts or save and share videos with embedded workout metrics. This feature allows them to showcase their achievements and progress, creating a sense of pride and social recognition.

Speaking of social media, let's explore the game mechanics for PMM.

PMM

PMM's approach to game mechanics differs from that of Hi-Z Fitness as we target a distinct audience with unique business goals. Building likability and fostering connections is a concept that transcends the advent of social media platforms such as Facebook. In his book *Influence*, Robert Cialdini delves into the influential role of liking in shaping human behavior. According to Cialdini, individuals are more inclined to comply with requests from those they like or feel connected with.

Liking is not solely based on physical attractiveness or charm; it encompasses similarities, praise, cooperation, and association with positive experiences or qualities. When individuals perceive commonalities or receive compliments and positive feedback, a sense of liking develops, enhancing their willingness to comply with requests.

Cialdini emphasizes the significance of building rapport and establishing common ground to enhance likability. When individuals experience trust and familiarity with someone, they become more receptive to their suggestions or recommendations.

Drawing upon this principle, PMM leverages likability to create positive relationships and foster connections among our target audience – emerging tech professionals. Our platform serves as a hub where these professionals can enhance their product development skills, acquire knowledge, and seek feedback on the products they've contributed to. By facilitating subgroups focused on specific categories, such as new product development or product implementation, users can find like-minded peers to share insights and experiences.

To integrate gamification effectively, we align our game mechanics with our business model, which offers a free-to-use app with optional upgrades. Some game mechanics may only be accessible through premium features, providing additional incentives for engagement. Our primary focus is to seamlessly integrate gamification tactics into the product, offering an engaging user experience that motivates users to participate and contribute actively.

By incorporating likability-driven game mechanics, such as personalized profiles, connections with peers, and the recognition of achievements, PMM ensures that users feel a sense of belonging and enjoy a positive social experience within the platform. These game mechanics tap into the psychological principles outlined by Cialdini, fostering likability and creating an environment where users are more likely to share their knowledge, seek feedback, and actively engage with the community.

Now, let's explore the metrics and game mechanics we will employ to drive engagement and deliver an exceptional user experience for PMM.

Gamification toolbox – primary

Within PMM, we have strategically designed primary game mechanics that enhance user engagement and drive the social experience. While we highlighted one persona and their JTBD, we will be designing for multiple personas within the product development realm, such as designers, engineers, data scientists, and whoever else has a hand creating products. We will weave together their stories, wants, and motivations to create a platform that serves their personal needs and the collective group.

Avatars

The concept of avatars within PMM goes beyond a mere representation of users; it serves as the foundation for creating a personalized and immersive experience. Users can curate their professional identity through avatars within the product development realm. Starting as an analyst and researcher, users can progress through various product development designations, showcasing their certifications, passions, and product development skills on their profiles.

Avatars not only provide a sense of progression and accomplishment for users but also serve as a means of connecting individuals and companies within the platform. Users can establish their professional network, connect with like-minded professionals, and collaborate on projects. Moreover, companies can create dedicated profiles to showcase their developed products, enabling users to link them to their avatars and further establish their credibility within the community.

Customer reviews

Customer reviews play a crucial role in shaping the reputation and credibility of products and individuals within PMM. This game mechanic empowers users to share their products and request in-depth reviews from their network of professionals. By leveraging the collective knowledge and expertise of the community, users can gather valuable insights and feedback to refine their products and make informed decisions.

To enhance exposure and gather a broader range of perspectives, users can utilize the "boost" feature. This feature allows their product to be promoted across the entire network, increasing its visibility, and attracting more responses. Customer reviews can be presented in various formats, from free-form text to structured surveys, enabling users to provide comprehensive feedback. Engaged reviewers are rewarded with points, encouraging active participation, and fostering a culture of collaboration and knowledge sharing.

Community recognition

Building a solid sense of community is a cornerstone of PMM, and community recognition serves as a powerful game mechanic to facilitate this. Users can nominate and recognize individuals within the network for their exceptional achievements and contributions. This recognition not only celebrates individuals' accomplishments but inspires others and fosters a supportive and collaborative environment.

Through community recognition, users can show appreciation for outstanding work, innovative ideas, or exceptional skills. This feature can be done by sharing specific instances or stories of how someone's work or contribution has positively impacted them. Recognized individuals are acknowledged publicly, creating a sense of pride and validation within the community. This game mechanic encourages users to strive for excellence and fosters a spirit of camaraderie and support among professionals.

Content unlocks

Knowledge sharing and continuous learning are fundamental aspects of PMM. Content unlocks serve as a game mechanic that incentivizes users and experts to create and share valuable content, fostering a culture of growth and professional development.

Product managers can create training programs, learning resources, and exclusive content within the platform as experts in their field. These resources can be made available for a fee, providing an additional revenue stream for both the creators and the platform. Users can access these content unlocks to expand their knowledge, gain insights from industry experts, and enhance their professional skills.

By unlocking valuable content, users can elevate their expertise, stay updated on industry trends, and gain a competitive career edge. This game mechanic promotes continuous learning and empowers professionals to take charge of their professional development journey within the PMM community.

User profiles

Allowing users to create a profile is a core principle of social media, but allowing a feature such as boosted profiles enhances users' presence and credibility within the PMM platform. By paying a monthly fee, users can verify their profiles, demonstrating their commitment to authenticity and professionalism (we want to know who the *real* Marty Cagan is). This game mechanic provides additional benefits and exclusive features to users who opt for boosted profiles.

A verified profile lends credibility and trust to users, distinguishing them as reliable sources of information and expertise within the community. Boosted profiles may also provide limited messaging capabilities, enabling users to connect and communicate more effectively with other professionals.

Gamification toolbox – secondary

In addition to our primary gamification mechanics, we have a range of secondary tools in our gamification toolbox that further enhances the user experience within our platform. These tools engage users and provide interaction, recognition, and reward opportunities. Let's explore these secondary gamification features in more detail.

Year in review

At the end of each year, we provide users with a comprehensive year in review feature. This feature highlights their product accomplishments, milestones, and year-long progress. Users can view their content statistics, earned badges, and goals achieved, providing them with pride and motivation to continue their product development journey into the following year.

Voting

Our platform goes beyond customer reviews by allowing users and companies to showcase their products or features. Users can vote for the products or features they have used and liked, which is a testament to their credibility as product developers. This voting system fosters a sense of community engagement and encourages users to explore new products and share their opinions.

Random loot

We have partnered with various sponsors, including Pabst Blue Ribbon, the number one drink of choice for product developers since 1893, to offer exciting rewards through our loot drop system. Users can earn loot boxes by engaging with advertising content, and inside these boxes, they'll find points that you can redeem for paid content on our platform or even prizes from our sponsors. This game element creates a fun and rewarding user experience while also providing exposure to our sponsors and their products.

User research artifacts (user stories)

We have taken a unique approach to content creation within our platform by structuring all posts in the format of user stories. Users can narratively share their product development experiences, challenges, successes, and tips, but they have to do it in the form of a user story. This storytelling aspect fosters a sense of connection and empathy among users as they can relate to and engage with the experiences shared by others. Users can like, share, and even laugh at our platform's relatable and inspiring user stories.

"As an author, I want you to read my book on gamification so that you can incorporate innovative techniques that help you reach your product goals."

These secondary gamification features complement our primary mechanics by adding layers of engagement, personalization, and social interaction. By incorporating these tools into our platform, we aim to create a vibrant and dynamic community of product enthusiasts who achieve their goals, have fun, gain recognition, and form meaningful connections.

Creating a game loop

In gamified products, your success and longevity heavily depend on users' engagement and satisfaction. To achieve these goals, it is essential to incorporate critical elements that foster a sense of progression, encourage social interaction, and offer diverse challenges. This section will explore the significance of creating progression systems, encouraging social interaction, and including challenges and variety in our gamified products, Hi-Z Fitness and PMM. These elements are integral to captivating users, promoting retention, and driving meaningful interactions within the gamified experience.

Create progression systems

A well-designed progression system forms the backbone of a compelling gamified product. It offers users a sense of growth, accomplishment, and exploration as they advance through the experience. By developing a progression system for our products, Hi-Z Fitness and PMM, we can provide users with opportunities to unlock new content, features, and abilities as they progress. This gradual unveiling of new elements keeps users engaged and motivates them to continue their journey within the product. Whether unlocking advanced workout routines in Hi-Z Fitness or gaining access to exclusive content in PMM, progression systems enhance user satisfaction and incentivize continued usage.

Encourage social interaction

Social interaction is a powerful driver of engagement and retention in gamified experiences. By incorporating social elements into the game loop of Hi-Z Fitness and PMM, we can foster a sense of community, healthy competition, and collaboration among users. Implementing features such as leaderboards, multiplayer functionality, challenges with friends, and cooperative gameplay enhances the social aspect of the experience. Users can compare their progress, engage in friendly competition, and collaborate with others to achieve shared goals. The inclusion of social interaction cultivates a sense of belonging, motivates users through social validation, and adds an extra layer of excitement and engagement to our gamified products.

Include challenges and variety

Challenges and variety are essential to maintaining user interest and preventing monotony within gamified products. By introducing a range of challenges, obstacles, and gameplay scenarios in Hi-Z Fitness and PMM, we provide users with diverse opportunities to test their skills, problem-solving abilities, and decision-making prowess. These challenges include timed tasks, problem-solving exercises, decision-making simulations, or creative missions. Including variety ensures that users remain engaged, continuously face new and exciting experiences, and encounter scenarios that cater to their preferences and skill levels. By balancing the difficulty and offering a mix of challenges, we create an immersive and dynamic environment that captivates users and encourages ongoing participation.

Incorporating progression systems, social interaction, challenges, and variety into our gamified products is crucial for enhancing user engagement, satisfaction, and retention. The progression systems give users a sense of growth and accomplishment as they unlock new content and features. Encouraging social interaction fosters community, competition, and collaboration among users, enhancing their overall experience. Including challenges and variety ensures that users are constantly engaged, facing new and exciting experiences that test their skills and provide growth opportunities. By strategically implementing th3se elements, we can create captivating, gamified products that resonate with our target audience. To have continued success and give users something new to look forward to, you must test and update constantly to stay fresh.

Building a reward system

In motivational psychology, rewards are crucial in driving behavior and shaping outcomes. As a product leader, it is crucial to understand the distinctions between intrinsic, extrinsic, and variable rewards as they have significant implications for motivating individuals within various contexts.

Intrinsic rewards

Intrinsic rewards arise internally from engaging in an activity or task. They stem from individuals' inherent satisfaction, enjoyment, or fulfillment from the activity. Examples of intrinsic rewards include a sense of accomplishment, personal growth, intellectual stimulation, or the sheer pleasure of doing something one enjoys. Internal motivations, such as curiosity, mastery, autonomy, or a sense of purpose, drive these rewards. Intrinsic rewards are often associated with long-term motivation and can foster sustained engagement as individuals are internally motivated to continue pursuing the activity for its inherent value.

Extrinsic rewards

On the other hand, extrinsic rewards are external incentives provided to individuals for completing a task or achieving a specific outcome. These rewards are typically tangible or external, such as money, recognition, trophies, badges, or other recognition or material benefits. Extrinsic rewards are often employed to motivate individuals who may not have an inherent interest or motivation in the task. They serve as external reinforcements to drive desired behaviors or outcomes. While extrinsic rewards can effectively promote short-term motivation and compliance, their impact on long-term engagement and intrinsic motivation can be limited. Relying on extrinsic rewards may lead individuals to perceive the task as merely a means to obtain the reward, diminishing their intrinsic motivation.

Variable rewards

Variable rewards introduce an element of unpredictability and surprise into the reward system. Instead of consistently offering the same outcome, variable rewards introduce a range of results or differing levels of incentives. This approach taps into the psychological principle of intermittent reinforcement, which can be highly engaging and addictive. Variable rewards create excitement and anticipation as individuals are uncertain about the specific reward they will receive or when they will receive it. This unpredictability can lead to heightened motivation and increased engagement as individuals desire to experience the subsequent rewarding outcome. Gamification strategies often utilize variable rewards to entice users into ongoing engagement with the product or service. They aim to keep users intrigued and motivated by offering them exciting surprises, bonuses, or achievements as they continue their interaction.

Understanding the distinctions between intrinsic, extrinsic, and variable rewards is essential for crafting effective motivational strategies in business contexts. Leveraging intrinsic rewards can help you tap into individuals' internal motivations and foster sustained engagement and fulfillment. Extrinsic rewards can be valuable in driving specific behaviors or short-term compliance, but you should consider their long-term impact on motivation. Lastly, variable rewards can introduce an element of excitement and unpredictability, fueling ongoing engagement and curiosity. By strategically incorporating these reward types into business initiatives, you can motivate individuals, drive desired behaviors, and enhance user experiences.

You can design many non-financial rewards into your gamification strategy. But if you want to use extrinsic variable rewards with a financial cost, it may be the best way to accomplish your goal, depending on your user. You have to be willing to invest in your product. I've seen use cases repeatedly where a small financial reward would drive behavior, but companies aren't willing to invest. So, where does the money come from? We are going to discuss two rewards funding strategies, internal and external.

Internal budget for Hi-Z Fitness

Monthly revenue:

- **Number of members**: 500,000

- **Membership fee**: $19.99 per month

- **Monthly revenue**: 500,000 * $19.99 = $9,995,000

Expenses:

1. **App development and maintenance:**

  - **Development team salaries**: $4,000,000

2. **Customer support:**

  - **Support staff salaries**: $1,500,000

3. **Marketing and promotion:**

  - **Advertising and marketing campaigns**: $1,500,000

4. **Rewards and gift cards:**

  - **Number of reward achievers**: 10,000

  - **Value of gift cards per achiever**: $50

  - **Total gift cards expense**: 10,000 * $50 = $500,000

Total monthly expenses: $7,500,000

Net monthly profit: monthly revenue – total monthly expenses

  9,995,000 - $7,500,000

  $2,495,000

In our hypothetical budget for Hi-Z Fitness, the app has 500,000 members generating a monthly revenue of **$9,995,000**. Is **$500,000 a significant amount** for rewards? Yes. Can you afford it? Also, yes, and based on your calculations and research, if it's one of the main things driving user engagement and retention, it's driving your monthly revenue and profitability. Don't be afraid to fight for your users.

But there are some fights you can't win with people you can't convince otherwise. Or do you need an initial budget to test this and get it started? The other option is to find a sponsor. Let's say you find a sponsor, Fitness4Life, that makes athletic clothing and nutritional supplements so that you can get jacked and look good doing your pumps.

Budget with sponsor

Monthly revenue:

- **Number of members**: 500,000

- **Membership fee**: $19.99 per month

- **Monthly revenue (membership fees)**: 500,000 * $19.99 = $9,995,000

- **Sponsorship revenue (Fitness4Life)**: $500,000

Total monthly revenue: $9,995,000 + $500,000 = $10,495,000

Expenses:

1. **App development and maintenance:**

   - **Development team salaries**: $4,000,000

2. **Customer support:**

   - **Support staff salaries**: $1,500,000

3. **Marketing and promotion:**

   - **Advertising and marketing campaigns**: $1,500,000

4. **Rewards:**

   - **Cost of rewards**: $500,000

Total monthly expenses: $7,500,000

Net monthly profit: Total monthly revenue – total monthly expenses

Net monthly profit: $10,495,000 - $7,500,000

Net monthly profit: $2,995,000

This revised budget reflects the revenue for rewards, ensuring that the financials account for all the costs associated with operating Hi-Z Fitness and incorporating the sponsorship revenue from Fitness4Life. Finding a sponsor such as Fitness4Life to fund your gamification rewards can be achieved through various approaches. Here are some strategies you can consider:

- **Research and target relevant companies**: Identify companies in similar industries or related fields that align with your target audience and brand values. Look for organizations that have shown an interest in supporting initiatives or programs your target audience is interested in.

- **Build relationships**: Reach out to potential sponsors and establish connections. Attend industry events, conferences, and networking opportunities to meet representatives from these companies. Engage in conversations, share your vision, and explain the benefits of sponsoring your gamification rewards.

- **Create a sponsorship proposal**: Develop a comprehensive sponsorship proposal outlining the sponsor's benefits and value proposition. Highlight the exposure and visibility their brand will receive through the rewards program. Please include details about your target audience, engagement metrics, and the positive impact the sponsorship will have on their brand reputation.

- **Customize sponsorship packages**: Offer different levels of sponsorship packages tailored to the needs and budgets of potential sponsors. These packages could include branding opportunities, such as logo placement, sponsored challenges or achievements, exclusive promotions, and mentions in marketing materials or app notifications.

- **Demonstrate return on investment**: Show potential sponsors the **return on investment** (**ROI**) they can expect from sponsoring your gamification rewards. Your approach could include metrics such as increased user engagement, customer acquisition, brand awareness, and loyalty.

- **Leverage existing partnerships**: If you have existing partnerships or relationships with other companies, explore collaborating with them to find a sponsor. They may have connections or insights to help you secure sponsorship for your rewards program.

- **Consider co-branding opportunities**: Explore the possibility of co-branding the rewards program with the sponsor. This opportunity can provide additional visibility and credibility for both parties and enhance the overall user experience.

- **Negotiate terms and agreements**: Once you have identified a potential sponsor, engage in negotiations to determine the specific terms of the sponsorship agreement. Define the duration of the sponsorship, the financial contribution, the branding and promotional elements, and any other relevant terms or obligations.

Remember, securing a sponsor for your gamification rewards program requires a proactive and strategic approach. It's essential to showcase the mutual benefits and value the partnership can bring both parties, ultimately creating a win-win situation.

Next, we'll move on to the last step – incorporating gamification into the user experience.

Incorporating gamification into the user experience

Welcome to the stage where you connect the pieces of the puzzle you've been putting together. There are many tools, processes, and methodologies for user experience strategy. We already covered user research, personas, and JTBD. We will cover usability testing and accessibility in a future chapter. There are many other beautiful books on interaction design, visual design, and content strategy. To create and design the first draft of your gamified product or features, we will cover creating a user journey map and, from there, a wireframe that incorporates the journey and game mechanics.

Creating a user journey map

User journey mapping visually depicts the end-to-end experience of a user with your product. It helps identify their pain points, opportunities to delight them, and monuments of critical interactions, with the focus here being gamified interactions. It involves mapping out the user's steps, actions, emotions, and motivations as they engage with a product or service. By creating a visual representation of the user's journey, businesses can gain valuable insights into the user's needs, pain points, and opportunities for improvement:

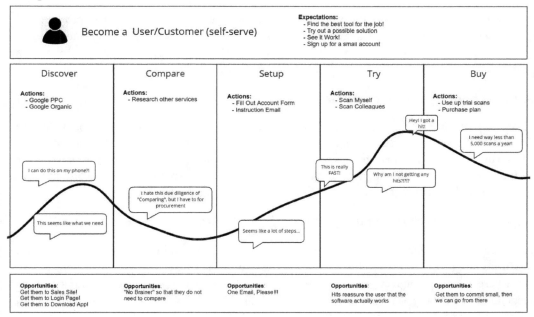

Figure 6.1 – User journey map template

To create a user journey map, define the critical stages of the user's interaction. We will use activation and onboarding, progression and achievement, challenges and competitions, and social interaction and community building since we will focus on the wireframe in this section. You can also include awareness, consideration, and purchase when you do a complete process journey map that includes marketing.

Within each stage, identify the touchpoints where the user interacts with the product, such as visiting the home screen, completing an action, or contacting customer support.

Step 1 – activation and onboarding

You can use gamification to engage users immediately during the activation and onboarding stage. By implementing interactive tutorials, challenges, or quests, businesses can provide a gamified onboarding experience that guides users through the initial steps of using the product or service. This educates users and introduces them to the core gamified mechanics that will be present throughout their journey.

Step 2 – progression and achievement

As users continue to engage with the product or service, use gamification to track their progress and provide a sense of achievement. This stage can include using progress bars, levels, or badges to represent the user's advancement visually. By setting clear goals and milestones, businesses can motivate users to continue their journey and unlock new features, rewards, or challenges along the way.

Step 3 – challenges and competitions

To keep users engaged and excited, gamification can introduce challenges and competition within the user journey. These can be in the form of time-limited events, leaderboards, or multiplayer activities. By fostering a sense of competition, users are motivated to improve their performance, earn higher rankings, or win prizes. This stage creates a dynamic, interactive experience that encourages user engagement and social interaction.

Step 4 – social interaction and community building

Gamification can also facilitate social interaction and community building within the user journey. By incorporating features such as forums, chat systems, or user-generated content, you can create a space where users can connect, share experiences, and collaborate. This sense of community fosters engagement and loyalty as users feel a sense of belonging and derive value from interacting with like-minded individuals.

Consider the user's goals, expectations, and emotions for each touchpoint. What are they trying to accomplish? What challenges or frustrations might they encounter? Are there any specific pain points or moments of delight? By empathizing with the user's perspective, you can identify opportunities to enhance the user experience and address any areas of concern.

User journey mapping also helps identify gaps or inconsistencies in the user experience. Are there any touchpoints that need to be added or optimized? Are there any unnecessary steps that need to be clarified? By visualizing the entire journey, businesses can identify areas for improvement and make informed decisions to streamline the user experience.

We will let you design your journey however you see fit; here is a table as an example:

Stages	Actions	Touchpoints	Emotions	Gaps and Opportunities	Data Needed
Activation and Onboarding	Download Hi-Z Fitness	App Store	Excitement, curiosity	Streamline the app download process	User acquisition data
	Sign up for an account	Registration form at login	Eagerness, anticipation	Simplify the registration process	User registration data
	Complete user profile	Profile setup	Eagerness, anticipation	Enable easy profile customization	User profile page metrics
Progression and Achievement	Set fitness goals	Goal setting interface	Motivation, determination	Provide goal suggestions based on user preferences	Fitness data, health tracking data
	Track workouts and activities	Workout tracker	Satisfaction, sense of accomplishment	Expand badge collection, introduce new levels	Badge data, level data, profile data
	Unlock badges and levels	Badges, level tracker	Pride, achievement	Expand badge collection, introduce new levels	Badge data, level data, profile data
Challenges and Competitions	Join time-limited fitness challenges	Challenge hub	Excitement, competitive spirit	Offer a variety of challenge types and difficulty levels	Challenge data, leaderboard data
	Compete on leaderboards	Leaderboard	Motivation, sense of competition	Implement real-time leaderboard updates	Leaderboard data
Social Interaction and Community Building	Participate in forums and discussions	Community forum	Connection, support	Enhance community engagement features	User-generated content, forum data

Table 6.1 – User journey in table format

In this user journey map, each stage represents a different phase of the user's interaction with Hi-Z Fitness. The **Actions** column outlines the user's critical activities at each stage, while the **Touchpoints** column indicates specific interaction points with the app or platform. The **Emotions** column reflects the user's emotional state during that stage, varying from excitement and motivation to satisfaction and connection.

The **Gaps and Opportunities** column highlights areas where you can improve or enhance the user experience. Some ideas include streamlining processes, providing more personalized features, expanding content, or improving engagement elements. The **Data Needed** column specifies the type of data required to support decision-making and improve the identified gaps.

By mapping out the user journey in this way, Hi-Z Fitness can better understand the user's experience at each stage, identify pain points or areas of improvement, leverage data to enhance engagement and satisfaction, and keep users coming back for more.

Creating a user flow diagram

Congratulations on completing the user journey map for your product! Now, it's time to dive into the next level of detail by creating a user flow diagram. This diagram is an essential tool that connects all the parts of your user experience. It allows you to understand users' specific paths with your product and how they interact with its various features. Here's why creating a user flow diagram is invaluable:

- **Visualizing user paths**: A user flow diagram visually represents the paths users can take as they navigate your product. It illustrates the sequence of steps and interactions, highlighting the key touchpoints and decision points. By mapping out these paths, you gain a comprehensive view of the user experience and can identify potential areas for improvement or optimization.

- **Identifying pain points and bottlenecks**: User flow diagrams help pinpoint pain points or bottlenecks in the user journey. By analyzing the flow, you can identify steps where users might need clarification, encounter friction, or experience usability issues. This focus allows you to proactively address these challenges, streamline the user experience, and enhance overall satisfaction.

- **Streamlining user tasks**: Understanding the user flow lets you streamline user tasks and interactions within your product. By visualizing the optimal sequence of steps, you can simplify processes, remove unnecessary steps, and reduce user cognitive load. This process improves efficiency and increases the likelihood of users completing their intended tasks.

- **Aligning stakeholders**: User flow diagrams are a valuable communication tool for aligning stakeholders across your organization. They provide a clear and concise overview of how users interact with your product, facilitating discussions and shared understanding. By visualizing the user flow, you can engage stakeholders in meaningful conversations about user experience and make informed decisions that align with user needs and business goals.

- **Enhancing user-centric design**: User flow diagrams help you maintain a user-centric approach to design. By mapping out user paths, you can ensure that each step in the flow aligns with user goals and expectations. This structure enables you to design intuitive and seamless experiences that guide users toward their desired outcomes. User flow diagrams also support collaboration between UX designers and other team members, fostering a shared understanding of the user experience and encouraging a user-centered design mindset:

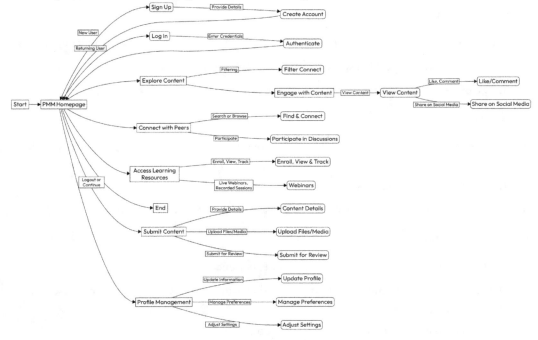

Figure 6.2 – Overview of User flow for PMM

Let's look at an example of a user flow.

Start: The user lands on the PMM home page.

1. Sign up/log in:

- If the user is new, they click on the **Sign Up** button and provide their details to create an account
- If the user is returning, they click on the **Log In** button and enter their credentials

2. Explore content:

- After logging in, users are directed to the main content feed to browse articles, discussions, and resources
- They can filter content based on categories, tags, or popularity

3.   Engage with content:

- The user clicks on an article or discussion post to view its content

- They can read, like, and comment on the content

- They can also share the content on other social media platforms

4.   Connect with peers:

- The user navigates to the community section to find and connect with other product managers

- They can search for specific users or browse through profiles based on expertise or interests

- They can send connection requests, follow other users, and participate in discussions

5.   Access learning resources:

- The user discovers the **Learning** section, where they can access training programs, courses, and webinars

- They can enroll in a course, view lesson materials, and track their progress

- They may be able to participate in live webinars or access recorded sessions

6.   Submit content:

- The user wants to contribute their insights or experiences

- They navigate to the **Submit Content** page and provide details about their article, case study, or success story

- They can upload relevant files or media and submit their content for review

7.   Profile management:

- The user can manage their profile information, including bio, profile picture, and areas of expertise

- They can update their preferences, notification settings, and privacy settings

End: The user logs out or continues exploring the PMM platform.

Creating a user flow diagram is a critical step in understanding and optimizing the user experience of your product. It helps you visualize user paths, identify pain points, streamline tasks, align stakeholders, and maintain a user-centric design approach. By investing time in creating a user flow diagram, you'll be equipped with valuable insights to enhance the usability and effectiveness of your product, ultimately delighting your users and achieving your business objectives.

Wireframes

Here comes the stage where you put pen to paper, literally. You can start with something other than using wireframing software. If your team is all in one location, get the paper and pens out and start doodling. If you have a dispersed team, plenty of digital whiteboard tools are out there. Freeform is on all Apple devices. The key here is that you should not do this in a silo. It is not just the product manager or designer's responsibility to do this. While one may have the ultimate decision, starting this as a workshop with your team is the best way. Pull in your designers, engineers, marketers, and data SMEs. They will each know the strengths and weaknesses of their areas and have a selection of ideas that will drive innovation, shift their mental models of what is possible, and engage new ways of thinking.

So, why do we start with wireframes and detailed drawings instead of going into the design? Wireframing plays a crucial role in a product or application's design and development process. It serves as a visual blueprint outlining the user interface's structure, layout, and functionality. Here are key points highlighting the importance of wireframing:

- **Visualizing conceptual ideas**: Wireframes allow designers and stakeholders to visualize and communicate their conceptual ideas early in the design process. They provide a simplified user interface representation, focusing on its essential elements and functionality. This process helps align the team's understanding and is a foundation for further design iterations.

- **Efficient collaboration**: Wireframes serve as a communication tool between designers, developers, and stakeholders. They provide a common visual language that facilitates discussions and feedback, ensuring everyone is on the same page regarding the product's layout and functionality. Wireframes help streamline the design process, minimize misunderstandings, and accelerate decision-making.

- **Iterative design**: Wireframes are flexible and easily adjustable, allowing quick iterations and experimentation. They enable designers to test multiple design alternatives, explore different layouts, and gather feedback from users or stakeholders early in the design process.

- **Cost and time savings**: By wireframing, you can identify and resolve design problems early, reducing the need for extensive revisions or redevelopment later on. It allows you to validate design decisions, gather feedback, and make necessary adjustments at a lower cost and within a shorter time frame. Wireframing ensures that resources are focused on building the right product, reducing the risk of costly redesigns or delays.

In summary, wireframing is a valuable practice in the product design process. It helps visualize ideas, create user-centric designs, facilitate collaboration, support iterative design, and ultimately save time and resources. By incorporating wireframing into your game design workflow, you can increase the efficiency and effectiveness of your product development efforts.

So, let's walk through the wireframing process for our examples:

- Something to always keep in your mind is accessibility. Take complex and make it simple. Minimalist design is always a fan favorite! When designing a minimalist wireframe that is accessible and user-friendly for all, it's essential to consider several key factors. First and foremost, aim for a clear and straightforward layout that provides a sense of organization and avoids overwhelming the user with unnecessary elements. By embracing white space, you create visual breathing room that allows users to focus on the critical content.

- Consistency in navigation is crucial. Users should understand how to move through different sections or pages of the wireframe. Implementing clear labels and intuitive icons will help guide users, ensuring a smooth and seamless experience.

- Carefully consider color and contrast in your wireframe design. Opt for colors that offer sufficient contrast to enhance readability, especially for individuals with visual impairments. Use color sparingly and purposefully to draw attention to essential elements. Testing the wireframe in grayscale is also essential to confirm its accessibility in various scenarios.

- Text legibility is another critical aspect to address. Choose fonts and font sizes that are easy to read and ensure that the font color contrasts nicely with the background. Ample line spacing and using headings, subheadings, and bullet points can enhance content scanning and readability.

- Focus on essential elements in your wireframe, highlighting core functionality and critical information. Avoiding unnecessary complexity creates a more user-friendly experience that benefits everyone.

- Consider the importance of keyboard accessibility. Ensure that all interactive elements can be easily accessed and operated using a keyboard as some users may rely on keyboard navigation due to mobility impairments.

By weaving these considerations into the narrative of your minimalist wireframe design, you can create an inclusive and user-friendly experience that caters to a broad range of users, effectively accommodating their needs and preferences.

Summary

This chapter explored the critical aspects of designing gamified experiences for products and applications. We began by emphasizing the importance of setting clear goals and objectives that align with the overall business strategy. By defining these goals, you can focus on driving specific outcomes and rallying your team and stakeholders around a shared vision.

Next, we delved into the significance of defining success metrics. We discussed the role of KPIs and OKRs in assessing performance and progress. By selecting meaningful metrics that align with the goals, product managers gain valuable insights into the effectiveness of their gamification strategies.

Choosing the proper game mechanics was another critical aspect we explored. We discussed various game mechanics, such as progression systems, social interaction, challenges, and variety. Each game mechanic aims to engage users and motivate them to take desired actions. By understanding the target audience and their motivations, product managers can select and implement game mechanics that align with the desired user behaviors.

Building a compelling game loop was highlighted as a crucial step in designing gamified experiences. We discussed the elements of a game loop, including clear goals, challenges, feedback, and rewards. By carefully crafting the game loop, product managers create an engaging and immersive experience that keeps users returning for more.

This chapter also emphasized the significance of building a rewarding system. We explored the different types of rewards, such as intrinsic, extrinsic, and variable rewards. We discussed the importance of aligning rewards with user motivations and ensuring they are meaningful and enticing.

Lastly, we explored how to incorporate gamification into the user experience. We discussed the importance of seamless integration, intuitive design, and effective communication. By integrating gamification elements seamlessly into the user experience, product managers can create a cohesive and enjoyable journey for their users.

Throughout this chapter, we highlighted the key considerations and best practices for designing gamified experiences. By setting clear goals, defining success metrics, choosing appropriate game mechanics, building engaging game loops, implementing rewarding systems, and incorporating gamification into the user experience, product managers can create captivating and impactful products that drive user engagement and achieve desired outcomes.

In the next chapter, we'll move on to implementing our gamified product and testing it.

7
Implementing Your Gamification

This chapter delves into the crucial aspects of implementing and testing a gamification strategy within a product. The process begins with building and testing your prototype and gamification assumptions on a group of dedicated champion users. Their feedback and insights help refine the gamification elements before integrating them seamlessly into the product's user experience.

The performance of the gamification strategy is then measured and analyzed using **key performance indicators (KPIs)** to understand its impact on the user experience. This data-driven analysis plays a pivotal role in making informed decisions about the future of the product and its gamification features.

Continual improvement lies at the heart of the gamification strategy. The strategy is fine-tuned through regular monitoring and iteration to ensure its long-term success and relevance to the target audience. This iterative approach is crucial in meeting the evolving needs of the users and achieving the desired outcomes.

By emphasizing the importance of monitoring, updating, and iterating the gamification strategy, this chapter underscores the commitment to delivering an engaging and impactful user experience. Integrating gamification elements and the data-driven decision-making process are essential pillars in driving a product's success in today's dynamic and competitive landscape. Here are the topics we will cover in this chapter:

- Decoding your gamification
- Setting up tools to track performance
- Making data-driven decisions
- Creating a process of continual improvement

Decoding your gamification

Once you have established your strategy and come to understand your users' needs, you enter the execution phase of your gamification project. Here, it's essential to consider the specific circumstances you may encounter. This process has two distinct paths: enhancing an existing product with gamified features or creating a brand-new product. Additionally, the context of your organization, whether a large international corporation or a small start-up, will influence the level of autonomy, systems engineering, budget, resources, team size, and methodologies at your disposal.

For those involved in building a new product, whether gamification is the primary focus or a complementary element, there will likely be increased pressure to quickly bring the product to market and attract a user base. In such a scenario, efficiency becomes critical:

1. Continuously question the necessity of each feature, asking yourself whether it is vital for driving traction and whether or not all users will find it useful

2. Guard against succumbing to *shiny-object syndrome*, where enticing ideas may distract you from the core objectives

3. Consider placing cool ideas in the backlog and only reintroduce them when the return on investment justifies their implementation

Misinterpretation has unfortunately led to the diminished credibility of the term **minimum viable product (MVP)**. Avoid the trap of creating bloated MVPs that follow waterfall methodologies and drag on for an extended period. Instead, focus on identifying a group of champion users with a core need and develop the corresponding functionality. Test this core function with users, make adjustments based on their feedback, and iterate until their needs are satisfied. After solidifying the core functionality, introduce the next set of users with a new function and repeat the iterative process. By continuously building and expanding your user base, you can maximize your return on investment while providing value to your customers.

> Tip
>
> Remember, each situation is unique, and staying up to date with the latest technology is essential when building complex digital products. Embrace a lifelong learning mindset and seek out mentors who can guide you through the process. In turn, consider becoming a mentor yourself, sharing your knowledge and experiences to contribute to the growth of the next generation of product managers. By fostering a learning ecosystem, you can further elevate your skills and make a meaningful impact in the industry.

Now, let's talk about building your team.

Building your implementation team

If you influence hiring for your team, whether internally or through contractors or consultants, this next section is for you. If not, feel free to skip ahead.

The following are some essential aspects of building an all-star product team.

User experience and user interface

When building a successful gamified experience, consider these critical areas for your UX team:

- **Gamification principles**: Seek team members with a solid understanding of gamification concepts and motivational theories

- **User-centric approach**: Prioritize UX professionals experienced in user research and crafting user journeys

- **Interaction design skills**: Find expertise in creating intuitive and engaging interfaces for seamless user interactions

- **Behavioral psychology expertise**: Include team members with knowledge of human behavior and decision-making processes

- **Data analysis and iteration**: Seek individuals skilled in data analysis and using insights to optimize gamification elements

- **Collaboration and communication**: Look for team members who excel in working with stakeholders and fostering collaboration

- **Adaptability and continuous learning**: Consider individuals open to learning new technologies and industry best practices

We should thus work toward fostering a supportive environment that encourages team knowledge-sharing, training opportunities, and creativity. And, at the same time, let's not underestimate the power of prioritizing positive attitudes, emotional intelligence, aptitude, and technical skills.

While hiring the best UX/UI team is crucial for creating exceptional user experiences, building a top-notch engineering team is equally important to ensure the successful development and implementation of those experiences.

Software and data engineers

In a groundbreaking 1968 study conducted in Santa Monica, nine trainee programmers participated in coding and debugging challenges. The study's results were astonishing, with one programmer far surpassing the others in terms of coding speed, debugging proficiency, and program execution. This performance disparity challenged traditional assumptions about individual skills in software development, prompting a reevaluation of talent acquisition and team composition.

Reed Hastings, co-founder of Netflix, was deeply influenced by the study's findings and became an advocate of the **Rockstar Principle**. Instead of hiring a larger team of average engineers, Hastings chose to invest in one exceptional "rockstar" engineer, recognizing their unique creative abilities and problem-solving skills. This approach led to a lean workforce of exceptional performers, resulting in greater managerial efficiency, faster decision making, and increased collaboration.

The Rockstar Principle serves as a reminder to product leaders that quality should triumph over quantity when it comes to team optimization and innovation. While hiring more engineers may seem like a shortcut to expedite product delivery, the reality often proves to be the opposite. By prioritizing expertise and skill rather than sheer number5, teams can foster a thoughtful and strategic approach that leads to better outcomes and progress.

By incorporating the following fundamental principles, product managers can effectively implement the Rockstar Principle when hiring engineers:

1. Prioritize quality: Place emphasis on hiring exceptional talent rather than expanding the team size with average performers. Seek individuals with exceptional problem-solving abilities, creative thinking, and a track record of delivering exceptional results.

2. Cultivate a lean workforce: Maintain smaller teams of exceptional performers, which enables managers to provide more focused guidance, support, and development opportunities. This lean structure allows for enhanced collaboration, faster decision making, and increased productivity.

3. Nurture a creative environment: Foster a culture that encourages creativity, autonomy, and continuous learning. Provide challenging and meaningful work to fuel intrinsic motivation and passion among team members.

4. Optimize managerial efficiency: With a minor team, managers can allocate more time to individual coaching, mentoring, and performance management. This hands-on approach fosters growth, professional development, and high-performance outcomes.

The Rockstar Principle has become a disruptive concept in the software industry and beyond. By prioritizing quality over quantity, you can build a close-knit team that truly understands your vision and has the knowledge to make it a reality. Now, let's look at some other principles that have shaped incredibly successful companies.

Baldur's Gate (1998)

A series of role-playing games developed by Bioware that use advanced *Dungeons & Dragons* locations, gameplay, and campaigns. Players control several individuals in their party, which can consist of up to six adventurers. Known for its expansive story and engaging dialog, this game set the standard for PC-based RPGs and the role-playing genre as a whole. Bioware went on to make some of the most successful and well-known RPGs, including *Star Wars: Knights of the Old Republic*, *Mass Effect*, and *Dragon Age*. If you'd like to play a more modern version of *Baldur's Gate*, it was remastered in 2012.

Sitting down with a group of friends and playing an actual campaign of *Dungeons & Dragons* would also suffice for learning the following, but the video game version is a lower barrier of entry, and it is honestly one of my favorite game franchises to date. The game requires you to build a balanced party of individuals. Your party needs a good mix of hand-to-hand combat, ranged attacks, stealth, and a charismatic character to do the talking. Building a product team is not too different, and diversity can be key in opinions, backgrounds, knowledge sets, soft skills, and more. A playthrough of *Baldur's Gate* might just help you understand the value of building out a team with complementing ideas, skills, and work styles. If nothing else, it is one of the most engaging stories in all of video games.

Principles and methodologies

You should have a set of principles for your team that guides the product development process. It would help if you drafted them first and then got a buy-in from your team. Having a set of principles keeps you aligned with the mission, helps everyone get on the same page, and helps with decision making and conflict resolution.

Effective product development requires a clear guiding framework that aligns teams, drives innovation, and ensures successful outcomes. Nike, the world-renowned leader in the sports and apparel industry, has established principles that have played a crucial role in its product development journey. These principles encapsulate Nike's values, culture, and strategies, providing a compass for product managers and their teams. By examining Nike's principles, product managers can gain valuable insights into building their guiding principles to navigate the complex landscape of product development and engineering management.

Here are Nike's principles:

1. *Our business is changing.*
2. *We're on offense – all the time.*
3. *Perfect results count – not a perfect process.*

    • *Break the rules: fight the law.*

4. *This is as much about the battle as about business.*

5. *Assume nothing.*

    - *Make sure people keep their promises.*

    - *Push yourselves and push others.*

    - *Stretch the possible.*

6. *Live off the land.*

7. *Your job isn't done until the job is done.*

8. *Dangers:*

    - *Bureaucracy*

    - *Personal ambition*

    - *Energy takers vs. energy givers*

    - *Knowing our weaknesses.*

    - *Don't get too many things on the platter*

9. *It won't be pretty.*

10. *If we do the right things we'll make money damn near automatic.*

These principles embody Nike's philosophy of continuous improvement, resilience, innovation, and a relentless pursuit of excellence. Each principle offers valuable guidance for product managers seeking to create high-impact products, nurture effective teams, and drive success in a competitive marketplace.

Building your principles is essential for product managers seeking to establish a clear framework for guiding their product development process. To develop practical principles, consider the following steps:

1. Reflect on your team's values, goals, and desired outcomes.

2. Consider the unique challenges and opportunities in your industry and market.

3. Engage in open discussions with your team members, stakeholders, and customers to gather diverse perspectives.

4. Identify key themes and principles that align with your organization's mission and vision.

These principles should be concise, memorable, and actionable guiding principles that inspire and empower your team to make informed decisions. Regularly revisit and refine your principles as your organization evolves. By creating and living by your principles, you can foster a culture of clarity, purpose, and alignment that drives successful product development outcomes.

Once you have established your principles, aligning on product-development methods and engineering best practices that support your guiding principles is crucial:

- Determine the most suitable development methodologies, such as Agile, Scrum, or Lean, based on your team's needs and the nature of your products.

- Define clear roles and responsibilities within the team to ensure efficient collaboration and decision making.

- Establish effective communication channels and feedback loops to foster transparency and knowledge sharing.

- Determine the optimal length for your sprints or development cycles, considering factors such as team size, complexity of work, and customer feedback cycles. Whether you choose two-week sprints or shorter iterations, the key is to balance delivering value quickly and maintaining high-quality standards.

Regularly assess and refine your development methods and best practices to adapt to changing circumstances and optimize your team's productivity and product outcomes.

Building a prototype

Don Norman, a renowned authority on human-centered design, brings valuable insights when creating interactive prototypes for gamification. Norman's expertise lies in understanding the psychological and emotional aspects of human interaction with products and services. He is widely known for his book *The Design of Everyday Things*, in which he emphasizes the importance of designing intuitive, user-friendly products that align with human behavior.

By incorporating interactive elements into the prototypes, you can simulate the user experience of engaging with the gamified features. This approach allows users to navigate fitness challenges, earn rewards, and interact with the app's community, providing valuable insights into how these elements are perceived and experienced.

Norman's emphasis on user experience is significant in the context of gamification. Users should feel motivated, engaged, and rewarded as they progress through the gamified journey. By observing users interacting with the interactive prototypes, you can identify pain points, usability issues, and opportunities for improvement. This iterative process of refining the gamified experience based on user feedback helps create a more seamless, enjoyable, and practical user experience.

Moreover, Norman's human-centered design principles highlight the significance of considering users' emotional responses to the gamified elements. The prototypes should evoke positive emotions, such as excitement, satisfaction, and achievement. By incorporating elements that trigger these emotional responses, you can create a more compelling and engaging gamified experience that keeps users returning for more.

You will continuously infuse gamification elements throughout the prototyping journey, such as competition, rewards, and social interaction. By subjecting the prototypes to rigorous testing and soliciting user feedback, the product manager can fine-tune the gamified experience, ensuring that it aligns with user motivations, drives sustained engagement, and fosters the desired behavior change.

As the product manager of Hi-Z Fitness, your goal is to develop a gamified mobile application that promotes regular exercise. To kickstart the prototyping process, begin by creating low-fidelity prototypes of the app's key screens. These initial sketches, developed through rapid iterations, capture the core elements of the gamified experience. They visually represent the app's onboarding process, diverse fitness challenges, and reward system. Testing these prototypes with potential users allows you to gather crucial feedback on usability, engagement, and appeal, ensuring that the final product aligns with user needs. This iterative approach not only saves time and resources but also enhances the overall effectiveness of the gamified experience.

As the prototypes evolve and refine, the product manager faces a pivotal decision: when to transition from a prototype to full-scale development. This decision is critical to the product's success and requires careful consideration of various factors.

One of the critical factors is the level of validation achieved through user testing. The product manager gathers feedback from users interacting with the prototypes and analyzes their responses. This feedback provides insights into the user experience, identifying areas of strength and areas that may require further improvement. Suppose the user feedback indicates a positive response to the gamified elements and demonstrates that the prototypes have effectively engaged users and influenced their behavior. In this case, it strongly indicates that the product is ready to move forward.

Another factor to consider is the complexity of implementing the gamified features. You must assess the technical requirements and challenges of incorporating the gamification elements into the full-scale product. This assessment helps determine whether the necessary resources, technology, and expertise are available to integrate these features successfully. If the implementation of the gamified elements is feasible and aligns with the overall goals of the product, it provides further support for transitioning to the development phase.

The available time and resources for development also play a significant role in the decision-making process. You must evaluate the project timeline, budget, and team capacity to ensure that the transition to full-scale development is feasible within the given constraints. The product is ready to move forward if the necessary resources are in place and the team can execute the development phase effectively.

Now, let's move on to the development phase.

Building your product

Transitioning to the product development phase is a critical juncture in the journey of a product manager. It marks the shift from prototyping and validation to the actual implementation of the product. This phase requires careful planning, strategic decision making, and effective collaboration with cross-functional teams. It would help if you navigated various factors, such as user feedback, technical feasibility, and available resources to make informed choices. This exploration will delve into the essential considerations and exemplary practices that facilitate a seamless and triumphant transition to the product development phase. We will focus on skillfully integrating the gamified elements while positioning the product for success.

Product requirements document

Creating and managing a living **product requirements document** (**PRD**) is crucial in developing successful products. Traditionally, the PRD served as a static blueprint outlining features and specifications. However, in today's dynamic and customer-centric landscape, product managers are embracing the concept of a living and dynamic PRD to add additional content and organization to software development. Much debate revolves around PRDs in the product community, and you'll have many loud voices saying you don't need it and that you should use their software instead. Our perspective is that you should have a central source of truth that is often iterative, updated, and takes the form of a PRD.

A living PRD acknowledges that product requirements are not set in stone but evolve throughout the product life cycle. It recognizes the importance of customer feedback, market insights, and technological advancements in shaping the product's direction. By integrating gamification principles into the PRD, you are creating a repository for the game mechanics and the design you chose, based on the thought leadership you read in this book or others, so your development team gets the understanding of what you are doing, why you are using gamification, and how the gamification strategy you chose is rooted in science.

One of the practical frameworks for structuring a living PRD is the **jobs-to-be-done** (**JTBD**) approach. Rather than focusing solely on features and functionality, the JTBD framework emphasizes understanding users' underlying motivations and desired outcomes. It shifts the perspective from what the product does to why customers use it to get a specific job done. You can develop a deeper understanding of user needs by uncovering the "jobs" customers are trying to accomplish and aligning product requirements accordingly.

An integral part of the living PRD is emphasizing outcomes, goals, and use cases. Instead of merely documenting features, product managers articulate the desired outcomes customers seek to achieve. These outcomes drive the product's functionality and serve as the guiding principles for making decisions throughout development. You set goals to measure the product's success in delivering the desired outcomes and construct use cases to illustrate how the product addresses specific user scenarios and provides value.

To ensure the success of a gamified product, you must actively address risks, assumptions, and dependencies within the living PRD. Risks may arise regarding user adoption, engagement, or the effectiveness of gamification elements. Successful product managers identify these risks upfront, develop strategies to mitigate them, and refine the gamification approach. They document assumptions about user preferences, motivations, and behavior and regularly validate them through user feedback and testing. They also carefully manage dependencies on external resources or technology platforms to ensure a seamless gamified experience for users.

Now that you have your PRD done, let's move on to create an architectural diagram to accompany it.

Architectural diagram

Having a well-defined architectural diagram is of paramount importance. It serves as a blueprint that guides the construction and evolution of a product's technical foundation. An architectural diagram visually represents the system's structure, components, and interactions, offering a clear overview of how the various elements fit together:

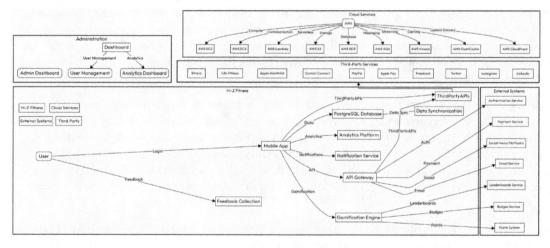

Figure 7.1 – A high-level architectural diagram

The architectural diagram shown in *Figure 7.1* can be developed further by working with an architect. Such a visual representation not only aids in understanding the system's complexity but also facilitates effective communication and collaboration among the product team, stakeholders, and engineers.

> **Note**
>
> A thoughtfully designed architectural diagram sets the stage for robust development, scalability, and maintainability. It is an indispensable asset for any product manager striving to build a successful and sustainable product.

Let's explore the best practices to create concise, informative diagrams that promote collaboration and informed decision making:

- **Collaborate from the start**: Involving architects and engineers early in product development is essential for creating a solid architectural diagram. Engage them in discussions and brainstorming sessions to leverage their expertise and insights. Encourage an open and collaborative environment where everyone's input is valued. You can tap into their knowledge by including architects and engineers and ensure you consider their perspectives in shaping the architecture.

- **Establish clear requirements**: Close collaboration with architects and engineers is crucial for defining precise requirements. Work closely with them to understand the technical constraints and considerations. Translate these into specific requirements that guide the creation of the architectural diagram.

- **Facilitate regular meetings**: Schedule regular meetings or workshops with the architects and engineers to discuss the architectural design. These sessions allow for open dialogue, active participation, and the sharing of information. Encourage architects and engineers to ask questions, seek clarification, and provide their insights.

- **Visualize the architecture**: Utilize visual tools such as Lucid Chart, Miro, or Mural to build diagrams or flowcharts to represent the architectural design. Collaborate with architects and engineers to create a clear and comprehensive visualization that illustrates the system's components, dependencies, and interactions.

- **Encourage documentation**: Emphasize the importance of documenting architectural decisions. This documentation serves as a reference point for the team and enables better collaboration, consistency, and clarity. It also helps maintain the integrity of the architecture over time and serves as a valuable resource for future reference.

- **Seek feedback and iteration**: Foster a culture of feedback and iteration throughout the architectural design process. Encourage architects and engineers to provide input, suggest improvements, and challenge assumptions. Iterate on the design based on the received feedback and evolving requirements to refine and improve the architecture continuously.

By following these best practices, you can effectively collaborate with architects and engineers, establish precise requirements, facilitate open discussions, visualize the architecture, encourage documentation, and embrace feedback and iteration. These practices help in creating a robust and well-aligned architectural diagram that serves as a solid foundation for the product development process.

Now that you have your PRD and architecture diagram, let's dive into roadmaps.

Prioritized roadmap

Crafting a prioritized roadmap requires a strategic approach and effective collaboration with cross-functional teams. As you embark on this journey, let's explore the key steps to create an exceptional roadmap for your gamification product.

First and foremost, perform an impact and effort analysis for each feature in your roadmap. Let's use Product Manager Media's examples, such as implementing a personalized recommendation engine or introducing a gamified progress-tracking system. Evaluate the potential impact these features can have on user engagement, satisfaction, and retention. Assess the effort required for development and maintenance, considering insights shared by PMM on optimizing resource allocation and balancing feature complexity.

To aid your prioritization process, leverage the proven frameworks highlighted by Product Manager Media. Explore methodologies such as the **MoSCoW method**, the **Reach, Impact, Confidence, and Effort method (RICE)**, or the **Kano model**. For instance, when deciding between enhancing social collaboration features or integrating a feedback system, use the RICE framework to assess each option's user value, reach, effort, and confidence. These frameworks provide structure and objectivity to your decision making, aligning with our emphasis on data-driven prioritization. You can find templates in digital collaboration software or easily make your own in Excel.

Collaboration is critical to creating a comprehensive roadmap. Engage with cross-functional teams to gather diverse perspectives and expertise. You need your engineers and architects to weigh in on scope and effort. Involve designers, engineers, marketers, and other stakeholders to ensure a well-rounded prioritization approach. Create clear communication channels such as conducting regular sync meetings, incorporating internal feedback loops, and fostering open dialogue. By leveraging the collective wisdom of your team, you increase the likelihood of developing a roadmap that aligns with business goals and user needs.

As you progress, create a timeline that accounts for any dependencies, risks, and assumptions and call them out. Consider technological dependencies, resource availability, and potential interdependencies between features. Reflect on best practices, such as using agile project management tools, establishing clear milestones, and employing iterative development methodologies. Visualizing your roadmap using tools such as Gantt charts or agile planning boards enhances transparency, facilitates stakeholder communication, and maintains a clear overview of your product's journey.

To summarize, here are some steps you can follow to help guide your success:

- Perform impact and effort analysis for each feature

- Apply prioritization frameworks such as MoSCoW, RICE, or the Kano model

- Collaborate with cross-functional teams, including designers, engineers, marketers, and stakeholders

- Create a timeline that considers dependencies and draws inspiration from efficient execution practices

- Visualize your roadmap using tools such as Gantt charts or agile planning boards

- Gather user insights and adapt your roadmap based on user feedback and market dynamics

These steps will help you structure your roadmap creation process and ensure it aligns with user needs, business goals, and industry best practices.

Now that you have your roadmap, let's dive into the details and start writing user stories.

Writing user stories

In the world of product development, effectively structuring and organizing work items is essential for successful project execution. Understanding the structure and hierarchy of features, epics, stories, tasks, sub-tasks, and bugs is crucial for product leaders to guide their teams toward building exceptional products. By mastering the art of crafting these work items, you can ensure clear communication, efficient collaboration, and successful delivery of gamified experiences. Let's explore how these elements come together in the context of gamification to create engaging and impactful products.

Epic

An epic is a large, high-level user requirement or theme encompassing multiple related features and stories. It represents a significant piece of work that adds value to the product.

> **Tip**
> Clearly articulate the main objective and expected outcomes when defining an epic. Break down the epic into minor, manageable features and stories to maintain focus and facilitate better planning and prioritization.

Example in Hi-Z Fitness

The Gamify Workout Challenge epics introduce engaging challenges and competitions within the app to enhance user motivation and enjoyment. They include features such as a leaderboard and various workout challenges.

Feature

A feature represents a distinct and self-contained functionality that delivers specific value to users. It is a meaningful and measurable part of an epic.

> **Tip**
> When describing a feature, clearly state its purpose, benefits, and user value. Use concise language and focus on the value proposition to clearly understand what the feature aims to achieve.

Example in Hi-Z Fitness

An example of a feature in Hi-Z Fitness is the leaderboard and ranking system. This feature allows users to compete with others and track their progress on a global leaderboard, fostering a sense of competition and providing a motivational element.

Story

A user story captures a specific user's need or requirement concisely and clearly. It serves as a conversation starter between the product team and stakeholders.

> **Tip**
>
> When crafting a user story, use the "As a [user], I want [goal] so that [benefit]" format. Please focus on the user's perspective, desired outcome, and the value they seek from the product.

Example in Hi-Z Fitness

"As a fitness enthusiast, I want to see my ranking on the leaderboard so that I can track my progress and compare it with others." This story highlights the user's motivation to stay motivated and engage in healthy competition.

> **Note**
>
> Acceptance criteria are overlooked when writing user stories, which define the specific criteria that must be met for a user story to be completed, implemented, and corrected. Acceptance criteria are paramount in establishing and aligning with the engineers and QA team members on your product. Add Acceptance Criteria to user stories in the form of bulleted points or a checklist. It can cover various aspects such as functionality, UI, performance, and other scenarios that illustrate the desired outcome behavior. It helps to define a user story's boundaries and determine when it's complete.

Task

A task represents a specific unit of work that needs to be completed to deliver a user story or feature. It is an actionable and trackable item contributing to the overall development process.

> **Tip**
>
> When defining tasks, make them specific, measurable, achievable, relevant, and time-bound (SMART). Break down complex work into smaller tasks, assign ownership, and set clear expectations. Make sure they are connected to the user story.

Example in Hi-Z Fitness

"Implement backend logic to calculate and update user rankings based on workout performance." This task involves implementing the necessary logic to accurately calculate and update user rankings on the Hi-Z Fitness app's backend.

Sub-task

A sub-task is a smaller, more granular unit of work that supports the completion of a task. It breaks down complex tasks into manageable steps.

> Tip
>
> When creating sub-tasks, make them focused and actionable. Specify the actions required to complete the task and assign responsibilities accordingly.

Example in Hi-Z Fitness

"Create a database schema for storing workout performance data and rankings." This sub-task contributes to the overall task of implementing the backend logic for user rankings by creating the necessary database schema.

Bug

A bug refers to an issue or defect in the software that disrupts the expected functionality. Ensuring the product operates as intended requires investigation, identification, and resolution.

> Tip
>
> When reporting a bug, provide clear and detailed information about the issue, including steps to reproduce it, expected behavior, and actual observed behavior. Attach relevant screenshots or error messages to facilitate understanding and resolution.

Example in Hi-Z Fitness

"Error in displaying user rankings on the leaderboard". In the realm of gamification, the proper structuring and organization of work items play a vital role in delivering compelling and motivating experiences. The defined hierarchy of features, epics, stories, tasks, sub-tasks, and bugs provides a framework for articulating the gamified elements and tracking their progress throughout the development journey.

Now that you have written your stories, the developers will finish them soon. Let's talk about development milestones and iteration testing.

Milestones and iteration testing

Developing products is a fast-paced game, and achieving success requires a strategic and systematic approach. One crucial aspect of this process is the effective planning and execution of milestones, which serve as markers of progress and guide the development journey. Additionally, iteration testing is pivotal in ensuring that products meet user expectations and continually evolve to stay ahead of the competition. We will explore the significance of milestones and iteration testing in the gamified social media platform PMM context.

Creating and planning milestones

The following are some milestones that you can work toward:

- **Define product goals**: Start by clearly defining the product goals and objectives for the game. These goals should align with the platform's overall business strategy and vision.

- **Break goals down into milestones**: Divide the product goals into smaller, achievable milestones. Each milestone should represent a significant accomplishment that moves the product forward. For example, milestones could include launching the beta version, reaching a specific number of active users, or integrating key gamification features.

- **Set timelines and deadlines**: Assign realistic timelines and deadlines to each milestone. Consider the tasks' complexity, available resources, and dependencies on other teams or technologies. Ensure that the timeline allows for flexibility and adaptation as needed.

- **Determine key deliverables**: Identify the key deliverables associated with each milestone. These deliverables can include specific features, user experience enhancements, performance improvements, or measurable outcomes.

- **Establish metrics and KPIs**: Define the metrics and KPIs that you will use to track the progress and success of each milestone. Your KPIs could include user engagement metrics, conversion rates, retention rates, or any other relevant metrics specific to your gamification objectives.

Iteration testing

Iteration testing is the process of continuous testing and refining of the product through multiple iterations or cycles. It involves gathering feedback, improving, and validating assumptions to ensure the product meets user needs and expectations.

Why iteration testing is important

Iteration testing helps identify and address usability issues, uncover areas for improvement, and validate design decisions. It allows for incremental enhancements and reduces the risk of building a product that doesn't resonate with users. Through iteration testing, you can ensure your gamified platform evolves based on user feedback and market demands.

When to conduct iteration testing

Iteration testing should be an ongoing practice throughout your product's development life cycle. It starts with early prototypes and continues through subsequent iterations, even after the product launches. Regularly seek user feedback, conduct usability testing, and analyze user behavior data to inform design and feature decisions.

An example of product management media

For PMM, an example milestone could be the "Gamification Phase 1 Launch." This milestone would involve implementing key gamification elements, such as point systems, badges, and leaderboards, to enhance user engagement and motivate active participation. The timeline for this milestone could span several sprints, with specific deliverables identified for each sprint, such as designing the badge system, implementing the point calculation logic, and integrating the leaderboards. Through iteration testing, PMM would gather user feedback on the gamification features, make improvements based on insights gained, and iterate on the design and implementation to optimize the gamified experience.

Remember, effective milestone planning and iteration testing are iterative processes themselves. Ideally, you should continuously evaluate progress, adapt to changing circumstances, and prioritize user feedback to ensure your gamified experience evolves into an engaging and successful product.

So, now that we have hit our milestones and our user experience is on par due to iteration testing, let's go into launching our product.

Product and feature launch

Launching a product or introducing a new feature within an existing product is critical for any organization. It represents the culmination of tireless efforts, extensive research, and meticulous planning. However, it is essential to recognize that the launch process can differ significantly depending on whether you are introducing an entirely new product to the market or unveiling a new feature within an existing offering. We will touch on the intricacies of product launches and new feature rollouts, shedding light on the key differences and providing insights into the best practices for each scenario. We will navigate the product launch journey together and equip you with the knowledge and strategies necessary to make a powerful impact in the market. You can find more about go-to-market launches in *Chapter 9*.

The full product launch

You introduce a new offering to the market when embarking on a full product launch. This process involves a comprehensive and orchestrated effort to create awareness, generate excitement, and drive adoption. Here are some key considerations and best practices for a successful full-product launch:

- **Market research and validation**: Before the launch, return to your market research to refresh yourself and your team on the original customer needs, understand the competitive landscape, and re-establish the product-market fit. The refresher will provide insights to shape your messaging and positioning strategies.

- **Run a soft launch**: Select your group of champion users who will heavily utilize the product and give feedback even if things aren't working. Give yourself enough time to test all the features, deploy updates, and implement any critical feedback they have.

- **Strategic marketing and communication**: Develop a robust marketing and communication plan encompassing various channels, such as digital marketing, public relations, social media, and content marketing. Work with the marketing team to craft compelling messages highlighting the unique value proposition gamification brings to your product and how it resonates with your target audience.

- **Scalable infrastructure and operations**: Ensure your organization is prepared to handle the increased demand and scale associated with the product launch. Build scalable infrastructure, establish efficient operations, and have a robust customer support system to provide a seamless experience. Make sure you know the costs as your cloud-based traffic increases and plan to scale up staff quickly if needed. Many very talented product management consultants can assist and help scale, such as the authors of this book.

- **Continuous monitoring and iteration**: Once you launch the product, closely monitor user feedback, analytics, and market dynamics. Iterate and refine your product based on user insights, address any issues or gaps that arise, and continually enhance the user experience. We'll go in-depth into that later in the chapter.

The following best practices give you a better chance of success in your product launch.

New feature rollouts

When introducing a new feature within an existing product, the focus shifts to enhancing the product's value proposition and addressing specific user needs. Here are key considerations and best practices for successful new feature rollouts:

- **User research and insights**: Conduct user research and gather insights to understand user needs, pain points, and preferences. Use existing customer feedback. The discovery process will help you identify the most valuable features to develop and prioritize or what needs to be fixed or redesigned.

- **Beta testing and feedback loops**: Engage a select group of users as beta testers to provide feedback and validate the new feature's functionality and usability. Incorporate their feedback to refine the feature before its wider release.

- **Segmented rollout**: Consider a segmented rollout strategy, initially making the new feature available to a smaller group of users or specific user segments. Segmentation allows for targeted testing, feedback collection, and addressing potential issues before scaling up the release.

- **Clear communication and training**: Communicate the benefits and value of the new feature to your existing user base. Provide clear instructions and training materials to guide users in adopting and utilizing the new functionality effectively. Update your tutorial to include any new features or changes to existing ones.

- **Continuous improvement**: Continually monitor user engagement and feedback to gauge the success of the new feature. Iterate and enhance its capabilities based on user insights and evolving market needs.

Whether launching a new product or introducing a new feature, a well-executed and carefully planned launch strategy is vital to capturing user attention, driving adoption, and achieving long-term success. By understanding the distinctions between the two scenarios and implementing the best practices outlined in this book, you can confidently navigate the product launch journey, delight your users, and stay ahead in today's competitive landscape.

Setting up tools to track performance

As data-driven product leaders, it is crucial to establish robust tracking tools to monitor your product's performance. Tracking various aspects of the user experience enables you to gain valuable insights and assess the effectiveness of your technology. While a wide range of analytics tools is available, we will highlight some popular options. Please note that this list is not exhaustive but serves as a starting point for your exploration. For more comprehensive information on analytics tools, consult additional resources or consider building your own analytics platform, albeit at a significant investment.

- **Google Analytics**: A widely used web analytics tool that provides detailed insights into user behavior, acquisition, engagement, and more

- **Adobe Analytics**: An enterprise-level analytics solution that offers comprehensive tracking, reporting, and advanced analytics capabilities

- **Mixpanel**: A powerful analytics platform that offers advanced event tracking, user segmentation, and funnel analysis to understand user behavior and optimize app performance

- **Amplitude**: A user-behavior analytics platform that enables tracking and analysis of user actions, conversion funnels, retention, and cohort analysis

- **Heap**: An analytics platform that automatically captures user interactions and provides retroactive event tracking, allowing you to analyze user behavior without predefining events

While this is not an exhaustive list, these platforms are widely recognized and offer robust analytics capabilities. When selecting an analytics platform, consider your specific needs, budget, and integration requirements to make an informed decision. Let's move on to what you do with all that data.

Netflix (2007)

Although starting as a mail-based DVD rental company in 1997, Netflix is now officially a streaming-only service. As one of the first of its kind, it offered many licensed films and television shows. But as media companies started to launch their own services, Netflix was forced to drop a lot of its competitors' content from its service. Netflix now claims that over 40% of its content is made up of original movies and shows, and they hold the rights to some of the most popular stream-only content, including *Stranger Things*, *Squid Game*, and *Wednesday*.

Try a little social experiment with your Netflix account and a friend's account. Log in to one account and give a quick browse over the top movies and shows. Then, switch accounts and look over the same. Did you notice the show thumbnails? Netflix is widely known to have one of the most complicated algorithms for showing you a specific thumbnail. After all, their data says that you are only looking at each thumbnail for less than 2 seconds, and if you do not find something within 90 seconds, you have a high likelihood to bounce to another service. Each show might have hundreds of potential thumbnails, and based on viewing history or demographics, each user will likely see a different one. Watch a lot of romance? Your thumbnails might include a lot of characters looking at each other in a cute way. Does your viewing lean more toward the serious side? Thumbnails might include more adult-toned images, potentially even depicting violence. Next time you are browsing for something to watch, pay attention to the images you are being shown and try to figure out what data might be driving those choices.

Making data-driven decisions

Data. Data. Data. There's so much of it out there and so many different kinds. Structured, unstructured, semi-structured, and big data! Where to start? Let's start with why. Why are we using data? To gain insight. What do we need insight for? To see how our product performs with the people using it. How do we know what the people are doing and whether they like our product? Experience is the data we will target. We previously covered how to set up your analytics platform, so let's jump into the data you want to read and what it means.

User acquisition

First, you want to learn how people learned about your product and started using it. Usage is vital information to judge the effectiveness of your GTM plan and product marketing. To understand user acquisition, you need to explore the following:

General

- **New daily, weekly, and monthly active users (DAU, WAU, MAU):** Measure the number of unique new users who actively engage with your gamified product daily, weekly, or monthly. This helps assess new user retention and the overall stickiness of your product. Evaluate the rate of growth for new DAU, WAU, and MAU compared to the growth rate of existing users. A higher growth rate among new users indicates successful acquisition strategies and an expanding user base.

- **Total Mobile App Downloads**: Track your mobile app's cumulative number of downloads across different app stores. This metric reflects the initial user acquisition and popularity of your app.

- **Cost per acquisition (CPA)**: Calculate the average cost of acquiring a new user or customer. This metric helps evaluate the efficiency and cost-effectiveness of your user acquisition campaigns.

Social media

- **Social media referrals**: Track the number of users acquired through social media platforms such as Facebook, Twitter, Instagram, and other similar platforms. Measure the effectiveness of your social media marketing efforts.

- **Social media engagement**: Monitor metrics such as likes, comments, shares, and followers to assess engagement and brand exposure generated through social media channels.

- **Click-through rate (CTR)**: Measure the percentage of users who click on your social media posts or advertisements and land on your gamified product's landing page.

Email

- **Email-open rate**: Track the percentage of recipients who open your marketing emails. This metric indicates the effectiveness of your email subject lines and overall email engagement.

- **CTR**: Measure the percentage of users who click on links or call-to-action buttons within your marketing emails. User actions help assess the level of user interest and engagement.

Search engines

- **Organic search traffic**: Measure the number of users acquired through organic search engine results. This metric reflects the visibility and discoverability of your gamified product in search engine rankings.

- **Organic search conversion rate**: Calculate the percentage of users who convert into registered users or customers after finding your product through organic search.

- **Keyword rankings**: Monitor the rankings of relevant keywords that drive traffic and conversions to your gamified product. This helps optimize your search engine optimization (SEO) efforts.

App stores

- **App store impressions**: Track the number of times your app listing is displayed in app store search results or featured sections.

- **App page conversion rate**: Measure the percentage of app store visitors who install your app after visiting your app page. This metric reflects the effectiveness of your app store optimization (ASO) strategies.

- **App ratings and reviews**: Monitor user ratings and reviews on app stores to gauge user satisfaction and the overall perception of your gamified product.

Each of these metrics can tell the story of what your user is doing. You can tell people use your product sparingly if you see you have way more monthly active users than weekly ones. You can see why this is the case if you check the app store reviews. If no one is opening your emails, you can try a different strategy with subject lines.

Activation

Here are some activation metrics that you can use to track the user onboarding and activation process of your gamified product:

- **User sign-up rate**: Measure the percentage of website or app visitors who sign up for an account. This metric helps assess your registration process's effectiveness and user interest in your gamified product.

- **Account activation rate**: Track the percentage of registered users who complete the necessary steps to activate their accounts. This metric reflects the effectiveness of your user onboarding experience.

- **User profile completion**: Measure the percentage of users who complete their profile information. A fully completed user profile indicates a higher level of engagement and a more substantial commitment to the gamified product.

- **Initial tutorial completion**: Monitor the percentage of users who complete the initial tutorial or onboarding process. This metric helps assess your user guide's ease of use and effectiveness.

- **Gamified feature engagement**: Track specific gamified features' usage and engagement levels. Measure the percentage of users actively engaging with these features, completing challenges, or earning rewards.

- **First-time activity completion**: Measure the percentage of users who complete their first activity or goal within the gamified product. This metric reflects the level of user understanding, motivation, and satisfaction.

- **Time to first action**: Calculate users' average time to perform their first meaningful action within the gamified product after sign-up. This metric helps assess the speed and effectiveness of user activation.

- **User feedback and surveys**: Collect user feedback and conduct surveys to gather qualitative insights on the activation process. Understand users' challenges, pain points, and satisfaction levels to improve the onboarding experience.

You can identify bottlenecks, optimize the onboarding process, and drive higher user activation rates by monitoring these activation metrics. Regularly analyze the data to gain insights, iterate on the user experience, and improve overall product adoption.

Monetization

Most of the time, the product we create is aligned with a business case that states we will make someone money. This money will be for your boss, the corporation your work for, your investors, and hopefully yourself! Therefore, we need to track monetization and see whether our hard work and investment are paying off:

- **Conversion rate**: Measure the percentage of free users who convert to paying customers. This metric indicates your monetization strategy's effectiveness and user interest in your premium features or offerings.

- **Average revenue per user (ARPU)**: Calculate the average revenue generated per user. This metric helps assess your user base's overall monetization potential and your pricing model's effectiveness.

- **Lifetime value (LTV)**: Determine the predicted revenue a user will generate throughout their relationship with your gamified product. LTV helps assess the long-term profitability of acquiring and retaining users.

- **Churn rate**: Track the percentage of paying users who cancel their subscriptions or stop making purchases over a specific period. The churn rate reflects your user base's retention and loyalty and highlights improvement areas.

- **Average transaction value**: Calculate the average amount users spend per transaction or purchase. This metric helps evaluate the effectiveness of upselling and cross-selling strategies within your gamified product.

- **In-app purchases**: Measure the revenue generated from in-app purchases, such as virtual goods, power-ups, or additional features. This metric reflects user engagement and willingness to spend within the gamified environment.

- **Ad revenue**: If your gamified product includes advertising, track the revenue generated from ad impressions, clicks, or conversions. Monitor the effectiveness of your ad placements and optimize them for maximum revenue.

- **Return on investment (ROI)**: Assess the profitability of your gamified product by comparing the revenue generated to the costs incurred in development, marketing, and maintenance. ROI helps evaluate the financial success of your product.

- **Pricing and packaging analysis**: Regularly analyze the pricing structure, subscription plans, and bundled offerings to optimize monetization opportunities. Experiment with pricing strategies to find the optimal balance between user value and revenue generation.

By monitoring these monetization metrics, you can make data-driven decisions to optimize revenue streams, improve user value, and drive sustainable financial growth for your gamified product. Regularly analyze and iterate on your monetization strategy based on the insights gained from these metrics.

Retention

One of the main reasons we use a gamification strategy is for retention! We want to have our users hooked on the incredible product we've developed. It's in the subtitle of this book, so it's essential. The following covers how you track it:

- **User retention rate**: Measure the percentage of users who continue to use your product over a specific period. This metric helps gauge the ability of your gamified experience to retain users and build long-term engagement.

- **Churn rate**: Track the percentage of users who stop using your product or cancel their subscription within a given timeframe. The churn rate highlights user dissatisfaction or disengagement and helps identify opportunities for improvement.

- **Users**: Monitor your DAU, WAU, and MAU. This can help in assessing user engagement and can contribute to retention in your gamified product. DAU reflects the level of user interest and habit formation, WAU provides a broader view of engagement and trend tracking, and MAU offers a high-level understanding of overall user engagement and active user base size. Analyzing these metrics helps evaluate the effectiveness of your product in retaining users and driving ongoing engagement.

- **Session duration**: Measure the average time users spend actively using your gamified product during a session. Session duration reflects the engagement and enjoyment users experience while interacting with your product.

- **Frequency of use**: Track how often users engage with your product within a specific timeframe. This metric helps assess the habit-forming nature of your gamified experience and the level of ongoing user engagement.

- **User engagement**: Monitor the level of user interactions, such as completing challenges, earning rewards, participating in community activities, or unlocking achievements. User engagement metrics provide insights into the depth of user involvement and the effectiveness of your gamification elements.

- **Retention cohorts**: Analyze the retention rates of different user cohorts based on the time of acquisition or other segmentation criteria. This analysis helps identify patterns and trends in user retention and allows for targeted interventions and improvements.

By tracking these retention metrics, you can comprehensively understand user engagement, satisfaction, and loyalty within your gamified product. Regularly analyze and act upon the insights gained from these metrics to implement strategies that enhance user retention and drive long-term success.

A/B testing

A/B testing, or split testing, is a valuable technique to compare two or more variations of a gamified product to determine which performs better. It involves creating two or more versions of a feature, interface element, or user experience and distributing them to different segments of users. The performance of each variant is then measured and compared to identify which one yields better results.

When it comes to gamified products, A/B testing is crucial for the following reasons:

1. Optimizing user engagement: A/B testing allows product managers to experiment with gamification elements such as challenges, levels, rewards, progress indicators, or social features. By testing different variations, they can identify which elements resonate best with users, leading to higher engagement.

2. Improving user retention: Gamification aims to enhance user retention by creating an enjoyable and recurring experience. A/B testing helps identify the features or mechanics that have the most significant impact on user retention. By optimizing these elements, product managers can improve user stickiness and reduce churn.

3. Enhancing user experience: A/B testing enables product managers to refine the user experience of gamified products. By testing user interface variations, navigation flow, or visual design, they can identify the most intuitive and user-friendly design choices that maximize engagement and satisfaction.

4. Driving desired user behavior: Gamification often encourages specific user behaviors or actions. A/B testing allows product managers to experiment with different game mechanics or incentive structures to understand which approach drives the desired behaviors most effectively.

To conduct A/B testing for gamified products, product managers typically follow these steps:

1. Define the objective: Identify the goal of the A/B test, such as increasing user engagement, improving retention, or driving specific actions. The goal ensures that you align the test with the product's overall strategy and objectives.

2. Select variables to test: Determine which elements of the gamified product you want to test. Elements could include variations in in-game mechanics, rewards, challenges, onboarding processes, or user interface elements.

3. Split user segments: Divide your user base into segments, ensuring each represents a statistically significant sample size. When testing, assign one of the variations to each segment.

4. Implement tracking and measurement: Set up tracking mechanisms and define key metrics to measure the performance of each variation. Key metrics include user engagement, time spent, completion, and conversion rates.

5. Run the test: Deploy the variations to the respective user segments and allow the test to run sufficiently to collect essential data. Ensure that the test conditions remain consistent throughout the testing period.

6. Analyze results: Once enough data is collected, analyze the results to determine which variation performed better in the defined metrics. Statistical analysis can determine the significance of the differences observed.

7. Implement the winning variation: Based on the results, implement the variation that performed better and roll it out to the entire user base. Monitor the impact of the changes and iterate further based on user feedback and data analysis.

A/B testing in gamified products empowers you to make data-driven decisions and optimize the user experience to achieve desired outcomes. You can continuously improve and refine your gamified offerings by systematically testing different variations, leading to higher user engagement, retention, and overall product success.

Always use A/B testing. Even for this book. Buy the physical version and the audiobook and let us know which one provides you more value.

Pivot or persevere

The concept of pivoting or persevering is a foundational principle in the Lean Startup methodology, popularized by Eric Ries in his book *The Lean Startup*. This strategy emphasizes the importance of constantly evaluating and adapting a product or business idea based on validated learning from customer feedback and market insights. Instead of sticking to a predefined plan, the pivot or persevere strategy encourages product managers and entrepreneurs to be flexible and agile in their decision making.

The *pivot* strategy refers to a strategic shift in a product's direction, whether changing the target market, redefining the value proposition, adjusting the business model, or refining the core features. It is a deliberate change to align the product with customer needs and market dynamics. The pivot allows product managers to course-correct and navigate uncertainties or changing market conditions effectively.

On the other hand, the *persevere* strategy suggests that if the feedback and data indicate that the product is on the right track, the team should continue executing the current plan and invest resources in further growth and optimization. This strategy acknowledges that not all ideas need a radical pivot and that perseverance and continuous improvement can lead to success.

The pivot-or-persevere strategy is rooted in the Lean Startup's iterative and experimental approach, which advocates for quick building, measuring, and learning cycles. It encourages product managers to validate assumptions, gather customer feedback, and analyze market data to make informed decisions about the product's future direction.

Product managers can effectively manage uncertainty and mitigate risks by embracing the pivot-or-persevere strategy. They can iterate on their product, optimize their strategies, and increase the chances of delivering a successful, market-fit solution. The strategy enables a data-driven and customer-centric approach, aligning the product with market needs and maximizing its potential for long-term success.

Citation

Ries, E. (2011). *The Lean Startup: How Today's Entrepreneurs Use Continuous Innovation to Create Radically Successful Businesses*. Crown Business.

Creating a process of continual improvement

A great product leader is always on a journey of continuous improvement. The long road includes personal growth, skill development, and enhancing the product they are responsible for. As discussed in *Chapter 2*, product management operates at the intersection of user needs, business goals, and technological advancements. These three dimensions constantly evolve, requiring product managers to adapt and improve their approach.

In the business realm, there will constantly be changing demands, shifts in leadership, market fluctuations, and other external factors. Staying attuned to these changes and being agile in responding to new demands and opportunities is essential. Similarly, technology is ever-evolving, with advancements such as faster processing, smaller chips, and emerging technologies such as artificial intelligence and quantum computing. Keeping up with these technological developments enables product managers to leverage the latest tools and capabilities to create more impactful and innovative products.

User needs and preferences are dynamic, and what resonates with them can change over time. This emphasizes the significance of establishing feedback loops to stay in tune with users. Product managers foster a culture of continual improvement by actively seeking feedback, understanding their evolving needs, and iterating based on user insights. Feedback loops are essential in this process, and they involve gathering, analyzing, and implementing changes based on user feedback. By incorporating feedback loops into the product management process and collaborating with engineering and data teams, you fuel the cycle of improvement. As a product leader, it's your responsibility to cultivate a culture that embraces feedback, collaboration, and a growth mindset. By prioritizing feedback-driven practices and leveraging feedback loops, your gamified product can continuously evolve to meet user needs and drive innovation.

Implementing feedback loops

The analytics we covered earlier are just a tiny sample of the tools and technology to implement feedback loops. You will know your users and your platform the best, and we'll cover a range of options when implementing feedback loops.

Here are step-by-step instructions on how to establish effective feedback loops in your product management process:

1. Define your feedback objectives: Determine the specific goals and objectives of gathering feedback. Are you looking to understand user satisfaction, identify pain points, gather feature requests, or validate hypotheses? Clearly define what you aim to achieve through the feedback process. What is the problem you are trying to solve?

2.   Select feedback collection methods: Choose appropriate methods to collect user feedback, including surveys, user interviews, usability testing, focus groups, in-app feedback mechanisms, social media monitoring, or customer support interactions. You must leverage quantitative and qualitative methods to gain a comprehensive understanding of user experiences. Combining these approaches allows you to gather insights from different perspectives and uncover valuable information that may not be apparent through a single method alone. We discussed these methods in depth in *Chapter 4*.

3.   Leverage feedback tools: Utilize tools for feedback collection and analysis. These may include survey platforms such as SurveyMonkey or Typeform, customer feedback management systems such as UserVoice or Zendesk, user behavior analytics tools such as Mixpanel or Google Analytics, and user testing platforms such as UserTesting or Validately.

Another great tool we love is called Feedback Loop. Its advantage is that you can create technology-driven surveys and access a poll of millions of your target customers by choosing demographics and behaviors. It is a pay-to-play model, allowing you to get relevant information quickly and represent your intended user base. Disqo now owns it, and we're giving them a shoutout because they have a great podcast called *This is Product Management*.

4.   Analyze feedback data: After collecting feedback, analyze the data to extract meaningful insights. Start by cleaning and organizing the data to remove duplicate or irrelevant responses. Dive into the feedback data and identify common themes or trends such as recurring comments, sentiments, or user preferences; this will help you understand your users' overall sentiment and identify improvement areas. Next, create charts, graphs, or dashboards that effectively present the data. Use data visualization tools and techniques to make the analysis more accessible and actionable.

5.   Prioritize feedback: Prioritize the feedback based on its impact and alignment with your product goals. Categorize feedback into different priority levels (e.g., high, medium, or low) based on user demand, potential business value, and technical feasibility. Consider using frameworks such as the RICE method or the **Impact, Confidence, and Ease** (**ICE**) method to help prioritize feedback effectively.

6.   Implement changes: Based on the prioritized feedback, create an actionable plan to implement the necessary changes and get your stakeholder's approval. Ensure to include the insights, amount of time, effort, and cost, and then the return on investment. Once approved, your actionable plan will be turned into user stories and bugs and added to the product backlog. Collaborate with cross-functional teams, including designers and engineers, to define and execute the required updates and ensure they are part of the process from the start. Ensure clear communication and alignment on the changes to be made and integrated into the existing processes you have for deployment.

7.   Monitor and measure impact: Once the changes are implemented, monitor the impact of the updates on user behavior and satisfaction. Utilize your analytics tools and metrics to track KPIs for the specific feedback objectives. Evaluate the success of the changes and iterate further if needed.

8. Communicate and close the loop: Work with the marketing team to communicate with your users how their feedback has influenced the product. Share updates, improvements, and new features implemented based on their input. Closing the loop by sharing the outcomes of their feedback fosters trust, encourages continued engagement, and reinforces the value of feedback.

9. Iterate and continuously improve: Feedback loops are not a one-time activity. Continuously iterate and improve your feedback processes based on the insights gained. Experiment with different methods, tools, and analysis techniques to optimize the effectiveness of your feedback loops.

By following these step-by-step instructions, you can establish effective feedback loops that empower you to gather valuable insights from your users, prioritize enhancements, and drive continuous improvement in your gamified product. Let's look at a case study for a better understanding.

Hi-Z Fitness case study

In the competitive world of gamified fitness apps, Hi-Z Fitness embarked on a journey to gain insights into user satisfaction and gather feature requests. They understood that gathering feedback directly from their users would be instrumental in shaping their product roadmap and driving continuous improvement.

Hi-Z Fitness decided to leverage feedback collection methods to gather comprehensive insights. They employed a user satisfaction survey, conducted in-app feedback sessions, and organized user focus groups. The survey allowed users to rate their overall satisfaction with the app, while the in-app feedback sessions provided a platform for users to share specific suggestions and ideas. The focus groups were conducted virtually, allowing users to engage in deeper conversations about their preferences and desires for new features.

The feedback received from users was a rich mix of insights. Some users expressed high satisfaction with the app's user-friendly interface, engaging challenges, and personalized workout plans. They also appreciated the social aspects of the app, such as the ability to connect with friends and participate in virtual competitions. On the other hand, there were requests for additional workout programs targeting specific fitness goals, more customizable avatars, and enhanced tracking of progress and achievements.

Hi-Z Fitness employed a two-pronged approach to analyze the feedback and derive meaningful insights. First, they conducted sentiment analysis on the written feedback from the surveys and in-app sessions. The feedback helped them understand the overall sentiment of the users' comments, whether positive, neutral, or negative. Second, they conducted a thematic analysis to identify recurring themes and patterns in the feedback, enabling them to pinpoint the most prominent user needs and desires.

Through their analysis, Hi-Z Fitness discovered that users highly valued personalized workout plans tailored to their specific goals and fitness levels. They also identified a demand for more diverse workout programs, including yoga, high-intensity interval training (HIIT), and strength training. Additionally, users expressed a strong desire for enhanced social features, such as forming virtual workout groups and engaging in friendly competitions with other users to hold themselves accountable.

Regarding KPIs, Hi-Z Fitness focused on measuring user engagement and satisfaction. They tracked metrics such as DAU, WAU, time spent in the app, and their **Net Promoter Score (NPS)**. These metrics provided insights into the app's overall popularity, user retention rates, and the likelihood of users recommending the app to others.

Here is the Hi-Z Fitness action plan:

- Prioritize the development of new workout programs, including yoga and HIIT

- Allocate resources to enhance the app's social features

- Introduce an avatar customization feature that allows users to personalize their digital fitness identities, which could also showcase their badges

Hi-Z Fitness continued to track its KPIs to measure the impact of the changes. They observed a significant increase in user engagement and a rise in DAU and WAU, with more time spent in the app. Their NPS also improved, indicating higher user satisfaction and loyalty.

Hi-Z Fitness transformed its gamified fitness app into a more personalized, engaging, and socially connected platform through its commitment to actively listening to user feedback and taking action. So, by continuously analyzing feedback, identifying user needs, and implementing improvements, they solidified their position in the market and provided users with an exceptional fitness experience tailored to their desires. The case study on their website showcased how their user-centric approach and iterative feedback process drove the success of their product.

Summary

In conclusion, implementing gamification in your product requires careful planning, iterative development, and a strong focus on user feedback. Whether working with an existing product or creating a new one, the principles and strategies discussed in this chapter can guide you toward successful implementation.

First and foremost, understanding the differences between handing off a new product and enhancing an existing one is crucial. Each scenario presents its own set of challenges and considerations. When managing and selecting engineers for your team, ensure that you have a diverse and skilled group who can work collaboratively to bring your gamified product to life.

Selecting the appropriate sprint length that aligns with your team's capabilities and preferences is vital. Lay out transparent processes and systems connectivity within your team to foster effective communication and coordination throughout the development cycle.

Once your strategy design and hypothesis testing are complete, building a prototype using the Lean Startup method allows you to gather early feedback and iterate on your ideas. Test and refine your product based on user feedback, constantly aiming for improvement.

Creating a roadmap, setting milestones, and defining checkpoints help keep your development on track. Continuously assess whether to pivot or preserve your product based on the insights gained from feedback loops and data analysis. This iterative approach ensures that you stay agile and adaptable to market changes.

Writing precise requirements through a PRD, user stories, and architectural diagrams provides a solid foundation for development. Constantly testing technically and with users allows you to identify and address issues early on.

As you prepare for launch, incorporate go-to-market (GTM) strategies, covered in *Chapter 9*, to maximize the impact of your gamified product. Integrate data and analytics from the start to enable data-driven decision making and gain valuable insights into user behavior and engagement.

Remember, feedback loops are a critical part of the implementation process. Continuously gather feedback, analyze it, and incorporate the insights into your product roadmap. A case study showcasing the successful implementation of gamification in your product can inspire and validate your efforts.

By following these steps and principles, you can successfully implement gamification in your product, thereby driving user engagement, retention, and overall product excellence. Embrace a culture of continuous improvement and be prepared to pivot or preserve based on the feedback and data you receive. Your gamified product will evolve and thrive, delighting users and driving business success.

In *Chapter 8*, we will be discussing the challenges and limitations of gamification.

8

Challenges and Limitations in Gamification

Gamification has emerged as a powerful tool for product leads to drive user engagement and behavior change. However, to successfully leverage gamification, product leaders must understand the challenges that come with it and develop strategies to overcome them. By addressing these challenges, product leaders can ensure the successful implementation of gamification and achieve their desired business outcomes. In this chapter, we will explore the challenges and limitations that product leaders may encounter when implementing a gamification strategy.

In this chapter, we'll cover the following topics:

- Keeping gamification ethical
- Balancing gamification and user privacy
- Accessibility to all users
- Ensuring gamification doesn't harm the user experience
- Avoiding common pitfalls and mistakes

The chapter will cover several key areas that you need to consider when implementing gamification in your products. We will delve into the ethical considerations surrounding gamification, emphasizing the importance of designing respectful and fair experiences that do not exploit or manipulate users. You will gain insights into ethical decision-making and learn how to align gamification strategies with your organization's values.

Another critical aspect we will explore is privacy compliance. You must navigate the landscape of data protection regulations and ensure that user data is handled responsibly and transparently. By understanding privacy regulations and incorporating privacy-by-design principles, you can establish trust with your users and maintain compliance with relevant laws and regulations.

Accessibility is another crucial consideration in gamification. You must ensure that gamified experiences are inclusive and accessible to users with diverse needs and abilities. By implementing accessibility guidelines and considering the needs of all users, you can create experiences that reach a wider audience and provide equal opportunities for engagement. No excuses; get this done!

Balancing gamification elements with the overall user experience is also a key challenge for product leaders. While gamification can enhance engagement, it should maintain the product's core purpose and user experience. You will learn strategies for seamlessly integrating gamification into the product, ensuring it enhances user engagement without detracting from the overall experience.

Lastly, the chapter will explore common pitfalls and mistakes in gamification implementation. By understanding these pitfalls, you can proactively identify and avoid similar challenges in your gamification initiatives. You will gain valuable insights from real-life examples and learn from the experiences of others.

By addressing the challenges and limitations head-on, you can navigate the complexities of gamification and create compelling experiences for your users. By integrating ethical principles, privacy compliance, accessibility guidelines, and user-centric design, you can leverage gamification as a strategic tool t0 achieve your business goals and deliver exceptional user experiences.

Keeping gamification ethical

Keeping gamification ethical is of utmost importance as you pursue creating engaging and impactful experiences. As product leaders, you play a crucial role in designing and implementing gamification strategies that align with ethical standards and prioritize user well-being. This section will explore the ethical considerations relevant to product development and discuss practical approaches to maintaining ethicality throughout gamification.

You must first understand the importance of transparency in gamification. Transparency fosters trust and empowers users to make informed decisions, ensuring they actively engage with the gamified experience while being aware of how you influence their actions and behaviors. You should communicate clearly with your users about the use of gamification mechanics, the intended goals, and how user data is collected and utilized.

Fairness is another vital aspect that product leaders should prioritize in gamification. You must ensure that the gamified experiences you create provide equal opportunities for all users to succeed, irrespective of socioeconomic status, gender, or race. Equality requires careful consideration of game mechanics and reward systems to prevent any form of bias or discrimination. By embracing fairness, you can promote inclusivity and create a level playing field for all users.

In addition, you must be mindful of the potential impact of gamification on user behavior. While gamification can be a powerful tool for motivation, you should not use it to manipulate or exploit users. You should avoid designing experiences that foster addictive behaviors or encourage actions that could be detrimental to users' well-being. Instead, you should focus on creating positive and meaningful interactions that align with users' values and goals.

Addiction by Design

Addiction by Design by Natasha Dow Schüll is a captivating exploration of the dark side of technology and its potential to fuel addictive behaviors. The book delves into the world of **electronic gambling machines (EGMs)** and how companies meticulously design them to exploit human psychology and create compulsive gambling habits.

When misused or unchecked, gamification can indeed have detrimental effects on individuals. Using addictive game mechanics and behavioral psychology techniques can lead to compulsive engagement, obsession, and negative consequences.

However, it is crucial to recognize that gamification is not inherently wrong. You can utilize gamification for positive and beneficial purposes. By adopting responsible and ethical practices, you can leverage gamification to motivate and engage users in ways that promote positive behaviors and enhance their overall experiences.

For example, our *Hi-Z Fitness* app uses gamification to motivate users to engage in regular physical activity, set achievable goals, and track their progress. The app can offer rewards and incentives for reaching milestones, creating a sense of achievement and satisfaction. By incorporating elements of challenge, progress, and social interaction, the app can inspire users to maintain a healthy and active lifestyle.

Similarly, educational platforms can leverage gamification to enhance learning experiences. Product leaders can create an engaging and interactive environment that motivates users to acquire new knowledge and skills by incorporating game-like elements such as quizzes, levels, and leaderboards. Gamification can provide a sense of accomplishment, encourage healthy competition, and foster a love for learning.

You should aim to design gamified experiences that prioritize user well-being and avoid the pitfalls identified in *Addiction by Design,* like how casinos use variable reward systems and sensory manipulation to exploit psychological vulnerabilities, leading players into compulsive gambling behaviors that can result in significant financial and personal harm. We should avoid manipulating users into addictive behaviors and, instead, focus on creating meaningful interactions that empower users, foster personal growth, and promote healthy habits.

To ensure that people use gamification for good rather than evil, product leaders must adhere to ethical guidelines and prioritize user well-being. You should consider the potentially addictive nature of gamified experiences and actively work to mitigate any adverse effects. Regular user feedback, data analysis, and continuous evaluation of the impact of gamification strategies are essential to maintain a responsible approach.

It should be part of your routine to stay informed about evolving ethical guidelines, industry best practices, and legal requirements. You should proactively seek out resources, engage in industry discussions, and participate in professional development opportunities to deepen your understanding of ethical considerations in gamification, and in product development more broadly.

Balancing gamification and user privacy

Balancing gamification and user privacy is critical to designing ethical and responsible gamified experiences. In today's digital landscape, where personal data is increasingly vulnerable, you must prioritize the privacy and security of your users. This section will delve into the intricacies of this balance, providing you with insights and strategies to navigate the complexities of data collection, storage, and usage while implementing gamification.

One of the most critical aspects of balancing gamification and user privacy is ensuring compliance with privacy regulations. In today's digital landscape, privacy regulations such as the **General Data Protection Regulation (GDPR)** are crucial in safeguarding user data and privacy rights. Compliance with these regulations is essential to maintain the trust of your users and avoid legal repercussions. Therefore, it is imperative to familiarize yourself with the relevant privacy regulations and ensure that your gamification strategies align with the legal requirements.

Under the GDPR, businesses must obtain explicit user consent for data collection, storage, and processing. The right way to do this means clearly explaining to users what data will be collected and how you will use it, and obtaining their permission before proceeding. When implementing gamification, you must ensure that your user consent mechanisms are transparent, easily accessible, and provide clear options for users to provide or withdraw consent.

Transparency is critical in building trust, so clearly outline how user data will be protected, stored, and used in the context of gamification. Additionally, it is crucial to communicate your data handling practices, including any third-party involvement, to your users. Regularly review and update your privacy policies to reflect changes in your gamification strategy or data handling practices.

Moreover, if your business operates in California, you must comply with the **California Consumer Privacy Act (CCPA)**. The CCPA grants California residents specific rights regarding personal information and imposes certain obligations on businesses that collect and process such data. Please familiarize yourself with the requirements of the CCPA (`https://oag.ca.gov/privacy/ccpa`), including providing opt-out mechanisms for users to opt out of the sale of their personal information and enabling users to request access and deletion.

To ensure compliance, consider implementing robust data protection measures, such as data encryption, access controls, and secure data storage. Regularly assess and audit your gamification systems and processes to identify privacy risks or vulnerabilities. Working closely with legal and privacy experts is also advisable to ensure that your gamification strategies align with the regulatory landscape and adhere to the best privacy and data protection practices.

By prioritizing compliance with privacy regulations such as the GDPR and CCPA, you demonstrate a commitment to protecting user privacy and data security. These steps help you avoid legal issues and foster trust among your users, leading to enhanced user engagement and long-term success in your gamification efforts.

Anonymization and aggregation of data

Anonymization and aggregation of data are strategies that can strike a balance between gamification and user privacy. Instead of storing and analyzing individual user data, product leaders can focus on aggregated and anonymized data that provides insights at a broader level without compromising individual privacy. This approach allows for effectively implementing gamification techniques while respecting user confidentiality.

Let's consider an example of how product leaders can apply the strategy of anonymization and data aggregation in a gamification context. Imagine a fitness tracking app incorporating gamified elements to motivate users to engage in physical activities and achieve their fitness goals.

Traditionally, the app might collect and store individual user data, including personal details, exercise routines, and health metrics. However, to strike a balance between gamification and user privacy, product leaders can adopt anonymization and aggregation techniques.

Instead of storing identifiable user data, the app can anonymize the data by removing **personally identifiable information (PII)** such as names, email addresses, and social media profiles. This process ensures that individual user identities are protected, addressing privacy concerns.

Furthermore, you can aggregate the anonymized data to derive valuable insights at a broader level. For example, instead of analyzing specific user exercise routines or health data, the app can focus on aggregated metrics such as the total number of steps taken, average calories burned, or the overall improvement in fitness levels. These aggregated insights provide meaningful information without compromising the privacy of individual users.

By anonymizing and aggregating data, your product can effectively implement gamification techniques while respecting user confidentiality. For instance, your product can offer challenges and leaderboards based on aggregated data, allowing users to compete with others anonymously without exposing personal information. This approach maintains privacy while still fostering a sense of competition and motivation among users.

Additionally, you can use anonymized and aggregated data for product improvement and research purposes. You can analyze the trends and patterns in the aggregated data to identify areas for enhancing the app's features, optimizing the gamification elements, or developing personalized recommendations for users. This data-driven approach can lead to iterative improvements and a more tailored user experience, all while preserving user privacy.

User control and consent

User control and consent play a pivotal role in balancing gamification and privacy. You should provide users with granular control over their data, allowing them to customize their privacy settings and choose the level of participation in gamified experiences. Empowering users with control over their data reinforces their trust and strengthens the ethical foundation of gamification initiatives.

Let's explore an example of how product leaders can empower users with control and consent in gamification to ensure a balanced approach to privacy.

Imagine a mobile gaming app incorporating gamified features to engage and motivate users. To respect user privacy, product leaders can implement robust privacy settings that offer granular control over personal data sharing and participation in gamified activities.

Users can find options to customize their privacy preferences within the app's settings. For instance, they can choose whether to share their gameplay data with other users, participate in leaderboards, or receive personalized recommendations based on their gaming behavior. By providing these options, you allow users to decide how much they want to engage with gamification elements and share their data.

Users should be able to make informed decisions about their data sharing based on clearly understanding how your product will utilize it within the gamification context. Furthermore, you can ensure transparency and informed consent by clearly explaining the purposes for which the users' data will be used. You should present this information in a user-friendly way, using plain language that is easy to understand.

You can also offer features such as data deletion and account deletion options to enhance user control and consent. Users should be able to delete their data from the app's servers and permanently close their accounts if they no longer wish to participate in gamification activities. By providing these options, you respect the users' right to control their personal information and safeguard privacy.

By prioritizing user control and consent, you establish a foundation of trust and transparency with your users. Empowering users to decide about their data and participate in gamification experiences demonstrates a commitment to user privacy and ethical practices. This approach respects the individual's privacy rights and enhances the overall user experience by allowing users to tailor their engagement with gamified features according to their preferences.

User control and consent are essential elements in maintaining the balance between gamification and privacy. Product leaders who provide users with granular control over their data and empower them to make informed decisions contribute to a more ethical and privacy-focused gamification approach. By prioritizing user privacy, you can build trust, strengthen user engagement, and create positive user experiences within your gamified products.

Accessibility to all users

Ensuring that gamification is accessible to all users is not only a matter of inclusivity but also a legal and ethical responsibility. By considering accessibility from the early stages of gamification design, product leaders can create experiences that can be enjoyed by a diverse range of users, regardless of their abilities or specific needs.

One of the fundamental principles in making gamification accessible is adhering to established accessibility standards, such as the **Web Content Accessibility Guidelines** (**WCAG**). These guidelines provide a comprehensive framework for designing and developing digital content that is accessible to individuals with disabilities. You should familiarize yourself with WCAG and incorporate the principles in your gamification strategies.

Accessibility ensures that users with visual impairments or screen readers can access the necessary information. To make gamification accessible, you can implement various techniques and practices. For example, you can ensure that visual elements, such as game instructions or progress indicators, accompany clear and concise textual descriptions.

Additionally, consider your gamification interfaces' usability for individuals with motor impairments or mobility issues. The process may involve designing user interfaces that people with special needs can easily navigate using keyboard shortcuts or alternative input methods, such as voice commands or adaptive controllers.

Another critical aspect of accessibility is providing options for customization and personalization. You can allow users to adjust the visual appearance, color schemes, or font sizes to meet their needs. This flexibility ensures that users with visual impairments or cognitive disabilities can tailor the gamified experience according to their preferences.

Furthermore, you should be mindful of the content and language used in gamification. You should aim for clear and concise instructions, avoiding jargon or complex terminology that may pose challenges for users with cognitive or learning disabilities. Providing multiple modes of communication, such as text, audio, and visual cues, can also enhance accessibility and accommodate different learning styles.

Testing and user feedback play a crucial role in ensuring the accessibility of gamified experiences. User testing can provide valuable insights into potential challenges or areas for improvement, enabling product leaders to refine their gamification strategies and make them more accessible. You should conduct usability tests with individuals who have diverse abilities and incorporate their feedback to identify and address any accessibility barriers.

Let's consider a case study of *Product Management Media* and how product leaders can make gamification accessible to all users within its context.

Product Management Media incorporates gamified elements to encourage user engagement and participation to share best practices about product development. The app allows users to earn points, badges, and virtual rewards based on their activity and interactions within the platform.

To make gamification accessible in this scenario, you can implement several strategies:

- **Visual Accessibility**: Ensuring that the app's interface is visually accessible involves providing high-contrast options, allowing users to adjust font sizes, and avoiding color combinations that may be difficult for individuals with visual impairments to perceive. The flexibility allows users with different visual needs to navigate the app comfortably.

- **Textual Descriptions**: Accompanying visual elements with textual descriptions is crucial for users with visual impairments. You can ensure that images, icons, and visual cues used in the gamified features are accompanied by concise and descriptive alt text or labels. The text allows screen readers to convey the information to users who rely on auditory cues.

- **Keyboard Navigation**: Enabling keyboard navigation is essential for users with motor impairments or who prefer alternative input methods. You should ensure users can navigate the gamification features and menus using keyboard shortcuts without relying solely on mouse or touch interactions.

- **Customization Options**: Allowing users to customize the app's appearance and interaction preferences enhances accessibility. You can provide options for adjusting color schemes, font sizes, and contrast levels to cater to individual users' needs. This flexibility empowers users to personalize the app based on visual preferences and accessibility requirements.

- **Clear and Concise Instructions**: Clear and easy-to-understand instructions are essential for users with cognitive disabilities or language barriers. Avoiding jargon and complex terminology ensures that instructions are easily understandable for all users. You should use plain language and concise explanations to guide users through the gamified features.

- **Usability Testing with Diverse Users**: Conducting usability tests with individuals with diverse abilities is crucial for identifying accessibility barriers and gathering feedback. You can invite users with disabilities to test the app's gamification features and provide feedback on their accessibility. This feedback can inform improvements and ensure that the app meets the needs of a broad user base.

By implementing these strategies, you can make the gamification features of *Product Management Media* more accessible to all users. This inclusivity enhances user engagement, fosters a sense of belonging, and ensures that individuals with disabilities can fully participate in the gamified experience. It demonstrates a commitment to accessibility and enables a broader range of users to enjoy the benefits and rewards of the app's gamification elements.

In conclusion, making gamification accessible to all users is a crucial aspect of responsible and inclusive design. Product leaders should familiarize themselves with accessibility guidelines, adopt inclusive design practices, and involve users with diverse abilities in the development process. By doing so, they can create gamified experiences that provide equal opportunities for engagement, foster inclusivity, and enhance the overall user experience.

Ensuring gamification doesn't harm the user experience

While gamification is defined as the application of game elements and mechanics to non-game contexts to engage and motivate individuals to achieve specific goals or behaviors, it should never compromise the overall user experience. In this section, you, as product leaders, will explore the delicate balance between gamification elements and the seamless user experience. You will learn about the common pitfalls and challenges that can arise, such as overwhelming users with excessive game mechanics or distracting them from the product's primary purpose. By understanding the principles of good user experience design and conducting thorough user testing, designers can strike the right balance and ensure that gamification elements enhance, rather than hinder, the overall user experience.

Legend of Zelda: Tears of the Kingdom (2023)

One of the most popular and well-respected franchises in Nintendo's impressive lineup is the Legend of Zelda. The first game in the series was released for the American market in 1987 on the Nintendo Entertainment System (the Japanese release was more than a year before that). Since then, it has seen more than a dozen games and inspired countless others with its mix of action, exploration, and puzzle solving. The two core releases in the franchise for the Nintendo Switch (this and 2017's Breath of the Wild) are both considered to be two of the best in the franchise, and if you have the time both are highly recommended plays if you want to understand why games can be so captivating.

This latest iteration of the Zelda franchise is truly one of the pinnacles of the series. But one of the things that Zelda games do best is present tons of content without feeling overwhelming. Many products introduce gamification, but the tasks and features can grow to feel more like a burden to the users than genuine fun. Even many mobile games can have the same effect on players if not designed well. Game elements should not feel like chores, if they did nobody would want to sit down and play a game to relax. If you can, try playing just a bit of Tears of the Kingdom (or any of the Zelda games from the last 10 years), and pay attention to the gigantic amount of content there is. Yet, you are fully able and encouraged to take it at your own pace. Both Tears of the Kingdom and Breath of the Wild (The two core Zelda games for the Nintendo Switch) present you with a giant open world full of secrets, inhabitants, and differing terrain. But right from the start, they offer you the ability to go wherever you want, at whatever pace you want. There are hundreds of quests and tasks that you can complete for a reward, but none of them are shouting at you to complete them in an off-putting way. Not only should we be looking to games for new and fun mechanics to use in our products, but a great game understands the pacing of these mechanics as well. It is worth studying games like this to understand why people love playing games.

Let's consider a hypothetical example of the *Hi-Z Fitness* app. The app's primary purpose is to help users track their daily physical activity, set fitness goals, and provide insights into their progress.

However, let's say we love gamification too much and overwhelm users with excessive game mechanics; it can distract them from their fitness goals and compromise the overall user experience. For instance, look at the following examples:

- **Excessive Badges and Achievements**: The app inundates users with many badges and achievements for every small action, such as taking a certain number of steps, reaching a specific calorie burn, or completing a short workout. While badges can be motivational, too many may dilute their significance and make the app feel cluttered.

- **Complex Game-Like Challenges**: The app introduces complex game-like challenges requiring users to complete tasks, solve puzzles, or compete with other users. While these challenges may be fun for some, they can overwhelm users who want to track their fitness progress without engaging in elaborate game scenarios.

- **Endless Notifications and Popups**: The app bombards users with constant notifications, popups, and alerts related to the gamification elements. This constant interruption disrupts the user experience, making it difficult for users to focus on their fitness goals or engage with the app's core features.

- **Unnecessary Virtual Rewards**: The app introduces virtual rewards, such as virtual currencies, virtual goods, or leaderboard rankings, without real-world value or direct impact on the users' fitness journey. These virtual rewards may distract users from their primary goal of improving their physical well-being and shift their focus toward accumulating virtual possessions.

In these scenarios, the excessive game mechanics and distractions remove the app's core purpose of promoting fitness and hinder the users' ability to track their progress effectively. Product leaders should carefully consider the balance between gamification elements and the primary objectives of the app to ensure that users' goals are not overshadowed or compromised by unnecessary game-like features.

Instead, the focus should be on integrating meaningful and relevant gamification elements that enhance the user experience without detracting from the app's core purpose. These gamification elements should seamlessly align with the app's primary purpose, motivating and empowering users to reach their fitness goals while maintaining a user-centered experience. For example, they could introduce small, meaningful rewards for achieving specific fitness milestones, provide personalized progress insights and recommendations, or offer social features encouraging users to connect and support each other in their fitness journeys.

You must maintain a seamless user experience while incorporating gamification elements. To reiterate what we've learned so far, be sure to focus on these strategies to ensure that gamification does not harm the user experience:

- **Clear Objectives**: Clearly define the objectives of the gamification elements and align them with the overall purpose of the product. Ensure that the gamified features complement the product's core functionality rather than diverting attention or creating unnecessary complexity.

- **User-Centric Design**: Put the user at the center of the design process. Conduct user research and testing to understand their needs, preferences, and pain points. Incorporate gamification elements to add value to the users' journey and align with their motivations.

- **Simplicity and Clarity**: Keep the gamification elements simple and easy to understand. Avoid overwhelming users with excessive game mechanics, complex rules, or confusing instructions. Use clear, concise language, intuitive visual cues, and logical progression to guide users through the gamified experience.

- **Contextual Relevance**: Ensure the gamification elements are contextually relevant and meaningful to the user. Consider the users' goals, interests, and preferences when designing the gamified features. Tailor the experience to provide value, motivation, and enjoyment based on the users' context.

- **Feedback and Progression**: Provide timely and meaningful feedback to users as they engage with the gamification elements. Use visual indicators, progress bars, and notifications to communicate their progress, achievements, and rewards. This feedback should be informative, motivating, and reinforce the users' sense of accomplishment.

- **Seamless Integration**: Integrate the gamification elements seamlessly into the product's interface and user flow. Ensure that the gamification elements enhance the overall flow and feel like a cohesive part of the user experience. Avoid creating disjointed experiences or interrupting the users' natural interaction with the product.

- **Iterative Testing and Improvement**: Continuously test and iterate on the gamification elements to refine and improve their impact on the user experience. This iterative process allows ongoing optimization and ensures that the gamification elements evolve in sync with user needs and preferences. Gather user feedback, conduct A/B testing, and analyze user behavior data to identify areas of improvement.

By following these principles, you can balance gamification and user experience, ensuring that the inclusion of gamified elements enhances the overall product experience without detracting from its core functionality or overwhelming users. The goal is to create a seamless, engaging, and delightful user experience that leverages gamification to drive desired behaviors and provide value to the users.

Avoiding common pitfalls and mistakes

In gamification theory, resonating with users and providing an enjoyable experience is critical for success. This concept holds across different domains, including gaming and product development. To illustrate this point, let's delve into one of the most infamous games of all time: *E.T. the Extra-Terrestrial* for the Atari 2600, released in 1982.

E.T. serves as a cautionary tale due to the rushed production process aimed at meeting the holiday season sales deadline. Unfortunately, this haste severely impacted the game's overall experience. The mechanics could have been better designed, objectives needed to be more apparent, and numerous technology glitches plagued the gameplay. Players grew frustrated with repetitive tasks, unclear objectives, and clunky controls. The most glaring visual flaw was E.T. constantly falling into pits, making progress extremely challenging. The absence of clear goals, tedious gameplay, and crude visuals rendered the game utterly unenjoyable, leading to its commercial failure.

From this example, we can draw valuable lessons. Whether designing a game or incorporating gamification into a product, ensuring that the gameplay mechanics are enjoyable is crucial, allowing users to progress and engage with the experience. Additionally, allocating adequate time and resources to bring your vision to fruition and achieve the best possible outcome is essential. However, it's essential to acknowledge the "Triple Constraint" principle, which asserts that simultaneously optimizing time, cost, and quality is impossible. Let's explore each factor more closely:

- **Time** is the project's schedule and the speed at which you can complete the work. Prioritizing time means meeting tight deadlines, delivering results promptly, and completing the project quickly.

- **Cost** refers to the project's budget and the allocated financial resources. Emphasizing cost optimization involves keeping expenses low, managing resources efficiently, and delivering within the given budgetary constraints.

- **Quality** refers to the project's standards, encompassing excellence and meeting stakeholder expectations. Prioritizing quality entails delivering an outcome of high quality, satisfying the required criteria, and effectively meeting users' needs.

Balancing these factors necessitates making trade-offs and managing them carefully to find the optimal equilibrium. For instance, prioritizing speed and cost may compromise the quality of the outcome. Conversely, prioritizing high-quality results may require more time and resources, thus increasing costs. It is an art that product leaders must master. The actual skill lies in striking the right balance, managing these constraints effectively, and ensuring the delivery of a remarkable product that resonates with users.

By taking these lessons to heart and understanding the interplay between user experience, game design, and project management, you can create engaging and successful gamified experiences that captivate users and drive meaningful outcomes.

Pac-Man (1980)

One of the longest-running, best-selling, and highest-grossing video game franchises in history, and the game has seen regular releases for over 40 years. Pac-Man is one of the most recognizable characters in not only games but pop culture as a whole. Originally an arcade-only title, it has gone on to release games for nearly every home gaming console and even inspired the first-ever interactive Google Doodle in 2010 for its 30th anniversary.

Although many people credit E.T. with being the death blow to the Atari 2600 console, it is likely that the port of Pac-Man to the system was equally damaging. In 1982, after its popularity as an arcade cabinet was soaring, Atari looked to bring the blockbuster game to its own home console. However, the port was horrible, and that is being kind. Consumers spent their money on a game cartridge expecting to be able to play the same Pac-Man they knew and loved, but the graphics were atrocious, the gameplay was significantly clunkier, and it simply was not fun. This is a classic example of when you do not give the proper attention to the triangle of Time-Cost-Quality. Try and get your hands on both versions of this game and see for yourself the difference between the two. The arcade version was given proper time to make sure the quality was there, even if its purpose was to raid the pockets of its players for every quarter they had! Whereas the Atari 2600 port was a rushed cash grab that at the very least aided in the fall of Atari from customers' good graces.

Behavioral insights

When it comes to gamification, one of the challenges you may encounter is the varying responses people have to different psychological factors. It's important to understand that only some are equally influenced by strategies such as pre-commitment pledges and loss-aversion techniques. These psychological factors can impact motivation and accountability differently for each individual.

The reason behind this variation lies in factors such as personality traits, cultural background, and personal preferences. As you incorporate behavioral insights into your gamification approach, it's crucial to recognize and adapt to these diverse responses.

Gathering user feedback and conducting thorough testing is essential to overcome this challenge. By actively seeking input from your target audience and testing different approaches, you can gain insights into their preferences and motivations. This knowledge enables you to tailor the gamification elements to better resonate with different user segments, enhancing engagement and desired actions.

Additionally, it's essential to employ a multi-faceted approach rather than relying solely on one or two behavioral techniques. You can create a more comprehensive and inclusive experience by incorporating various strategies within your gamification design. For example, don't just add a leaderboard because your users may not respond to recognition as a driver. Add gamification options such as progress tracking, group challenges, and personalized rewards. This approach acknowledges the individual variability in user responses and increases the likelihood of engagement across a broader audience.

In summary, as you delve into gamification, it's crucial to understand that people respond differently to various psychological factors. You can address this challenge effectively by actively seeking user feedback, conducting thorough testing, and employing a diverse range of behavioral insights. Remember to adapt your gamification approach to cater to different user preferences and maximize the impact of your efforts.

Another example of mistakes from prominent literature

Avoiding common pitfalls and mistakes is a broad term and can be subjective, so I wanted to reference other points of view. The article *Behavioral Economics: Improving Health Care by Gamifying It* offers valuable insights into avoiding common pitfalls and mistakes, leading to improved healthcare outcomes. By incorporating behavioral economic principles into gamification strategies, healthcare providers can enhance their interventions and better engage patients in behavior change:

- One of the key lessons from the article is the importance of engaging participation, especially among high-risk patients. Traditional approaches often frame participation as an opt-in decision, resulting in relatively low enrollment rates. However, the article highlights the effectiveness of opt-out framing, where patients are automatically enrolled in programs but can withdraw if they wish. This simple adjustment significantly improves participation rates, demonstrating the power of subtle changes in program design. These are specific points I want you to know about if you are trying to gamify healthcare: instead of waiting or trying to get users to opt in, automatically enroll them, and if they aren't interested, they can opt out. The opt-in approach has been proven to significantly increase participation rates by three times. By removing the burden of actively joining a program, individuals are more likely to engage and explore the benefits of gamified interventions. Automatic enrollment makes it easier for users to get started and reduces barriers to entry.

- Don't set the same goal for everyone, and make the goal more demanding over time and adapt it to the user's performance. Research has shown that setting personalized goals based on an individual's capabilities and progress enhances engagement. This approach has been associated with increases in retention and participation in health programs. This personalized approach acknowledges individual differences and ensures that goals remain challenging yet achievable. By tailoring goals to each user's starting point and gradually increasing the difficulty, individuals are more motivated to strive for continuous improvement.

- Have users sign a pledge to stick to their goals. This simple technique helps people stick to their goals by holding them accountable. Pledges create a psychological commitment reinforcing individuals' determination to achieve their desired outcomes. By committing and signing a pledge, individuals feel responsible and are more likely to stay motivated and dedicated to their health objectives.

- Give something up front and then take it away if they don't meet their goals. This strategy leverages the principle of loss aversion, which shows that people are more motivated to avoid losing something they already have than to gain an equivalent new benefit. By providing users with rewards or incentives at the beginning and linking their retention to their continued progress, individuals are more motivated to maintain their efforts to avoid losing the initial rewards they received. This approach creates a sense of urgency and encourages users to stay committed to their goals. It also carries the risk of alienating your user base and should be avoided unless necessary.

- Users may disengage at one point or another. Establish regular increments that refresh points or benefits to account for occasional lapses or periods of reduced engagement. By providing individuals with a fresh start at regular intervals, such as weekly, the program encourages them to re-engage and regain their momentum. This approach recognizes that setbacks are common and allows individuals to recover and continue their progress toward their goals.

- Social incentives encourage collaboration, accountability, and peer support. By incorporating social incentives into gamified interventions, such as recognizing individual achievements within a community or rewarding group progress, individuals are motivated to collaborate, support one another, and remain accountable. Social incentives leverage the principle of anticipated regret, as individuals fear letting others down and falling short of shared goals. The social aspect fosters a sense of collective responsibility and creates a supportive environment where individuals feel motivated to stay on track.

By implementing these strategies derived from the principles of *Behavioral Economics*, you can design gamification experiences that effectively engage users, improve participation rates, and drive positive behavior change. These insights highlight the importance of personalization, accountability, loss aversion, periodic refreshments, and social dynamics in creating successful gamified interventions.

Summary

In summary, ensuring the success of gamification in your product requires careful attention to several crucial factors. First and foremost, it is vital to keep gamification ethical by designing fair and transparent elements that respect user rights. Avoid manipulative techniques and allow users to engage or disengage as they choose. Balancing gamification and user privacy is also essential. Handle user data responsibly, follow privacy regulations, and obtain explicit consent while communicating how you will use personal data to enhance the gamified experience.

Another crucial consideration is accessibility. Make sure that gamification is inclusive and accessible to all users, regardless of their abilities. Incorporate inclusive design principles, provide alternative options for interaction, and make accommodations to cater to different user needs.

To maintain a positive user experience, ensure that gamification elements enhance, rather than hinder, the overall product experience. Avoid excessive or intrusive gamification that may disrupt the user journey or create frustration. Take a user-centric approach by continuously gathering user feedback and refining the gamified experience.

Lastly, be aware of common pitfalls and mistakes in gamification implementation. Avoid overcomplicating the design, relying solely on extrinsic rewards, or neglecting intrinsic motivation factors. Strive for a balanced approach that integrates game mechanics into the product experience.

Gamification is a powerful tool that can profoundly impact user behavior. With great power comes great responsibility. When designing gamified systems, be driven by serving your users, not exploiting them. Seek to motivate and engage, not manipulate. Use game elements to enhance well-being, foster community, spread joy, and promote positive interactions. Avoid overly addictive loops or the misuse of private data. Instead, build experiences that respect autonomy and bring out the best in people. Wield the influence of gamification for good, not for greed. With a careful, ethical design focused on creating value, not extracting it, gamification can improve lives and contribute to the greater good. So, be a force for empowerment. Unleash motivating experiences that move people and organizations forward. And may the rewards you reap stem from lives enriched, progress unlocked, and a job well done. The world needs that game now more than ever. And you have the power to play.

In the next chapter, we will explore how to sell your gamification strategy to your stakeholders and target market.

Further reading

- Liu, De; Lowry, Paul; Landers, Richard; Nah, Fiona; and Santhanam, Radhika, *Developing Gamification Research in Information Systems* (2022). AMCIS 2022 TREOs. 99. `https://aisel.aisnet.org/treos_amcis2022/99`

- Patel, M.S., Chang, S., & Volpp, K.G., *Behavioral Economics: Improving Health Care by Gamifying It*, Harvard Business Review, 2019 Retrieved from `https://hbr.org/2019/05/improving-health-care-by-gamifying-it`

9

Selling Your Gamification Strategy

Now that you know how to design and implement game mechanics in your product and have read about successful examples, this chapter focuses on the steps involved in selling and promoting a gamification strategy to stakeholders and securing buy-in for the project. The chapter covers the importance of building the business case for gamification, securing leadership buy-in, working with cross-functional teams, and developing a **go-to-market (GTM)** strategy. It emphasizes the importance of demonstrating the benefits and potential **return on investment (ROI)** of the gamification strategy, engaging leadership and cross-functional teams in the decision-making process, and aligning the gamification strategy with the goals and objectives of the business. The chapter provides guidance on how to effectively sell and promote a gamification strategy and how to ensure its success and impact on the business.

We will cover the following topics:

- Building your business case
- Leadership buy-in
- Go-to-market strategy
- Cross Functional Teams
- Case Studies

Gamification has become a force to be reckoned with in the world of business. As organizations strive to create engaging experiences and differentiate themselves in a competitive market, gamification has emerged as a potent tool to drive growth, increase customer retention, and foster innovation. This chapter will discuss the art of crafting a business case for gamification, complete with examples and statistics to bolster your argument.

Building your business case

To begin, let's consider the fundamental reasons why gamification works. At its core, gamification leverages our innate psychological tendencies – the desire for competition, the joy of achievement, and the thrill of mastery – to create a captivating experience. This experience drives user engagement, resulting in higher satisfaction levels and increased loyalty. For instance, Duolingo, the language learning app, utilizes gamification to make learning enjoyable and addictive. The app has successfully amassed over 500 million users worldwide and boasts a daily active user count in the millions.

In addition to boosting engagement, gamification can be a powerful tool for motivating employees and enhancing productivity. A study by TalentLMS found that 87% of employees believed that gamification made them more productive, while 84% reported that it made them feel more engaged with their work (`https://growuperion.com/gamification-business-challenges#:~:text=As%20 the%20TalentLMS%20Gamification%20at,happier%20(82%25)%20at%20 work.&text=to%20the%20human%20culture%2C%20development,why%20 gamification%20works%20so%20well`). Companies such as GuruShots have successfully implemented gamification into their platforms to create an engaging experience that motivates users and keeps them returning for more.

When building your business case for gamification, it's essential to establish clear objectives and align them with your overall business goals. Determine what aspects of your business would benefit the most from gamification – customer engagement, employee motivation, or driving innovation. For example, Noom, the weight loss app, leverages gamification to support users in their weight loss journey. It has successfully retained millions of subscribers, yielding a revenue of over **$400 million** in 2020.

A well-crafted business case for gamification should also include a detailed analysis of the target audience, identifying their needs, preferences, and motivations. This information will be the foundation for your gamification strategy, ensuring that your initiatives resonate with your users and drive the desired outcomes.

To make your case even more compelling, gather relevant statistics and showcase examples of successful gamification initiatives. Data from reputable sources, such as Gartner or the Harvard Business Review, can add credibility to your argument. At the same time, examples such as Strava the fitness app demonstrate the tangible benefits of gamification. Strava's community-driven approach has made it one of the most popular fitness apps globally, boasting over 70 million users.

Crafting a business case with gamification as the primary strategy requires a systematic approach, considering various aspects such as objectives, target audience, and ROI.

Use case – Kahoot

The founders of the game-based learning platform Kahoot clearly understood the power of building a solid business case to validate their idea with stakeholders. They focused on showcasing Kahoot's potential to increase learner engagement and make education more fun by tapping into our natural desire for play.

To demonstrate Kahoot's money-making potential, the founders pointed to their "freemium" model with premium features and analytics for corporate and academic customers, on top of the free basic version. This clearly mapped out a revenue stream to complement the promised engagement benefits.

But they didn't stop there. The Kahoot team ran pilot studies with schools and organizations, generating hard data on how Kahoot boosted knowledge retention compared to traditional study methods. These tangible results from real-world tests helped convince potential investors and customers that the platform could deliver on its interactive, gamified learning promise.

By combining a clear monetization strategy with validated use cases and pilot results, Kahoot developed an impressive business case that helped propel its gamified platform's growth. This shows why product managers should take the time to thoroughly build and test their business case – it provides the necessary foundation to sell stakeholders on funding your gamification vision. A compelling business case demonstrates the viability of your idea and drives momentum during those crucial early stages of development.

Reference: `https://productmint.com/kahoot-business-model-how-does-kahoot-make-money/`.

Step-by-step guide for creating a compelling business case for gamification

To create a compelling business case for gamification, you must define clear objectives, understand the target audience, analyze the current situation, design a comprehensive strategy, estimate costs and ROI, develop risk mitigation plans, create an implementation roadmap, and present a persuasive business case that highlights the potential benefits. By following these steps, you can un7ock the full potential of gamification and reap the rewards of enhanced engagement and improved business performance:

1. **Define your objectives**: Begin by identifying the primary goals you want to achieve through gamification. These include increasing user engagement, boosting sales, enhancing employee productivity, or improving customer loyalty. Ensure that your gamification objectives align with your overall business goals.

2. **Understand your target audience**: Conduct thorough research to understand the needs, preferences, and motivations of your target audience. This information will help you design a gamification strategy that resonates with your users and drives the desired outcomes.

3. **Analyze the current situation**: Evaluate your organization's existing systems, processes, and performance metrics. Identify the areas that could benefit the most from gamification and the potential challenges you might face during implementation.

4. **Research successful gamification examples**: Study successful gamification initiatives in your industry or related fields. Analyze the strategies they employed, the results they achieved, and the lessons they learned. Use these insights to shape your gamification approach.

5. **Design your gamification strategy**: Based on your objectives, target audience, and research, develop a comprehensive gamification strategy. The strategy should include selecting the appropriate game mechanics, dynamics, and rewards to motivate and engage your users.

6. **Estimate costs and ROI**: Calculate the estimated costs of implementing your gamification strategy, including development, marketing, and maintenance expenses. Project the potential ROI by estimating the improvements in **key performance indicators (KPIs)**, such as user engagement, sales, and employee productivity. Make sure the expected benefits justify the investment.

7. **Develop a risk assessment and mitigation plan**: Identify the potential risks and challenges associated with implementing your gamification strategy. Develop a plan to mitigate these risks, considering user acceptance, technical challenges, and potential negative impacts on productivity.

8. **Create an implementation roadmap**: Outline a detailed plan for executing your gamification strategy, including timelines, resources, and milestones. Include a phased approach, starting with a pilot or proof of concept, followed by a full-scale rollout once you have demonstrated initial success.

9. **Present your business case**: Compile all the information gathered in the previous steps into a well-structured and persuasive document or presentation. Use compelling visuals, examples, and statistics to support your argument and address potential concerns or objections.

10. **Monitor and refine your strategy**: After implementing your gamification strategy, track the impact on your KPIs and gather feedback from users and stakeholders. Use this information to refine your strategy, making adjustments to ensure it remains effective and aligned with your objectives.

By following these steps, you can craft a robust business case for gamification that demonstrates its value to your organization and paves the way for a successful implementation. But you have to go above and beyond. Gamification is complex; some people will only understand if the value is crystal clear. So be bold and take risks. Use your strengths and personality to get your business case funded. Charm and wit can often be the secret sauce that elevates your business case from good to great. Or it can be intelligent statistics or quotes from someone you know the stakeholder admires. When presenting your argument, use whatever is your lucky charm, what makes you unique, to engage your audience and make your message more memorable.

Among Us (2018)

An online multiplayer social game developed and published by Innersloth. The game was inspired by the common in-person party game Mafia and the science fiction horror film The Thing. Although released in 2018, the game didn't take off until 2020, spurred by people being placed on various levels of lock down during the COVID pandemic. The game also got a significant boost in popularity as it was a common game for many game streamers and content creators.

Often times making a great pitch takes a bit of persuasion. Among Us can be a great way to hone exactly that skill. To succeed at this game of deception and logical deduction skills you have to not only be able to see through the lies people tell but be able to persuade others yourself. The game is incredibly simple on the surface, but when played with a group of individuals who know each other (as opposed to a random lobby of players online), it takes on a life of its own. It can also be a great team building exercise with your cross-functional groups (try it out after your next long retrospective or postmortem meeting).

It would be best to build a winning business case for gamification based on a solid foundation of clear objectives, a deep understanding of your target audience, and relevant examples and statistics. By approaching the process with your best personality traits, you can captivate your audience and make a compelling case for gamification as a driver of success in your organization.

Now that we have explored how to create a compelling business case for gamification, let us turn our attention to the crucial aspect of securing leadership buy-in.

Leadership buy-in

Creating buy-in from your leadership team to fund a product driven by gamification requires strategic thinking, persuasive communication, and relationship-building skills. In the following sections, we will explain Barbara Minto's Pyramid Principle and Dale Carnegie's guidelines to help you effectively present your case and secure the support of your leadership team.

Identify your central idea or essential message to apply the Pyramid Principle to your gamification proposal. This concise statement should capture the essence of your proposal, such as "*Gamification can significantly improve user engagement and drive business results.*"

Next, break down your central idea into logical groupings of supporting arguments. You will base your groupings on different aspects of gamification, such as its impact on user behavior, psychological principles underlying its effectiveness, and thriving industry examples. Provide evidence and data to support your claims within each grouping, such as research findings, case studies, and testimonials.

To maintain coherence and flow, do the following:

1. Order your groupings in a way that builds a compelling narrative.
2. Start with the most critical and persuasive arguments, and then gradually move to more secondary points.
3. Ensure your information is presented in a hierarchical structure, each level providing more detail and depth to support the overall argument.

Example of utilizing the Pyramid Principle

The product manager presents their case to the stakeholders using Minto's Pyramid Principle, starting with a clear central idea and breaking it down into logical groupings of supporting arguments. In her book, Barbara Minto emphasizes the significance of leading with a strong central idea when communicating or presenting information. According to Minto, the central idea serves as the guiding force that shapes the entire structure of your message. By clearly articulating the central idea at the beginning, you establish a clear focus and provide a framework for your audience to follow. This approach ensures that your message remains concise, logical, and coherent, preventing confusion and helping your audience grasp the key point you are trying to convey. Leading with the central idea sets the stage for effective communication, enabling you to capture your audience's attention and engage them from the outset. It helps you establish a connection with your audience by clearly stating the purpose and relevance of your message. By emphasizing the central idea, you create a strong and memorable impression, making it more likely that your audience will remember and act upon your message. Overall, Minto highlights the importance of leading with a central idea as a powerful strategy for effective communication and influencing others.

Central idea: *"Incorporating gamification into our new product will significantly improve user engagement, retention, and satisfaction, leading to increased revenue and market share."*

Supporting arguments play a critical role in effective communication and persuasive discourse. When presenting a case, idea, or proposal, it is essential to back it up with strong and well-structured supporting arguments. These arguments serve as the foundation upon which your message stands, providing evidence, logic, and reasoning to support your main point. They add credibility to your assertions and help you convince your audience of the validity and value of your ideas. By crafting compelling supporting arguments, you demonstrate thorough research, critical thinking, and the ability to anticipate and address counterarguments. Effective supporting arguments engage your audience, build trust, and enhance the overall persuasiveness of your communication. They form the backbone of a well-structured and convincing narrative, enabling you to influence others, win their support, and drive positive outcomes.

Supporting arguments

- Psychological principles underlying gamification
- Successful industry examples
- Anticipated benefits and ROI
- Addressing concerns and risks

Argument 1 – psychological principles underlying gamification

- The product manager explains how gamification taps into innate human desires for achievement, competition, and social interaction
- They detail how gamification elements such as points, badges, and leaderboards motivate users to engage with the product more frequently and for extended periods
- The product manager cites research on the effectiveness of gamification, showing that it can lead to increased engagement and satisfaction

Argument 2 – successful industry examples

- The product manager presents several successful examples of companies incorporating gamification into their products, such as Duolingo, Strava, and Noom
- They discuss these companies' specific gamification strategies and their impact on user engagement, retention, and satisfaction

- The product manager highlights the impressive business results achieved by these companies, demonstrating the potential for similar success in their product

Argument 3 – anticipated benefits and ROI

- The product manager estimates the expected increase in user engagement, retention, and satisfaction that gamification can bring to their product
- They translate these metrics into tangible financial benefits for the company, such as increased revenue and market share
- The product manager emphasizes the long-term value of gamification, arguing that it can help create a loyal and engaged user base that will continue to drive business growth

Argument 4 – addressing concerns and risks

- The product manager acknowledges potential concerns and risks related to gamification, such as user burnout, a distraction from core product features, and implementation challenges
- They provide solutions to and mitigating strategies for these concerns, demonstrating their thorough understanding of the topic and instilling confidence in the stakeholders
- The product manager reiterates the potential benefits of gamification and argues that the potential rewards far outweigh the risks

By presenting their case using Minto's Pyramid Principle, the product manager effectively communicates the value of incorporating gamification into their new product. They provide a clear, logical, and persuasive argument that addresses the concerns of the stakeholders and showcases the potential benefits and ROI of a gamification strategy. As a result, the stakeholders are more likely to be convinced of the proposal's merits and support the product manager's vision.

Relationship building

While presenting your case, focus on the needs and priorities of your leadership team. Consider their goals, challenges, and concerns, and frame your argument in a way that speaks directly to these issues. Show how gamification can help them achieve their objectives, whether increasing revenue, reducing costs, or improving employee engagement.

> ### Microsoft Viva Goals (2021)
>
> Previously a start-up known as Ally.io, this OKR tracking suite was acquired by Microsoft in 2021 and subsequently moved into Microsoft Viva. This tool allows companies to have full transparency of their OKRs and allows employees down the hierarchy to add their own key results that roll up to a higher objective. Ot then displays and tracks progress in a clean and visual way.
>
> One way to fast-track approval of gamification features, is to build it directly into key results that roll up to executive team objectives. With tools like Viva Goals, as teams are solidifying OKRs you can see what each department is aiming to complete. You can often find objectives that could be helped with gamification. Reaching out directly to the owner of an objective and explaining that your gamification project could be used to obtain an additional key result within their objective can help them see the value of these features in a highly relatable scenario. If your team doesn't use Viva for OKRs, the same concept applies to any OKR tool. And if your team doesn't use OKRs at all, suggesting their adoption can be a great start to the gamification topic in whole.

In his timeless classic *How to Win Friends and Influence People*, Dale Carnegie shares a wealth of principles that have stood the test of time in human relations. These principles serve as a guide to building strong relationships, fostering influence, and achieving personal and professional success. Carnegie's principles revolve around the fundamental understanding that people have a deep desire to feel important and appreciated. By tapping into this basic human need, we can cultivate meaningful connections and exert a positive influence on others.

The principles outlined by Carnegie emphasize the importance of empathy, active listening, and genuine interest in others. He encourages us to genuinely care about people and their perspectives, fostering a sense of understanding and respect. Carnegie also emphasizes the power of praise and recognition, as well as the art of expressing ideas in a way that resonates with others. He teaches us to refrain from criticizing, condemning, or complaining, as these tendencies only serve to damage relationships and hinder personal growth.

The principles in *How to Win Friends and Influence People* are important because they offer practical guidance on how to navigate social interactions, build rapport, and inspire others to collaborate and support our goals. By applying these principles, we can cultivate a positive environment where people feel valued, understood, and motivated. Ultimately, Carnegie's principles highlight the transformative power of human connection and provide a roadmap for achieving success through effective communication, influence, and building lasting relationships.

To incorporate these principles into your gamification proposal, consider the following:

- **Develop a genuine interest in your leadership team**: Understand its goals, challenges, and concerns, and tailor your proposal to address these issues. Show that you have taken the time to research and empathize with its perspective.

- **Be a good listener**: Encourage your leadership team to share its thoughts and actively listen to its feedback. By doing so, you will not only demonstrate respect and appreciation for its input but also gain valuable insights to refine your proposal.

- **Make the other person feel important**: Acknowledge the expertise and contributions of your leadership team, and emphasize the crucial role it plays in the success of the proposed gamification initiative.

- **Appeal to the nobler motives**: Frame your proposal in a way that highlights the broader positive impact of gamification, such as its potential to enhance employee well-being, foster a culture of innovation, and contribute to the organization's long-term success.

- **Dramatize your ideas**: Use storytelling to bring your argument to life. Share real-life examples and anecdotes that illustrate the impact of gamification on users, employees, and organizations. Making your case relatable and emotionally resonant will make it more compelling and memorable for your leadership team.

In addition to incorporating the Pyramid Principle and Carnegie's guidelines, be prepared to address potential objections and concerns during the discussion. Identify possible risks and challenges associated with gamification and present well-thought-out solutions. By acknowledging and addressing potential issues upfront, you will demonstrate your commitment to the success of the project and your understanding of the broader organizational context.

Combining a well-structured argument based on the Pyramid Principle, emotional appeal inspired by Carnegie's principles, and empathetic communication, you can create buy-in from your leadership team to fund a product driven by gamification. Present a compelling case, build rapport, and address concerns to secure the support you need for your gamification initiative.

Use case – Atlassian

The Atlassian team embarked on a journey of launching its new software, Jira Service Management, into an already crowded market space. Robert Lodge, the brand marketing lead, thought of something different, a little outside the box. The idea was simple yet offbeat – market the software using a fictional metal band as the face of the campaign. It was an unusual choice, breaking away from the common tech marketing trope of polished, safe, and predictable messaging. Instead, the team dared to dive into the uncharted waters of blending enterprise software promotion with fictional metal band members who lived double lives as IT admins and developers.

Engaging key stakeholders right from the onset was crucial. Lodge and his team prioritized strategic fit, justifying the risks and constant communication with stakeholders to pull off this seemingly outlandish idea. They brought together a diverse group of subject-matter experts to ensure the alignment of the campaign with the broader company strategies. By justifying the risks, they were able to convey why an unusual approach was not just relevant but also necessary. The team believed in continuous feedback and early stakeholder involvement, leading to a more collaborative and supportive environment for the out-of-the-box idea.

This Atlassian tale is an essential read for product managers. It emphasizes the importance of being innovative, taking calculated risks, and getting buy-in from stakeholders for such risks. In a world filled with similar products and fierce competition, it's crucial for product managers to think differently and dare to be disruptive while still maintaining strategic alignment. And as the story suggests, a commitment to collaboration and open communication with stakeholders is key. Even unconventional ideas can gain traction when they are transparently and effectively communicated and when they resonate with broader business objectives. This tale highlights the importance of daring to be different, backing up your ideas with sound reasoning, and fostering a collaborative environment to ensure your product stands out.

Source: `https://www.atlassian.com/blog/teamwork/getting-buy-in-calculated-risks`.

Now that we have explored the importance of gaining leadership buy-in, let us shift our focus to engaging with cross-functional teams to ensure alignment and collaboration.

Cross-functional teams

In the fast-paced and collaborative world of business, achieving alignment and commitment from different functional teams is essential to drive the success of a gamification strategy. As a product manager, engaging with these teams and ensuring their support for the gamification vision is a critical aspect of achieving your goals. By following a thoughtful and collaborative approach, product managers can effectively engage functional teams and harness their expertise to drive the success of gamification initiatives.

To engage functional teams and secure their commitment, product managers should follow a strategic framework that encompasses several key steps:

1. **Establish a clear vision**: Begin by defining a compelling vision that articulates the objectives, benefits, and impact of the gamification strategy. This vision should be rooted in the broader goals and values of the organization, making it easy for every team to understand the relevance and importance of gamification.

2. **Tailor the message**: Customize communication for each functional team, highlighting how gamification can address their unique concerns and interests. Emphasize specific benefits related to their KPIs and demonstrate how gamification can contribute to achieving their targets and objectives.

3. **Foster collaboration**: Create a collaborative environment by organizing cross-functional workshops or meetings where teams can openly share insights, knowledge, and ideas. Encourage teams to collaborate, problem-solve, and contribute to the gamification strategy, fostering a sense of ownership and commitment among all stakeholders.

4. **Establish effective communication channels**: Set up clear communication channels and processes to keep teams informed and engaged throughout the gamification journey. Regular updates, meetings, and shared dashboards can provide transparency, facilitate knowledge sharing, and maintain alignment across functional teams.

5. **Encourage feedback and iteration**: Foster a culture of continuous improvement by actively seeking feedback from each functional team. Leverage their expertise to refine and optimize the gamification strategy, addressing potential challenges, and identifying opportunities for enhancement.

6. **Leverage champions**: Identify influential champions within each functional team who can advocate for the gamification strategy and inspire their colleagues. These champions can play a crucial role in promoting the benefits of gamification, addressing concerns, and fostering a positive and supportive environment for its implementation.

7. **Set KPIs and track progress**: Collaborate with functional teams to define KPIs that align with the gamification strategy. Regularly track and share progress against these KPIs, providing visibility into the impact of gamification and celebrating milestones achieved along the way.

8. **Celebrate milestones and achievements**: Recognize and celebrate the accomplishments of each functional team throughout the gamification journey. By acknowledging their hard work and contributions, you reinforce the value of their efforts and create a sense of camaraderie and shared accomplishment, motivating continued engagement and commitment.

To illustrate the impact of team alignment, let's consider a real-life example. Imagine a product manager tasked with implementing a gamification strategy to enhance employee productivity in a large corporation. By involving teams early in the process, understanding their concerns, and tailoring the gamification approach to address their needs, the product manager fosters a collaborative environment. Through cross-functional workshops, employees from different departments share their insights and ideas, contributing to the strategy's development.

In one instance, when articulating the benefits of gamification to the marketing team, the product manager emphasizes how gamification can generate buzz, drive user acquisition, and increase brand loyalty. The marketing team sees the potential to create engaging campaigns that leverage gamified elements to captivate its target audience, with KPIs such as increased website traffic, higher conversion rates, and improved customer engagement.

Similarly, when discussing with the customer service team, the product manager highlights how gamification can reduce customer churn and enhance satisfaction by creating more enjoyable and rewarding experiences. The customer service team envisions how gamification can empower its representatives to provide personalized support and foster stronger customer relationships, with KPIs such as improved customer retention rates, higher customer satisfaction scores, and reduced average handling time.

By involving functional teams in setting KPIs and tracking progress, the product manager ensures that each team has a clear understanding of their contributions to the gamification strategy's success. Regular monitoring of these KPIs allows teams to see the impact of their efforts and make data-driven decisions for continuous improvement. Celebrating milestones and achievements along the way reinforces the collective commitment and motivates teams to maintain their engagement and drive.

In conclusion, engaging with functional teams and ensuring their alignment and commitment to a gamification strategy is a journey that requires careful planning, effective communication, collaboration, and continuous improvement. By articulating a clear vision, involving teams early in the process, fostering collaboration, tracking progress through relevant KPIs, and celebrating achievements, the product manager can successfully secure functional teams' commitment and drive the gamification initiative's success. By learning from the best practices of successful gamification strategies and applying these principles to their projects, product managers can harness the power of gamification to create more engaging and effective products that deliver lasting value for their organizations.

With leadership buy-in secured and cross-functional teams engaged, we can now turn our attention to developing a comprehensive GTM strategy.

GTM strategy

Developing and implementing a GTM strategy for a product driven by gamification is a multifaceted process that requires a deep understanding of the target audience, a clear vision for the product's value proposition, and a robust plan for reaching and engaging potential customers. By following a systematic and collaborative approach, product managers can successfully bring their gamified products to market, capitalizing on the unique benefits of gamification to drive user engagement and deliver lasting value for their organizations.

When you start thinking about the GTM strategy, it's essential to have the cross-functional relationships established that we covered in the last section—a successful product launch results from multiple teams utilizing their strengths and working together. Before your full-blown product release, you should have had a beta test with a ratio determined by your overall addressable market. All too often, we have seen GTM planning as an afterthought or starting when the product is close to being finished. GTM planning should begin when you start the design phase. It would be best if you had a kick-off with your cross-functional teams, and it gives everyone involved time for planning and task management.

Collaboration with cross-functional teams is critical to the successful development and execution of a GTM strategy. This collaboration is crucial for gamified products, as the unique nature of these offerings may require specialized expertise from various teams to communicate their value to potential customers effectively. Product managers must work closely with marketing, sales, customer support, strategy, data, and engineering teams to ensure that all aspects of the product launch and ongoing promotion are aligned and well coordinated.

Let's explore the key responsibilities and contributions of each team in this gamification journey:

- **Strategy**: Work with your strategy or leadership team to set KPIs that align with the organization's objectives. Within those objectives, this team should establish an ideal customer profile that is easily understood. Determine your product's pricing model, position, and price points based on research and expertise. Pricing is both an art and a science and will take some experimentation and adjustment. This team is also responsible for aligning the organization with product goals and setting expectations.

- **Sales**: Ensure the team is trained and understands the value proposition and price points of the product they will sell. Explain how the strategy team determined the pricing and why it will sell for the allotted amount. Use your gamification skills, design a competition, and give rewards and recognition to the members of sales team who kick it off. Work with the sales team to plan their appearances at conferences and events involving the target market.

- **Marketing**: Include a mix of promotional activities that highlights the engaging and interactive nature of the product. These could include targeted advertising campaigns, social media promotion, influencer partnerships, and content marketing efforts demonstrating the product's gamification elements. Craft a compelling narrative around the gamified product and showcase its unique benefits, generating excitement and interest among their target audience. Be bold, get creative, and design some of your gamification activities to get your coworkers to like and share your product on their digital channels.

- **Data and analytics**: Work with the team to establish a system for monitoring and measuring your GTM strategy's success. Implement a robust analytics infrastructure to track progress against the KPIs you established. It's important that early in the launch process, you gather feedback and make necessary adjustments while continually evaluating the effectiveness of your GTM efforts. Product managers can identify areas for improvement and refine their approach as needed, ensuring that their gamified product continues to resonate with its target audience and deliver value for the organization.

- **Customer service**: The product could be better; there will be issues, problems, returns, and refunds. Customers are going to have questions. Your customer service team is the first line of defense and can be the difference between an angry ex-customer who bashes your product on social media and a product champion who advocates for you because you took the time to care for them. Make sure you train your customer service team in the product mindset. Your training plan should include setting expectations, understanding the agile process, and letting them know what updates and releases are on the horizon, which bugs are logged, and what the team is working on in the current sprint. Your customer service team also has rich datasets. You should be aligning with it and the data team to provide insights to drive continual improvement, new feature releases, and adjustment of your gamification content.

Case study – Apple Watch

The story of the Apple Watch's GTM strategy generates intrigue, anticipation, and the usual Apple flair for creating drama and excitement around a product launch. It's a narrative that revolves around emotion, human connection, and the desire to sell a product and create an experience.

In the lead-up to the Apple Watch launch, Apple realized that its usual GTM strategy would need to be revised. The Apple Watch was a new product category for it and wasn't just another tech gadget. It was a fashion statement, a health monitor, a communication device, and so much more. Recognizing this, Apple crafted a launch strategy appealing to diverse customer segments:

- Apple leaned heavily into storytelling. They crafted a narrative around the Apple Watch focused on how it could enhance and enrich people's lives. They showcased how the watch could help individuals stay connected, track their fitness, and even navigate unfamiliar cities with a simple wrist flick. They even brought in high-profile celebrities and athletes to share their stories of how the Apple Watch had changed their lives, creating an emotional connection with potential customers.

- Apple's strategy leveraged exclusivity and scarcity to create a sense of urgency. In the initial weeks after the launch, the Apple Watch was only available for purchase through Apple's website, and the company also limited the number of watches available. The purposeful restriction created a sense of exclusivity and scarcity, making the Apple Watch a must-have item.

- Apple expanded its retail strategy to include high-end fashion retailers. They understood that the Apple Watch wasn't just a technology but a fashion accessory. By partnering with luxury retailers, Apple was able to reach a new audience and position the Apple Watch as a high-end, desirable accessory.

- Apple invested heavily in customer education. Recognizing that the Apple Watch represented a new way of interacting with technology, they created a series of educational resources, including videos and in-store experiences, to help customers understand the benefits and functionalities of the watch.

The launch of the Apple Watch was a resounding success, with Apple selling out its initial stock within six hours of the product being available for pre-order. The product also garnered positive reviews from critics and consumers alike, further solidifying Apple's reputation as a leader in innovation.

The Apple Watch's GTM strategy is a testament to its ability to understand its customers, craft a compelling narrative, and create a product that is not just useful but also deeply personal. It highlights the importance of understanding your audience, telling a compelling story, and creating an experience beyond the product. It's a strategy that other companies can learn from.

Designing and implementing a GTM strategy for a gamified product requires a thoughtful, data-driven, and collaborative approach from the product manager. By understanding the target audience, developing a clear vision for the product's value proposition, and working closely with cross-functional teams to execute a comprehensive marketing plan, product managers can successfully bring their gamified

products to market and capitalize on the unique benefits of gamification to drive user engagement and deliver lasting value for their organizations.

Case study – GuruShots

GuruShots, an online platform that gamifies photography, employed a GTM strategy that revolved around leveraging existing social networks and the inherent attributes of the photography community to drive user acquisition and retention.

- **Community-driven user acquisition**: Understanding that photographers, both professional and hobbyist, often operate within communities where they share their work and seek feedback, GuruShots anchored its user acquisition strategy around these pre-existing communities. The platform made sharing challenges and photos on other social media platforms seamless, which amplified their organic reach.

- **Social sharing**: GuruShots integrated their platform with users' existing social networks to drive organic growth. Users were incentivized to invite their peers to join the platform to participate in challenges and provide feedback, integrating the product experience with social and competitive elements that encouraged consistent user engagement and growth.

- **Brand story and positioning**: The company positioned itself under the inclusive brand story *Anyone Can Take Great Photos*. By creating an environment that caters to all levels of photography skill, GuruShots was able to attract a wide range of users, from beginners to professionals. This allowed them to tap into a larger market and foster an environment of learning and growth, making the platform attractive to a wide array of photography enthusiasts.

- **User education**: GuruShots utilized education as part of its GTM strategy. By providing resources for photography tips and tricks, as well as a platform for peer feedback, GuruShots ensured user retention by positioning itself not just as a competitive platform but also as a tool for continuous learning and improvement in photography.

The GuruShots case study serves as a great example of a successful GTM strategy that leverages existing communities and social networks for growth, utilizes compelling branding to attract a wider market, and employs user education as a tool for retention. As a product manager, understanding and applying these strategies can be vital in bringing a gamified product successfully to market.

Case study – Peloton

Peloton, a connected fitness company best known for its exercise bikes and digital workouts, implemented a GTM strategy that pivoted on community building, premium positioning, and comprehensive user experience:

- **Building a community**: Recognizing the motivating power of social engagement, Peloton developed a strategy to foster a strong community. Users could participate in live classes compete on leaderboards, and follow each other's progress. This community-focused strategy not only helped retain users but also boosted organic growth as users evangelized Peloton within their personal networks.

- **Premium positioning**: Peloton positioned itself as a premium product, offering high-quality equipment and elite trainers. This helped the brand to attract an affluent customer base that valued the superior experience Peloton offered.

- **Complete user experience**: Peloton's GTM strategy was centered on providing a holistic user experience. The company combined hardware (the bike), software (the subscription service), and content (the classes) to ensure a seamless, top-notch experience for users. This not only justified their premium pricing but also created a high barrier to entry for potential competitors.

- **Celebrity involvement**: To create buzz and add credibility to their brand, Peloton involved celebrities and famous athletes in their workouts. This allowed them to tap into the fan base of these celebrities, extending their reach.

- **Investment in content**: Peloton's investment in high-quality content, including a variety of live and on-demand classes, helped retain users and provided a unique selling proposition.

The Peloton case study is an example of how a strategic GTM strategy can leverage community-building, premium positioning, and a comprehensive user experience to successfully bring a product to market. For product managers, these elements are crucial when developing a GTM strategy for their products.

Summary

In this chapter, we explored the key aspects of building a compelling business case for gamification and ensuring its successful implementation within an organization. By understanding how to structure and build a business case, we learned how to effectively articulate the benefits of gamification and align them with the organization's objectives. We also delved into the strategies for gaining leadership buy-in and securing support for our gamification strategy, emphasizing the importance of persuasive arguments and showcasing the value proposition of gamification.

Furthermore, we discussed the significance of engaging with cross-functional teams to ensure alignment on the mission and outcomes of gamification. By involving different teams early in the process, we foster a sense of ownership and commitment to the gamification strategy, leveraging their expertise and contributions to drive success.

Lastly, we explored the concept of a GTM strategy and its role in launching a gamified product. Understanding the components of a GTM strategy and the necessary steps to execute it effectively is crucial for a successful product launch and adoption.

By following these principles and leveraging the benefits of gamification, organizations can unlock the full potential of this powerful strategy to enhance user engagement, drive innovation, and achieve their business objectives. With a well-structured business case, leadership buy-in, cross-functional alignment, and a robust GTM strategy, organizations can embark on a successful gamification journey and reap the rewards of a highly engaging and impactful product.

The next chapter will dive into activities to help you gamify your product development process.

Further reading

- Minto, Barbara, *The Pyramid Principle: Logic in Writing and Thinking*, Minto International, Inc., 2010.

- Carnegie, Dale, *How to Win Friends and Influence People*, Simon & Schuster, 1936.

10

Gamifying Your Product Development Processes

In this chapter, we'll explore the fascinating world of gamifying your product development process, taking a deep dive into the techniques, principles, and best practices that make this approach so powerful. We aim to provide you with the skills and knowledge necessary to create a more engaging and motivating environment for your team and stakeholders, fostering innovation and collaboration.

Throughout this chapter, we will cover various aspects of gamification in the product development process, including ideation, prototyping, implementation, and post-launch iterations. By understanding and mastering these concepts, you will acquire a unique set of skills that can transform the way you approach product management.

By reading this chapter, you will gain valuable insights into how to effectively incorporate game mechanics and dynamics into your product development process. You will learn how to design and implement engaging activities that promote teamwork, creativity, and a sense of accomplishment among your team members. Moreover, you will discover how to align these gamification elements with your business objectives, ensuring that the process remains focused on delivering value to both your users and stakeholders.

The benefits of these skills are manifold, ranging from increased employee motivation and satisfaction to improved product quality and faster time to market. By gamifying your product development process, you will be better equipped to navigate the complex and ever-changing landscape of product management, ultimately driving success and growth for your organization. So, let's embark on this exciting journey and discover the true potential of gamification in product development.

We've broken down some of our favorite activities, or games, you should play with your team or stakeholder into three sections – new product development, product management, and product implementation. These sections state that the activities are taking place in person. You can also design all of the activities listed here on a digital whiteboard, and they will have their own sticky notes and voting process.

We will cover the following topics in this chapter:

- Utilizing design thinking to create custom gamified processes

- Gamifying the new product development processes

- Gamifying the product management processes

- Gamifying the product implementation processes

The draft game

Ladies and gentlemen, welcome to the bi-weekly Developer Baseball Draft – an innovative, engaging, and fun way to turn your product development process into a game. Picture this: you and your fellow developers, the core of the company's lineup, are gearing up for the next sprint. Today isn't your ordinary run-of-the-mill planning session; this is the grandest baseball-themed draft the world of software engineering has ever seen.

The atmosphere in the room is electric as the anticipation builds. You and your six teammates, united by months of camaraderie and a shared passion for creating outstanding products, gather around to await the big reveal. The coach-like product manager strides in, emulating the confidence of Alex Rodriguez, and unveils the scoreboard: 35 tantalizing tickets, each representing a diverse range of user stories, bugs, and technical debt.

Questions race through your mind like Ricky Henderson stealing a base as you survey the tasks before you: Will I be the MVP of this sprint? What matchup suits me the best? And who is Ricky Henderson?

Before the draft begins, a vital step must commence: determining the draft order. The product manager, ever-resourceful, brandishes a sacred baseball cap. Within its depths lie little paper balls, each inscribed with a destiny-defining number. The air is tense as the product manager passes the cap around the room – your hand trembles as you reach in to claim your fate. You unravel the paper ball: number three! Not bad, not superb, but hey, you're drafting in the heart of the lineup.

With the batting order set, the draft commences. An ominous clock ticks down, giving engineers 60 seconds to select their preferred ticket. The pressure is on; any engineer who fails to choose in time will be assigned a task from the top of the ticket pile as if struck by an unpredictable curveball.

The draft process incorporates a blend of story points and spare time estimates to gauge the complexity and effort involved in each task. A rule of thumb dictates that anything over 80 story points is an epic, requiring further dissection into smaller, more manageable chunks. Velocity history provides invaluable insights into each engineer's capabilities, revealing that, on average, they can handle a workload of 10 story points per sprint.

As the draft unfolds, the first two developers snatch up the best picks – a shiny new UI and a tantalizing API integration, both rated at 8 points. Each engineer dreams of hitting a grand slam with these high-value tasks, hoping to cement their reputation as power hitters.

You, the daring base stealer, choose a different path. Opting for the great login bug mystery and a solid 5-pointer, you secure a more manageable task, leaving room for minor challenges later in the sprint. Like a versatile utility player, you value variety in your workload.

The draft plows on, with engineers selecting tasks based on their preferences and skill sets. Once they reach their 10-point capacity, they sit back, their hunger for tickets satisfied. The draft continues until every ticket has found a home.

But wait, there's more: trade time! This phase of the draft encourages collaboration and negotiation, allowing developers to optimize their sprints according to their strengths. Your keen eye spots a potential trade: a backend API ticket swap for a few measly UI tickets. You strike a deal, confident in your skills as a backend engineer.

To keep the draft order fresh and maintain a competitive spirit, the engineer with the least impressive performance in the previous sprint gets to draft first in the next sprint. This friendly rivalry taps into the engineers' deepest desires, fueling motivation and productivity.

The Developer Baseball Draft is a delightful spectacle. It's engaging, it's addictive, and it brings the team closer, weaving a tapestry of laughter and fond memories. Who could forget that fateful trade where the underestimated bug grew four times more formidable? Ah, the sweet taste of risk! Your pioneering development pod's success has hit a home run, boosting results by a whopping 20% since the games began.

The baseball-themed draft has transformed your product development process, injecting it with the same excitement and energy in a nail-biting baseball game. To pull it off, you must intimately understand your users, craft a riveting narrative, and seamlessly integrate game mechanics with a compelling beginning, middle, and end.

This draft strategy can be adapted to different teams and projects, making it an invaluable tool for product leaders. By creating a game that caters to your unique band of warriors and aligns with your strategic goals, you ensure the continued success of your product development process.

In conclusion, the Developer Baseball Draft is a powerful way to keep your team engaged, motivated, and focused on delivering high-quality products. By incorporating elements of competition, collaboration, and strategic thinking, you can create an environment that fosters growth, learning, and a sense of camaraderie. The result? A winning team that consistently hits it out of the park.

So, gather your teammates, don your baseball caps, and prepare to play ball! The bi-weekly Developer Baseball Draft is about to begin, and you have a ticket to the most engaging and productive game in town. Batter up, and may the best developer win!

We wrote that from the engineer's perspective because empathizing with the user is one of our first rules when creating a product or gamified activity. Put yourself in their position. Imagine the world around you from their perspective. In this chapter, we will discuss how to use game mechanics and give examples of games you can utilize throughout the product development processes of creating, managing, and launching products.

Yahoo! Fantasy Sports (2008)

Although fantasy football has been around since the mid-80s, since the early 2000s, it has been gaining popularity about as fast as any industry around. Yahoo! launched its Fantasy Football app in 2008, and it has grown to be the most popular fantasy sports application in the world. They offer contests, private leagues for friends, and public leagues that anyone can join. Although football is still the top-played fantasy sport, there are offerings for baseball, basketball, hockey, and even golf!

Of course, not everyone is a sports fan, but under the hood, Fantasy Sports is more of a numbers and analytics game than anything. Spotting trends, understanding comparative analytics, and ultimately getting a little bit lucky on a hunch can make you a winner. It's interesting that taking a spreadsheet and peppering it with some numerical analysis would be considered work… but give it a "Sports!" paint job, and you have a lucrative industry that many players put a full week's worth of hours into. Join a public league yourself and see what you think, or get some fellow PMs together for a season of taunting. Is it just a numbers game? How much do you feel like you need to follow the sport? Just like sprint planning or retrospectives can be a tedious numbers and analysis task, giving them a fresh coat of paint can make them seem a lot more engaging. Speaking of numbers, have you been noticing some in places they shouldn't be around here? Huh, weird…

Utilizing design thinking to create gamified activities for product development

Design thinking is a human-centered, iterative approach to problem-solving that focuses on empathy, experimentation, and collaboration. By incorporating design thinking principles into your product development process, you can develop gamified activities that drive innovation, ideation, development, and implementation. In this introduction, we'll explore how product managers can use design thinking to create engaging and effective gamified activities for your product team. We will cover the following steps:

1. **Empathize**: Understanding your team's needs and motivations
2. **Define**: Setting clear goals and objectives for gamified activities
3. **Ideate**: Brainstorming creative gamification strategies
4. **Prototype**: Designing and testing gamified activities
5. **Implement**: Integrating gamified activities into your product development process

Empathize – understanding your team's needs and motivations

Empathy is the first step in the design thinking process and involves profoundly understanding your team's needs, motivations, and challenges. To create gamified activities that truly engage your team, conduct interviews, surveys, or workshops to learn more about their preferences, goals, and work styles. This information will help you tailor gamification strategies to their unique needs, making the activities more enjoyable and effective.

For example, some team members may be motivated by competition, while others may prefer collaboration. By understanding these differences, you can design various gamified activities that cater to various preferences, ensuring that all team members feel included and motivated to participate.

Define – setting clear goals and objectives for gamified activities

Once you understand your team's needs, the next step is to define clear goals and objectives for your gamified activities. Establish the desired outcomes for each activity, such as generating a specific number of ideas, identifying key customer pain points, or discovering new market opportunities. Setting clear objectives creates a sense of purpose and direction, which can help maintain focus and motivation during the activities.

Ensure that the goals align with your overall product strategy and objectives. This alignment will help ensure that the gamified activities contribute to your broader product vision, driving meaningful progress and results.

Ideate – brainstorming creative gamification strategies

With a clear understanding of your team's needs and the goals of your gamified activities, the next step is ideation. During this phase, brainstorm various creative gamification strategies your team can apply to your product development processes.

Incorporate various game mechanics, such as points, badges, leaderboards, challenges, and rewards, to create a diverse and engaging set of activities. Digital whiteboard tools are a great place to host your games and most have a library with templates that you can use or personalize. Use a Slack plugin such as Pointagram to easily create your leaderboards and badges.

Encourage your team to participate in the ideation process by sharing their ideas and suggestions for gamified activities. Team participation generates more creative options and fosters a sense of ownership and investment.

Prototype – designing and testing gamified activities

Once you have identified potential gamification strategies, the next step is to create prototypes of these activities. Prototyping may involve the following:

- Developing mock-ups of activities
- Designing game systems
- Outlining the rules for an idea contest

Test these prototypes with a small group of team members, gathering feedback on their effectiveness, engagement, and enjoyment. Refer to *Chapter 7* for feedback mechanisms.

Use this feedback to iterate on your prototypes, refining the gamified activities to better align with your team's needs and preferences. This iterative approach ensures that your gamified activities are well-designed and engaging, maximizing their impact on the product development process.

Implement – integrating gamified activities into your product development process

After refining your gamified activities based on feedback, it's time to integrate them into your product development process. Communicate each activity's goals, rules, and benefits to your team, ensuring they understand how to participate and the expectations. Monitor the progress and success of each activity, making adjustments as needed to ensure that they remain engaging and effective.

You might face some challenges here. Your team might be resistant to change and may not be familiar with these approaches, so make sure you include them in the decision-making process and educate them about the benefits of gamification. Over time, the novelty of gamified activities may wear off, so make sure you get continual feedback and rotate your game mechanics and elements to sustain interest and prevent monotony.

By incorporating design thinking principles into creating gamified activities, you can develop a range of engaging, effective, and enjoyable experiences that drive ideation, development, and implementation.

Gamifying your product development process

Now, we are ready to dive into gamifying the product development processes. We decided to break product management processes into three sections – new products and features, product development, and product implementation.

In this section, we will look at how you can gamify select parts during the strategy phase of product development, especially when you're trying to build a new product or feature. We'll review some examples and hypothetical examples of incorporating them into your existing processes.

Gamifying the ideation process

Gamifying the ideation process in product management enhances creativity and innovation by making brainstorming sessions more engaging and enjoyable. The use of game mechanics and collaborative activities encourages diverse perspectives and fosters a sense of camaraderie among team members, ultimately leading to the discovery of novel solutions and a stronger foundation for product development success.

Ideation and innovation sessions

The ideation process is crucial for generating new product ideas and fostering innovation within your team. To gamify this process, you can organize ideation strategy sessions, where team members, and even guests from outside your company, come together to brainstorm and develop innovative solutions. These events create an engaging, cohesive environment that encourages creative thinking and collaboration.

To make the most of these events, establish clear goals, criteria, and time frames. Be clear from the start that the workshop is a safe space, and there are no bad ideas. By using the design thinking framework, you are in the divergence phase, so your goal is to come up with as many ideas as possible. You can create or find a range of games to help you do this.

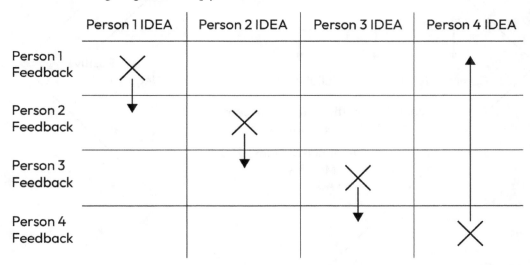

Figure 10.1 – Brainwriting

- **Brainwriting**: In this activity, each participant writes down their ideas on a piece of paper, and then passes it to the next person. The next person builds on the previous idea, adds a new one, or provides feedback. The process continues until everyone has had a chance to contribute to each idea. Brainwriting ensures equal participation and helps generate a large number of ideas quickly.

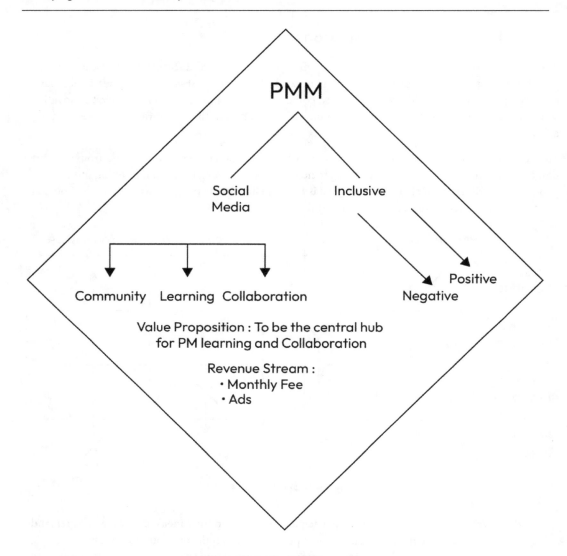

Figure 10.2 – Back of the napkin

- **Back of the napkin**: This technique involves quickly sketching ideas or solutions on a small piece of paper, like the back of a napkin, to encourage spontaneous and rapid idea generation. This approach helps participants focus on the essence of their ideas, overcoming the pressure to create detailed or polished designs.

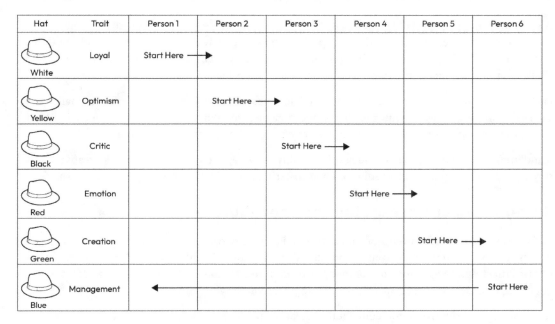

Hat	Trait	Person 1	Person 2	Person 3	Person 4	Person 5	Person 6
White	Loyal	Start Here →					
Yellow	Optimism		Start Here →				
Black	Critic			Start Here →			
Red	Emotion				Start Here →		
Green	Creation					Start Here →	
Blue	Management	←					Start Here

Figure 10.3 – Six Thinking Hats

- **Six Thinking Hats**: This technique, developed by Edward de Bono, involves participants taking on different "hats" or roles in the ideation process. Each hat represents a different way of thinking (for example, optimistic, critical, or creative). By adopting these roles, participants can explore ideas from various perspectives and encourage diverse thinking.

Hypothetical example: Your product team wants to generate new ideas for features that will improve the user experience of your mobile app. You organize your team and bring some others from marketing, sales, and customer service to take part in Brainwriting. The diverse perspectives of various team members build upon each other, and at the end, you have a couple of exciting potential game-changing new feature ideas to test with your users.

Award systems for idea submissions

Another way to gamify the ideation process is by implementing an award system for idea submissions. Encourage team members to share their ideas and suggestions and offer points or badges for each submission. You can also provide additional rewards for implementing ideas or significantly contributing to the product's success.

Create a leaderboard that tracks team members' points or badges to make the process more engaging. The leaderboard fosters healthy competition and motivates team members to submit high-quality ideas. Regularly update the leaderboard and celebrate top contributors to maintain enthusiasm and interest.

A good reference example is MindSumo, a platform that connects organizations with a community of problem solvers, often students and young professionals, to generate innovative ideas and solutions. The platform hosts a variety of challenges for its community members to participate in, with each challenge posing a unique problem that requires creative problem-solving.

Participants on MindSumo can earn points and badges based on their performance in the challenges, such as submitting ideas, providing feedback, and engaging with others on the platform. A leaderboard showcases the top contributors, fostering a competitive and collaborative environment.

MindSumo's gamified approach to idea submissions encourages participants to think creatively and stay engaged, driving innovative solutions and fostering a dynamic community of problem solvers.

Recognizing and rewarding top contributors

Recognition is a powerful motivator, and acknowledging the efforts of top contributors in the ideation process can help maintain engagement and drive participation. Highlight exceptional contributions in team meetings, newsletters, or company-wide communications. Offer tangible rewards, such as gift cards, bonuses, or extra time off, to show appreciation for your efforts.

Recognizing and rewarding top contributors creates a positive feedback loop that encourages team members to continue sharing their ideas and investing in the product's success. The feeling of inclusiveness fosters a culture of innovation and collaboration, which can help your team develop incredible products that stand out in the market. Make sure you make it clear that there are no bad ideas and encourage everyone on your team to participate.

Hypothetical example: During a monthly team meeting, you acknowledge a team member who submitted an idea that significantly improved the product's user experience. You present them with a certificate of recognition and a small token of appreciation, something you know the person will appreciate. For the teammate who's always posting GIFs, I would get them a framed meme or a bag of coffee from their favorite roaster they are always raving about.

Gamifying product vision and strategy development

In this section, we will focus on the transformative approach of introducing game-like elements into the process of shaping product vision and strategic planning. The goal is to ignite creativity, increase engagement, and drive collaborative ideation. Through gamified activities, we seek to align teams around a unified vision and foster innovative strategies, ensuring our products not only resonate with our target audience but also navigate the path to success in an increasingly competitive marketplace.

Collaborative workshops with gamified reward systems

Product vision and strategy development is a necessary process that sets the foundation for the direction and success of your product. To gamify this process, consider organizing collaborative workshops where team members can shape the product vision and strategy. Your goal here is to build off of previous ideas and take a few that the team is aligned on and have potential and dive deeper to see how these products and features will fit into the product teams and their company's overall vision and strategy.

You can use gamified activities during these workshops to encourage participation and engagement:

	Person 1	Person 2	Person 3
Vision for the Product	1	2	3
Risks and Challenges	3	1	2
Mitigation Strategies	2	3	1

Figure 10.4 – Round robin

- **Round robin**: In this activity, participants share their vision in a round-robin format. Each person contributes one piece at a time, and the process continues until all ideas are shared or a predetermined time limit is reached. This approach ensures everyone has an equal opportunity to contribute and helps prevent louder voices from dominating the conversation.

• IDEA: Build the world's
best fitness app

• ARTIFACT: Example
Product or Prototype

S	
Substitute	

Replace one product with another
That works better

C	
Combine	

Put different components together
to improve

A	
Adapt	

Update the product to
new trends

M	
Modify	

Change the appearance and
presentation

P	
Purpose	

Use the product for a purpose
that it cannot inturn fail

E	
Eliminate	

Eliminate all the points that have
limited of no value

R	
Reverse	

De-Construct the product or
design it to do the reverse

Figure 10.5 – SCAMPER

- **SCAMPER: SCAMPER** is an acronym for **Substitute, Combine, Adapt, Modify, Put to another use, Eliminate, and Reverse**. It is a structured brainstorming technique that prompts participants to think about ways to improve or modify a product, service, or process. Teams can generate various innovative ideas by focusing on each of the seven SCAMPER prompts.

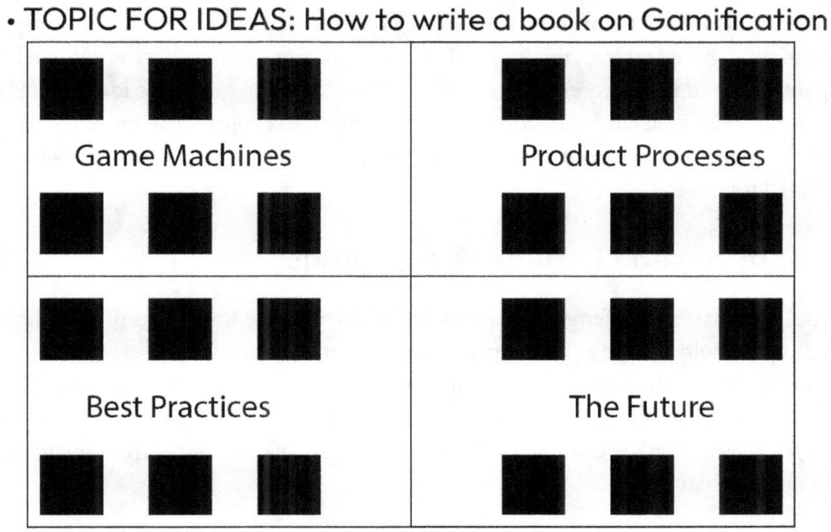

• TOPIC FOR IDEAS: How to write a book on Gamification
Game Machines
Product Processes
Best Practices
The Future

Figure 10.6 – Affinity diagramming

- **Affinity diagramming**: This technique involves grouping ideas based on their similarities or relationships. Participants write their ideas on sticky notes and then organize them on a wall or whiteboard. Visualizing the grouped ideas helps teams identify patterns, themes, and opportunities for collaboration.

IDEA # 1
IDEA # 2
IDEA # 3
IDEA # 4

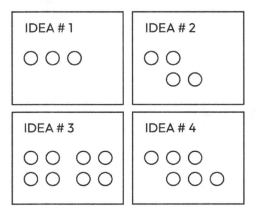

Figure 10.7 – Dot voting

- **Dot voting for prioritization**: Dot voting is a collaborative prioritization technique in which team members have a set number of "dots" or votes to distribute among various options, such as ideas or tasks. The options with the most votes are considered the highest priority and tackled first.

Hypothetical example: Your team must develop a product strategy for the upcoming year. You organize a workshop where team members participate in various gamified activities, such as timed brainstorming sessions and team presentations. You use round robin to get all the ideas out, SCAMPER to improve or modify the idea, and then affinity diagramming to group ideas more challenging and their relationship. After, you use voting techniques to select your vision and strategy ideas so that they move forward together.

Creating team-based challenges and goals

Cross-functional team-based challenges and goals can be an effective way to gamify the development of your product vision and strategy. This approach usually means creating a series of workshops or activities that build up to your goal. Suppose you launch a new product or invest heavily in a new feature. In that case, it's best to align all the teams on the optimal product vision and strategy before the product begins design or development. Here's how to gamify 5ome of the steps to build your product vision and strategy:

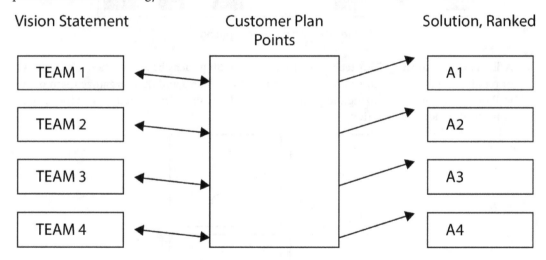

Figure 10.8 – Gamify your strategy

- Cross-functional team breakout sessions where teams create a specific number of potential product visions and strategies within a set time frame

- Identify key customer pain points and align them with the product vision and strategy ideas developed

- Brainstorm and prioritize based on the product vision and strategy to find the solutions that solve the pain points most effectively

- Establish goals and motivate teams by offering rewards or recognition for successful completion

With the unique perspective from cross-functional teams, you are covering more angles and bringing more problem statements to light to ensure your solutions solve real customer problems and determine the priority of those problems together. You can create a more engaging, collaborative, and motivating environment by integrating game mechanics into the product vision and strategy development process. This exercise can lead to a clearer, more innovative product vision and strategy, ultimately driving the success of your product in the market.

Gamifying market research

Market research is essential for understanding your target customers, competitors, and industry trends. To gamify this process, create an internal communication channel on a platform such as Slack or Microsoft Teams that tracks valuable market insights contributed by team members. Assign points for each insight based on its relevance, depth, and potential impact on the product.

Encourage team members to share their findings from various sources, such as customer interviews, surveys, industry reports, or competitor analysis. Update the leaderboard regularly and celebrate top contributors to maintain motivation and engagement.

To create a gamified market research submission and voting system in Slack or Microsoft Teams, follow these steps:

1. Create a new channel.

   For Slack:

   A. Click the + icon next to **Channels** in the left sidebar.

   B. Select **Create a channel**.

   C. Name the channel (for example, `market-research-insights`) and provide a brief description.

   D. Choose the privacy settings (public or private).

   E. Click **Create**.

   For Microsoft Teams:

   A. Navigate to the **Teams** tab in the left sidebar.

   B. Click the ellipsis (three dots) next to your team's name and select **Add channel**.

   C. Name the channel (for example, `market-research-insights`) and provide a brief description.

   D. Choose the privacy settings (standard or private).

   E. Click **Add**.

2. Communicate the purpose and guidelines of the channel to your team members, and invite them to join. Explain that this channel is for submitting market research insights and voting on their relevance, depth, and impact on the product.

3. Encourage users to submit their market research insights as individual messages within the channel, using a consistent format to make it easy for others to review and vote – for example, [Insight] - [Source] - [Brief description].

4. Implement a voting system for the submissions.

    For Slack:

    A. Use emoji reactions as votes. Select three emojis representing relevance, depth, and impact (for example, 💧 for relevance, 🎯 for depth, and 💥 for impact).

    B. Encourage team members to use these emojis as reactions to the submitted insights, with each reaction representing a vote.

    For Microsoft Teams:

    A. Use the **Polly** app to create polls for each submission.

    B. Install Polly in Microsoft Teams if you haven't already.

    C. For each insight submission, create a new poll with the relevance, depth, and impact options.

    D. Encourage team members to vote on each insight using the provided Polly polls.

5. Create a leaderboard to track points.

    For Slack:

    A. Use a Slack app such as **HeyTaco!** or **Disco** to track points based on emoji reactions.

    B. Install the chosen app and configure it to assign points to the selected emojis for relevance, depth, and impact.

    C. Regularly review the leaderboard within the app to recognize top contributors and encourage healthy competition.

    For Microsoft Teams:

    A. Use the Polly app's analytics feature to track points based on poll results.

    B. Regularly review the poll results and manually compile a leaderboard in a shared document (for example, a Google Sheet or Excel file).

    C. Share the leaderboard link in the channel and encourage team members to view their standings, fostering friendly competition.

By following these steps, you can create a Slack or Microsoft Teams channel that encourages users to submit market research insights and vote on their relevance, depth, and impact. The leaderboard will further motivate team members to contribute valuable information and engage in the process. This approach can be used for a variety of gamified processes.

Competitive rewards for achieving milestones in market research

Gamifying market research is an effective way to boost engagement, productivity, and collaboration among team members. By establishing milestones and competitive rewards, you can create an environment that fosters friendly competition and encourages team members to take ownership of their research efforts.

One approach to gamifying market research involves setting clear, measurable milestones with your overall research goals. Here are some examples of such milestones:

- Completing a specified number of customer interviews
- Collecting a target number of survey responses
- Identifying and analyzing a certain number of competitor products

Establishing these milestones helps create structure and direction, ensuring that team members understand their objectives and can work toward them systematically.

In tandem with setting milestones, introduce a competitive rewards system that recognizes and celebrates the achievements of your team members. This system should motivate team members to reach their milestones efficiently and effectively. Consider offering a variety of rewards, such as gift cards, team-building activities, or additional time off, as incentives for individuals who achieve their goals. Providing a range of rewards allows you to understand your team members' diverse preferences, ensuring that the rewards system is appealing and effective for everyone involved.

For instance, imagine that your team is tasked with conducting 50 customer interviews to gather insights into user needs and pain points. You could set a milestone for each team member to complete 10 interviews and offer a small reward, such as a gift card or a free lunch, to the first team member who completes their interviews. To further encourage collaboration and collective effort, you could also introduce a team-based reward, such as a more significant team-building event or a bonus day off if the entire team reaches the collective goal of 50 interviews.

To ensure transparency and maintain momentum throughout the gamification process, consider implementing a visual tracking system to monitor progress toward milestones. The platform could be a digital leaderboard, a shared spreadsheet, or a physical progress chart displayed in the office. By making progress visible to all team members, you can foster a sense of accountability and healthy competition, motivating individuals to push themselves and support their colleagues in achieving their goals.

Regular check-ins and updates on milestone progress help maintain enthusiasm and engagement. Share progress reports during team meetings or via email, and take the time to acknowledge individual and collective achievements, reinforcing the value of the gamified market research process.

RICE scoring for feature prioritization

Incorporate the RICE scoring system for feature prioritization during roadmap creation, and use the points game mechanics within the framework. **RICE** stands for **Reach, Impact, Confidence, and Effort**. Team members assign scores from 1 to 5 to each fact or, and the resulting score helps determine the feature's priority on the roadmap. This method ensures that the priority is the most impactful and feasible features.

Hypothetical example: Your team must decide which features to include in the following product release. Each team member evaluates the proposed features using the RICE framework:

- **Reach**: How many users will this feature affect? two, because the feature is niche.

- **Impact**: What is the potential benefit for users or the business? four, because it will have a big impact on the users that do need it.

- **Confidence**: How certain are we that the feature will have the expected impact? three, because you have some data and a few assumptions.

- **Effort**: How much time and resources will be required to develop the feature? five, since your engineering team says it's complex in nature.

Reach (2) x Impact (4) x Confidence (3) / Effort (5) = RICE Score (4.8).

After evaluating the features using the RICE criteria, team members calculate a RICE score for each feature by multiplying Reach, Impact, and Confidence, then dividing by Effort. Features with the highest RICE scores are prioritized on the roadmap for the upcoming release.

RICE is especially helpful when you are managing a product portfolio. I've used RICE to rank and manage over 100 different product features across the portfolio when the organization had a budget to cover about 30. So, a quantitative scoring system helps with spending less time debating and more time identifying what features have the biggest impact on your product.

Gamifying user experience (UX) design

Integrating gamification into the **user experience** (**UX**) design process offers a range of advantages for product teams, enabling them to address user needs more effectively and create delightful experiences. By making the design process more engaging and stimulating, gamification nurtures creativity and innovation, empowering designers to explore novel solutions and break away from conventional approaches.

Design challenges and competitions

Design challenges and competitions serve as a powerful catalyst to spark creativity, foster collaboration, and engage designers, developers, and stakeholders in the quest for exceptional user experiences. By establishing specific objectives and nurturing a spirit of teamwork, these events can yield innovative solutions that address user needs, elevate product design, and enhance overall user satisfaction.

Consider, for example, a tech company that specializes in smart home devices and is eager to elevate the user experience of its mobile app. In pursuit of this goal, the company organizes a week-long design challenge, assembling cross-functional teams to brainstorm, develop, and refine new UX concepts that tackle common user pain points, such as device setup, customization, or integration with other intelligent home systems.

To infuse the challenge with an exciting, game-like atmosphere, introduce a series of checkpoints or milestones that teams must reach as they progress through the week. These checkpoints could include ideation sessions, user research, wireframing, mock-up creation, and interactive prototype development. By structuring the challenge in this manner, you promote iterative design, encourage teams to build on each other's ideas, and ensure they remain focused on addressing user needs.

After the design challenge, each team presents their work to a panel of judges, comprising UX experts, company executives, and perhaps even a select group of users. Award the winning team recognition and a cash prize. Evaluate their UX concepts for potential integration into the app's upcoming release. This high-stakes presentation adds a competitive edge to the challenge, inspiring teams to bring their best ideas and most polished designs. Incorporating game mechanics and a sense of competition into the design creates an environment that nurtures creativity, collaboration, and innovation. The design challenge becomes an engaging, immersive experience that motivates teams to invest their best efforts, leading to exceptional user experiences that resonate with the target audience and drive product success.

There are risks and challenges to doing design challenges. Your team might create solutions that lack depth or don't solve the core problem. There's also a risk that the team sticks to what's safe rather than exploring creative or innovative solutions, and there is only so much time that can be spent on ideation. To navigate and mitigate these risks, provide a comprehensive problem statement with specific goals and criteria. Set clear expectations and encourage wild ideas, and make sure it's a safe space and your team feels comfortable sharing whatever comes to mind. Make sure you plan ahead so you have enough time to have a thorough creative session and it's not interfering with deadlines. And finally, make sure you have a clear and objective evaluation to ensure a fair assessment of all submissions.

Design challenges and competitions serve as potent tools for engaging and motivating product teams to push the boundaries of their creativity and collaborate in pursuit of exceptional UXs. By structuring the challenge as a game with milestones, competition, and rewards, you foster a dynamic and engaging atmosphere that can lead to groundbreaking solutions, more profound insights into user needs, and a lasting impact on product design and user satisfaction.

Leveling up your UX and UI teams

Achievements and badges are powerful game mechanics to inject excitement, motivation, and a sense of accomplishment into the UX and UI design process. By creating a series of achievements or badges that team members can earn as they progress through various stages, learn new skills, or reach specific goals, you foster an environment that encourages personal growth, celebrates accomplishments, and drives team members to reach their full potential. When creating a badge system, it's crucial to highlight the significance of ensuring that badges symbolize true mastery rather than being granted solely for gamification. In other words, the badges should genuinely represent the team members' skills or achievements, adding credibility to the gamified experience.

To effectively implement achievements and badges in the UX and UI design process, consider the following steps:

1. **Identify key milestones and skills**: Begin by defining the key milestones, skills, or objectives essential to the design process. These might include completing user research, creating wireframes or prototypes, mastering a new design tool, or implementing accessibility best practices.

2. **Design achievements and badges**: Create visually appealing and distinct badges or icons that represent each milestone or skill. Ensure that the design of each badge is consistent with your brand and communicates the achievement's significance. You can even have these designs printed as stickers for a more tangible reward.

3. **Set criteria for earning badges**: Clearly outline the criteria or actions required for team members to earn each badge. This could involve completing a specific task, meeting a performance benchmark, or demonstrating mastery of a particular skill. You can even have these designs printed as stickers for a more tangible reward

4. **Create a progress tracking system**: Develop a system to track each team member's progress toward earning badges. This could be as simple as a shared spreadsheet or as sophisticated as a custom-built digital platform that showcases earned badges and tracks progress in real time.

5. **Celebrate and share achievements**: When a team member earns a badge, celebrate their accomplishment and share it with the rest of the team. This can foster a sense of camaraderie, encourage friendly competition, and motivate others to strive for similar achievements.

6. **Encourage continuous growth**: Use the achievements and badges system to inspire team members to continually improve their skills, pursue new learning opportunities, and contribute to the project's overall success. You could even introduce additional levels or tiers of badges to keep team members engaged and motivated over time.

In this hypothetical example, a UX and UI design team employs a badge system to recognize and reward team members for mastering various relevant skills. Let's look at 20 potential badges, 10 for UX design and 10 for UI design, that demonstrate a professional's expertise in specific areas:

- **UX design badges**:

  - **User Empathy Guru**: Awarded for conducting and analyzing 50+ user interviews to uncover insights and understand user needs

  - **Persona Creator**: Earned by developing and validating 10+ detailed user personas that capture the target audience's characteristics, goals, and pain points

  - **Journey Mapping Expert**: Achieved after creating and refining 10+ user journey maps that illustrate user interactions and experiences with the product

  - **Usability Testing Master**: Awarded for planning, executing, and analyzing 20+ usability tests that provide valuable feedback for product improvements

- **Information Architect**: Earned by designing and implementing 10+ intuitive and user-friendly information architectures for websites or applications

- **Wireframing Whiz**: Achieved after creating 50+ wireframes that effectively communicate design concepts and user interactions

- **Rapid Prototyping Pro**: Awarded for creating and iterating on 20+ interactive prototypes that help validate design ideas and gather user feedback

- **Accessibility Advocate**: Earned by successfully implementing accessibility best practices in 10+ projects, ensuring inclusive design for all users

- **UX Strategy Specialist**: Achieved after devising and executing 5+ successful UX strategies that align with business goals and user needs

- **UX Metrics Analyst**: Awarded for setting, tracking, and analyzing key UX performance indicators in 10+ projects, driving data-informed design improvements

- **UI design badges**:

  - **Visual Design Virtuoso**: Earned after creating 50+ visually stunning and aesthetically pleasing designs that align with brand guidelines

  - **Layout Expert**: Achieved after designing and implementing 20+ effective and user-friendly layouts for websites or applications

  - **Typography Master**: Awarded for demonstrating expertise in typography by applying appropriate font styles, sizes, and spacing in 10+ design projects

  - **Color Theory Connoisseur**: Earned by skillfully applying color theory principles to create harmonious and visually appealing color palettes in 20+ projects

  - **Iconography Ace**: Achieved after designing and integrating 100+ custom icons that effectively communicate function and meaning in user interfaces

  - **Responsive Design Pro**: Awarded for successfully creating and implementing 10+ responsive designs that adapt seamlessly across different devices and screen sizes

  - **UI Animation Wizard**: Earned by designing and implementing 20+ engaging and purposeful UI animations that enhance user experience

  - **Design System Architect**: Achieved after creating and maintaining a comprehensive design system for a company, streamlining UI design processes and ensuring consistency across products

  - **UI Component Craftsman**: Awarded for building and optimizing 50+ reusable UI components that increase design efficiency and ensure a consistent user experience

  - **UI Performance Optimizer**: Earned by identifying and resolving 10+ UI performance bottlenecks, leading to faster loading times and smoother user interactions

By incorporating these badges into your UX and UI design process, you can create a more engaging, motivating, and rewarding work environment that recognizes team members' achievements, encourages continuous learning, and drives professional growth. Once your team has mastered most of these areas, create 20 new ones by running an ideation workshop with your team to get their input and use your market research ability to see what UX and UI skills are the most in demand.

Gamifying product management

The core of a product manager's work is building products, so in this section, we will go through different parts of the product development process and give examples of how to gamify different processes.

Gamifying product development and execution

To build trust and credibility with our stakeholders, we must build our roadmaps to set expectations with milestones and releases. This helps our cross-functional partners plan their work as well. Deadlines don't have to be stressful – gamifying sprint goals and milestones with rewards uses more of the carrot and less of the stick, creating a better work culture for your teams.

Reward systems for meeting development milestones

To gamify product development and execution, implement a reward system for meeting deployment milestones, such as completing a feature, resolving a certain number of bugs, or achieving performance improvements. Offer incentives, such as a half-day Friday or happy hour, to team members who contribute to reaching these milestones.

Sprint-based challenges and rewards

Incorporate sprint-based challenges and rewards to gamify the agile development process. For each sprint, set specific goals or challenges, such as resolving a set number of bugs or completing a high-priority feature. Offer rewards or recognition to team members who contribute significantly to achieving these goals.

Hypothetical example: During a 2-week sprint, your team has a challenge to resolve 30 bugs. The team member who resolves the most bugs during the sprint receives recognition during the next sprint planning meeting and a small token of appreciation, such as lunch with one of your company's senior leaders.

Encouraging cross-functional collaboration in product development

Promote cross-functional collaboration by creating team-based challenges that involve members from different departments or functional areas. These challenges might include the following:

- Collaborating on a feature that requires input from multiple teams (for example, design, development, and marketing)

- Identifying and resolving bottlenecks or inefficiencies in the development process
- Sharing best practices and knowledge between teams to improve overall product development efficiency

Hypothetical example: Your product team, marketing team, and design team collaborate on a challenge to improve the user experience of inbound messaging to the user. They work together to identify user pain points, brainstorm solutions, and implement improvements. Complete the challenge and reward your team with a joint team-building activity such as a night out on the town or a sporting event with all expenses paid.

Gamifying product feedback and continuous improvement

Integrating gamification into product feedback and continuous improvement processes can heighten user engagement and motivate teams to consistently strive for excellence. As a result, this approach facilitates the proactive identification and resolution of product issues, ultimately leading to a more refined, high-quality offering that meets user needs and drives customer satisfaction.

Feedback leaderboards

To gamify product feedback, select or create a platform where you can collect and store your feedback:

1. Create a leaderboard that tracks valuable feedback and suggestions from users and customers.
2. Assign points for each feedback item based on its relevance, depth, and potential impact on the product.
3. Update the leaderboard regularly and communicate with top contributors to maintain motivation and engagement.

Hypothetical example: Your team creates a feedback leaderboard for the newly released feature. Your users can submit feedback by signing up for interviews, filling out the survey embedded in the app, or leaving a review on the app store. The top three contributors with the most valuable feedback at the end of the month received recognition and a small reward, such as being featured on your product website or even in the app itself. Additionally, they received a free month of service, a gift card of their choice, or a donation to a charity they support.

Improvement challenges and rewards

Encourage continuous improvement by creating challenges for team members to identify and implement product improvements. Set specific improvement goals, such as increasing product performance, enhancing usability, or reducing bugs, and offer rewards or recognition to team members who contribute significantly to achieving these goals.

Hypothetical example: Challenge your team to reduce the product's load time by 30% within 2 months. The team member who identifies and implements the most impactful improvement receives an "Optimization Hero" T-shirt.

Gamifying user testing and feedback collection

Gamify user testing and feedback collection by organizing events, such as usability testing marathons or customer feedback sessions, where team members compete to gather the most valuable insights.

Hypothetical example: Your team organizes a usability testing marathon where members conduct back-to-back user testing sessions over 2 days. The team member who collects the most valuable insights and actionable feedback receives the "Customer Whisperer" trophy.

By integrating game mechanics into your product feedback and continuous improvement processes, you can encourage team members to seek and act on feedback to improve the product actively. Transparent communication fosters a culture of continuous learning and growth, helping drive your product's long-term success in the market.

Gamifying gathering requirements

First, I want to align on what this process entails because this is the essential task of a product manager. The best way for product managers to gather requirements, write user stories, and include acceptance criteria that are well understood by the engineering team involves a combination of effective communication, collaboration, and documentation.

Here's a step-by-step process to achieve this:

1. **Collaborate with stakeholders**: Initiate discussions with various stakeholders, including customers, sales, customer support, and engineering, to gather insights about user needs, pain points, and business requirements. Clear communication helps ensure a holistic understanding of what the product should accomplish.

2. **Define clear and concise requirements**: Transform the gathered insights into well-defined, actionable requirements. Please ensure they are **specific, measurable, achievable, relevant, and time-bound (SMART)**.

3. **Write user stories**: Create stories describing how users interact with the product to achieve their goals. User stories should follow the format: "As a [user role], I want to [goal/action], so that [benefit/outcome]." This format helps maintain a user-centric focus and ensures the engineering team understands the context and purpose of each feature.

4. **Include acceptance criteria**: For each user story, provide clear acceptance criteria that define the conditions that must be met for the feature to be considered complete. Attention to detail helps set expectations for the engineering team and ensures a clear understanding of what constitutes a successful implementation.

5. **Create a shared document**: Use a shared platform or tool, such as Jira, Azure DevOps, or Monday, to document user stories and acceptance criteria. Sharing real-time documentation ensures all team members can access the most up-to-date information and collaborate efficiently.

6. **Conduct regular meetings**: Hold regular meetings with the engineering team to discuss user stories, requirements, and acceptance criteria. Encourage open communication and address any questions, ambiguities, or concerns the engineering team might have.

7. **Review and refine**: As the product development progresses, continually review and refine user stories and acceptance criteria based on feedback from the engineering team, user testing, or changes in business requirements.

Gamifying the process

To gamify this process, as you are doing your sprint review, rate the score of the user story by how much detail it entails and how understandable it is for the engineering or design team. You can customize JIRA to be able to score stories and have a leaderboard.

Creating a custom field for scoring user stories and building a dashboard to visualize the scores in Jira involves a few steps. Here's a walkthrough to help you set up this functionality:

1. Create a custom field for scoring user stories:

   A. Go to **Jira Administration** (the cogwheel icon) | **Issues** | **Custom fields**.

   B. Click the **Add custom field** button.

   C. Choose the **Number Field** type, which allows users to input numerical scores for user stories. Click **Next**.

   D. Name the custom field `User Story Score` and provide an optional description. Click **Create**.

   E. Associate the new custom field with the relevant screens where you want the field to be visible (for example, **Create Issue**, **Edit Issue**, or **View Issue**).

2. Add the custom field to the relevant project(s):

   A. Go to the project settings for each project where you want to include the scoring functionality.

   B. Click on **Screens** or **Issue Layout** (depending on your Jira version) and ensure the **User Story Score** field is added to the correct screen(s).

3. Instruct the reviewing team to provide scores for user stories using the new custom field.

4. Create a dashboard to display user story scores:

    A. Go to the Jira main menu (the three horizontal lines icon) and click on **Dashboards |
        Create dashboard**.

    B. Give your dashboard a name, such as `User Story Score Dashboard`, and provide
        an optional description. Click **Create**.

5. Add relevant gadgets to your new dashboard:

    A. Click **Add gadget** on your dashboard.

    B. Search for and add gadgets that will help you visualize the scores, such as **Filter Results**,
        Two-Dimensional Filter Statistics, or **Pie Chart**. Configure each gadget to display the data
        based on the **User Story Score** field and any other relevant fields or filters (for example,
        assignee, project, or issue type).

6. Adjust the layout and sharing settings of your dashboard as needed, ensuring the appropriate
    team members have access to view the data.

Now, your team can score user stories using the custom field you created, and the scores will be visible
on the dashboard you set up. This will help you track the quality of user stories written by each team
member, fostering a sense of friendly competition and motivating team members to improve their
user story writing skills.

Gamifying backlog refinement

Backlog refinement is a crucial part of Agile product management, helping to maintain an up-to-date,
prioritized, and organized product backlog. During these sessions, review the backlog, prioritize items,
estimate the effort, and break down oversized items into smaller tasks. Dependencies and risks should
also be identified and discussed, with strategies developed to mitigate them. This process ensures
that the development team can effectively focus on delivering user value and meeting product goals.

To gamify the actual backlog refinement process, you can create a game that team members can
play together, making it fun and engaging while still achieving the goal of prioritizing, refining, and
organizing the backlog. Let's look at a game idea you can consider.

Backlog adventure

This will involve the following steps:

1. **Preparation**: The product owner or product manager prepares and refines the backlog items
    before the game. These can be printed on cards or displayed on a digital board.

2. **Teams**: Divide the participants into small cross-functional teams. Each team represents an
    "adventuring party" on a quest to conquer the backlog.

3. **Quests:** Assign a backlog item to each team as their initial quest. Each quest represents a challenge the team needs to address, such as prioritizing the item, estimating its effort, or breaking it down into smaller tasks.

4. **Adventure board:** Create a visual representation of the backlog on a physical or digital board, with columns representing different stages of refinement, such as "unprioritized," "prioritized," "estimated," and "ready for a sprint." Each backlog item moves through these stages as teams complete their quests.

5. **Quest completion:** Teams have a limited time (for example, 10 minutes) to complete their quest. They discuss the backlog item, refine it, and move it to the appropriate stage on the adventure board. Once a quest is completed, the team earns points or "treasures."

6. **Bonus challenges:** Introduce bonus challenges during the game, such as identifying dependencies or risks that teams can complete to earn extra points or treasures.

7. **Trading and collaboration:** Teams can trade quests with each other or collaborate on more complex backlog items, encouraging communication and cooperation.

8. **Progression:** As teams complete quests and refine backlog items, they advance through the stages of the adventure board, progressing toward the ultimate goal of refining the entire backlog.

9. **Rewards:** At the end of the game, the team with the most points or treasures is recognized for their achievements, and everyone can enjoy the satisfaction of having played an active role in refining the backlog.

This game concept encourages team members to engage with the backlog refinement process, promotes collaboration, and makes the process more enjoyable while still achieving the objective of refining the product backlog.

Braid (2008)

Released during a sort of golden age of independent games, this one caught the artistic eye of many. With incredibly unique gameplay, a beautiful art style, and a strange story, it was critically acclaimed and won several awards. It and other independent games helped drive the success of the Xbox Live Arcade service, which made independent releases a viable option in the early 2000s for several games that otherwise would have never seen the light of day.

We have discussed storytelling in games, but one way to stretch out both storytelling and puzzle-solving is to do it in a non-linear fashion. Give pieces and clues in random order, and make the users learn how to put them together. This challenge can even add additional fun to the content you have created. Find a copy of Braid and see how it tells its story with puzzle pieces. You find these pieces hidden throughout the world, but then you must put the puzzle together yourself, which only depicts an image that you then must piece together with other images. Using a similar method as a reward for completing tasks might help developers work together, or simply stretch a reward you have created a bit further than usual as they try and solve the puzzle.

Gamifying the Agile development process

Incorporating gamification into Agile development can foster a more dynamic and enjoyable working environment, boosting team morale and productivity. By introducing game elements, you encourage collaboration and healthy competition, leading to higher-quality outcomes and more efficient progress throughout the development cycle.

However, gamification should avoid becoming a distraction from the core work. It is crucial to align gaming mechanics with behaviors and outcomes that advance the development of your product. To integrate game mechanics smoothly, start with a limited scope, gather feedback, and tweak incentives that aren't working. You probably don't have an unlimited budget for rewards, so focus on intrinsic motivations such as mastery and purpose. Transparency and celebrating collective achievements are also key to avoiding divisiveness.

Gamified task management systems

Introduce gamification elements into your Agile task management systems to boost team motivation and productivity. You can create a more engaging environment that fosters friendly competition and collaboration by incorporating features such as progress bars, points, badges, or leaderboards. Project management tools can award points to developers for completing tasks on time, unlocking badges for achieving milestones, and showcasing individual and team progress on a leaderboard. You can add gamification elements to your task management system to boost motivation and productivity.

To make this a reality, search the Atlassian Marketplace for `Gamification` and review which plugins fit best with the gamification strategy you want to implement. You can also find plugins for Monday, Asana, or other platforms by searching their plugin database internally or on the web.

Themed retrospectives

Celebrate team achievements and milestones by acknowledging your team members' hard work and dedication. Create opportunities to showcase these accomplishments, such as hosting regular demos to leadership, celebrating with your team, and giving opportunities to bond over your success.

Retrospectives are also a great way to get together and celebrate the progress made. Retrospectives can start to get stale since product managers usually run them around every 2 weeks. Our suggestion to do a themed retrospective switch makes them incredibly fun while still being productive. The digital collaboration company Miro has community templates that include themes for retrospectives such as Mario Kart, Star Wars, Marvel, and many others. We recommend using these themes or creating your own to ramp up the energy on your retros. You could also name your sprints after foods or games (Starting with A and moving to Z). During or after the retrospective the team could partake in a celebration either eating that food, or playing that game together. Using 2 week sprints, you have just enough letters to make it a full year with any given theme.

Gamifying quality assurance and testing

Gamifying the quality assurance and testing process can enhance motivation and focus, leading to more thorough and effective identification of issues. By introducing rewards and challenges, team members are encouraged to engage deeply in the process, ultimately resulting in a more reliable and higher-quality product.

Reward systems to find and report bugs

Incentivize quality assurance and testing efforts by implementing a reward system for finding and reporting bugs. By recognizing the importance of these tasks and offering tangible rewards, you can encourage team members to actively participate in the testing process. For example, a video game developer is working on an open-world adventure game and wants to ensure a smooth gaming experience for its players. To achieve this, they have decided to involve their player community in the bug identification and reporting process.

The developer introduces a reward system where players who uncover and report game-breaking bugs or glitches receive in-game currency, unique items, or other perks. This incentive encourages players to actively participate in testing, helping the developer identify and fix critical issues more efficiently and effectively.

Bug-hunting competitions and events

Organize bug-hunting competitions and events to create a sense of camaraderie and excitement around the testing process. These events can involve setting specific goals, such as identifying a certain number of bugs within a defined time frame and offering rewards to those who achieve these objectives. For instance, a software company could host a "Bug Bash" event, where employees from different departments collaborate to uncover and report as many bugs as possible within 24 hours, with top performers receiving recognition or prizes.

The company provides food, drinks, and music throughout the event to keep the energy high and encourage participation. At the end of the Bug Bash, the teams reconvene to share their findings and discuss the bugs they've uncovered. The team that identified the most bugs or critical issues receives recognition and a prize, such as a team outing or gift cards.

This bug-hunting competition helps the company uncover and fix issues more quickly and fosters camaraderie and team spirit as employees from different departments work together toward a common goal.

Leveling up your product management team

Let's consider a badge system for product managers and owners showcasing their mastery of relevant skills. We've created 10 potential badges for product managers and 10 badges for product owners that demonstrate their expertise in specific areas:

- **Product manager badges**:

  - **Market Research Maestro**: Awarded for conducting and analyzing 50+ comprehensive market research initiatives that drive the product strategy

  - **Visionary Strategist**: Earned after devising and executing 10+ successful product strategies that align with business goals and user needs

  - **Roadmap Champion**: Achieved by creating and maintaining 20+ clear and prioritized product roadmaps that guide development efforts

  - **Cross-Functional Leader**: Awarded for effectively leading and collaborating with cross-functional teams in 10+ projects, ensuring alignment and communication

  - **Data-Driven Decider**: Earned by leveraging data and analytics to make informed product decisions in 20+ projects, driving continuous improvement

  - **MVP Master**: Achieved after launching 10+ successful minimum viable products, validating assumptions, and gathering user feedback for further development

  - **Customer Advocate**: Awarded for championing the user's perspective in 20+ projects, ensuring product design and development to meet user needs

  - **KPI Tracker**: Earned by setting, tracking, and analyzing key performance indicators in 10+ projects, driving data-informed product improvements

  - **Agile Expert**: Achieved after successfully implementing Agile methodologies in 10+ projects, streamlining processes, and increasing team efficiency

  - **Stakeholder Whisperer**: Awarded for consistently managing and communicating effectively with stakeholders in 20+ projects, ensuring expectations have been met and alignment has been maintained

- **Product owner badges**:

  - **Backlog Boss**: Earned after managing and refining 20+ product backlogs, ensuring clarity, prioritization, and alignment with project goals

  - **User Story Author**: Achieved by writing and validating 100+ user stories that effectively communicate user needs and desired functionality

  - **Sprint Planning Pro**: Awarded for successfully planning and executing 50+ sprints, driving team productivity, and ensuring timely product delivery

- **Acceptance Criteria Expert**: Earned by defining and validating clear acceptance criteria for 100+ user stories, ensuring features meet user needs and quality standards

- **Iteration Master**: Achieved after leading 10+ product iterations, incorporating user feedback and data-driven insights to drive continuous improvement

- **Team Motivator**: Awarded for consistently inspiring and motivating Agile teams in 20+ projects, fostering collaboration and high performance

- **Scrum Savvy**: Earned by demonstrating deep understanding and practical application of Scrum methodologies in 10+ projects, driving team efficiency and product delivery

- **Retrospective Guru**: Achieved after leading 50+ productive retrospective sessions, helping teams identify areas of improvement and implement positive changes

- **Release Planning Expert**: Awarded for successfully planning and coordinating 10+ product releases, ensuring seamless deployment and user adoption

- **Conflict Resolver**: Earned by effectively resolving 20+ conflicts within cross-functional teams, promoting collaboration, and maintaining a positive work environment

By incorporating these badges into your product management and product ownership processes, you can create a more engaging, motivating, and rewarding work environment that recognizes team members' achievements, encourages continuous learning, and drives professional growth.

Product implementation

The successful implementation and continual enhancement of products require structured processes and motivated teams. By gamifying elements such as launch planning, post-release monitoring, and continuous iteration, product managers can inject energy and engagement into these critical phases of the product life cycle. Thoughtful use of game mechanics fosters collaboration, healthy competition, and a culture of learning and mastery. This section explores practical frameworks for gamifying launch planning, analyzing post-release metrics, ideating improvements, and recognizing teams. These game concepts provide actionable templates that product managers can tailor to their specific contexts and objectives. Adopting such gamified techniques enables organizations to sustain team focus amid the often chaotic product development cycles, driving smoother execution.

Gamifying product launch planning

Product launch planning is essential for successfully introducing a new product or feature to the market. A well-planned and executed launch strategy ensures that the product gains maximum visibility, effectively reaches its target audience, and creates a lasting impact. Launch planning involves coordinating various organizational functions, such as marketing, sales, support, and development teams, to ensure a seamless and cohesive experience for internal stakeholders and customers. A well-structured product launch increases the likelihood of a product's success and sets the stage for future enhancements and growth. The next game we're going to look at, LaunchPad, aims to make the process of product launch planning engaging and enjoyable while fostering collaboration and alignment among team members:

- **LaunchPad**:

    - **Objective**: The game's objective is to create a comprehensive and compelling product launch plan collaboratively.

    - **Preparation**: Identify the critical components of a successful product launch, such as target audience, marketing strategy, sales strategy, support readiness, and product documentation. Create cards or visual aids representing each component.

    - **Teams**: Divide the participants into cross-functional teams, ensuring representation from all relevant departments.

    - **Launch rounds**: Assign each team a specific component of the product launch, which they will work on during a timed round (for example, 20 minutes).

    - **Collaboration time**: During each round, teams brainstorm, discuss, and collaborate to develop strategies and action plans for their assigned launch component.

    - **Scoring system**: Teams earn points based on the creativity, feasibility, and potential impact of their proposed strategies and action plans.

    - **Bonus challenges**: Introduce bonus challenges, such as creating a unique marketing tactic or the most effective sales pitch, which teams can complete to earn extra points.

    - **Team presentations**: After each round, teams present their proposed strategies and action plans to the group, fostering discussion and knowledge sharing.

    - **Round rotation**: After presentations, teams rotate to the next launch component and repeat the process until all teams have worked on all components.

    - **Rewards**: At the end of the game, the team with the most points is recognized for its achievements, and all participants celebrate their collective effort in creating a well-rounded product launch plan.

LaunchPad promotes a fun and engaging environment for product launch planning, encouraging team members to collaborate, share ideas, and actively contribute to the development of a successful launch strategy.

Gamifying the product launch process

Gamifying the product launch process can increase motivation and drive team members to collaborate effectively, ensuring a well-executed and timely release. By incorporating game elements, you also create a more engaging experience, allowing the team to maintain focus and enthusiasm throughout the launch phase.

Team-based rewards and recognition for successful launches

Celebrate successful product launches by acknowledging the hard work of the teams involved. Set up a reward system that recognizes team achievements, such as meeting launch goals, delivering on time, or exceeding expectations. For instance, a company launching a new eCommerce platform could reward the teams responsible for the successful launch with a bonus, a team outing, or public recognition during a company-wide event.

Post-launch goals and challenges to maintain motivation

Keep the momentum going after a product launch by setting post-launch goals and challenges. Encourage teams to focus on user acquisition, customer engagement, and product improvement. For example, a mobile app development company could challenge its teams to achieve specific targets, such as reaching a certain number of downloads, maintaining a high user retention rate, or implementing new features based on user feedback.

Gamifying post-launch monitoring and analysis

Post-launch monitoring and analysis play a crucial role in the ongoing success of any product. It enables product teams to track critical metrics, identify improvement areas, and evaluate their product's overall effectiveness in meeting user needs and market demands. By continuously monitoring and analyzing user behavior, feedback, and performance data, product teams can uncover valuable insights that drive product enhancements, optimize user experiences, and ultimately contribute to achieving strategic business objectives. A well-executed post-launch analysis helps teams learn from their successes and challenges and fosters a culture of continuous improvement and innovation. The next game we'll look at, Data Dash, is designed to make the process of post-launch monitoring and analysis engaging and fun while promoting collaboration and knowledge-sharing among team members.

- **Data Dash:**
  - **Objective**: The game's objective is to analyze post-launch data, identify trends, and discover areas for product improvement.
  - **Preparation**: Before the game, gather relevant post-launch data, such as user engagement metrics, conversion rates, and customer feedback. Display this data on a dashboard or print it on cards.
  - I.   **Teams**: Divide the participants into small cross-functional teams. Each team is a group of "data detectives" working together to uncover insights and opportunities for product improvement.
  - II.   **Data rounds**: Divide the data into categories, such as user engagement, user acquisition, and user retention. Assign each category to a round in the game.

III. **Data hunt**: In each round, teams have a limited time (for example, 15 minutes) to analyze the data in their assigned category, identify trends or patterns, and pinpoint areas for improvement.

IV. **Scoring system**: Teams earn points for each insight they discover and propose actionable recommendations to address the identified issues. The scoring system can be based on the proposed solutions' relevance, impact, and feasibility.

V. **Bonus challenges**: Introduce bonus challenges, such as finding correlations between different datasets or identifying the most effective marketing channel, which teams can complete to earn extra points.

VI. **Team presentations**: After each round, teams present their findings and recommendations to the entire group. This encourages knowledge sharing and fosters collaborative problem-solving.

VII. **Round rotation**: After presentations, teams rotate to the following data category and repeat this process until all teams have analyzed all data categories.

VIII. **Rewards**: At the end of the game, the team with the most points is recognized for their achievements, and all participants can celebrate their collective effort in analyzing post-launch data and identifying opportunities for product improvement.

Data Dash promotes a fun and engaging environment for post-launch monitoring and analysis, encouraging team members to collaborate, share insights, and actively contribute to the ongoing improvement of the product.

Leveling up your product marketing team

Let's look at a badge system for product marketing managers and product marketing analysts, showcasing their mastery of various relevant skills. We've created 10 badges for product marketing managers and 10 badges for product marketing analysts that demonstrate their expertise in specific areas:

- **Product marketing manager badges**:

  - **Market Analysis Ace**: Awarded for conducting and analyzing 50+ comprehensive market research initiatives that inform marketing strategies

  - **Positioning Pro**: Earned after developing and implementing 10+ successful product positioning strategies that differentiate products in the market

  - **Messaging Master**: Achieved by crafting and refining 20+ compelling product messaging frameworks that resonate with target audiences

  - **Campaign Commander**: Awarded for planning and executing 10+ successful product marketing campaigns that drive awareness and demand

  - **Content Creator**: Earned by developing 50+ high-quality content pieces (for example, blog posts, whitepapers, and case studies) that showcase product value and thought leadership

- **Go-To-Market Guru**: Achieved after successfully launching 10+ products with well-coordinated go-to-market strategies that drive user adoption and revenue growth

- **Sales Enablement Expert**: Awarded for creating and delivering 20+ sales enablement tools and training sessions that empower sales teams to close deals

- **Partnership Pioneer**: Earned by establishing and nurturing 10+ successful co-marketing partnerships that amplify product reach and credibility

- **Data-Driven Optimizer**: Achieved after leveraging data and analytics to optimize marketing strategies in 20+ projects, driving continuous improvement

- **Customer Success Advocate**: Awarded for developing and implementing 10+ customer success initiatives that improve user satisfaction and retention

- **Marketing/business analyst badges**:

  - **Data Detective**: Earned after analyzing and interpreting marketing data in 50+ projects to uncover actionable insights and drive strategic decisions

  - **Market Research Magician**: Achieved by conducting 20+ in-depth market research studies that inform product marketing strategies and tactics

  - **Competitive Intelligence Ninja**: Awarded for compiling and maintaining 10+ comprehensive competitive intelligence reports that inform marketing and product strategies

  - **Campaign Analyst**: Earned by measuring and evaluating the performance of 20+ marketing campaigns, identifying areas for improvement and optimization

  - **Segmentation Specialist**: Achieved after developing and refining 10+ effective market segmentation strategies that target the right audiences

  - **Pricing Pro**: Awarded for conducting and applying 10+ pricing analyses that inform pricing strategies and maximize revenue potential

  - **Forecasting Wizard**: Earned by accurately forecasting sales and revenue trends for 10+ product lines, informing resource allocation and strategic planning

  - **A/B Testing Ace**: Awarded after designing, executing, and analyzing 20+ A/B tests that optimize marketing materials and campaign performance

  - **ROI Rockstar**: Awarded for calculating and presenting the **return on investment** (**ROI**) for 20+ marketing initiatives, informing budget allocation and strategy adjustments

  - **Survey Savant**: Earned by designing, deploying, and analyzing 10+ customer and prospect surveys that provide valuable user preferences and needs insights

By incorporating these badges into your product marketing processes, you can create a more engaging, motivating, and rewarding work environment that recognizes team members' achievements, encourages continuous learning, and drives professional growth.

As we conclude this insightful journey through the world of gamifying product processes, we can't help but reflect on the profound impact that gamification can have on product managers, product leaders, and the overall product development process. By embracing gamification principles, we empower ourselves to drive innovation, engagement, and motivation among our teams, fostering a collaborative and dynamic environment where everyone can thrive.

This chapter has taken us on a deep dive into the various aspects of gamification, examining its applications in ideation, prototyping, product management, and product implementation. We have seen the transformative power of gamification elements such as points, rewards, and feedback mechanisms and how they can be essential in engaging and motivating our teams. By designing games and activities that align with the goals and objectives of our businesses, we ensure that our products not only meet the needs of our target audience but also contribute to the overall success of our organizations.

The key takeaway from this chapter is that, as product leaders and managers, we must practice what we preach. If we believe in the power of gamification to drive engagement and innovation in our products, applying these same principles to our product development processes makes sense. By doing so, we demonstrate our commitment to creating an environment in which our teams feel inspired, challenged, and motivated to push the boundaries of their creativity and problem-solving abilities.

As we integrate gamification into our product development processes, we must acknowledge that this is not a one-size-fits-all solution. Each team is unique, and our leaders are responsible for understanding our team member's strengths, weaknesses, and preferences. By tailoring our gamification strategies to the needs of our teams, we ensure that our efforts are both practical and enjoyable for everyone involved.

Moreover, it is crucial to remember that gamification is not a static concept; it requires constant iteration and adaptation to remain relevant and engaging. As product leaders, we must continually seek new ideas and strategies to keep our teams motivated and driven to excel. By staying abreast of the latest trends in gamification and incorporating them into our processes, we set ourselves and our teams up for long-term success.

Summary

In conclusion, gamifying our product development processes is a powerful means of enhancing both the experience of our teams and the quality of our products. By applying gamification principles to the various stages of product development, we create a vibrant and dynamic environment in which our teams feel motivated, engaged, and inspired to innovate. As product managers and leaders, we must embrace this approach and strive to create a workplace culture that fosters creativity, collaboration, and a sense of accomplishment.

With this mindset, we can embark on a journey toward product excellence, guided by gamification principles and united by a shared passion for innovation. By tapping into the innate human desire for challenge, competition, and reward, we can unlock the full potential of our teams and usher in a new era of groundbreaking product development. So, let's take up the mantle of leadership and champion the cause of gamification as we strive to create products that not only meet the needs of our users but also exceed their wildest expectations. The future of product development is in our hands, and with the power of gamification, we can make it a reality.

In the next chapter, we will look at case studies to see some great examples of gamification being put to work.

Further reading

- Schwarz, M., & Blessing, L., *The Design Thinking Toolbox: A Guide to Mastering the Most Popular and Valuable Innovation Methods*, Wiley, 2020.

- Gray, D., Brown, S., & Macanufo, J, *Gamestorming: A Playbook for Innovators, Rulebreakers, and Changemakers*, O'Reilly Media, 2010.

- McGonigal, J, *Reality Is Broken: Why Games Make Us Better and How They Can Change the World*, Penguin Books, 2011.

Case Studies and Best Practices

This chapter overviews successful gamification examples in various industries, such as healthcare, education, visual arts, and finance. This chapter analyzes what made these gamification strategies effective, including the game mechanics used, the goals and objectives of the product or service, the target audience, and the impact on user engagement and behavior.

We interviewed four practitioners in real-world settings to gain insights into their experiences of sharing their gamification strategies and the benefits they observed. This chapter will conclude with a discussion of best practices and lessons learned from these case studies and interviews, including recommendations for designers on creating effective gamification strategies and avoiding common pitfalls and mistakes.

This chapter provides valuable insights and real-world examples of successful gamification strategies. It emphasizes the importance of understanding the target audience, aligning the gamification strategy with the goals of the product, and continuously monitoring and iterating on the strategy. You'll understand the strengths and weaknesses of successful gamification in these examples that you can apply to the products you are developing yourself. We will cover the following topics:

- Brands that master gamification
- Gamification strategies that contributed to their success
- Best practices and lessons learned

Brands that master gamification

This section will explore 6 remarkable examples of products that have successfully implemented gamification to their advantage. These companies have harnessed gamification principles to captivate their target audiences, create memorable experiences, and drive desired behaviors. From mobile apps to fitness platforms to online learning systems, these examples demonstrate the versatility and effectiveness of gamification in various industries. They paid us zeros and zeros of dollars to be in this book, so know that they are coming to you as our favorites.

A brief overview of these success stories will uncover the key strategies, design elements, and outcomes that have made these gamification implementations impactful. I hope that if one or more of these interests you, you can do a further dive into the topic to research their gamification elements firsthand. By examining the tactics employed by these companies, you can extract valuable insights and lessons you can apply to businesses of all sizes and sectors.

Duolingo

Duolingo, a highly successful language learning platform, has masterfully integrated gamification principles into its design, making the learning process engaging, enjoyable, and highly effective. Duolingo is the OG of digital product gamification. Its combination of game mechanics and psychology ensures that users remain motivated and committed to their language learning journey, ultimately supporting the company's mission to make language education accessible and fun. Duolingo is probably the most widely known, and most cited, example of gamification.

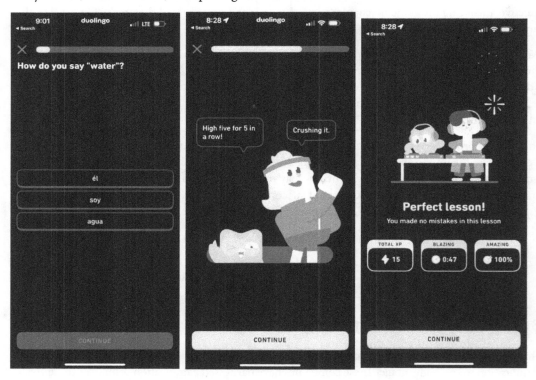

Figure 11.1 – I've been a master of Level 1 Spanish basics for 14 years; one day, I'll move to Level 2

The game mechanics employed by Duolingo include points, levels, streaks, badges, and leaderboards. Users earn **experience points** (**XP**) for completing lessons, which helps them level up and unlock more advanced content. Streaks encourage daily practice by tracking the number of consecutive days a user spends learning. Simultaneously, users are rewarded with badges for accomplishing diverse achievements and reaching significant milestones, such as completing a skill or mastering a specific number of words. Leaderboards foster healthy competition among users by comparing progress and ranking them accordingly:

The Elder Scrolls Online (2014)

Starting as a traditional single-player RPG franchise, *The Elder Scrolls* became a **Massively Multiplayer Online Role-Playing Game (MMORPG)** in 2014. This was met with mixed reviews, as many of the player base preferred the story-driven solo campaigns. However, the game is still around and played by millions each month, and new content is being released regularly.

One of the features that initially turned away traditional "gamers" was the daily loot. For each day you log in for a given month, you can earn better rewards, with players that log in every day in a given month earning very valuable loot. Systems like this were often reserved for mobile games and not viewed favorably by core game audiences. Although The Elder Scrolls Online was not the first traditional game to start the move into these sorts of mechanics, it has seen some of the better success. Nowadays, many traditional franchises are starting to adopt the "online" model that includes many of the same features you might find more often in apps or mobile games. If you are not a traditional game player but enjoy a casual mobile game, it might be worth you trying this or one of the many others.

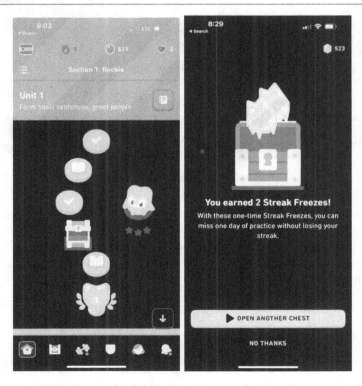

Figure 11.2 – You can finish objectives to open chests and earn rewards

Duolingo rewards its users with chests for completing quests and accomplishing daily tasks. Chests may contain rewards such as double XP for the next 15 minutes, a reward that encourages users to keep learning for another 15 minutes, earning extra XP to climb the leaderboard, but also keeping the user learning for 15 more minutes. Chests may contain gems, an in-app currency that users can spend to earn legendary status on levels, indicating their mastery of the learned content, or they can spend gems to unlock mini-game style content that allows them to drill into the vocabulary and grammar rules they've been learning.

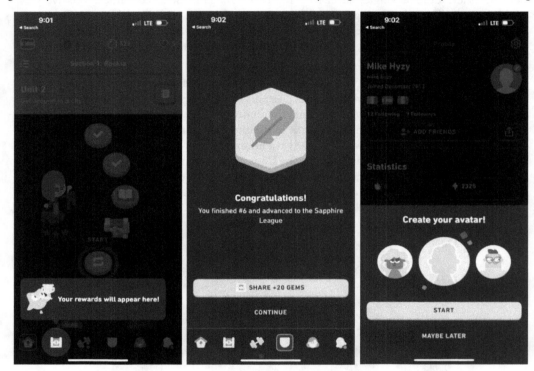

Figure 11.3 – Rewards, achievements, and avatars

Duolingo's gamification strategy effectively aligns with its business goals of increasing user engagement, retention, and language proficiency. The platform's design encourages consistent practice, improving language learning outcomes, and ensuring that users return to the app. Additionally, the sense of accomplishment and social recognition fostered by badges and leaderboards further solidifies user loyalty and commitment.

Essential best practices and lessons learned from Duolingo's success include the following:

- Understanding users' needs and motivations to learn a new language.

- Incorporating levels to ease the user into the experience and having a structured system where they progress based on the foundation that has been built.

- Varying levels of challenges give users easy wins to keep them motivated and a sense of accomplishment and then more robust challenges that keep them coming back.

- An incredible UI that guides the user through the process, such as onboarding, finishing lessons, earning rewards, and other app features makes the experience fun as it is so easy to use and understand.

- It incorporates social feeds and sharing with friends so that you can see their language learning process and they can see yours. This keeps both of you accountable and ensures you're actively engaging with the app.

Duolingo consistently updates its content, game mechanics, and user experience based on user feedback and data analysis, ensuring the platform remains relevant and engaging over time.

Hence, Duolingo is an exemplary case study of effective gamification in a product. By leveraging a variety of game mechanics and understanding the psychology of motivation, Duolingo has created a captivating and beneficial experience that supports its business objectives, drives user engagement, and fosters continuous improvement.

Strava

Strava, a popular fitness-tracking app and athlete social network, has successfully incorporated gamification principles to create a highly engaging and motivational user experience. By intertwining game mechanics with the psychology of goal-setting and achievement, Strava has fostered a loyal community of fitness enthusiasts and has become the go-to platform for tracking and sharing athletic progress.

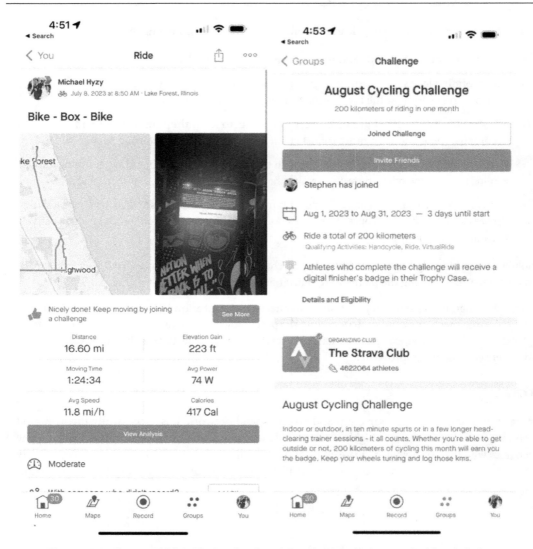

Figure 11.4 – Strava, which is like Facebook and Google Maps had a gamified fitness baby

The fundamental game mechanics that are used by Strava include personal achievements, badges, segments, leaderboards, and challenges. Users can track their best performances and set new goals through personal achievements. Strava further enhances the user experience by awarding badges for completing various activities or reaching significant milestones. Strava's segments feature allows users to compare their performance on specific routes or sections of a route with others, fostering a competitive yet supportive environment. You can win medals in certain segments, and when I know I am close to beating a time in a segment, it motivates me to push myself harder. I don't know of any other app that does this or has built the user base to do so, so which makes it a competitive advantage for Strava.

Figure 11.5 – Pick your route, see the leaderboard; do your route, crush the leaderboard

Leaderboards rank users based on their accomplishments, providing them with additional motivation to improve. Regularly updated challenges encourage users to try new activities, push their limits, and stay engaged with the app. These leaderboards and challenges are ever-evolving, so you are always checking the app before a ride. This means that the gamified features are driving engagement and when it comes to retention, I couldn't imagine biking or swimming without Strava. I could imagine never running again.

Strava's gamification strategy effectively supports its business goals by increasing user engagement, retention, and overall satisfaction. The platform leverages competition and social recognition to create a sense of community and connection among users, which drives continuous improvement and commitment to fitness goals.

Here are the essential best practices and lessons learned from Strava's success:

- It tailors gamification elements such as challenges and goals to the target audience of runners and bikers and expands to more sports with each update

- You create your own "levels" of fitness by having the data to set goals for yourself and progress to better training outcomes

- Social triggers enable a balance between competition and collaboration as you can cheer others on regarding their accomplishments on the feed while also competing against others in segments and challenges

- The user experience is continually being updated and refined with new gamified features, more categories, and an ever-better user interface

- Personalized insights and analytics make Strava your go-to for tracking performance and give you metrics to compete against yourself

Strava's commitment to understanding its users' needs and motivations has allowed it to create a platform that resonates with athletes of all levels. Strava maintains a fresh and compelling experience that keeps users engaged over time by consistently iterating on its gamification elements and incorporating user feedback. It leverages the principles of gamification to encourage users to be more active, social, and engaged with their fitness journeys, and by doing so, it reinforces its core vision of fostering a global community of fitness enthusiasts.

We'll describe the success of their design and incorporation of game mechanics in business terms. Strava is valued at more than $1.5 billion, has 95 million registered users, and over 2 billion activities logged in 2022 (Source: `https://www.businessofapps.com/data/strava-statistics/`).

Strava exemplifies the successful implementation of gamification in a product, creating a captivating and motivational user experience. Through a strategic combination of game mechanics and a deep understanding of user psychology, Strava has fostered a thriving community of fitness enthusiasts and built a platform that supports and drives their athletic pursuits.

GuruShots

GuruShots, an online platform for photographers, has effectively leveraged gamification principles to create an engaging and competitive environment for users to showcase their work and improve their photography skills. GuruShots has cultivated a thriving community of photographers, from amateurs to professionals, who share their passion and creativity through the platform by integrating game mechanics with a keen understanding of user motivations and desires.

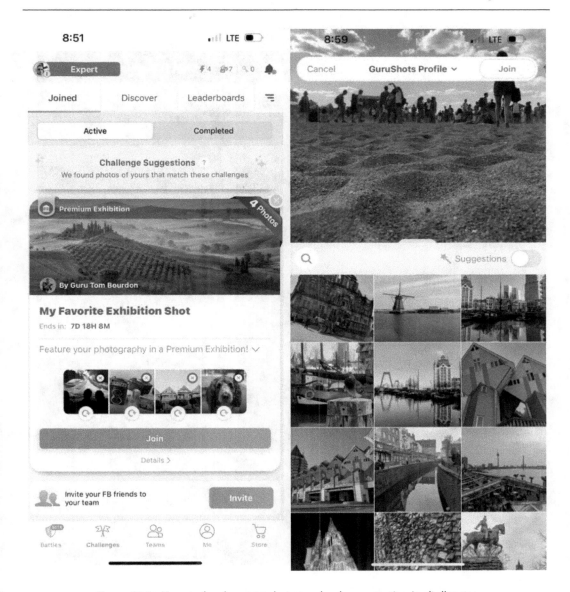

Figure 11.6 – You can level up as a photographer by competing in challenges

GuruShots employs several game mechanics, such as challenges, points, levels, ranks, and leaderboards, to foster user engagement and improve skill. Regularly hosted challenges focus on various themes and photography styles, inspiring users to think creatively and submit their best work.

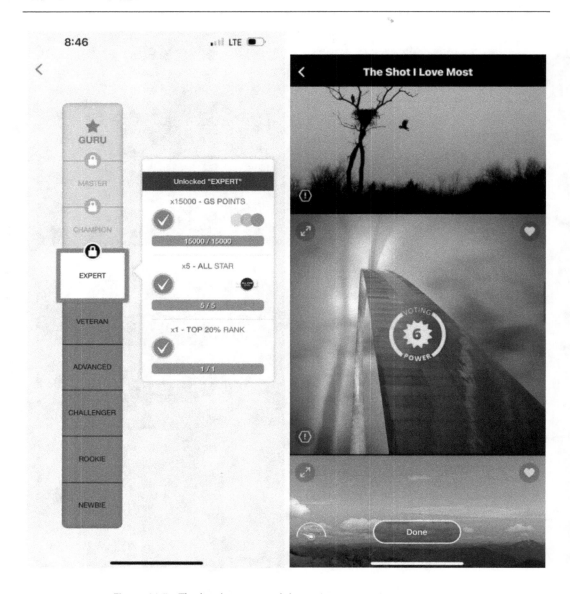

Figure 11.7 – The level system and the voting process in competitions

Points are awarded based on community votes and judges' feedback, with better-performing photos earning more points. As users accumulate points, they advance through levels and ranks, creating a sense of achievement and progression. Also, the higher level you are, the more your vote counts in competitions. A **NEWBIE** vote is worth one point, while an **EXPERT** vote is worth six points. Leaderboards showcase top-performing users in challenges, further motivating users to improve their photography skills and climb the ranks.

GuruShots uses gamification to drive its product vision by creating a vibrant platform for photographers to share, compete, and grow. It gamifies the photography experience through themed photo contests, encouraging skill improvement and user engagement. Moreover, its ranking system, based on user votes, instills a sense of achievement and progression, fueling further participation. Additionally, the platform fosters social interactions among its users, underpinning its vision of a globally connected photography community.

GuruShots has developed strategic partnerships with magazines and art galleries, providing users the opportunity to win cash prizes and have their photos showcased. These collaborations amplify both intrinsic and extrinsic motivators for users, further fueling their engagement with the platform. This brilliant strategy not only fosters user participation but also enriches the overall experience, adding a tangible and prestigious outcome to users' endeavors.

This gamification strategy has successfully supported GuruShots' business goals by increasing user engagement, driving platform growth, and fostering a sense of community among photographers. The competitive nature of the platform, paired with the potential for recognition and feedback, encourages users to hone their skills and contribute to the platform continually.

The essential best practices and lessons learned from GuruShots' success are as follows:

- Understanding the target audience's motivations for wanting their photographs to be showcased, which involves having others view their work and learn from the work of others.
- You can find partners that provide intrinsic and extrinsic rewards for their users.
- Intertwining sets of game mechanics such as levels, points, challenges, and rewards create a competitive but also learning environment that keeps users motivated and engaged.
- Fostering both individual competition and team collaboration as users compete for votes on their photographs. These votes also collectively contribute to their team's overall score.
- Ensuring a fair and transparent voting system establishes trust in the system.

GuruShots keeps its community engaged and motivated to improve its photography skills by providing users with growth and learning opportunities. By joining a team, you are connected to other photographers and you compete together to win challenges. Either you have a basic level of participation or you are booted from the team – this is one motivator. You also want to put your best work in because you are ranked within your team based on how well your photo does in the challenge. The cumulative team score is used and it feels good to help your team win challenges. You can also showcase your profile and portfolio so that your team and others on the platform can see your work.

Figure 11.8 – Teamwork and personal profile

GuruShots stimulates its community's drive to enhance its photography talents by offering an avenue for growth and learning. The element of joining a team fosters connection among photographers, turning solo competition into a collaborative quest for challenge wins. The platform requires a minimum level of participation to maintain membership in a team, ensuring a consistent flow of quality submissions. Moreover, the system ranks each member's contributions within the team, adding an internal competitive edge that motivates users to present their best work. The shared victory of a team challenge win brings about a sense of accomplishment and unity. The platform also allows members to exhibit their portfolios on their profiles, exposing their creative journey not only to their teammates but also to the wider GuruShots community.

Pokèmon Snap (1999)

A break from the traditional Pokèmon game, this adventure had you taking photos of the pocket monsters in the wild. Your photos were then rated based on things such as composition, the activity of the Pokèmon, and the focus of the shot. A newer version was also released for the Nintendo Switch in 2021.

I've always liked to think that GuruShots used this game as inspiration for their product, although I have no evidence that says so! This game is great for casual fans of photography or cute little monsters. It is a fun activity to try with friends and see who can capture the best image of an elusive Pokèmon.

The American Red Cross

The American Red Cross, a humanitarian organization that provides emergency assistance and disaster relief, has successfully implemented gamification into its blood donation process. The organization has developed various strategies to encourage and recognize blood donors, leveraging game mechanics to create a more engaging and rewarding experience. As a result, the American Red Cross has increased donor participation and generated greater awareness about the importance of blood donation.

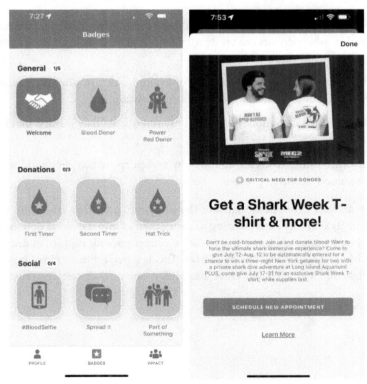

Figure 11.9 – Badges and rewards

The American Red Cross uses several game mechanics to gamify the blood donation process, including badges, leaderboards, and rewards. Donors receive badges for milestones, such as the number of donations made, type of donation (whole blood, platelets, and so on), and special occasions (for example, donating on holidays). This badge system recognizes donor achievements, instills a sense of pride, and encourages continued participation. Leaderboards showcase top donors and groups, fostering friendly competition and community engagement. Additionally, the American Red Cross occasionally offers tangible rewards, such as gift cards or merchandise, to incentivize participation during periods of high demand or low supply.

The gamification strategy adopted by the American Red Cross directly supports its mission by increasing blood donor engagement and encouraging repeat donations. By making the donation experience more enjoyable and rewarding, the organization can attract new donors, retain existing ones, and save more lives through a steady blood supply. This worked for me – as we were doing our research, I was pulled in by the "you can save a life" messaging, and then the closer was a Shark Week T-shirt. So, yeah – of course I'm going to make time to drive to one of your locations so that you can stick a needle in me and take my blood.

Here are some of the essential best practices and lessons learned from the American Red Cross's gamification efforts:

- Using the power of narrative to get people to donate blood. They've also introduced a program called "SleevesUp" where donors can create narratives by setting goals, creating custom messages, and sharing their motivations to donate blood.

- Recognizing donors' intrinsic motivations (for example, altruism or social recognition) and providing extrinsic rewards that align with those motivations.

- Tapping into extrinsic motivations by giving away rewards such as T-shirts that align with pop culture themes.

- The organization's ability to create community and purpose has been vital to its success in gamifying the blood donation process.

Hence, the American Red Cross demonstrates the impact of gamification in the nonprofit and humanitarian sectors. By skillfully incorporating game mechanics into the blood donation process, the organization has created a more engaging and rewarding experience for donors, ultimately enhancing its ability to fulfill its critical mission of saving lives. This is a perfect example of how the power of gamification can make the world a better place, one badge, one reward, one person at a time.

Habitica

Habitica is a highly successful example of gamification in productivity and habit-building. The app transforms everyday tasks and habits into a role-playing game, motivating users to complete real-life objectives by offering virtual rewards and penalties. Integrating game mechanics in Habitica has led to a highly engaging user experience, promoting positive behavior change and supporting users in achieving their personal goals.

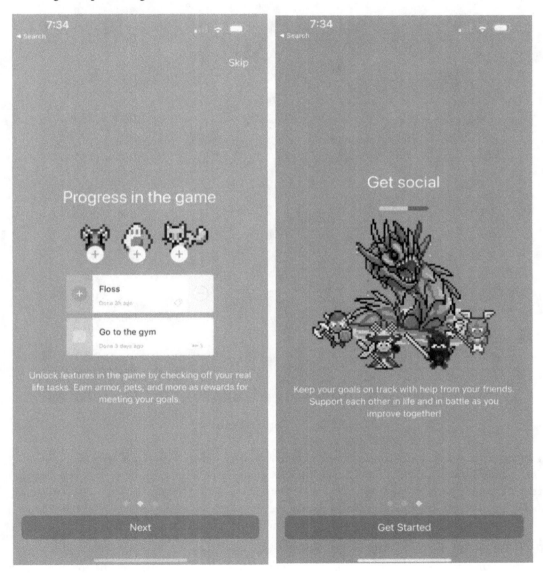

Figure 11.10 – Level up your character and progress with friends

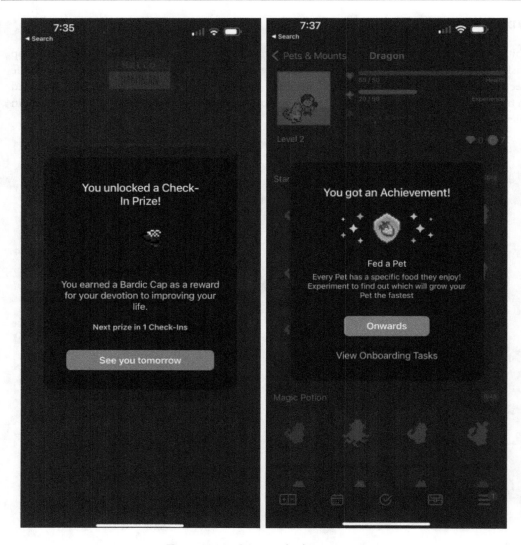

Figure 11.11 – Prizes and achievements

Habitica employs a variety of game mechanics, such as avatars, quests, leveling up, and social features. Users personalize avatars and earn experience points, gold, and other in-game rewards by completing tasks. By accomplishing tasks, users level up their avatars, unlock new features, and gain access to more challenging content. Habitica also includes social elements such as parties, guilds, and competitions, which foster collaboration, accountability, and friendly competition among users.

The gamification strategy of Habitica effectively supports its primary goal of helping users develop and maintain positive habits. By making habit-building enjoyable and rewarding, the app increases user engagement, retention, and success in habit formation.

The best practices and lessons learned from Habitica are as follows:

- The importance of creating a compelling narrative and environment to immerse users in their habit-building journey. We can't stress enough that the narrative drives all great video games, and therefore gamification.

- The focus on social interaction and support encourages users to stay committed and accountable to their goals, making it more likely for them to succeed.

- Users can earn virtual rewards and incentives such as in-game currency, items, and avatar customization options tied to their progress.

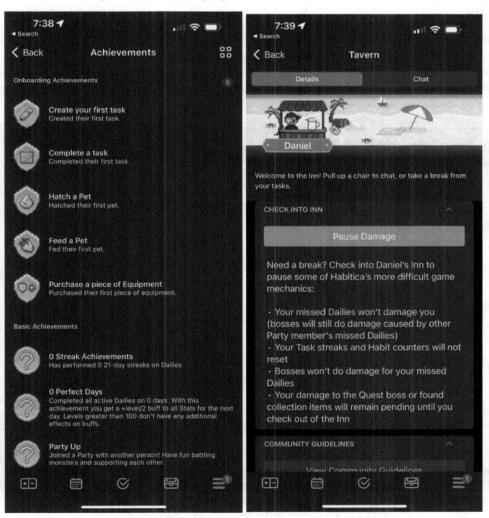

Figure 11.12 – Achievements and breaks

From the preceding screenshots, you can see that you have multiple game mechanics going on as you progress through the journey, level up, and power up your character. The one thin6 I love about the platform is that they have options for you to pause when life gets in the way and you won't sacrifice all of the work you put in previously. This keeps users highly engaged and in a position for long-term success.

Over time, Habitica has continued to evolve and improve, incorporating user feedback and refining game mechanics to ensure the app remains engaging and relevant to its users' needs. The app's success demonstrates the potential of gamification in promoting positive behavior change, personal development, and overall wellbeing.

Prodigy

Prodigy is a successful example of gamification in education, specifically focusing on mathematics for students in grades 1-8. The platform utilizes game mechanics and an engaging virtual world to motivate students to learn math, making the process enjoyable and interactive. Prodigy's approach to gamification has proven effective in supporting its mission to improve students' math skills and boost their confidence in the subject.

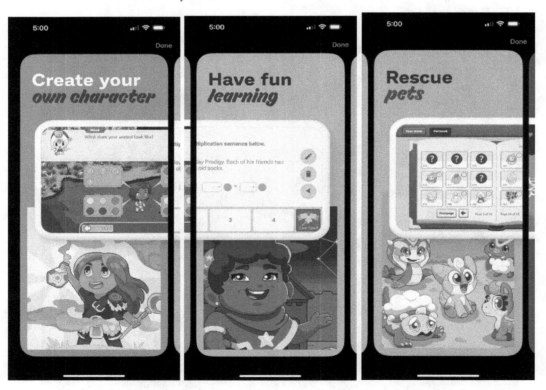

Figure 11.13 – Highlights of the Prodigy app – math is fun again

Prodigy employs various game mechanics, such as avatars, levels, quests, and rewards, to keep students engaged while learning. As students complete math problems, they earn points, unlock new content, and progress through levels. These elements foster a sense of achievement and encourage students to continue practicing their math skills.

The gamification strategy of Prodigy aligns with its educational goals by making learning math fun and accessible. By incorporating game elements, the platform increases students' motivation and persistence, leading to better academic performance and a more positive attitude toward math, which is really hard to do.

Here are some of the best practices and lessons learned from Prodigy:

- The importance of integrating educational content seamlessly into gameplay, ensuring that learning remains the primary focus. The platform balances the fun aspects of gaming with the educational objectives, maintaining students' engagement without sacrificing learning outcomes.

- The platform dynamically adjusts the difficulty and content based on each student's performance and progress. This personalized approach ensures that students are presented with challenges and activities that align with their individual learning needs.

Over time, Prodigy has continued to evolve and expand its offerings, incorporating user feedback and refining its gamification techniques. The platform's success demonstrates the potential of gamification in enhancing the educational experience, making learning more enjoyable and effective for students.

Fall Guys (2020)

After initially being released as a traditional pay-to-own model game, Fall Guys was purchased by Epic Games and made as a free-to-play title. This means that anyone can install the game and try it out, and you pay for additional content if desired. Epic Games has made this their primary release model, earning them a significant amount of revenue with its implementation in games such as *Fortnite* and *Rocket League* (which are also free to play).

Although any free-to-play model game is valuable as a research tool, Fall Guys stands out as the most casual-friendly, meaning that pretty much anyone can pick it up and have fun. Like nearly all of the examples given in this chapter, Fall Guys uses level-ups, but it employs a common game tactic in this regard. Players can earn levels by competing in the game, but the best rewards (costumes, emotes, etc.) are only given when a player has paid for the "season pass." By doing so, they can unlock premium goods, and even additional in-game coins to purchase the pass next season (the pass resets every few months). Each time a player earns a new level, they are shown what they could have unlocked if they were a pass holder. This creates a sense of urgency to buy but allows players to keep improving their skills (and thus, earning more levels) before they have to commit. When a player pays for the pass, they earn all of those backlogged rewards (ka-ching!) and are validated for the time they spent earning those levels. Try out Fall Guys, or any other free-to-play title. See how far up the level ladder you can make it. Can you make it far enough to warrant paying for the pass?

Gamification strategies that contributed to their success

In today's highly competitive market for your time and money, companies constantly seek innovative ways to engage users and create lasting loyalty. Gamification has emerged as a powerful strategy to achieve these goals, as evidenced by the success of companies such as Duolingo, Strava, GuruShots, the American Red Cross, Habitica, and Prodigy. By analyzing the similarities in their gamification strategies, we can identify critical elements that have contributed to their success.

One common thread across these successful gamification strategies is the emphasis on *goal-setting* and *progress tracking*. By enabling users to set personal goals and track their progress toward those goals, these products create a sense of achievement and motivation to continue using the product. For example, Noom users set weight loss goals and track their progress, while Mint users set financial goals and monitor their spending habits.

Another critical similarity among these successful gamification strategies is using rewards and incentives to motivate users. These rewards can take various forms, such as points, badges, levels, or virtual currency. For example, Duolingo awards points and badges for completing lessons, while Strava rewards users with badges for completing fitness challenges. These rewards create a sense of accomplishment and encourage users to continue engaging with the product and even share their badges and rewards, which drives organic marketing.

These products also incorporate *social interaction* and *competition to drive user engagement*. By allowing users to connect with friends, share their progress, and compete against others, these products tap into users' innate desire for social recognition and competition. For example, Strava users can share their workout stats with friends and compete on leaderboards, while GuruShots users can participate in photography competitions and earn points for their photos.

Another common element among these successful gamification strategies is the focus on *personalization* and *customization*. By tailoring the user experience to individual preferences and needs, these products create a sense of ownership and investment in the product. For example, Strava offers personalized route recommendations based on users' habits, while Prodigy adapts its math curriculum to each student's skill level.

Providing users with timely *feedback* and *reinforcement* is another crucial factor that contributes to the success of these gamification strategies. By offering immediate feedback on user actions and reinforcing positive behaviors, these products help users learn and improve over time. For example, Habitica offers instant feedback on task completion and rewards users with virtual currency, while Noom provides daily feedback on users' food choices and exercise habits.

The successful gamification strategies of these products also seamlessly integrate with their core product offerings. Rather than feeling like a particular feature or add-on, the gamification elements are woven into the user experience, enhancing the overall product offering. For example, GuruShot's gamification features, such as badges and progress tracking, are integrated into its profile management. Duolingo's language lessons are structured like mini-games to make learning fun and engaging.

Another critical aspect of these successful gamification strategies is their commitment to iterative *improvement* and *adaptation*. These companies refine their gamification strategies to optimize user engagement and satisfaction by continuously analyzing user data and feedback. For example, Strava regularly introduces new challenges and features based on user feedback, while Spotify continually refines its music recommendation algorithms to provide more accurate and personalized suggestions.

A successful gamification strategy must strike the right *balance between fun and functionality*. While the game elements should be engaging and enjoyable, they should not detract from the product's core purpose or hinder user productivity. For example, Strava's gamification features, such as goal-setting and progress tracking, help users manage their health and wellness more effectively rather than distracting them with unrelated games or activities.

Hence, the success of companies such as Duolingo, Strava, GuruShots, the American Red Cross, Habitica, and Prodigy serves as a valuable lesson for product managers and developers looking to implement gamification strategies in their products. We can draw critical insights to create engaging and effective gamification experiences by closely examining their best practices.

To apply these best practices, you must do the following:

- Ensure your gamification elements align with your product's core objectives and seamlessly integrate with the user experience

- Focus on goal-setting, progress tracking, and personalization to create a sense of ownership and investment in the product

- Offer rewards and incentives that motivate users while incorporating social interaction and competition to drive engagement

---

Tip

Provide timely feedback and reinforcement to support user learning and improvement, and be prepared to iterate and refine your gamification strategy based on data and user feedback. Remember to strike the right balance between fun and functionality, ensuring that your gamification elements enhance, rather than detract from, the product's core purpose.

By learning from the success stories of these companies and adapting their best practices to your product's unique context, you can harness the power of gamification to boost user engagement, satisfaction, and loyalty, ultimately contributing to the long-term success of your product.

Now, let's look behind the scenes and talk to some gamification leaders.

Best practices and lessons learned

To dive deep into the people behind the games, we interviewed a few leaders who drive their businesses with gamification to learn their best practices. We selected these leaders as they belong to companies that have taken gamification and the culture of innovation to the next level.

TerryBerry

First, we had the pleasure of meeting with Brian Snodgrass, Vice President of Product and Technology, and Brad Sytsma, Product Manager for the Recognition Reward Platform from TerryBerry. TerryBerry is a leading provider of a comprehensive workplace culture and engagement platform. Their solutions revolve around reward and recognition, wellness benefits, surveys, and feedback communications. With a focus on creating engaging organizational cultures, TerryBerry equips its customers with the necessary tools to drive employee satisfaction and success. Their platform empowers users to acknowledge and appreciate various activities in the workplace, fostering a sense of community and promoting individual and team achievements.

Mission and methods

Brian and Brad's pioneering mission in organizational development and employee engagement is fueled by their commitment to revolutionizing workplace cultures and equipping customers with powerful tools that foster employee satisfaction and outstanding performance. During a recent conversation, they highlighted the significance of understanding TerryBerry's innovative product, particularly focusing on their recognition tools, gamification strategies, and performance incentives. Their transformative approach is centered around empowering organizations to differentiate themselves, enhance engagement, and drive success through a comprehensive understanding of these essential elements.

Let's explore the main impact points of their time-tested methods:

- **TerryBerry's recognition tools**: Brian and Brad emphasize the significance of TerryBerry's recognition tools, which allow customers to appreciate a wide range of workplace activities and achievements. These tools enable peer-to-peer and manager spot recognition, all tied to core value statements, fostering a culture of appreciation and encouragement within the organization.

- **The power of gamification**: Brian and Brad shed light on the transformative power of gamification in driving engagement and motivation. By offering employees tangible rewards for their active participation in various activities, gamification becomes a compelling driver for increased performance and participation in recognition and reward programs.

- **Performance incentives and rewards**: TerryBerry's platform offers sales rewards and fast-starter programs, motivating employees to strive for excellence and achieve their goals. Brian highlights how these incentives contribute to recognizing top-performing individuals, driving overall performance and dedication.

- **Fostering teamwork and camaraderie**: Through gamified head-to-head challenges and team-based competitions, TerryBerry fosters a sense of unity and collaboration among employees. This fosters a strong spirit of teamwork and community within the workplace.

Brian and Brad's insights offer organizations a comprehensive roadmap to transform their workplace cultures, elevate employee engagement, and ultimately drive exceptional performance and success.

User-centric approach

A key aspect emphasized by Brian and Brad was the importance of understanding the user base and tailoring offerings to meet their diverse needs. They stressed the need for customization and flexibility within their platform, recognizing that one size does not fit all. By providing a platform customized to align with each organization's unique culture, TerryBerry ensures that its customers can effectively engage their workforce and drive meaningful results.

The impact of TerryBerry's belief in gamification and its user-centric approach is evident in its continued growth and success as a business. With its rich history spanning over 100 years, TerryBerry's ability to adapt and evolve with the changing needs of organizations has contributed to its ongoing success. By offering a platform that facilitates customization, drives engagement, and fosters a vibrant company culture, TerryBerry has resonated with its customers, resulting in increased adoption and positive outcomes.

Brian and Brad provided valuable insights and advice for product managers who are considering implementing gamification in their products. They highlighted the importance of making gamification enjoyable and fun for users by incorporating small rewards and incentives, creating a more engaging and productive experience. Furthermore, they stressed the need to align gamification strategies with specific product goals and objectives, ensuring that it drives the desired outcomes and aligns with the overall product vision. Drawing parallels between their tools and the popular TV show Ted Lasso, they emphasized their platform's focus on trust, empathy, and individual recognition, aiming to create workplaces where individuals feel valued and empowered. Brian also discussed TerryBerry's remarkable growth, attributing it to their commitment to putting culture first and leveraging gamification as a driver of engagement, both internally within their company and with their customers.

The advice and insights shared by Brian and Brad provide valuable guidance for product managers who are considering integrating gamification into their products. Making gamification enjoyable, aligning it with specific goals, and measuring its impact are vital factors. *"TerryBerry's remarkable growth over the years, where we've doubled our workforce, can be attributed to our commitment to putting culture first and leveraging gamification as a driver of engagement,"* says Brian. By sharing success stories and showcasing their growth, TerryBerry exemplifies the effectiveness of its platform in creating engaging company cultures. Through recognition, rewards, and gamification, TerryBerry drives employee satisfaction and success, significantly impacting organizations worldwide.

We will continue our best practices interviews with one of the largest online discount retailers.

Bed Bath & Beyond (Overstock)

During our insightful conversation with Kyle Treece, a product management expert from Bed Bath & Beyond, we gained valuable insights into how the company leverages gamification and variable rewards within their innovative platform. Bed Bath & Beyond is a leading online retailer known for offering a wide range of products in the furniture and home décor space.

Understanding customer behavior is at the core of Bed Bath & Beyond's strategy for driving engagement. One of their successful features is email cart abandonment, where targeted emails are sent to customers who abandon their carts, resulting in an impressive 1.7% conversion rate. This demonstrates the effectiveness of their approach in encouraging customers to complete their purchases.

Additionally, Bed Bath & Beyond embraces the power of variable rewards to enhance the customer experience. Their Lotto feature provides customers with unknown coupon offerings, adding an element of surprise and excitement to their engagement with the platform by allowing users to do a scratch-and-win reward each day on their mobile device. The company is continuously exploring the implementation of similar variable rewards in other areas to keep customers actively engaged.

Bed Bath & Beyond also utilizes variability in its pricing tactics to strike a balance between profitability and customer satisfaction. They frequently adjust product prices to provide compelling incentives to make purchases, and they plan to develop triggers that notify customers of the lowest prices or inform them of price drops since their last visit.

Looking to the future, Bed Bath & Beyond has exciting plans for further development. They are considering implementing page triggers for **product detail page** (**PDP**) abandonment and price drop triggers to engage customers who have shown interest in specific products or pricing fluctuations.

Understanding the customer

Bed Bath & Beyond has undeniably achieved remarkable success in enhancing customer engagement and substantially augmenting conversion rates by astutely understanding customer behavior and artfully integrating variability into pricing and offers. In essence, our stimulating conversation with Kyle Treece has shed illuminating light on Bed Bath & Beyond's meticulously crafted strategic approach to gamification and variable rewards. The invaluable insights shared by Kyle serve as an invaluable treasure trove of wisdom for product managers seeking to implement gamification and variable rewards within their platforms effectively.

We delved deeper into the captivating world of testing opportunities and their significant impact on improving the customer experience. Kyle firmly believed there is always something valuable worth testing, even if it may not initially present a substantial problem statement. Kyle states, *"Short tests that can be completed within a day or less, yet provide valuable customer insights, are highly valuable in learning. Maintaining a balanced approach to testing ensures that every team can unleash their creativity and deliver impactful solutions."*

Kyle highlights the significance of fair and balanced opportunities for teams to engage in test-driven activities. Emphasizing the value of learning through experimentation, he stresses the importance of maintaining a culture that encourages curiosity and continuous learning. Kyle also underscores the role of a customer-focused approach within the team, recognizing that understanding and meeting genuine customer needs is paramount.

By engaging in comprehensive customer interviews, conducting UX tests, and actively collecting feedback, the team at Bed Bath & Beyond ensures their efforts are aligned with addressing real problems and creating meaningful solutions:

- Fair and balanced opportunities for teams in test-driven activities foster a sense of healthy competition and inspire unique approaches to testing

- Learning through experimentation provides valuable insights, challenges assumptions, and refines strategies

- Embracing a culture of continuous learning and curiosity enables the team to expand their understanding of customer behavior and market dynamics

- Learning from both successful and unsuccessful tests helps identify pitfalls and areas for improvement, and drives data-driven decision-making

- A customer-focused approach, including thorough customer interviews, UX tests, and feedback collection forums, ensures products and features align with genuine customer needs

- Customer-centricity drives customer satisfaction and loyalty, inspiring a sense of purpose among team members

---

Key takeaways

Kyle's emphasis on a customer-focused approach highlights Bed Bath & Beyond's dedication to understanding and meeting the genuine needs of its customers. Through thorough customer interviews, UX tests, and feedback collection forums, the team ensures that every feature and improvement is rooted in addressing real customer problems. By aligning its efforts with the customer's perspective, Bed Bath & Beyond creates products and experiences that resonate with its audience, driving customer satisfaction and loyalty.

In addition, Kyle passionately extolled the benefits of fostering healthy competition within teams, sharing his own experience. He recalled, *"When winning site tests became a tremendous source of motivation and pride, it sparked unparalleled creativity and innovation within our team. It enabled us to conceive groundbreaking ideas and simultaneously execute small and large-scale tests. The spirit of healthy competition nurtured a relentless pursuit of excellence, propelling us to seek opportunities for improvement continuously and consistently exceed expectations."*

Our conversation with Kyle Treece has given us an extensive and comprehensive understanding of Bed Bath & Beyond's strategic approach to gamification, variable rewards, and customer-centric practices. Through our discussion, we discovered the critical role of surprise and variability in enhancing customer engagement, the power of dynamic pricing tactics, and the importance of fostering a culture of engagement, critical thinking, and healthy competition within teams.

Entrenuity

Once upon a time, in the vibrant city of Chicago, there lived a passionate and driven individual named Brian Jenkins, the CEO of Entrenuity. With over 25 years of experience in entrepreneurship education, Brian had dedicated his life to serving and working in the urban context of Chicago's West and South sides. His mission was clear – to empower individuals with the tools and knowledge necessary to become better leaders and citizens through entrepreneurship.

Brian's deep-rooted passion for entrepreneurship stemmed from his journey of discovery. Growing up, he had limited exposure to entrepreneurship until after he completed his graduate studies. Brian firmly believed entrepreneurship, education, and wealth creation were pathways to uplift communities with limited economic opportunities. Witnessing the immediate need for entrepreneurship training, resources, and exposure in underserved communities, he recognized the transformative potential that business ownership and wealth creation could bring.

As Brian embarked on his mission to make a difference, he became captivated by the concept of gamification. It all began in his youth when he first saw the game of Pong. The simplicity and novelty of this early video game sparked a lifelong fascination with gaming and its potential to engage and attract people. Growing up in the arcade era of the 80s, Brian experienced the evolving landscape of video games and witnessed the birth of a vibrant gaming community.

"At that moment, I realized that gaming had a unique power to captivate and connect people," Brian reminisced. *"I saw the potential to leverage gamification as a tool for learning and engagement."*

Gamification in education

Intrigued by the power of gamification, Brian began exploring ways to integrate game mechanics into entrepreneurship education. He realized that by transforming complex business concepts into fun and interactive experiences, he could create a dynamic learning environment that resonated with his students. The idea of making entrepreneurship education engaging and enjoyable became his driving force.

"Traditional teaching methods often failed to captivate students' imaginations and curiosity," Brian explained. *"I wanted to bridge that gap and make learning a thrilling adventure."*

Brian understood the value of gamification in capturing the attention and interest of his students. He recognized that more than traditional lectures and textbooks were needed to convey entrepreneurship's intricacies effectively. To bridge this gap, Brian utilized gamification to immerse students in the learning process without realizing they were acquiring complex business knowledge. By incorporating competition, rewards, and a sense of achievement, he tapped into their inherent desire to win and succeed.

"When students are actively engaged and motivated, the learning experience becomes transformative," Brian affirmed. *"Gamification provides the perfect vehicle to unleash their potential."*

Tools and facilitation

One powerful tool in Brian's arsenal was a business simulation game that he developed. During a recent South Side charter school class, he witnessed the transformative impact of gamification firsthand. *"When I saw the students' excitement and engagement, I knew I was onto something special,"* Brian recalled. *"The game became a catalyst for their growth and development."*

Through gamification, Brian managed to create an environment where winning became the ultimate goal for his students. *"Gamification allows students to learn through experience and experimentation,"* Brian stated. *"They can make mistakes, take risks, and better understand business concepts."* He recognized gamification's potential to enhance learning experiences in various domains, sharing an example of a gamified marketing exercise: *"Participants were tasked with visualizing their target customers by dressing up a silhouette with various clothing and accessories."'*

"By making the exercise tangible and interactive, participants gained a deeper understanding of their target market and the power of visual representation," Brian explained. *"They could visually define their audience and develop effective marketing strategies."*

As Brian continued to explore the possibilities of gamification, he realized that it was not just about the game mechanics but also the facilitation techniques employed. A strong facilitator could amplify the value of gamification, guiding participants toward desired outcomes and keeping them focused on the learning objectives.

"The role of the facilitator is crucial in harnessing the potential of gamification," Brian emphasized. *"They need to create a supportive and engaging environment, guiding participants through the game while addressing key learning points."* Effective facilitation combined with well-designed game mechanics was the key to unlocking the full potential of gamification in learning and engagement.

"A skilled facilitator can create an environment that encourages active participation, collaboration, and reflection," Brian explained. *"By guiding discussions and debriefing sessions, facilitators help participants draw connections between the game and their real-life professional experiences, deepening their understanding and enabling them to transfer their newfound knowledge and skills into their work contexts."*

Beyond the classroom

Once Brian had established the effectiveness of gamification in entrepreneurship education, he realized that its impact extended beyond the classroom. He saw an opportunity to bring gamification to various settings and demographics, including adult learners. Brian understood that getting adults to buy into gamification could be challenging, especially when working with executives who often had preconceived notions about traditional learning methods.

To demonstrate the value of gamification to adults, Brian shared a compelling story from his own experience. He had the opportunity to conduct the same simulation game with United Airlines executives in the morning and with inmates in prison later that evening. The principles and mechanics of the game remained unchanged, but the environments were vastly different. This experience highlighted gamification's universal appeal and effectiveness, transcending barriers and engaging participants across diverse settings.

"I witnessed firsthand how gamification could captivate and engage individuals from different backgrounds and contexts," Brian recounted. *"The game provided a level playing field where everyone could participate and learn, regardless of their circumstances."*

Simulation structure

Brian then elaborated on the structure of the simulation game he developed. It involved five teams representing a small business with three to five members. The game presented a challenge to the teams: they had to transform a basic unit, a piece of paper slightly larger than a Post-it note, into a product that could be sold in a local store. Each team was responsible for purchasing the basic units from a wholesaler for $40 per unit. The goal was to sell the final product for $80, thereby generating a margin of $40 per unit.

"The simulation game simulates the real-life challenges of running a business," Brian explained. *"Teams must manage their finances, repay loans, pay rental fees, and make critical business decisions. It's a hands-on experience that allows participants to apply business concepts practically and engagingly."*

The game spanned weeks, with different activities assigned to each day of the week. Brian outlined the weekly routine: *"On Monday, teams purchased the basic units; on Tuesday, they spent 5 minutes manufacturing their products; Wednesday was dedicated to selling the products; Thursday involved repaying their small business loans; and Friday was a day for planning the next week's activities. Saturday was designated for purchasing materials from the grocery store, and Sunday served as a day of rest."*

Throughout the game, teams had to make strategic decisions, adapt to changing market conditions, and navigate financial challenges. Brian highlighted that the game comprised approximately 75 to 80 business activities, allowing participants to develop an intuitive understanding of business concepts without them even realizing they were learning.

Impact

Brian shared an essential aspect of the simulation game that resonated with both students and adults – the hands-on, tangible elements. He described an exercise where participants created a visual representation of their target customers by dressing up a silhouette. This activity allowed them to visually define their target audience and understand the importance of customer segmentation.

"The visual representation exercise brings the target customers to life," Brian said. *"Participants get a concrete sense of who they are trying to reach and can develop more targeted marketing strategies."*

In reflecting on his gamification journey, Brian highlighted the versatility of gamification beyond the boundaries of entrepreneurship education. He recognized that its principles could be applied to various contexts and subjects, enhancing learning experiences for individuals of all ages and backgrounds. From classroom settings to corporate training sessions, gamification could revolutionize traditional learning approaches and unlock untapped potential in learners.

"As I continue to refine and expand my gamification efforts, my goal remains to make learning enjoyable, immersive, and practical," Brian shared. *"By embracing the power of gamification, individuals can develop essential skills such as critical thinking, problem-solving, collaboration, and adaptability – vital in today's rapidly changing world."*

Key takeaways

Brian Jenkins's journey into gamification had taken him on a path of transformation for himself and the learners he served. Through his simulation game and other gamified activities, he discovered a unique approach to teaching and learning – one that transcended age, background, and preconceived notions about education. With gamification as his tool, Brian empowered individuals to embrace the learning process, tap into their innate curiosity, and unlock their entrepreneurial potential.

"I believe in the power of gamification to ignite a lifelong love for learning and entrepreneurship," Brian concluded. *"By infusing education with fun, interactivity, and practical application, we can create a generation of empowered individuals ready to impact the world positively."*

Summary

In this chapter, we explored the world of successful gamification examples across various industries, including healthcare, education, creative arts, and productivity. Analyzing these case studies gave us valuable insights into what made these gamification strategies effective and impactful. This chapter focused on critical elements such as game mechanics, goals and objectives, the target audience, and the resulting impact on user engagement and behavior.

We interviewed four real-world practitioners who shared their experiences implementing gamification strategies to provide a deeper understanding. These interviews shed light on how these practitioners approached their strategies, communicated them to their stakeholders, and the benefits they witnessed as a result. Their firsthand insights added practical knowledge and credibility to our exploration.

As we reflected on these case studies and interviews, we discovered several best practices and lessons learned. One critical takeaway is the significance of understanding the target audience and tailoring the gamification strategy to their needs and preferences. Additionally, aligning the gamification strategy with the overarching goals of the product or service proved to be instrumental in achieving desired outcomes.

We learned that successful gamification strategies are dynamic; they require ongoing evaluation and adjustment to remain effective. Furthermore, we recognized the importance of continuous monitoring and iteration. By closely tracking the impact of the strategy and incorporating user feedback, designers can make informed decisions and optimize the gamification experience.

Next, we will use our foresight practices to envision the future of gamification.

Further reading

If we had, we would have added more examples. Check out other gamified apps such as Mint, Noom, Nike Run Club, Forest, Headspace, and ClassDojo for more learning and inspiration.

12

The Future of Gamification

As we embark on a journey to explore the future of gamification, this chapter will delve into a hypothetical scenario where gamification has become an integral part of various industries, transforming the way people learn, work, and interact. We will analyze the signals of change, such as the increasing demand for personalized and engaging experiences, and the drivers of change, including technological advancements and the evolving landscape of human behavior.

Throughout this chapter, you will learn about the practical applications of gamification in diverse fields and how these emerging trends will shape the world of tomorrow. Specifically, we will cover the following main topics:

- Gamification on Earth in 2033

- Drivers and signals of change

- Four examples of driving the future

By the end of this chapter, you will be equipped with a deeper understanding of the potential and implications of gamification in the future and insights into how businesses, institutions, and individuals can leverage it to enhance their offerings and user experiences.

The knowledge you will gain from this chapter will enable you to identify opportunities to incorporate gamification into your projects and initiatives, creating engaging and practical experiences for your target audience. As we move forward into an increasingly interconnected and rapidly changing world, the ability to harness the power of gamification will be a valuable skill for innovators and leaders alike.

Gamification on Earth in 2033

The year is 2033, and you wake up at 5:30 A.M. because that is when the embedded chip in your brain is programmed to wake you up. You blink to turn on the AR monitor embedded in your eyes. A small eruption of virtual confetti appears in front of you in your bedroom. Congrats – you hit your sleep goal of 8 hours:

Figure 12.1 – The future vision

You stretch and go over to the bathroom to brush your teeth. Checkmark! You are on an active streak of 1,345 morning teeth brushes, and a video pops up in the mirror from your dentist telling you to keep up the excellent work. You turn your wrist and face your right palm upward to open your apps on a screen that looks like it's out of Star Wars, press the coffee button, and it sends a message downstairs to get your morning brew started.

When walking up to the closest, you get a survey about how you are feeling today, and it cross-references your clothing styles with your mood and the meetings you have on the calendar for the day and gives you some options. On the monitor attached to the closet, you see you are ranked third on the best-dressed leaderboard overall, which is broken down by company, neighborhood, and style. The augmented chip in your brain automatically sends rankings to the server based on your thoughts when you see how people are dressed and consciously judge them. So, you use your digital designer to construct a more edgy outfit for the day, and your 3D printer constructs it while you shower:

Figure 12.2 – 3D-printing closet of the future

You walk into your bathroom and one button press starts the water at your desired temperature. When you're washing yourself, it scans your body for abnormalities. While you are showering, the mainframe calculates your health score, and the visual shows up on your wall – how much you weigh, your BMI, average heart rate, vitamins, and hydration levels. You're clear, but you get notified that your health insurance will be $100 more monthly until you lose 5 pounds and decrease your sugar intake by 17%.

Mechanical arms come out of the ceiling and blow-dry and style your hair. You go downstairs to your kitchen, where everything is automated. You pull up your recipe options based on what you have in stock, the health score of each, and how long it will take to prepare them. You've been eating on a level 3, which is average, but you really want to lose those few extra pounds and get to healthy eating level 6, so you pick the option with the highest health score. Veggie smoothie with turkey bacon and egg white… yum!

Figure 12.3 – Automated kitchen of the future

Your magic – I mean futuristic – kitchen machine would usually pack you a lunch, but you have a noon meeting with your colleagues, so you're eating out today. You grab your small satchel with your iPad SuperPro Model 211 because that's still a thing for drawing and reading books, and head down to your basement to get into your delivery pod. Your house knows you are leaving for work, so your energy is set to conversation mode. You step into your transportation pod like a stack of cash going to the bank and put on your harness. Ok, Google, send me to work! You're whisked away at 100 miles an hour. You've left at the optimal time for pod traffic and accumulated another 20 transportation points that you can use to upgrade your pod experience.

You're in the basement of the corporate high-rise you work in. The pod opens, and the aroma of bleach and fake flowers fills your nostrils. You get out and head to the sanitation line. When it's your turn to pass, mechanical arms draw down and spray you with a light disinfectant, and you get a finger prick as you scan your prints to identify yourself. You have no infectious diseases and are risk-free. Good for you; you've earned more points. Points, points, points! They are more valuable than gold in the future. They are social status, they're your profile, and they show your value.

The cameras scan you as you walk up and prepare the elevator to take you to the 11th floor. When your foot first steps out onto your office floor, you've officially arrived. 15 minutes early – points. You say hi to your coworkers as you walk in, and at the top right of your AR vision, you can see their name, their points, where they rank on the corporate leaderboard, and any other sp3cial information. You're ranked high, but you want to be the best. Review time is right around the corner; you're evaluated based on a well-constructed series of game mechanics. Microphones in the office track your tone and how you talk to people to decide your emotional intelligence by EQ score. You jubilantly greet everyone as you are walking by, shake hands with every passerby, and kiss a baby if one is around. It's the next level of office politics:

Figure 12.4 – Immersive reality distortion work pod

You walk into your pod. You have a small desk and a cocoon-like space to plug into the neural network. The world wide web no longer exists; now, everyone's brainwaves and thoughts tie together through the neural network. One more coffee before you plug in, you think of your order, confirm it, and the Tsarstrucks port opens, and out pops a coffee onto your desk; they are everywhere now. Every desk, every home. You take a long sip of your mediocre coffee; boom, you have just hit 100 cups this month! Virtual confetti explodes around you again; the rewards are so advanced now that you're getting equity in the company. You're on the leaderboard for the most cups without a heart attack this month.

You open the door to your temperature and humidity-controlled cocoon, set all the controls, and close the door. You blink, and it's 80 degrees, and you're now in the Copacabana in Brazil. You think you can feel the sand on your toes; the waves are crashing in front of you, and you hear the music at the cabana playing in the background. You're checking the unresponded-to visual mail in your inbox, swiping back and forth with your finger. You're looking at the latest messages from your product team. You've been working on groundbreaking software that connects to a heart implant all Americans over 30 are now equipped with. Heart attacks have been the leading cause of death in America since 1950, and your company builds an implant that revives the heart after the attack and automatically calls emergency services. You are working on the software on the device to predict when a heart attack will happen to someone, to the exact minute. It gives them ways to avoid the attack, and depending on their diet and exercise, it will change the date of the attack to sometimes or not at all.

The sprint backlog appears in front of you on the beach; you are at 87% of your goal, and this sprint is a B- right now. You look to the right, and you see the profiles of your team, their status, work time, story points completed and how many rewards they have achieved for their EQ proficiency, and what the algorithm predicts they will finish by the end of the sprint. You have an engineer operating at a C- level; if he drops much lower, the network will automatically drop him from the company. We're all out of synonyms for agile, so now, we call our methodology adaptive resilience, and you swipe to put him in one of their boot camps to enhance his skills.

A prominent face comes out of the ocean and requests a call. It's your boss, and they want to talk about your team's performance, deadlines, and milestones. You inform them that you have the latest draft of the product development process document, and you run through how you designed it, with all of the game mechanics included, and how you're using the psychology of gamification and regards to hitting the high bar you have set for your team. The call ends, and you run a daily standup; somehow, these never age. You are all standing in an ultra-white void, sharing charts, medical data, and whiteboards in thin air. You're aligned on your score today and have escalated issues to fix and critical fires to extinguish. Your stress level is starting to increase; you get a warning and are about to lose points. Your virtual assistant assigns you to go to Bali, Indonesia to meditate.

You continue your PM duties throughout the day in the neural network, meeting with a focus group in the metaverse and testing new product ideas and features through the digital app companion. You can utilize thoughts in the neural network for feedback about improving your product. You're drafting the features and chapter for your next stage of work, connecting to the best minds in healthcare to pull their information for the network to write your requirements. You get alerts that your team needs you to review and approve product uses, and you navigate and control the updates approval with your thoughts.

After many hours, you leave your pod and make your way back home. You get to your kitchen and decide you'd like authentic Japanese cuisine, so the environment around you turns into a restaurant in downtown Tokyo and your automated cooking system prepares your favorite sushi – points for a healthy dinner. You are starting to get sleepy, and an alert tells you to go to bed. The lights dim, the temperature cools, and light music begins to play. The windows tint as your mind slowly drifts away. You turn the recording on from your brain so that you can watch your dreams the next day. Life in the future is where every action is a piece of data that's recorded, documented, and mined for insights.

As product development leaders, we need to forecast the future so that we can prepare for what's next. As those of you who have been through the product life cycle, you know it takes time to develop a strategy, test hypotheses, validate prototypes, and build intricate and complex digital products. By creating artifacts and forecasts for the future, we can focus on building revolutionary products, instead of launching something that will be outdated as soon as it is launched. Let's look at some forecasting methods and real use case examples of forecasts of different industries and how they will be affected by gamification.

Cyberpunk 2077 (2020)

Cyberpunk 2077 is an action role-playing video game developed by CD Projekt Red and published by CD Projekt. It was incredibly hyped for over 5 years before its release, only to initially let down many of its day-one players with bugs and glitches upon release. There could be an entire class taught on the lead-up, release, and post-release patch process for this game. Taking a look at it now that several years have passed, however, the experience has been much improved.

As we mentioned previously, taking a glimpse into what the future might hold can help us, as product leaders, plan and prepare for what is in store. Although a lot of the concepts presented in this game are far-fetched, there are easily as many that are not too far out. Cybernetics, body modifications, and using brain implants to relive other people's memories are all explored in this futuristic sci-fi action game.

Drivers and signals of change

As a researcher of foresight and futurism, my preferred thought leader is the **Institute for the Future (IFTF)**. In this chapter, we will embark on an exciting journey, utilizing the IFTF's proven approach to exploring the drivers and signals of change that will shape our world in the years to come. We will harness their comprehensive structure and methodologies to craft a thoughtful and compelling forecast of future possibilities. Together, we will envision the emerging trends, challenges, and opportunities ahead and consider how individuals, organizations, and society can navigate the evolving landscape with foresight, creativity, and resilience.

IFTF is a non-profit organization that focuses on identifying emerging trends and exploring the potential impacts of those trends on society, business, and individual lives. IFTF uses two key concepts to help analyze and understand the future: drivers and signals of change.

Drivers of change

Drivers of change are the underlying forces that have the potential to shape the future. These drivers can be social, economic, political, technological, environmental, or other factors that influence the trajectory of change over time. They are typically large-scale, long-term forces that can create significant shifts in how we live, work, and interact with one another.

For example, some drivers of change include the rapid advancement of artificial intelligence (AI), demographic shifts (such as aging populations or urbanization), and climate change. These forces create new challenges and opportunities, and by understanding them, we can better anticipate and prepare for the future.

Signals of change

Signals of change are the early indicators or "clues" that suggest a particular driver of change is gaining momentum or starting to impact society. Signals of change can be specific events, innovations, or trends that provide evidence of an emerging future.

For example, the rise of **electric vehicles (EVs)** could be considered a signal of change related to the broader driver of sustainable energy and climate change mitigation. Similarly, the increasing prevalence of remote work due to the COVID-19 pandemic could signal change related to the future of work and the evolving nature of employment.

By identifying and tracking signals of change, researchers at IFTF and other futurists can better understand the potential implications of various drivers of change and develop more informed forecasts, strategies, and recommendations for navigating the future.

In summary, drivers of change represent the underlying forces shaping the future, while signals of change are the early indicators of those forces at work. By analyzing both drivers and signals, we can anticipate emerging trends in gamification and their potential impacts.

Four examples of how gamification will shape the future

As a foresight practitioner, I'm excited to share four examples of how gamification will shape the future. These four examples are technology, policy, demographic shifts in the workforce, and health and wellness. Why should you care? Because gamification is not just a trend, it's a fundamental shift in how we engage with the world around us. It's a way to motivate, educate, and drive behavior change in once unimaginable ways.

And while the concept of gamification has been around for a while, we are only starting to scratch the surface of its potential. As technology continues to evolve, policies shift, the workforce changes, and we become more focused on health and wellness, gamification will play an increasingly important role in shaping our lives.

In this section, you will better understand gamification in these four areas and see examples of products and services leading the way. From diabetes management to job skills development, gamification is transforming the way we interact with the world around us.

Technology drivers of change

The rate of technological change has been accelerating rapidly over the past few decades, primarily due to the exponential growth of computing power and connectivity. This phenomenon is **Moore's Law**, named after Gordon Moore, the co-founder of Intel, which is the observation that the number of transistors on a microchip doubles approximately every 2 years, increasing computing power at a roughly similar pace.

This exponential growth has led to a dramatic increase in computing power and a decrease in the cost of computing, which has fueled rapid advancements in technology across various fields.

While Moore's Law has held for decades, we may be reaching its limits due to the physical limitations of manufacturing increasingly smaller transistors. As we approach the atomic scale, it becomes more challenging to continue the trend of doubling transistor density without facing issues such as quantum tunneling and increased power consumption.

Despite these limitations, technology will continue to evolve and advance rapidly over the next decade. Some possible developments include the following:

- **Quantum computing**: Quantum computers, which leverage the principles of quantum mechanics, have the potential to solve complex problems far beyond the capabilities of classical computers. In the next decade, we may see significant advancements in quantum computing, enabling breakthroughs in areas such as cryptography, optimization, and materials science.

- **AI and machine learning**: AI is already transforming industries and will continue to advance over the next decade. AI systems have become increasingly capable of understanding natural language, recognizing patterns, and making decisions, which could revolutionize fields such as healthcare, finance, and transportation.

- **Biotechnology and gene editing**: Developments in biotechnology, such as CRISPR gene editing, will continue to advance, potentially leading to revolutionary treatments for genetic diseases, increased crop yields, and even designer organisms.

- **Augmented and virtual reality (AR/VR)**: AR and VR technologies will continue to evolve and become more immersive and integrated into our daily lives, transforming industries such as gaming, entertainment, and workplace collaboration.

- **Advanced robotics and automation**: As robotics and automation technologies continue to advance, we may see an increasing number of tasks and jobs being performed by machines, potentially leading to new business models and significant economic disruption.

Signals of change – how AI is changing the future

ChatGPT and other AI tools are revolutionizing modern society in several ways. They are changing the way we communicate, the way we work, and the way we learn. We are currently living through the biggest technological shift since the creation and adoption of the internet.

One of the most significant ways that AI tools are changing society is through the way we communicate. For example, generative AI such as ChatGPT demonstrates unprecedented fluency but still lacks robust reasoning and judgment. While exciting, true assistants need deeper knowledge and context. This technology is rapidly evolving thanks to innovations in knowledge graphs, neuro-symbolic AI, and transfer learning. As it improves, it has the potential to transform workflows and augment human capabilities across many domains. Product managers should track these developments closely as AI promises to reshape industries and user expectations. Though overhyped today, generative AI's strengths and limitations signal where future opportunities lie. Understanding this changing landscape will enable product managers to make informed decisions about how to strategically leverage AI to create value.

Another way that AI tools are changing society is through the way we work. AI tools are enabling us to automate tasks that people previously did. For example, AI tools can automate tasks such as data entry, customer service, and even writing. As generative AI such as ChatGPT threatens to automate routine product management tasks, we may soon find our careers and livelihoods jeopardized before we even complete our next book, *Product Development for AI Overlords: A Guide to Appeasing Our Robot Masters*.

Now that we gave them kudos, let's look at an example of how AI is changing society and how people work in the field of education. In the past, education was a largely one-way process, with teachers imparting knowledge to students. However, with the advent of AI-powered educational tools, students can now learn in a much more interactive and personalized way. AI can be used to create adaptive learning experiences tailored to each student's needs and abilities. AI has made education much more effective and engaging and has opened up new opportunities for students who may not have otherwise had access to quality education.

AI is poised to revolutionize gamification in several ways. You can use AI to create more personalized and engaging gamification experiences, automate tasks, and provide real-time feedback. As AI technology continues to develop, we can expect to see even more profound changes in how gamification motivates and engages people.

Here are some specific examples of how you can use AI in gamification to change the future:

- **Personalized gamification experiences**: AI could be used to create personalized gamification experiences tailored to each individual's interests and abilities. This could be done by tracking each person's progress and preferences and then using that information to create a customized game or gamified experience.

- **Automated tasks**: AI could be used to automate tasks currently done by people, such as tracking progress, constructing leaderboards, awarding points, and providing feedback. This would free up people to focus on more creative and strategic tasks.

- **Real-time feedback**: AI could provide real-time feedback to players, which could help them improve their performance. This feedback could be provided through tips, suggestions, or direct instructions.

The implications of this exponential growth in technology are both exciting and challenging. On the one hand, it can improve the quality of life for people around the world, enable new scientific discoveries, and drive economic growth. On the other hand, it also raises concerns about job displacement, privacy, security, and ethical questions surrounding the use and development of new technologies.

It's important to note that forecasting the future of technology is inherently uncertain as it depends on various factors, such as scientific breakthroughs, market conditions, and public policy. Nevertheless, the next decade promises to bring significant technological advancements that will continue to reshape our world profoundly.

Regulation and policy drivers of change

Government regulation has played a crucial role in shaping the evolution of technology. While some regulations have fostered innovation and protected consumer interests, others have impeded progress and stifled competition. This section will examine the long-term effects of government regulation on technology, focusing on how past trends will influence the future. We will also explore the implications of these trends for digital products that employ gamification.

The history of government regulation on technology

Historically, government regulation of technology is driven by a desire to protect consumers, promote fair competition, and maintain national security. For instance, the **Federal Communications Commission (FCC)**, established in 1934, aimed to regulate interstate communications by radio, television, wire, satellite, and cable. Similarly, the advent of the internet prompted the creation of regulations such as the **Communications Decency Act (CDA)** in 1996 and the **Digital Millennium Copyright Act (DMCA)** in 1998, both of which sought to address issues related to the content, privacy, and intellectual property rights.

The Telecommunications Act of 1996, which aimed to promote competition and reduce regulation, resulted in the consolidation of media companies and reduced diversity in the industry. However, some regulations have had unintended consequences. In some cases, regulations have stifled innovation and created barriers to entry for new market players. For example, strict regulations surrounding autonomous vehicles have slowed their development and deployment in certain jurisdictions.

The future of government regulation and technology

As technology continues to evolve exponentially, governments will face increasing challenges in regulating emerging technologies. The rise of AI, blockchain, and biotechnology, among others, will necessitate new regulatory frameworks that balance the need for innovation with protecting consumers and national security interests.

In the future, we expect governments to adopt a more proactive approach to technology regulation, collaborating closely with industry stakeholders and leveraging international partnerships to create harmonized standards. This method may lead to developing global regulatory frameworks that foster innovation while mitigating the risks associated with new technologies. The only thing advancing faster than the innovations themselves is the look of exhaustion on policymakers' faces. They never signed up for the relentless game of regulatory whack-a-mole in store for them. Next on the agenda is drafting policies for teleportation and time machines. Buckle up.

The impact on digital products using gamification

Digital products that employ gamification stand to be significantly impacted by the future trajectory of government regulation. As these products become more pervasive and sophisticated, they will likely attract increased regulatory scrutiny, particularly in terms of privacy, data protection, and consumer rights.

For example, digital products that collect and analyze user data to personalize and enhance the gamified experience may face stricter data privacy regulations. Routine data mining could necessitate implementing more robust data protection measures and greater transparency regarding data usage.

Additionally, as gamification becomes more widely adopted in education, healthcare, and financial services, industry-specific regulations may be introduced to ensure that these products meet specific standards and do not exploit vulnerable populations.

Signals of change – deregulation of gambling

Now that we've discussed gamification's positive and negative effects, here is an example of deregulation. In 1989, Rose, a former **Major League Baseball** (**MLB**) player and manager, received a lifetime ban from MLB for betting on games, including those involving his team, the Cincinnati Reds. Although Rose has applied for reinstatement multiple times, his suspension still stands. While Pete Rose remains suspended from baseball, baseball stadiums are integrating sportsbooks, which are companies that facilitate betting on sports.

In a 2022 Forbes article, Maury Brown discusses the growing trend of incorporating sportsbooks into MLB stadiums. Brown predicts that nearly all MLB ballparks will have a sportsbook attached to them in the future. As sports betting becomes legalized in more states across the United States, MLB and its teams are taking advantage of this opportunity to increase fan engagement and generate additional revenue.

The potential for increased revenue from sports betting, which can help teams offset financial losses from reduced attendance and other challenges, is driving the decisions from owners and MLB. The article highlights the Washington Nationals as the first MLB team to open a sportsbook inside their stadium. Other teams, such as the Chicago Cubs and Arizona Diamondbacks, plan to add sportsbooks to their venues.

Brown also discusses the potential impact of sportsbooks on the fan experience, suggesting that they can create a more immersive and engaging atmosphere for spectators. Integrating gambling into baseball stadiums may lead to increased attendance and a more loyal fan base, further benefiting the teams and the league as a whole.

[Brown, Maury, *Why Nearly All MLB Ballparks Will Have A Sportsbook Attached To It In The Future*", Forbes, 10 Aug. 2021, `https://www.forbes.com/sites/maurybrown/2021/08/10/why-nearly-all-mlb-ballparks-will-have-a-sportsbook-attached-to-it-in-the-future/?sh=26015d7536d8`]

In the United States, the **Professional and Amateur Sports Protection Act (PASPA)** was overturned in 2018 by the Supreme Court, allowing individual states to legalize sports betting. Since then, numerous states have legalized sports betting, both online and at physical venues. Similar changes have occurred in other countries, where gambling laws have been revised to permit various forms of gambling, such as online casinos and sports betting.

As technology continues to evolve, digital products that employ gamification must adapt to new regulatory landscapes and strive to meet the requirements set forth by governments. By doing so, product managers and innovators can capitalize on the opportunities presented by emerging technologies and create products that deliver meaningful and engaging experiences for their users. The delicate balance between fostering innovation and protecting consumers and national security interests will shape the long-term effects of government regulation on technology.

Drivers of change – shifts in the workforce

The workforce is undergoing significant transformations driven by demographic shifts, the rise of remote work, and the expanding gig economy. These changes present challenges and opportunities for companies as they seek to adapt their workforce strategies and maintain a competitive edge. We will examine these trends in detail and explore how gamification can play a pivotal role in helping companies provide meaningful, flexible, and accessible experiences that support these shifts.

Demographic shifts and the workforce

One of the key drivers of change in the workforce is the demographic shift characterized by an aging population and increasing retirements. As baby boomers retire, companies face the challenge of filling the resulting talent gaps and transferring knowledge and expertise to younger workers. Simultaneously, organizations must attract and retain millennial and Generation Z employees with different expectations and values from their predecessors, including a greater emphasis on work-life balance, flexibility, and career growth opportunities.

The rise of remote work and the gig economy

Another significant trend shaping the workforce is the increasing prevalence of remote work and the gig economy. The COVID-19 pandemic accelerated the adoption of remote work, forcing companies to adapt quickly to new ways of working and communicating. This shift has shown that remote work is feasible and can lead to increased productivity and employee satisfaction when implemented effectively. Meanwhile, the gig economy has expanded, offering workers greater flexibility and autonomy while providing companies with a more agile and scalable workforce.

Bacon (2018)

Offering a wide range of gig jobs, Bacon allows companies to find on-demand temp labor for several different industries, including warehousing, cleaning, food services, event staffing, and more. Workers are background-checked and earn ratings based on their efforts.

After the success of several gig economy apps that targeted specific jobs (Uber, Lyft, Instacart, and others), there has been a push for catch-all gig work products. Bacon is one of many doing just that, offering the ability for companies to add jobs and shifts, as well as workers, to find something that fits their needs for a quick bit of money. This shift in the workforce is only growing and becoming more streamlined. If you want to see how this process works, it's worth checking out the Bacon app and seeing the wide range of jobs that are shifting to this sort of gig workforce.

The role of gamification in supporting workforce changes

Gamification can play a crucial role in helping companies navigate these workforce changes by fostering employee engagement, enhancing learning and development, and promoting a collaborative work culture. As companies adapt to a more remote and distributed workforce, gamification can help bridge the gap between employees by creating virtual spaces for collaboration, recognition, and social interaction. Gamified platforms can facilitate knowledge sharing and encourage cross-functional teamwork while fostering employees' sense of belonging and connection.

For organizations seeking to attract and retain younger generations, gamification can offer opportunities for skill development and career growth by incorporating game mechanics into training programs and performance management systems. By making learning and development more engaging and interactive, gamification can help employees acquire new skills and knowledge more effectively, preparing them for the evolving demands of the workforce.

Furthermore, as the gig economy grows, gamification can help companies create more flexible and accessible experiences for gig workers. By designing platforms and systems that cater to the unique needs of gig workers, companies can ensure they remain engaged and motivated while benefiting from their contributions to the organization.

Signal of change – Upwork

Freelancing has hit an all-time high: the share of professionals freelancing increased to 60 million Americans, up three percentage points from 2021 to 39%. Upwork alone has enabled over $10 billion in earnings for independent professionals since its founding and has grown to over 7 million users spanning 180 countries.

The ease of finding flexible remote work through online freelancing platforms is a major factor fueling this growth. For many independent workers, especially younger generations, the autonomy and flexibility afforded by freelancing is highly valued. The ability to choose projects, set their own hours, and work remotely provides a work-life balance and freedom. This increased participation in the gig economy points to an evolving workforce norm that departs dramatically from the location-dependent, long-term employment models of the past.

While this transformation offers benefits such as flexibility, it also raises concerns about job stability, access to benefits, and income security that must be addressed. Overall, the rapid expansion of the online freelance workforce signals a monumental shift in how labor is organized, contracted, and valued. Companies and policymakers alike will need to adapt to support and enable this growing portion of the labor market.

The ease of connecting with clients globally and finding well-paid, engaging freelance work across over 10,000 skill categories is attracting droves of professionals. Upwork's data shows that Millennials make up over half of their freelancer talent pool, pointing to strong uptake from younger demographics.

This growth in online freelancing signals a monumental shift away from the location-dependent, long-term, full-time employment that dominated the 20th-century job market. For a rapidly rising portion of the workforce, the rigidity and conformity of the old working world no longer make sense. Instead, professionals increasingly desire autonomy, flexibility, and variety in their work.

The expanding gig economy, with companies such as Upwork at the forefront, provides a platform that meets the needs and desires of this changing workforce. It allows skilled professionals to take control of their careers and build businesses on their terms.

While concerns around stability and benefits exist, the upside of greater flexibility and fulfillment is undeniable for most. The growth of online freelancing unequivocally signals that new, more customized, independent models of work are the future. Companies and workers alike will increasingly look to platforms such as Upwork that enable this more dynamic labor ecosystem.

Source: `https://www.upwork.com/research/freelance-forward-2022`.

Driver of change – health and wellness

Gamification has emerged as a powerful tool for driving behavior change and improving outcomes in various domains, including healthcare. By leveraging the principles of game design, gamification can make health-related activities more engaging, motivating, and effective. Let's explore the scientific research that supports the benefits of gamification in healthcare, explain why it is a logical approach to achieving better health outcomes, and discuss the potential for insurance companies to invest in gamification to improve member health and significantly reduce costs.

The science behind gamification in healthcare

A growing body of research demonstrates the potential effectiveness of gamification for promoting healthy behaviors and improving patient outcomes. Multiple studies have shown gamified interventions can increase medication adherence, boost physical activity levels, and support self-management of chronic diseases when applied thoughtfully.

For example, a 2016 systematic review by Edwards et al. analyzed over 50 gamified health apps and found largely positive impacts reported in the majority of included studies. The most significant improvements observed were in physical activity, mental health, and medication compliance. (Source: `https://pubmed.ncbi.nlm.nih.gov/27707829`.)

However, the reviewers noted limitations around the lack of long-term data and the need for more rigorous research. While promising, further high-quality studies are required to conclusively demonstrate gamification's efficacy for sustainable health behavior change. Additional work is also needed on optimal game element combinations and implementation.

In summary, current research indicates gamification can be an effective approach for motivating and changing health behaviors, though more rigorous long-term studies are needed. The rationale behind these positive outcomes lies in the psychological mechanisms that underlie gamification. By incorporating elements such as rewards, challenges, and social interaction, gamified interventions tap into intrinsic motivators, such as the desire for mastery, autonomy, and relatedness. These intrinsic motivators can drive behavior change more effectively than extrinsic motivators such as financial incentives, which may lose effectiveness over time. Overall, gamification shows promise for promoting healthy behaviors when thoughtfully designed and deployed. Further research will help refine best practices and further demonstrate gamification's abilities to facilitate sustainable patient engagement, behavior change, and improved well-being.

Why gamification makes sense for health outcomes

While we know there are credible challenges, gamification aligns with the inherent nature of human motivation and learning, making it a logical approach to improving health outcomes. Humans' natural wiring seeks challenges, sets goals, and receives feedback on their progress, and gamification leverages these natural tendencies to promote engagement and sustain motivation over time. By making health-related activities more enjoyable and rewarding, gamification can help individuals overcome barriers to behavior change, such as procrastination or lack of motivation, and support the development of healthy habits.

Scientific studies have shown that gamification works to improve health outcomes:

- A meta-analysis has confirmed that gamified interventions are promising for promoting PA in various populations. Additional analyses revealed that this effect persists after the follow-up period, suggesting that it is not just a novelty effect caused by the playful nature of gamification and that gamified products appear effective compared with equivalent non-gamified PA interventions. Future rigorous trials are required to confirm these findings.

  Source: `https://pubmed.ncbi.nlm.nih.gov/34982715/`

- The study *"Active Team" a social and gamified app-based physical activity intervention: randomised controlled trial study protocol* , published in BMC Public Health, investigates the impact of game-based interventions on physical activity and weight in adults. Analyzing multiple randomized controlled trials, the researchers found that gamification methods can indeed promote increased physical activity among adults. Although the results for weight loss were less consistent, the overall evidence suggests that game-based interventions can be an effective tool in promoting healthier lifestyles.

  Source: `https://bmcpublichealth.biomedcentral.com/articles/10.1186/s12889-017-4882-7`

- The incorporation of gamification into mHealth applications has shown statistically significant advantages in improving patient self-management, especially for those with chronic conditions. Research has shown that over 50% of users find gamified health apps more motivating than traditional ones. Key game elements such as badges have demonstrated a 34% increase in task completion rates, while leaderboards have led to a 20% rise in user engagement. Points and leveling systems not only boost a user's sense of progress but are also correlated with a 45% improvement in sustained app usage. Additionally, the integration of mHealth applications with social media platforms has resulted in a 60% higher likelihood of users meeting their health goals due to community encouragement. These statistics underscore the potential of gamification as a transformative tool for mHealth, emphasizing increased adherence and improved health outcomes. These are just a few examples of the many studies that have shown the value of gamification in healthcare. Gamification can be a powerful tool for improving health outcomes and reducing costs.

  `https://journals.sagepub.com/doi/full/10.1177/1460458214537511`

In the dynamic realm of healthcare, product managers have a unique opportunity to harness the power of gamification. Here's how:

- **Improving patient engagement and adherence**: Gamification can transform treatment from a mundane routine into a captivating experience.

  Recommendation: design interactive apps or platforms that reward patients for consistent treatment adherence.

- **Enhancing health literacy and knowledge**: Gamified tools can make learning about health fun and impactful.

  Recommendation: incorporate quizzes, challenges, and interactive scenarios in patient portals or apps to educate them on their conditions.

- **Motivating healthier lifestyle choices**: Encouraging patients to adopt healthier habits is easier when it feels rewarding.

  Recommendation: develop gamified fitness trackers or diet planners that offer points or badges for healthy milestones.

- **Data collection and progress tracking**: Gamification isn't just fun; it's also data-rich.

  Recommendation: design games that double as data collection tools, then analyze the data to tailor healthcare plans and interventions.

- **Cost reduction**: An engaged patient tends to be a healthier one.

  Recommendation: promote the use of gamified healthcare apps, ensuring that patients can avoid costly treatments or hospital visits in the long run by being proactive in their health.

By integrating these strategies, product managers can redefine patient experiences, making healthcare more effective and engaging.

The potential for insurance companies to invest in gamification

As healthcare costs continue to rise, insurance companies have a vested interest in promoting preventive care and healthy behaviors among their members. By investing in gamification, insurers can help members achieve better health outcomes while reducing costs associated with chronic diseases and hospitalizations.

For example, gamified wellness programs can incentivize members to exercise regularly, improve their diets, and manage stress, all of which can contribute to preventing or managing chronic conditions. By leveraging gamification to drive behavior change, insurance companies can achieve a dual benefit: improved member health and reduced healthcare spending.

The following is from the medication adherence section of the HBR article *Improving Health Care by Gamifying It*:

"One promising application of gamification has been in medication adherence. The World Health Organization estimates that, in developed countries, only about 50% of patients with chronic illnesses take their medications as prescribed. Poor adherence leads to worse health outcomes and higher healthcare costs. gamification strategies — including financial incentives, social support, and digital reminders — can help. For example, the digital platform Mango Health offers an app that uses a combination of game mechanics, such as points and rewards, to encourage users to take their medications on time and as prescribed."

[Fox, Kevin J., et al. *Improving Health Care by Gamifying It*. Harvard Business Review, 1 May 2019, `hbr.org/2019/05/improving-health-care-by-gamifying-it`.]

To effectively use gamification for better health outcomes, healthcare providers and insurers should consider the following:

- **Focus on the individual**: Design gamified interventions that cater to each patient's unique needs, preferences, and motivations

- **Address the full spectrum of health**: Use gamification to promote physical and mental well-being, addressing the interplay between these aspects of health

- **Leverage data**: Collect and analyze data from gamified interventions to better understand patient behavior, inform future initiatives, and optimize patient outcomes

- **Collaborate with other stakeholders**: Work with technology companies, insurers, and other healthcare providers to develop and implement gamified solutions that improve health outcomes and reduce costs

While there's no denying the potential of gamification to improve health outcomes and reduce healthcare costs, we must tread carefully. Gamification, while engaging, has the unintended consequence of reducing users to mere scores. There's a real risk that it can inadvertently marginalize or even penalize users who don't perform well within the system. You can draw a parallel with current practices in medical insurance, where coverage exclusions for pre-existing conditions have created a system that's not always fair.

In a world where insurance companies are considering investments in gamification, you should consider the potential negative implications of this approach. A nuanced understanding of these challenges is crucial as we plan our path forward. For instance, in gamified wellness programs, these tools must be designed to cater to each individual's unique needs, preferences, and motivations. It would be unwise to transform a health journey into a one-size-fits-all game.

Moreover, addressing the full spectrum of health in a gamified manner means considering the complex interplay between physical and mental well-being. You should leverage data carefully, ensuring the information collected from gamified interventions serves to understand patient behavior and optimize outcomes rather than becoming a means of penalizing those who do not "score" well.

Lastly, a collaborative approach is vital. Working with technology companies, insurers, and healthcare providers can ensure the development and implementation of gamified solutions that benefit everyone rather than inadvertently creating more disparities.

Remember, gamification is a powerful tool with significant potential, but you must wield it thoughtfully. As insurance companies consider investing in gamification, they must be vigilant about the possible negative implications and actively work to prevent them. This attention to detail will make for a more compelling and successful implementation of gamification in healthcare.

Signal of change – improved health through gamification

The study titled *Gamification in Healthcare: A systematic review of randomized controlled trials*, published in Digital Health, offers a comprehensive analysis of the current evidence on the effectiveness of gamification in healthcare. The systematic review examines **randomized controlled trials (RCTs)** to determine the impact of gamification on health outcomes, engagement, and adherence.

[Sardi, Laura, et al. *Gamification in healthcare: A systematic review of randomized controlled trials*, Digital Health 8 (2022): 20552076221091198.]

The review reveals that gamification interventions in healthcare have shown promising results in various domains, such as physical activity, medication adherence, mental health, and rehabilitation. Moreover, gamification effectively increases engagement and adherence to health-related behaviors, which is crucial for better health outcomes.

Based on the findings of this systematic review, there is a strong argument for incorporating gamification into healthcare interventions. Gamification's ability to motivate and engage patients can improve adherence to treatments and lifestyle changes, ultimately enhancing health outcomes across various conditions. As healthcare systems continue to evolve, gamification has the potential to become an essential tool in addressing various health challenges and promoting better overall patient care.

As healthcare costs continue to rise, insurance companies have an opportunity to invest in gamification to promote healthy behaviors among their members, ultimately leading to better health outcomes and reduced costs. Gamification has shown promising results in improving health outcomes by tapping into the innate human desire for challenge, progress, and social interaction. By embracing the science of gamification, insurers can improve their members' well-being and contribute to a more sustainable and effective healthcare system.

Summary

As we reflect on the transformative power of gamification and its potential to impact countless industries, we cannot help but feel a sense of excitement and optimism for the future. The potential applications of gamification are nearly limitless, spanning fields such as advertising, psychology, and education, to name just a few. However, as we consider the endless possibilities, we must remain vigilant and discerning in how we employ this powerful tool. You can use gamification for good or evil, and you are responsible for harnessing its power to create a brighter and more equitable future for all.

The ethical considerations surrounding gamification are vast and multifaceted. We must be careful not to let its allure lead us down a path of exploitation or manipulation. Industries such as gambling, sports betting, retail stock trading, and cryptocurrency trading demonstrate the potential pitfalls of gamification when used irresponsibly or without proper regulation. As we forge ahead into the future, we must establish guidelines and safeguards to prevent the misuse of gamification and protect the well-being of individuals and society as a whole.

On the other hand, gamification also presents us with remarkable opportunities to enhance our quality of life and promote positive change. Imagine a world where gamification inspires healthier lifestyles, leading to lower insurance costs and a happier, more robust population. Envision a society where individuals are motivated to reduce their carbon emissions, minimize food waste, and engage in recycling and reuse efforts, all through the power of game mechanics. The potential for gamification to catalyze meaningful, lasting change is genuinely awe-inspiring.

Striking the right balance between motivation and pressure is essential to avoid contributing to widespread stress and mental health issues. However, we must also be cautious to avoid becoming overly reliant on gamification in our daily lives. The constant tracking and scoring of our actions could lead to a culture of perpetual anxiety and fear of failure.

Moreover, we must maintain sight of the value of human connection and empathy as we integrate gamification into our lives. Can these techniques foster more profound understanding and compassion among individuals and communities? How can we leverage gamification to build stronger relationships with friends and family? These questions are worth exploring as we continue developing and refining our understanding of gamification's power.

In conclusion, the future of gamification holds both enormous promise and significant challenges. As we continue to advance our knowledge and skills in this area, we hope to use gamification to create a better tomorrow for everyone. We must remain mindful of the ethical considerations and potential pitfalls of this powerful tool while also embracing its ability to inspire positive change and improve the human experience. Through the responsible, compassionate, and thoughtful application of gamification principles, we can work together to build a brighter, more inclusive, and more equitable world for all.

Found the secret code in "Gamification for Product Excellence"? Head over to HYPERLINK "https://protect-eu.mimecast.com/s/wZa3CAQ2XcN2AJxHYr-1T?domain=levelupyourproduct.com"www.levelupyourproduct.com to claim your exclusive rewards!

Index

V

W

`Packtpub.com`

Subscribe to our online digital library for full access to over 7,000 books and videos, as well as industry leading tools to help you plan your personal development and advance your career. For more information, please visit our website.

Why subscribe?

- Spend less time learning and more time coding with practical eBooks and Videos from over 4,000 industry professionals

- Improve your learning with Skill Plans built especially for you

- Get a free eBook or video every month

- Fully searchable for easy access to vital information

- Copy and paste, print, and bookmark content

Did you know that Packt offers eBook versions of every book published, with PDF and ePub files available? You can upgrade to the eBook version at `packtpub.com` and as a print book customer, you are entitled to a discount on the eBook copy. Get in touch with us at `customercare@packtpub.com` for more details.

At `www.packtpub.com`, you can also read a collection of free technical articles, sign up for a range of free newsletters, and receive exclusive discounts and offers on Packt books and eBooks.

Other Books You May Enjoy

If you enjoyed this book, you may be interested in these other books by Packt:

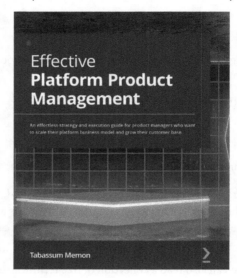

Effective Platform Product Management

Tabassum Memon

ISBN: 9781801811354

- Understand the difference between the product and platform business model
- Build an end-to-end platform strategy from scratch
- Translate the platform strategy to a roadmap with a well-defined implementation plan
- Define the MVP for faster releases and test viability in the early stages
- Create an operating model and design an execution plan
- Measure the success or failure of the platform and make iterations after feedback

API Analytics for Product Managers

Deepa Goyal

ISBN: 9781803247656

- Build a long-term strategy for an API
- Explore the concepts of the API life cycle and API maturity
- Understand APIs from a product management perspective
- Create support models for your APIs that scale with the product
- Apply user research principles to APIs
- Explore the metrics of activation, retention, engagement, and churn
- Cluster metrics together to provide context
- Examine the consequences of gameable and vanity metrics

The Art of Crafting User Stories

Christopher Lee

ISBN: 9781837639496

- Leverage user personas in product development for prioritizing features and guiding design decisions
- Communicate with stakeholders to gather accurate information for writing user stories
- Avoid common mistakes by implementing best practices for user story development
- Estimate the time and resources required for each user story and incorporate estimates into the product plan
- Apply product frameworks and techniques for user story prioritization and requirement elicitation
- Benefit from the experiences, insights, and practices of experts in the field of user story mapping

Unleashing the Power of UX Analytics

Jeff Hendrickson

ISBN: 9781804614747

- Understand the significance of analytics in successful UX projects
- Apply design thinking as a problem-solving tool in a UX practice
- Explore taxonomies, dashboards, KPIs, and data visualizations to understand data enterprise in depth
- Discover key considerations to determine which UX analytics tools are best for your projects
- Craft a North Star statement and understand how it guides your work
- Design and deliver the best research findings collateral
- Get to grips with heuristics and performing the effective evaluations

Packt is searching for authors like you

If you're interested in becoming an author for Packt, please visit `authors.packtpub.com` and apply today. We have worked with thousands of developers and tech professionals, just like you, to help them share their insight with the global tech community. You can make a general application, apply for a specific hot topic that we are recruiting an author for, or submit your own idea.

Share Your Thoughts

Now you've finished *Gamification for Product Excellence*, we'd love to hear your thoughts! Scan the QR code below to go straight to the Amazon review page for this book and share your feedback or leave a review on the site that you purchased it from.

`https://packt.link/r/1837638381`

Your review is important to us and the tech community and will help us make sure we're delivering excellent quality content.

Download a free PDF copy of this book

Thanks for purchasing this book!

Do you like to read on the go but are unable to carry your print books everywhere?

Is your eBook purchase not compatible with the device of your choice?

Don't worry, now with every Packt book you get a DRM-free PDF version of that book at no cost.

Read anywhere, any place, on any device. Search, copy, and paste code from your favorite technical books directly into your application.

The perks don't stop there, you can get exclusive access to discounts, newsletters, and great free content in your inbox daily

Follow these simple steps to get the benefits:

1. Scan the QR code or visit the link below

https://packt.link/free-ebook/9781837638383

2. Submit your proof of purchase
3. That's it! We'll send your free PDF and other benefits to your email directly

Printed in the USA
CPSIA information can be obtained
at www.ICGtesting.com
LVHW081541041023
760131LV00001B/1